IN THE SIGN OF THE GOLDEN WHEEL

SANGHARAKSHITA

•

IN THE SIGN OF THE GOLDEN WHEEL

•

INDIAN MEMOIRS OF AN ENGLISH BUDDHIST

•

WINDHORSE PUBLICATIONS

Published by Windhorse Publications
Unit 1-316 The Custard Factory
Gibb Street
Birmingham
B9 4AA

© Sangharakshita 1996
Cover design Dhammarati
Printed by The Cromwell Press, Melksham, Wilts.
Cover photograph © Clear Vision Trust Picture Archive

The epigraph is taken from
Krishna Kripalani, *Rabindranath Tagore: A Biography*, OUP 1962, p.211

British Library Cataloguing in Publication Data
A catalogue record for this book is available from the British Library

ISBN 1 899579 14 1

PUBLISHER'S NOTE: Since this work is intended for a general readership,
Pali and Sanskrit words have been transliterated without the diacritical marks
that would have been appropriate in a work of a more scholarly nature.

Contents

ABOUT THE AUTHOR

SANGHARAKSHITA WAS BORN DENNIS LINGWOOD in South London, 1925. Largely self-educated, he developed an interest in the cultures and philosophies of the East early on, and realized that he was a Buddhist at the age of sixteen.

The Second World War took him, as a conscript, to India, where he stayed on to become the Buddhist monk Sangharakshita ('protector of the spiritual community'). After studying for some years under leading teachers from the major Buddhist traditions, he went on to teach and write extensively. He also played a key part in the revival of Buddhism in India, particularly through his work among the ex-Untouchables.

After twenty years in India, he returned to England to establish the Friends of the Western Buddhist Order (FWBO) in 1967, and the Western Buddhist Order (called Trailokya Bauddha Mahasangha in India) in 1968. A translator between East and West, between the traditional world and the modern, between principles and practices, Sangharakshita's depth of experience and clear thinking have been appreciated throughout the world. He has always particularly emphasized the decisive significance of commitment in the spiritual life, the paramount value of spiritual friendship and community, the link between religion and art, and the need for a 'new society' supportive of spiritual aspirations and ideals.

The FWBO is now an international Buddhist movement with centres in sixteen countries world-wide. In recent years Sangharakshita has been handing over most of his responsibilities to his senior disciples in the Order. From his base in London, he is now focusing on personal contact with people, and on his writing.

'Life's memories are not life's histories, but the original work of an artist'

Rabindranath Tagore (1861-1941)

Chapter One

THE SCENT OF GARDENIAS

ONE MORNING IN EARLY MAY, my devotions being over, I closed the summer-house door behind me and made my way back to The Hermitage by the path that ran between the ornamental trees. On passing the gardenia bush I noticed among the glossy evergreen leaves two white double flowers. They were the first gardenias of the year. Having plucked them I bore them indoors and placed them in a jar in the centre of my table, whence they diffused their rich scent through the room as I had my tea and toast, taught first a Nepalese and then a Tibetan student, and finally continued working on my new article 'The Religion of Art'. I was glad the gardenias had begun to appear. *Vaishakha Purnima*, the full moon day of the month *Vaishakha*, corresponding to April–May in the Western calendar, was little more than two weeks away, and flowers would be needed for the decoration of the shrine.

Vaishakha Purnima was the most important festival in the Buddhist year. It was the anniversary of the day on which the wandering, freelance ascetic Gautama had attained supreme, perfect Enlightenment and become the Buddha or Enlightened One. According to late Sinhalese traditions it was also the anniversary of his birth thirty-five years earlier and his *parinirvana* or final passing away forty-five years later, so that throughout Buddhist South-east Asia, as well as in modern India, Vaishakha Purnima was known as the 'thrice-sacred' festival. It would be the fourth time I had celebrated it in Kalimpong since my arrival in the little Himalayan township in 1950, and the first time I had celebrated it at The Hermitage since the Young Men's Buddhist Association (India) had become the Kalimpong branch of the Maha Bodhi Society with me, the Association's founder, as bhikshu-in-charge, and I wanted this year's celebrations to attract as many people as possible and to be an inspiration to Buddhist and Hindu alike. I therefore booked the Town Hall for a public meeting on the first Sunday after the Vaishakha Purnima, started preparing The Hermitage for the specifically religious observances of the thrice-sacred day itself, and sent out hundreds of printed invitations and programmes. I also wrote to the Sub-Divisional Officer asking him to give the pupils in government schools a holiday on Vaishakha Purnima, and to Monsignor and Mother Superior with a similar request in respect of Buddhist pupils attending the Catholic Mission schools.

Our full moon day meetings were usually held in the summer-house, where the place of honour was occupied by the wooden image of the standing Buddha given me by Lama Govinda, but as the place was rather small I decided that the biggest room in The Hermitage should be turned into a temporary shrine. This room normally functioned as the games room, where our younger members played ping-pong, and since it had not seen paint for a good many years and looked decidedly shabby I asked our Nepalese landlady to get it painted. She agreed, but did nothing, and in the end I bought a couple of tins of white paint and did the job myself. At least, I did most of it myself. Joe did the rest the following day, which was Vaishakha Purnima eve, while Miss Rao stitched curtains and other members and friends decorated the place with greenery (I was not in favour of the usual paper flags), as well as decorating in a similar manner the bamboo arch that I had caused Man Bahadur to erect at the front gate and for which I had made a 'welcome' sign from red cloth and cotton wool.

At this point there was a catastrophe. After going home for lunch, Joe had returned to help me finish setting up the temporary shrine, which was already resplendent with electric-blue hangings, rows of brass offering bowls, and (borrowed) silver butter-lamps. Intending to do something to our alabaster Buddha-image, he set it down on the edge of the ping-pong table, which was being used as a worktable. Unable to bear the weight of the heavy image, the top of the table at once see-sawed violently, precipitating the image on to the floor and breaking off its head. Everyone was horrified, especially our Tibetan and Nepalese members, for whom the breaking of a Buddha-image was inauspicious in the extreme and bound to bring bad luck, and strange looks were cast at the wretched upasaka, who stood petrified with confusion and chagrin. One who could be responsible for something as inauspicious as the breaking of a Buddha-image must be highly inauspicious himself, the looks seemed to say, and it was obvious that the incident had served to confirm the impression, which I knew some of our members had formed, that there was something uncanny about the elderly Canadian Buddhist who wore colourful American clothes that were several sizes too big for him, who waggled his bottom when he walked, and who accosted young men in a way they found acutely embarrassing. After the celebrations Joe stuck the head of the Buddha-image on with glue, but unfortunately he failed to get the upper and lower portions of the neck quite flush, and since the glue was of the super-adhesive variety the mistake could not be rectified. The alabaster image, given me four years ago by a devout couple in Burma, was therefore relegated to one side of the shrine, a position it retained when the latter was moved back to the summer-house. Visitors rarely noticed the dark ring round its neck, but it was some years before those who had been present forgot how Joe had broken a Buddha-image, and some years before the aura of inauspiciousness that came to surround the eccentric Canadian upasaka was entirely dispelled.

At the time of its occurrence, the catastrophe cast a damper on our preparations for the thrice-sacred festival, and it was not until the follow-ing day that spirits were fully recovered. After an early morning puja in the summer-house, held for the benefit of our more regular members and friends, we gave the first wave of visitors tea and started putting the finishing touches to the decorations. In the case of the temporary shrine, this mainly consisted in arranging flowers in the various vases we had managed to collect, as well as in scattering them, Indian style, on and around the image table. Many more double white flowers having ap-peared among the glossy evergreen leaves of our gardenia bush, I had, besides other flowers, plenty of velvet-petalled, richly scented gardenias at my disposal. While I was trying to place them where they would show to the greatest advantage, a little girl brought me a bunch of gardenias from her mother. In the course of the morning more bunches of gardenias arrived, as well as two or three small basketfuls of the same exotic flower, until I had far more of them than were needed for the vases and image table. Yet still the gardenias continued to come. The gardens of Kalim-pong seemed to be raining gardenias upon us, the deluge culminating in the arrival of a perfectly enormous basketful sent down from Krishnalok by Princess Irene of Greece. Gardenias lay in fragrant white heaps on the floor. There must have been thousands of them. I therefore began sticking them into the greenery with which the temporary shrine had been covered, so that eventually the room was practically lined with garde-nias. Those left over I stuck in the greenery surrounding the entrance, the windows, and the veranda posts – stuck them, indeed, in every nook and cranny. By the time I had finished the place was a veritable paradise of gardenias, and the rich scent of gardenias filled the air.

That night the former games room was packed, and the silver butter-lamps cast a warm glow over eager, expectant faces and colourful national costumes, as well as over the solid walls of gardenias on either side. The meeting should have begun at six o'clock, but the Governor of West Bengal, who happened to be staying in Kalimpong and whom I had invited through the SDO, did not turn up until more than an hour later. Dr Mookerji was a retired college professor whose appointment to the governorship had taken everybody by surprise, but who with his simple, unassuming ways had soon won for himself a place in people's affections. He was also a Christian (not a convert, but a member of an 'old' Anglican family), and I was concerned lest he should not know that shoes had to be removed before entering the shrine, and dropped a hint to that effect. But I need not have worried. Dr Mookerji knew very well what to do, and in fact sat through the puja and through my own sermon on the significance of Vaishakha Purnima, as well as through the musical items that followed, with as great an appearance of devotion as any of the older Buddhists or Hindus present. After he had left there was more music, and it was with the sound of the sitar, and of youthful voices raised in praise of the Buddha, that the meeting eventually came to an end.

I had originally intended to dismantle the temporary shrine the next day, but in such numbers did people continue to come in order to worship that I decided to leave it as it was for the time being. In any case, though Vaishakha Purnima itself was over, the year's celebrations were far from being concluded. The public meeting in the Town Hall was still to come, and organizations that were also celebrating *Buddha Jayanti*, as the thrice-sacred festival was generally known in India, had invited me to address them. One of these was the Maitri Sangha, the Bengali cultural organization where I had already given a number of lectures and where I had a small following of educated Bengalis sympathetic to Buddhism. On the present occasion, however, I was not the only speaker, there being three others on the platform with me: Bhadant Anand Kausalyayan, the elderly Punjabi monk who took me on long walks whenever he was in Kalimpong; Swami Gangeshwarananda, the incumbent of the local Ramakrishna Mission ashram, and Dr George Roerich, the Tibetologist. I was more than a little surprised that Gangeshwarananda had been invited to speak, since he was very unpopular in Kalimpong on account of his evil temper and was known to be hostile to Buddhism. I could only assume that the organizers had invited him because he was the religious representative of the Bengali Hindu community, so to speak, and because they were confident he would observe the proprieties. But if such was their confidence, it proved to have been misplaced. When it was his turn to speak the swami launched into a virulent attack on Buddhism, an attack which ended with his exclaiming, in tones of the utmost contempt, 'But what sort of religion can you expect from someone who died from over-indulgence in pork!' The little audience was deeply shocked. I said nothing at the time, but after the meeting I protested to the secretary of the Sangha, as did several other people. I also called on the president of the Sangha on my way back to The Hermitage and protested to him too. Genial Dr Boral was quick to promise that such an incident would not occur again. A few days later I heard that Mrs Charu Mitter, the influential Bengali lady whom some called the Queen of Kalimpong, was extremely displeased with the swami's behaviour and that, like Dr Boral, she intended there should be no repetition of the incident.

Whether prompted by Gangeshwarananda's attack on Buddhism, or for some other reason, the morning after the Maitri Sangha meeting I started writing a satirical sketch on Brahminism entitled 'How Buddhism Disappeared from India'. Bhadant Anand, to whom I read extracts, thoroughly enjoyed this little *jeu d'esprit*, but though I finished it a couple of weeks later the work was far too scathing to be publishable in India and I never gave it a final revision.

The lectures at the Maitri Sangha were all in English, but at our public meeting in the Town Hall (which in fact preceded the Maitri Sangha meeting by a week) the lectures were in four or five languages. The reason for the diversity was that the population of Kalimpong was a polyglot one, and I wanted everybody to be able to hear the Dharma in his mother tongue or, at least, in a language with which he was familiar. This policy – or rather principle – of mine was well known in the town and our Vaishakha Purnima public meeting was therefore attended by people from all sections of the community, whether Buddhists or Hindus, hill people or plainsmen. Though the lectures were in so many languages, there was no disharmony between them in point of content, much less still any disharmony between one speaker and another, and when after the three-hour programme my helpers and I took down the decorations we could congratulate ourselves on a truly successful meeting. The day before there had, however, been a little disharmony between one of the speakers and Joe. The speaker in question was Miss Barclay, an elderly Englishwoman of generous disposition but uncertain temper who had arrived in Kalimpong earlier in the year and was now one of The Hermitage's most frequent visitors. The scene of the disharmony was my room. Joe had come to discuss the next day's public meeting with me, and Miss Barclay was furious with him for taking up my time, as she saw it, when she wanted to talk with me herself. Her outburst astonished the poor Canadian upasaka, who was accustomed to being at the originating rather than at the receiving end of such displays of temperament, and I had to intervene to restore the peace between these two Western followers of the Dharma (Miss Barclay had recently become a Buddhist, much to the annoyance of the local missionaries). Later I explained to Joe that it was by no means unusual for Miss Barclay to fly into a tantrum and that he should not take it too seriously.

The good people of Kalimpong had hardly finished celebrating Buddha Jayanti when there came news of an event that for many days intermitted all other topics of conversation. Everest was conquered. Edmund Hillary and Tenzing Norgay had succeeded in reaching the top of the highest mountain in the world, where hitherto no human foot had trod. The Nepalese, in particular, were wildly excited, for Tenzing Norgay was a Sherpa, and inasmuch as the Sherpas were Nepalese by nationality, even if not by ethnic origin (they were in fact of Tibetan stock), his achievement could be regarded as demonstrating, in the eyes of the whole world, the superiority of the Nepalese people in at least one field. They might not have produced an internationally renowned writer or scientist, or even an internationally renowned politician, but they had produced Tenzing Norgay, the conqueror of Everest. So proud were the Nepalese of their hero, and to such an extent did they identify with him, that they were impatient of any reminder that Tenzing Norgay was technically an Indian citizen and that he had not stood on the summit of Everest alone. Among younger Nepalese the name of Edmund Hillary was hardly ever mentioned, while that of Sir John Hunt, the leader of the expedition, was not mentioned at all. Listening to them, one could easily have thought that Sherpa Tenzing, as he was generally called, had reached the top of Mount Everest by his own unaided efforts.

I myself felt little or no excitement when, on the morning of Tuesday 2 June, Miss Barclay brought the news that Everest had been conquered. Though I could appreciate the courage and determination that had made such an achievement possible, the idea that a mountain, or any other part of nature, was something to be 'conquered', was foreign to my whole way of thinking and feeling. Mountains were alive. Indeed there were mountains, Everest itself being one, which could be said to have personality, in the sense of having the power to attract people and influence them. A mountain of this kind was a sacred mountain, and the proper attitude towards it was one of reverence and worship. In the words of a modern pilgrim to Mount Kailas, the most sacred of all the mountains in the Himalayan system:

> This worshipful or religious attitude is not impressed by scientific facts, like figures of altitude, which are foremost in the mind of modern man. Nor is it motivated by the urge to 'conquer' the mountain. Instead of conquering it, the religious-minded man prefers to be conquered by the mountain. He opens his soul to its spirit and allows it to take possession of him, because only he who is *inspired* or 'possessed' by the divine spirit can partake of its nature. While the modern man is driven by ambition and the glorification of his own ego to climb an outstanding mountain and to be the first on top of it, the devotee is more interested in his spiritual uplift than in the physical feat of climbing. To him the mountain is a divine symbol, and as little as he would put his foot upon a sacred image, so little would he dare to put his foot on the summit of a sacred mountain.

Lama Govinda's sentiments were very much my own, and I was therefore unable to share the jubilation of our Nepalese members and friends that Everest had been conquered and that a man of their own blood had been the first to stand on the untrodden snows of its summit.

But Tuesday 2 June, the day on which I received the news of the conquest of Everest, was also Coronation Day. Later it was rumoured that the news of Hillary and Tenzing's achievement had been deliberately held back in order that its release on that day might be a present, as it were, to the new monarch, Elizabeth II, on the occasion of her coronation. Be that as it may, I was as little excited by the Coronation as I was by the news of the conquest of Everest. Nine years had passed since my departure from England, and I had no thought of returning. Moreover, I was a monk, and since that be-rainbowed August morning six years ago when I had gone forth 'from home into the life of homelessness' it had been my conviction that one who had renounced the world had no exclusive mundane loyalties, whether national or racial. Though known in Kalimpong as 'the English monk' I did not really think of myself as such. Language and literature apart, my links with the country of my birth were tenuous, being more or less limited to the occasional exchange of letters with English Buddhists. It was therefore hardly surprising that I should not have been excited by the Coronation or that I should have given it no more thought than did my Nepalese and Tibetan friends. The only people who were at all excited by it were the handful of elderly

British residents who had stayed on after Independence and, of course, the occupants of that stronghold of Scottish Presbyterianism, Dr Graham's Homes, where 500-odd children of mixed parentage were brought up as Christians and taught to think of the United Kingdom as 'home' and where, not surprisingly, the film of the Coronation was soon being shown. I did not see the film. Not only was I not interested in seeing it, but monks were not supposed to see films and in any case I knew that I was *persona non grata* at the Homes. Miss Barclay saw it, however, and afterwards gave me an account of the feudal pomp and ecclesiastical circumstance by which the coronation ceremony had been surrounded. She also lent me her copy of the *Daily Mirror* Coronation number.

Of only one picture of the coronation do I retain even a faint recollection – a picture of the Queen, newly crowned and sceptred, sitting in the Coronation Chair and looking strangely young for so great a responsibility. More vivid is my recollection of another picture, which I may actually have seen not in the *Daily Mirror* Coronation number but in an earlier issue of the same popular newspaper. This was a picture of three women in deep mourning standing together, heavily veiled, in attitudes expressive of sorrow, shock, and resignation. Below was the caption 'Three Queens – One Grief'. The occasion was the funeral of King George VI, and the three queens were Queen Mary, Queen Elizabeth the Queen Mother, and Queen Elizabeth II, one of whom had just lost a son, one a husband, and one a father. There was a quality of timeless, archetypal tragedy about this triple image that I found deeply moving. It was as though the three Fates or three Norns were mourning doomed humanity. I had seen Queen Mary during the War, walking over Westminster Bridge accompanied by a single lady-in-waiting. Then too she was in mourning, the Duke of Kent, her youngest son, having been killed recently in a flying accident. Years earlier I had seen the future Queen Elizabeth II, then Princess Elizabeth. Riding with my father on the top of a red double-decker London bus, when I was six or seven years old, I had found myself looking down over the wall of a West End mansion. In the garden two little girls were playing, one slightly bigger than the other. 'Look,' said my father, as the bus moved on, 'there are the two little princesses, Elizabeth and Margaret Rose.'

But these were only memories. Not long after Vaishakha I had a visitor who came straight from the Britain of the second Elizabethan Age, as it was hoped the new reign would prove to be, and who provided me with a more direct and tangible link with my native land. The visitor was a very small, very upright, very severe-looking woman in traditional

Tibetan dress, complete with rainbow-apron. She was Dawa's mother. Dawa Tsering Bhutia was one of our oldest and most faithful members. Though in government service, he was secretary of our little branch of the Maha Bodhi Society, as he had been of its predecessor the Young Men's Buddhist Association (India) in his student days. Reliable and conscientious to a fault, he was at the same time inclined to be anxious, and it was with considerable trepidation that he brought his formidable little mother to see me. Had her Dawa been behaving himself while she was away, she wanted to know, or had he been wasting his time hanging round the bazaar and getting into bad company? She hoped he had not been drinking, or smoking, or chewing tobacco, since otherwise she would have to give him a good thrashing. Fortunately I was able to reassure her on all these points, and her rigid features relaxed a little. What I would have said had she also hoped that her son was keeping clear of women I do not know. My young friend was desperately in love with a Nepalese girl whom he wanted to marry and was terrified lest his mother should find out, since she had often declared that under no circumstances would she allow him to marry anyone but a Tibetan. During his mother's visit Dawa was very much on tenterhooks, in case I should inadvertently let slip something about him that he did not want her to know; but luckily this did not happen, and mother and son were able to leave The Hermitage apparently reassured, in her case, and relieved, in his.

The strait-laced, strong-minded little Tibetan woman made quite an impression on me. Our conversation was carried on mainly in English, a smattering of which she had picked up from the family for whom she worked as an *ayah* in England and to whose service she would soon be returning. But although her very limited English was decidedly of the fractured variety, with occasional lapses into Nepali, she spoke it not only with the utmost aplomb but with an upper-class accent and intonation that would have done credit to a duchess. Listening to her, I could at times have fancied that I was in a drawing-room in the Home Counties rather than amid the foothills of the Eastern Himalayas. The link with my native land with which she provided me, at least for half an hour, was a direct and tangible one indeed.

Not that Dawa's mother was my only visitor during this period, that is, my only visitor from outside Kalimpong (visitors from the town itself came every day, at all hours). There were visitors from Poland and America, France and Germany. The French visitor was Miss Delannoy, the short, untidy Sorbonne alumna who had spent a couple of weeks in

Kalimpong earlier in the year and who even then had seemed to be more interested in Buddhism than in the subjects she was supposed to be studying. Having made a trip to Nepal, she was in fact now staying in Ghoom, and shortly after her arrival in Kalimpong took the Three Refuges and Five Precepts from me. She was, I noticed, more balanced than she had been at the time of her previous visit. The German visitors were Dr and Mrs Liebenthal. Frail and evidently poor, the gentle old couple had not come direct from Germany, which they had left in the thirties. They had come from China via Shantiniketan, at whose Cheena Bhavan Dr Liebenthal was now teaching. A Sinologist of international repute, he had translated the Chinese version of the *Sutra of the Lord of Healing* into English and on his second visit to The Hermitage he presented me with a copy of this work, by which he clearly set great store. My most interesting visitor, however, was not from Poland or America, France or Germany. He was from Japan.

Dr Kajiyama arrived at The Hermitage two days after Vaishakha Purnima, when the temporary shrine was as yet undismantled and the scent of gardenias still filled the air. He arrived at the end of our evening puja, and after showing him his room (he was an expected guest rather than a casual visitor) I accompanied Miss Barclay and Miss Delannoy to the bazaar, both those ladies having attended the puja. While I was out the young Japanese scholar must have sat and meditated in the deserted shrine-room, between the walls of gardenias, for he afterwards told me that even in the Zen monasteries of his native Japan he had not experienced so peaceful an atmosphere. During the month he stayed with me he gave not the slightest trouble. He was an ideal guest. Slim and self-effacing, he flitted about like a shadow, being particularly careful not to disturb or interrupt me when I was busy. One afternoon I took him and Anand-ji (as Bhadant Anand was generally called) to see Dr Roerich, and the veteran Tibetologist was glad to have news of the Pali Institute at Nalanda, where Dr Kajiyama was studying and teaching and whence he had travelled up to Kalimpong to escape the burning heat of the plains. The Institute had been started two years earlier by my teacher Bhikkhu Jagdish Kashyap, and though the ever-sceptical Anand-ji had doubted of its success it was now doing well and had attracted some distinguished scholars. Half-way through his stay Dr Kajiyama spent a few days in Darjeeling, which was eight thousand feet above sea level to Kalimpong's four thousand. It was as though Kalimpong was not cool enough for him, and probably the misty, pine-clad slopes of the Queen of the Hill Stations were more reminiscent of Japan than were the maize-planted terraces of her more tropical younger sister. However that might have been, Dr Kajiyama must have thought of his native land quite a lot, for we talked about Japan, and discussed Japanese Buddhism, on more than one occasion. In particular we discussed Ashvaghosha's *Awakening of Faith in the Mahayana*.

I had come across this seminal work, in Suzuki's translation, during my wandering days in South India. I had found it in the library of a Hindu ashram where I was staying, and so great an impression did it make on me that I at once copied the entire text into my notebook. That notebook I still had with me and I still reflected, from time to time, on the teachings of the profound and cryptic little work, which according to some modern scholars was an original Chinese composition, but which had in any case exerted a strong influence on practically all the major schools of Far Eastern Buddhism. I was particularly struck by the concept – or rather image – of 'perfuming', distant reflections of which even found their way into my poetry. In Early Buddhism samsara and nirvana were mutually exclusive realities, which left unresolved the question of how they were related. According to Ashvaghosha, or whoever wrote under that name, the relation between them is one of mutual perfuming. Clothes have no scent in themselves, but if they are permeated with perfumes then they come to have a scent. Similarly, the pure state of Suchness (Ashvaghosha's term for the Absolute) is without defilement, but upon its being 'perfumed' by ignorance there appear on it the marks of defilement. In a corresponding manner, the defiled state of ignorance is devoid of any purifying influence, but upon its being 'perfumed' by Suchness it comes to have such an influence. Indispensable though the help of Buddhas, Bodhisattvas, and spiritual friends may also be, a man is able to renounce samsara and realize nirvana primarily because his deluded mind is permeated by the perfume of Suchness – a perfume far surpassing the scent of gardenias.

Chapter Two

TEA GARDENS, TAMANGS, AND A TALKING CALF

LONGVIEW WAS ONE OF THE BIGGEST TEA ESTATES in the Darjeeling District, but I had heard of its existence only recently, when I received a visit from its new, South Indian manager. R.A. Padmanathan was a reader of the *Aryan Path*, to which I was a regular contributor; the *Aryan Path* was printed and published in Bangalore by the Indian Institute of Culture, and the director of the Institute was Padmanathan's cousin. On learning from this cousin that the Buddhist monk whose name appeared so frequently in the pages of the Institute's journal lived in Kalimpong, thus being virtually his next-door neighbour, Padmanathan lost no time in coming to see me. The visit was followed by an exchange of letters between us, an exchange which culminated, towards the end of June, in his inviting me to Longview and my accepting the invitation. Though I had been living in the District for over three years I had as yet had no more than a glimpse of the world-famous tea gardens, and the idea of spending a few days in one of them appealed to me.

I did not go to Longview alone. Sachin accompanied me. He was one of my oldest pupils, having attended the evening tutorial classes which, shortly after the establishment of the now defunct YMBA, I had started for the benefit of those of our members who were fearful of not passing their school or college examinations. After an unsuccessful attempt at a science degree in Darjeeling (his father had wanted him to be a doctor) he was back in Kalimpong, attending the Scottish Universities Mission (Arts) College, and now came to me for tuition in Logic and English Literature. Logic we both found interesting, at times even fascinating, but English Literature – especially English poetry – was sheer, unadulterated delight. Besides going through the Calcutta University's IA Prose and Poetry Selections page by page and line by line, I dictated paraphrases of the poems to him, the ability to reproduce 'in your own words' the meaning of Wordsworth's 'Immortality Ode' or Shelley's 'To the West Wind' being, apparently, highly prized by the examiners. Not that we confined ourselves to the Selections. Sachin's love of literature was hardly less than my own, and we often wandered, in the course of these tutorials, far beyond the limits of what was academically prescribed. Love of literature constituted, indeed, a strong bond between us. It had been a major factor in the development of our friendship, which now that Sachin was back in Kalimpong was flourishing more vigorously than ever. Rarely did a day pass without our seeing each other, either at The Hermitage or at the bungalow in the Scottish Mission compound where he lived and where, if he happened to be out, I sometimes talked with his father, who was a doctor in the Mission hospital. When Padmanathan invited me to Longview it was therefore natural that I should tell Sachin, natural that he should want to accompany me, natural that I should be willing for him to do so, and natural, finally, that we should decide to extend the scope of our excursion and return to Kalimpong via Kurseong and Darjeeling.

The evening before our departure I learned that Gyan Jyoti's jeep would be going down to Siliguri in the morning. Gyan Jyoti was the prominent Newar Buddhist merchant who had invited Kashyap-ji (as my teacher was generally known) to Kalimpong and who, since Kashyap-ji had taken me there with him and then left me to 'work for the good of Buddhism', was indirectly responsible for my presence in the town. Though we did not often meet, he was always ready to oblige me, and thus it was that I travelled to Siliguri in the front seat of his jeep, while Sachin followed by bus. Within half an hour of our leaving The Hermitage we had crossed Teesta Bridge, three thousand feet below Kalimpong, and were speeding along the muddy potholed track that wound between the foothills to the plains. The rainy season was well advanced, and I saw that the Teesta had risen dramatically and that its waters were no longer jade green or turquoise in colour but a dull ochre laced with soapsuddy yellow. There had already been a few landslides, but the road had been cleared, and the other occupants of the jeep and I were beginning to congratulate ourselves on an uneventful journey when, only a few miles from the plains, we suddenly found our passage blocked by three enormous boulders. These had to be dynamited out of the way before we could proceed, with the result that it took five hours instead of the expected three to reach the would-be-industrial shanty town that was Siliguri, where the Longview jeep was waiting. Half an hour later, having been swallowed by the rolling green acres of the tea gardens, which extended up into the first range of foothills, Sachin and I were being deposited at the entrance to the manager's bungalow and welcomed by Padmanathan.

According to the dictionary a bungalow was a one-storey house, but the building in which we now found ourselves, and where we were soon partaking of a late lunch with our host, was more like a country mansion than the modest suburban dwelling that, in England at least, the Hindi-derived term had come to designate. The table at which we sat could have accommodated twenty people, while the enormous dresser that stood against one wall and the massive sideboard that stood against another held, respectively, dinner services, and glass- and silverware, that must have been shipped from England decades ago. Obviously in the spacious days of the Raj the manager of a Darjeeling tea estate had lived in considerable splendour, waited on by a horde of servants, and entertaining lavishly. In this respect, at least, Padmanathan was far from emulating his imperial predecessors. He lived very simply, making use of only a few of the twenty-odd lofty rooms, keeping only a handful of servants, and doing little or no entertaining. Though clad, as no doubt his predecessors had been clad, in khaki shorts and open-necked shirt, he did not really give the impression of being the manager of an important tea estate. With his serious expression, and mild manners, he gave the impression, rather, of being a college professor or not very successful lawyer.

Lunch was not only late but lengthy, Padmanathan having a lot to say to me, and after the meal Sachin and I barely had a chance to try out the bungalow's ping-pong table before it was time for afternoon tea and a visit to the temple. When he took over, Padmanathan explained, there was not a single place of worship in the whole estate. He had therefore built the labourers a temple, and from the way he showed this to us it was clear he was quite proud of the little whitewashed structure on the edge of the labour force's assembly ground. It was open-fronted, and divided into two compartments, each with its own bell. One compartment contained images of Radha and Krishna, both standing; the other, a sedent image of the Buddha. Having shown us the temple Padmanathan took us to see first the tea gardens, with their thousands of rows of flat-topped bushes, and then the various offices. Though our host drove us round for quite a while, we were far from seeing the whole estate which, he informed us, comprised 1,500 acres and had a labour force of 3,000. Most of the labourers were Tamangs, which meant they were Buddhists, but according to Padmanathan they were totally ignorant of Buddhism and had, in fact, no interest in religion. The rest of the labourers were either Thapas or other Nepalese Hindus or – though there were very few of these – Nepalese Christian converts.

By the time we returned to the bungalow Sachin and I had seen and heard so much that was new to us that we felt quite tired, and were content simply to sit on the veranda without speaking. Situated on a ridge as it was, the bungalow commanded a breathtakingly extensive view of the plains, and as darkness fell – the 'embalméd darkness' of the tropics – we could see the lights of Siliguri twinkling in the distance. How was it, I wondered, that a place that looked so sordid by day could contrive to present so magical an appearance at night! But I did not wonder for long. The air was cold, my mosquito-curtained bed was inviting, and we had to be up at 05.00 in order to accompany Padmanathan to the assembly ground and see the labour force being given its orders for the day.

If I had expected to see dawn break, next morning, on 3,000 heads, then I was disappointed. Only four or five hundred men, women, and children actually turned up, many of them carrying the traditional *tokri* or cone-shaped wicker basket. They were, I had to admit, an unattractive lot. Though sturdily built, they were for the most part squat, bandy-legged, low-browed, and broad-featured, with expressions that ranged from the dull and apathetic to the coarse and brutal, so that one had to remind oneself that these were human beings and, as such, one's brothers and sisters – even one's brother and sister Buddhists. When the force had assembled, and it was obvious no more labourers would be turning up that day, Padmanathan made his way to the temple, stepped inside the first compartment, rang the bell, put on his spectacles, and read out two verses from the *Bhagavad-gita*. He then stepped into the second compartment, rang the bell there too, read out two verses from the *Dhammapada*, took off his spectacles, and rejoined the little band of assistants and overseers with whom he had been talking. The assembled labourers took no interest in these proceedings. 'Burra Saheb's job is to run the estate,' their sullen looks seemed to say, if they said anything at all. 'Religion is the job of brahmins and lamas.' For Padmanathan had engaged a Nepalese brahmin to officiate in the Hindu half of the temple and a Tamang lama to officiate in the Buddhist half, and the two functionaries were in obsequious attendance upon him as he performed his own supernumerary ministrations. These ministrations over, he was free to give the labour force, or as much of it as had turned up, its orders for the day, which he did through the medium of the overseers, his own Nepali being insufficient for that purpose. The overseers then led off their respective contingents to various parts of the estate, while Padmanathan took Sachin and me to his office for breakfast.

After breakfast our host showed us more of the estate, this time initiating us into the mysteries of the tea-producing process, from the picking of the 'two leaves and a bud' with which the process began to the dispatching of the big, fragrant wooden chests with which it concluded. Picking was usually done by women, Padmanathan explained, as we looked out over one of the gardens, where scores of pairs of female hands were working with incredible rapidity, right hand and left hand alternately tossing the young shoots and leaves back over the picker's shoulder into her tokri. Women were in any case more reliable than men, he continued; because they had children to feed they worked regularly, whereas the men worked only when they needed liquor money and were often drunk for days on end. The bushes on which the shoots and leaves grew were, I noticed, all no more than breast high, for though the tea plant was really a tree, belonging to the same family as the camellia, in cultivation its growth was restricted for the convenience of the picker. It was no doubt for the same reason that the tops of the bushes were kept perfectly flat. Planted out as they were at regular intervals, in long straight rows, the neat little bushes gave the hillside something of the appearance of a Dutch formal garden of clipped yew.

Each time a picker filled her tokri she took it to the overseer, who weighed it and entered the weight against her name in a little book. At the end of the day the weights were added up and she would be paid according to the total. Thus the faster she worked the greater would be the number of times she filled her tokri, and the greater the number of times she filled her tokri the more she would be paid. In this way an active young woman could earn what by local standards was a good wage.

From the gardens the freshly-picked shoots and leaves were transported to a factory, where they went through the remaining stages of the tea-producing process, all of which Padmanathan showed us. The unfortunate herb was spread on trays, rolled, fermented, baked, and tortured in a variety of other ways, before being sifted into grades and packed ready for dispatch to Calcutta. For the whole time we were inside the factory I was not only conscious of the extreme humidity; I was also conscious of a pervasive, overpowering odour – the odour of tea. It was an odour reminiscent, not of the delicate aroma wafted from the four o'clock incarnation of 'the cup that cheers but does not inebriate', but rather of the stench emanating from yesterday's used tea-leaves. I was therefore not sorry when, our initiation into the mysteries of tea-production being complete, Sachin and I eventually emerged with Padmanathan into the comparative coolness of the air outside and were taken back to the bungalow, where my host and I at once plunged into a serious discussion – a discussion that lasted until lunchtime and was continued in the evening.

The fact of the matter was that I was deeply concerned about the Tamang labourers, who after all comprised by far the greater part of the Longview labour force. They were Buddhists, in the sense that they had been born into 'Buddhist' families. More precisely, they were Nyingma Buddhists, that is, followers of Padmasambhava, the Precious Guru, one of the two co-founders of the Tibetan Buddhist tradition. Yet according to Padmanathan they were totally ignorant of Buddhism and had no interest in religion. Something had to be done, and done quickly, since otherwise they might cease in the course of another generation to be Buddhists even in name. The idea that eventually occurred to me, as Padmanathan and I talked, and which I at once communicated to him, was that he should establish a branch of the Maha Bodhi Society at Longview, a branch that would be responsible for spreading the basic teachings of Buddhism among the labour force and which I myself would visit regularly. Within a few years the Tamangs would be completely changed; they would be Buddhists in fact as well as in name and true followers of the Precious Guru. Though Padmanathan did not mislike the idea of there being a branch of the Maha Bodhi Society at Longview, he was far from sharing my confidence that it could be a means of changing the Tamangs. I had seen for myself, he commented ruefully, how little interest the labourers took in what went on inside the temple. It had been a great disappointment to him. At least some of them, he had thought, would get into the habit of going to the temple to pray, whether to the Buddha or to Radha-Krishna (it didn't really matter to whom), and to offer the lama or the brahmin a few annas. But none of them ever did. A few of the Hindu office staff sometimes went to the temple, but the Tamang and other labourers gave it a wide berth. The nearest the latter ever got to it was when they came to the assembly ground to be given their orders for the day, and even then they took no more notice of the temple than if it had been an ordinary building. It was as though they did not appreciate what he had done for them.... Later on, Sachin having joined us, Padmanathan returned to the theme. Not only had he built the labourers a temple. He had also provided them with a free dispensary; but they steadfastly refused to avail themselves of its services, preferring to rely instead on old wives' remedies of their own when they fell sick or were injured. It was the same in the case of the shop he had opened for their benefit. This too they refused to patronize, even though they could buy provisions there at wholesale prices. He couldn't understand them. They seemed not to respond to kindness. Why, when asked which of his various predecessors they had liked best they invariably mentioned the name of Mr—, a British manager who abused them and swore at them, who was very free with his fists, and who was not above laying into them with a whip. Sometimes he thought, our host added, that if they had a voice in the matter the labourers of Longview would vote to bring back Mr—, whip and all.

Next day I had another serious discussion, this time with the Deputy Commissioner, Sri Dutt-Majumdar, whom I had already met once or twice. He arrived a couple of hours before lunch, having come to confer with Padmanathan on a problem that had lately arisen and with which he was having to deal: the problem of the infiltration of some of the tea estates by Communist agitators. The Communist Party – or parties – was not illegal in India: those were in any case the heady days of Indo-Chinese friendship, when according to the popular slogan the peoples of India and China were brothers, friends, mates; but agitation in the tea estates could lead to strikes, strikes to loss of production, and loss of production to loss of foreign exchange, tea being one of India's most valuable exports. As Deputy Commissioner, Dutt-Majumdar was therefore concerned with the matter. Infiltration by Communists was also of concern, it seemed, to the good Fathers of North Point, the famous Catholic college on the outskirts of Darjeeling. One of their number had recently called on him at his office, so Dutt-Majumdar informed me, to report that the English Buddhist monk who lived in Kalimpong was, in fact, a Communist spy, and to suggest that in the interest of national security he should be expelled from the District. 'I know very well why he reported you,' Dutt-Majumdar smilingly assured me. 'You have nothing to worry about.'

I too knew why the Jesuit Father had reported me. Indeed, I thought I knew the reason for his action better than Dutt-Majumdar himself did. It was not merely that, in accordance with my teacher's behest, I was working in Kalimpong for the good of Buddhism, thus diminishing the influence of the missionaries, Catholic and Protestant alike, in what they were accustomed to regard as their very own territory. A few months earlier I had sent to the Calcutta English-language dailies a letter exposing a particularly odious method of obtaining conversions to Christianity that had come to my notice in Kalimpong, and the publication of this letter had aroused the wrath of the missionary fraternity throughout north-eastern India and made me even more notorious among them than I was already. The method in question was that of 'conversion through pregnancy', as I termed it. A Christian girl would be encouraged to associate with a non-Christian boy who, when she became pregnant, would be pressurized by the Mission authorities first into agreeing to marry her, then into agreeing to marry her in church, and finally, since only Christians could be married in church, into agreeing to become a Christian. Sometimes the pressure included threats of physical violence. All this I explained to Dutt-Majumdar, who was naturally interested, the more especially since the boys whose cases I mentioned came from communities entitled to official protection from exploitation by outside agencies. He therefore asked me to let him have the facts in writing, at the same time promising to take action in the matter.

When Sachin and I took leave of Padmanathan that afternoon I was well content with the success of our visit, and had much to think about as the Longview jeep zigzagged up the succession of hairpin bends that led to Kurseong. In Kurseong we spent an hour or two at the TB Sanatorium visiting Lachuman, an old pupil of mine who was now a patient there, then caught the bus to Darjeeling. On my previous visits to Darjeeling I had been the guest of a hospitable Punjabi shopkeeper, but he was out of station (as the phrase went) and I decided to stay at the Gandhamadan Vihara instead. Situated on the sheer hillside below the main road into Darjeeling, the Gandhamadan Vihara was the religious and cultural centre of the town's two or three dozen Barua families, the Baruas being Theravadin Buddhists from East Bengal. It comprised a small shrine-cum-lecture hall, a row of guest rooms, and a one-room wooden *kuti* for the use of the resident bhikshu. At that time there was no resident bhikshu, nor had there been one, I gathered, for several years. There was, however, an orange-robed guest, in the person of the same Burmese Maha Thera or 'Great Elder' who had once visited me in Kalimpong and whom I had put up for the night. With him I therefore renewed acquaintance, having breakfast with him next morning and accompanying him to the house of Kali Kinker Barua, the secretary of the local Bengal Buddhist Association, for a *bhojana-dana* or ceremonial food-offering. I also renewed acquaintance, during that and the following day, with two leading members of the Tamang Buddhist Association, besides spending time with personal friends and visiting the town's English bookshops with Sachin, who was staying with his maternal grandmother.

The two members of the Tamang Buddhist Association were brisk, dapper little P.T. Lama and his big, pan-chewing brother Inspector T. Moktan. The latter, who was in the West Bengal police, was the more religious-minded of the two, and always came to see me when his duties took him to Kalimpong. A widower with two small daughters, he had decided, most uncharacteristically for a Nepalese, not to remarry. Though the two brothers were looking for me, and I was looking for them, we did not meet until we happened to bump into each other in the bazaar. They at once took me to the Tamang Gompa, as the pagoda-style Nyingma temple was called, and showed me the new *mani* chamber they were constructing there. A mani was a prayer-wheel or, more accurately, a prayer-cylinder, and a mani chamber was a chamber containing, not a prayer-cylinder such as was twirled by old-fashioned Tibetans as they took their evening stroll, but a giant version of the same devotional aid, a version which in this case would stand eight or ten feet high and occupy practically the entire chamber. They were constructing the mani chamber in memory of their mother, the brothers explained; it was nearly completed, as I could see, and they would like me to speak at the opening ceremony. I at once accepted the invitation. The principal object of worship in the Tamang Gompa was the enormous sedent image of Padmasambhava that had given me, three years ago, so overwhelming an impression of the spiritual reality of the Precious Guru, and I was happy to renew my connection with the place. I also accepted the invitation because I knew that even educated Buddhists like P.T. Lama and Inspector T. Moktan knew very little about Buddhism, and I was glad, while remaining personally not keen on prayer-cylinders, to have the opportunity of explaining the meaning of an ancient Buddhist tradition.

A few weeks later, therefore, I was back in Darjeeling and back at the Gandhamadan Vihara. This time Sachin did not accompany me. He was more than willing to do so, but according to the Hindu calendar both the days for which I would be away were inauspicious and his mother did not want him to be away from home then. On arriving in Darjeeling I again renewed acquaintance with the Burmese Maha Thera, then spent the remainder of the day seeing people, visiting bookshops, and executing various small commissions for Sachin and Miss Barclay. The day concluded with a three-cornered philosophical discussion between me and two Bengali Hindu friends – a discussion which lasted until the stroke of midnight. Next morning, after an early *bhojana-dana* at the home of Kali Kinker Barua, I made my way down the hillside to the Tamang Gompa, my host escorting me. The opening of the new mani chamber public occasion, with the Deputy Commissioner, Sri Dutt-Majumdar, presiding, and my own lecture as the principal item on the programme.

I had decided to speak on the meaning of the mantra *om mani padme hum hri*, this being the mantra embossed on the great copper cylinder that stood awaiting the push that would give it its first ponderous revolution on its axis. A good part of my lecture was devoted to explaining the significance of the Jewel (mani) and the Lotus (padma), which were, I said, universal symbols, being found, in different forms, all over the world. In the words of the summary I afterwards wrote of the lecture:

> The lotus grows in water, and water always represents life. Philosophically speaking, life is what we call *Samsara*, the repeated process of birth and death. Life and birth are closely connected, and for this reason the Lotus stands for the Garbha, the feminine principle, as well. It also represents the heart, and the emotions, since these are both associated with the feminine principle.
>
> The jewel, on the other hand, symbolizes light. Light represents knowledge. The source of light is the sun, the heat of which fecundates the earth. The Mani or Jewel therefore represents the active generating power, the masculine principle. Since reason is supposed to predominate in man, it also stands for reason, intellect and spiritual understanding.

In explaining the significance of these two symbols I was careful to insist that whereas a concept had only one meaning a symbol suggested innumerable meanings, so that the significance of a symbol could never be exhausted intellectually. It was therefore possible to interpret the words *mani padme*, literally 'the Jewel (is) in the Lotus', in a number of ways. They could signify the presence of a spiritual reality behind the veil of appearances, or the fact that every man and woman possessed the potentiality for Enlightenment, or the desirability of harmonizing the rational and emotional sides of our personality. Thus the meaning of *mani padme* was not abstract and philosophical but concrete and practical, and might be summarized as follows:

> All our thinking is in terms of pairs of opposites. We think of the true and false, right and wrong, etc. The Jewel and the Lotus represent the ultimate duality of existence. In China these two principles are called Yang and Yin; in India they are sometimes called Purusha and Prakriti, Shiva and Shakti. When we say that

the Jewel is in the Lotus, we are reminding ourselves that things are not really separate from each other, and that our dualistic way of looking at things is a delusion. When we realize, by spiritual practice, that duality is only the creation of our own minds, we become enlightened.

The references to Purusha and Prakriti, and Shiva and Shakti, were for the benefit of the Hindu members of the audience, the opening of the new mani chamber being not only a very public occasion but something of an inter-faith one as well. It was not that I really believed in the possibility of establishing an exact correspondence between Buddhist and Hindu symbols.

Besides explaining the meaning of the mantra I sought to account for the effect produced by its repetition. Words were sounds, and sounds consisted of vibrations. Every word we uttered not only conveyed a meaning but set up certain vibrations, which could be either harmonious or discordant. It was these vibrations, and not the rational content of the words, which influenced us most deeply, and it was possible for us to be influenced in this way because we, too, were made up of vibrations. Not only our physical bodies, but our minds as well, were vibrating at a certain rate. Everything in the universe vibrated. Buddhism and science agreed that nothing in the world was solid, but that everything was in a state of perpetual oscillation. At this point I referred to an American scientist's success in measuring the power of mantra vibrations numerically by means of radiation (particularly radiesthesia). The highest rate at which a mantra could vibrate, according to this authority, was 250,000 times a second. Several mantras vibrated at this rate, the mantra *om mani padme hum* being among them. This information, which I had gleaned from the writings of the Tantric scholar Dr Benoytosh Bhattacharya, was music to the ears of my Tamang Buddhist friends, as was the information, gleaned from the same source, that the revolution of a mani-cylinder released beneficial cosmic forces in favour of the person revolving it. When I sent a copy of the printed summary of my lecture to Lama Govinda, however, he responded with a flat rejection of the idea that the emotional and spiritual effect of a mantra had anything to do with its vibrational value as measured by a scientific device. Mechanistic interpretations of this kind, he roundly declared, were rank materialism, and as such quite inconsistent with the principles of true Buddhism. In deference to his superior understanding of the subject I therefore never reprinted the little article in which I had summarized my lecture at the opening of the Tamang Gompa's new mani chamber, but years later, particularly after becoming acquainted with Pythagoreanism, I sometimes wondered, *pace* Lama Govinda, whether there might not be a correlation, even a correlation expressible in mathematical terms, between the numerical frequencies and ratios that obtained in the outside world and human emotions, and whether the one might not, conceivably, have an effect on the other.

The new mani chamber having been opened and the massive cylinder given its initial push, I returned to the Gandhamadan Vihara and spent the next few hours absorbed in one of the books I had bought the previous day. It was T.S. Eliot's *The Use of Poetry and the Use of Criticism*. In my lecture I had spoken of the desirability of harmonizing the rational and emotional sides of our personality. There were certainly sides of my own personality that needed to be harmonized and integrated, though these were not so much the rational and the emotional as the religious and the aesthetic. Sometimes the two overlapped, even coincided, but more often they remained separate and distinct, even mutually antagonistic. This meant that usually they tended to alternate, sometimes even within the space of a single day, with now one now the other predominating, whether in respect of my inner preoccupations or my outward activities. On the day of the opening ceremony this was certainly the case. Having given a lecture on the meaning of a Buddhist mantra in the morning, and spent the afternoon absorbed in English literary criticism, in the evening I attended the full moon day puja in the Vihara's shrine-cum-lecture hall, administering the five precepts to the assembled Baruas and delivering my first sermon in Hindi.

On returning to Kalimpong next day I found the town in an uproar. At least the Hindu part of it was in an uproar. A butcher had been about to cut the throat of a calf when the innocent creature opened its mouth and said, apparently in good Nepali, 'Have mercy. Don't kill me. I am Holy Mother Cow.' News of the miracle spread like wildfire. Pious Hindus flocked from all parts of the town to have *darshan* of the calf, to prostrate themselves before it, and to implore its blessing. Neck profusely garlanded with marigolds, and forehead smeared with vermilion, it was taken in procession through the bazaar amid scenes of tremendous enthusiasm. Whenever it stopped for a moment, people pressed forward to dip their fingers in the precious deposit and apply it to their foreheads, cow-dung being endued, for orthodox Hindus, with all kinds of purificatory properties. Money was also collected on behalf of the now deified calf, and at the end of an hour the fortunate quadruped was the richer by

35,000 rupees. The principal contributors were the saffron-turbaned Marwari merchants, who occupied a prominent position in the town's economy and who were known as much for their strict Hindu orthodoxy as for their business acumen. A piece of land was being purchased for the calf, I was told, and a shed-cum-temple erected where it would be able to live out its days in peace. As for the butcher who had been the witness of the miracle, he had forsworn his sanguinary trade and become a vegetarian, and was going to spend the rest of his life in the calf's service as its priest and personal attendant.

The majority of our members, especially the younger ones, did not believe the calf had actually spoken, least of all that it had claimed to be Holy Mother Cow in person. There was general agreement, though, that something strange must have happened in the butcher's shed. Perhaps the butcher experienced a sudden revulsion as he lifted his knife against the innocent creature, a revulsion so strong that he *thought* he heard the calf speaking and begging him to spare its life. A few of our members rejected even this rationalistic explanation. The whole thing was a deliberate hoax, they declared. There had been no talking calf, no repentant butcher. The story had been fabricated by the local branch of the All-India Cow Protection Society; they had fabricated it in order to whip up support for their flagging anti-cowslaughter campaign, and Hindu popular sentiment, always volatile, had done the rest. To me it was obvious the cow-protectionists had been involved, if only to the extent of taking advantage of a rumour favourable to their cause, and I was pleased some of our members had seen through their machinations. A few weeks earlier I had started a new series of weekly lectures at The Hermitage. One lecture was entitled 'How to Develop Discrimination', and it had led to some lively discussion. In Kalimpong, as elsewhere, one had to learn to discriminate between religion and superstition, between individual devotion and collective hysteria, and the knowledge that some of my closer associates were beginning to do this was very heartening.

Chapter Three

DEATHS AND ENTRANCES

LESS THAN A HUNDRED YEARS EARLIER Kalimpong had been part of Bhutan, just as Darjeeling had been part of Sikkim, the Raj having nibbled at the corners of both kingdoms. None the less there were very few Bhutanese living in the town, though with their striped *chubas* (knee-length in the case of the men), cropped hair, and bare feet those that did live there made a particularly colourful contribution to the ethnic and cultural diversity of the place. What they lacked in numbers they more than made up in weight, at least where the Buddhist community was concerned, Kalimpong's leading Buddhist family being Bhutanese. This family was the Dorji family. The head of the family, Raja Sonam Topgay Dorji, lived in princely style at Bhutan House, which was situated three miles up the road from me, on the other side of town. Though his official designation was that of Trade Agent to the Government of Bhutan, he functioned as both prime minister and foreign minister of his undeveloped country, as well as being its *de facto* ambassador to India. Moreover, he controlled trade between Bhutan and India by the simple expedient of keeping as much of it as possible in his own hands, with the result that besides being the most powerful man in Bhutan, next to the king, he was extremely wealthy. Indeed, the Dorji family was reputed to be wealthier than the royal family. But powerful and wealthy though he now was, Raja Dorji's origins were distinctly plebeian. His father, who was the son of a syce, had rendered important services to the British and been suitably rewarded, while Sonam Topgay himself, following in his father's footsteps, had been made a titular raja, had married a Sikkimese princess, had become Trade Agent to the Government of Bhutan, and had built Bhutan House.

During my first months in Kalimpong I visited Bhutan House more than once, and met both Raja and Rani Dorji, as well as meeting their eldest son and their two daughters, one of whom was to become queen of Bhutan. While Topgay Raja, as he was generally known, mingled freely with the citizenry of Kalimpong and was a popular figure in the lower bazaar, his wife, who was the sister of the Maharaja of Sikkim, held herself icily aloof and was far from popular. Her unpopularity was due less to her aloofness, which in any case was expected from a member of the aristocracy, than to her extreme tightfistedness and the utter ruthlessness with which she distrained upon debtors and evicted tenants the minute they were in arrears. She was in fact a formidable personage, and few people dared cross her path. Unfortunately, I had been obliged to cross it when, some three years earlier, she was the chairman and I the general secretary of the Sacred Relics Reception Committee (the relics in question were those of Shariputra and Maudgalyayana, the Buddha's chief disciples, which were then touring India after being returned by the Victoria and Albert Museum). For purely personal reasons Rani Dorji was determined that the relics of the two Arahants should not be lodged at the Tharpa Chholing Gompa, the biggest and most important Buddhist monastery in Kalimpong, and there exposed for the veneration of the public, whereas I was no less determined that they should be lodged there and succeeded, eventually, in winning the support of the other members of the committee. Since then Rani Dorji had refused to have anything to do with me, with the YMBA (she had attended a lecture or two in its very early days) or, more recently, with the Kalimpong branch of the Maha Bodhi Society.

One morning towards the end of September, however, a few days after we had celebrated the birth anniversary of Anagarika Dharmapala, the founder of the Maha Bodhi Society, Gyan Jyoti came with an invitation to lunch at Bhutan House. As I already knew, Raja Dorji was dead. He had died two nights ago, a condolence meeting had been held at the Town Hall, and I had myself written to Jigme Dorji, the late Raja's eldest son, expressing my sympathy for him and the rest of the family. Anand-ji was also invited, Gyan Jyoti informed me, as was the Venerable Mahanama, the latter being a cousin of Gyan Jyoti's who had recently arrived in Kalimpong and who, though a monk, cherished aspirations to stardom in the world of films. Four days later I accordingly walked half a mile up the road to the Dharmodaya Vihara, the English-style family house which was the religious and cultural centre of the local Newar Buddhists, where Anand-ji and Mahanam-ji were staying and where I had myself spent the first ten months of my life in Kalimpong. From there the three of us were driven to Bhutan House, passing beneath the enormous *vajra* or thunderbolt-sceptre that lay across the top of the front gate and gave the whole place, I always thought, a sinister and threatening look. Rani Dorji and her children were waiting on the veranda to receive us. Though black was not the traditional Buddhist colour of mourning, they all wore black chubas, knee-length in the case of Jigme and his brothers, which served to accentuate the pallor of their countenances. Not surprisingly, they looked not only grief-stricken but deeply shocked. Raja Dorji had died, it seemed, rather unexpectedly. According to Gyan Jyoti it was unclear what he had died from, how long he had been ill, or even if he had been ill at all, and rumour was already rife in the bazaar. Grief and shock were however mingled, in the family's looks, with a third expression which I found it more difficult to identify but which was almost one of horror. What could this mean? But I had no time to speculate. After they had silently saluted us and we had silently responded to their salutations, the stricken family conducted Anand-ji, Mahanam-ji, and me first to the dining-room for the ceremonial food-offering and then up-stairs to Raja Dorji's room for the more specifically religious part of the proceedings.

The body was laid out on a richly decorated bed in the middle of the room with its head, only the top of which was visible, towards the glass-fronted shrine on the right. Silver butter-lamps were burning and the resinous fragrance of Tibetan incense filled the air. On the far side of the body, facing us, were a large framed photograph of Raja Dorji and masses of flowers. On this side were three chairs, and on these my brother monks and I were invited to take our seats while Rani Dorji, Jigme, Tashi, Kesang, and the two younger sons, who were barely out of their teens, together with the servants of the house, all stood behind us. Anand-ji being very much my senior in ordination, I had naturally assumed that he would be giving the funeral sermon; but to my surprise he asked me, in an undertone, to give it instead. According to monastic convention a request from a senior to a junior monk had the force of a command, and for the next twenty-five or thirty minutes I therefore spoke, as the custom was, of the merits of the deceased, of the shortness of human life, of the inevitability of death, and of the necessity for practising the Dharma while there was still time and while one was still possessed of health, strength, and mental energy. Though I had not really known Raja Dorji, having met him only once, and though my contact with his wife had ended unfortunately, I spoke with considerable feeling, as I could sense that Rani Dorji and her children stood at one of those junctures in human life where only the Dharma is of any avail, and I wanted them to realize this. Perhaps they did realize it, to an extent, for I felt a relaxation in the atmosphere behind me, as if my words had helped lighten the load of grief, shock, and something akin to horror, by which they were oppressed. When I had finished speaking Anand-ji softly started up the *paritta-gathas* or 'verses of protection', in the chanting of which Mahanam-ji and I joined, after which he 'transferred merits' to the deceased Raja by pouring water into a bowl to the accompaniment of the appropriate formulae. Rani Dorji, Jigme, and the rest of the family, then offered each of us a robe and, one by one, prostrated themselves before us three times in the Tibetan fashion.

A funeral sermon often makes quite a deep impression on its auditors at the time, but the impression rarely lasts. In Rani Dorje's case, however, the words I had spoken over her dead husband's body seemed to have had an effect that was more than usually durable. At any rate, after the ceremony at Bhutan House her attitude towards me underwent a slight but definite modification. No longer refusing to have anything to do with the young monk who had dared cross her path, she now came to see me occasionally, each time bringing with her a small offering (sometimes it was a *very* small offering). For a person of Rani Dorji's rigid and unforgiving disposition this represented a change of heart indeed, and though the general opinion in Kalimpong was that Rani Dorji was not capable of a change of heart, but only of a change of tactics (some opined she did not have a heart at all), as representing a change of heart I for one was willing to regard it. Not that she modified her attitude towards me immediately. It was a year or more before the modification was sufficiently marked for me to be sure I was not imagining things and that there actually had been a change of heart on her part. Meanwhile, it did not occur to me to speculate on the possible effects of my sermon. In the days following the ceremony at Bhutan House two other questions occupied my mind. What was the reason for the expression of near horror I had seen on the faces of the Dorji family, and that continued to haunt me, and why had Anand-ji asked me to give the funeral sermon instead of giving it himself?

An answer to the first question was not long in coming. The rumours that had circulated in the bazaar since Raja Dorji's death condensed into a single rumour, that rumour hardened into a general belief, and the belief, in its turn, into an accepted fact. Raja Dorji had not died a natural death. He had been killed by means of black magic. If such was the case, or if Rani Dorji and her children believed it to be the case, then it explained the expression, unidentifiable but almost one of horror, that I had seen mingled, in the latter's faces, with the grief and shock. Black magic was practised throughout the Himalayan region, and Nepalese Hindu *jakris* or witch doctors and Bhutanese Dukpa Kagyu lamas alike were popularly credited with fearsome powers. (Mme Blavatsky's 'dread Dad-Dugpa clan' may well have been not the product of her fertile imagination, as sometimes alleged, but of her contact with Bhutanese lamas of the Dukpa Kagyu School.) Moreover, the Dorji family was not without enemies, both inside and outside Bhutan, and it was entirely feasible that someone who was unable or unwilling to attack it openly should have decided to have recourse to a weapon traditionally employed by the weak against the strong. If they believed that this was what had happened, and that Raja Dorji had indeed been killed by means of black magic, the Rani and her children would have had a sense of dark, destructive forces having been unleashed against them by they knew not whom. They would have felt that hovering above Bhutan House there was a black cloud, lightning from which had already struck down the head of the family and might at any moment strike down one or more of them.

The question of why Anand-ji had asked me to give the funeral sermon took longer to answer. Certainly he had not asked me to give it because of any incapacity on his own part; as I well knew, he was an accomplished speaker, in both Hindi and English, not to mention Sinhalese and his native Punjabi. Neither had he asked me, I felt sure, because I needed practice in the art of speaking, since he was aware I had quite enough of that anyway. Why then had he asked me, especially when his relegating the central role in an important religious ceremony to the juniormost monk present could have been seen as constituting a slight to the rich and powerful family at whose invitation that ceremony was being performed? Anand-ji must certainly have had a reason for so obvious a departure from protocol. Since he was very much my senior it would hardly have been in accordance with monastic etiquette for me to ask him point blank what that reason was, and though he was in the habit of taking me for long walks whenever he was in Kalimpong (he had been semi-resident in the town since early spring), and though he was friendly and communicative, I felt I did not yet know him well enough to be able to dispense with etiquette to that extent. But if I did not know him very well, I knew quite a lot about him. I knew about his studies at a monastic college in Ceylon, about his two years in the West, about his association with Kashyap-ji (with whom and Rahul Sankrityayana he had formed a famous trio), about his work as a translator of Pali canonical texts and modern English novels, about his high-level involvement with the movement for the propagation of Hindi, the national language, and about his Communist sympathies. Anand-ji's was in fact a many-sided personality, and if I did not know him very well it was partly because it was difficult to tell which of his numerous activities and interests were more expressive of the 'real' Anand-ji or even whether there existed, behind them, a 'real' Anand-ji at all. Not surprisingly, different people saw him in different ways. The German pilgrim Hans-Ulrich Rieker, who had met him two or three years earlier in 'the great monastery of the Buddhist monks', as he terms the Maha Bodhi Society's Calcutta headquarters, describes him as having 'the glance of a wise and mature man' and as being 'adverse to trivialities', as well as being quiet and amiable and possessed of a fundamental conscientiousness. (Mahanam-ji, whom he also met, is described, under the name of Kaccana, as attaching considerable importance to an elegant appearance and as leaving a trail of cheap perfume behind him wherever he went.) What struck me about Anand-ji, in the course of our long walks along the less frequented roads of Kalimpong, was his communicativeness (up to a point), his highly rationalistic approach to Buddhism, his ready wit, his proneness to mockery, and his profound cynicism. I also noticed that he had, in common with other cynics, a streak of sentimentality in his make-up, the beneficiaries of this weakness being his various young protégés. One of these had already spent a few weeks in Kalimpong with his patron, and at Anand-ji's request I had taken him to Darjeeling and had him admitted to the Government College, the principal of which happened to be a friend of mine. Two or three months later, and only a few days before the death of Raja Dorji, another of these protégés turned up, and it was from this young man that I eventually discovered why Anand-ji had asked me to give the funeral sermon instead of giving it himself.

Dinesh was small and slightly built, with dark brown skin, thick, wavy black hair, close-set brown eyes, a rather prominent nose, and a big, sensual mouth. Since the Newar monks at the Dharmodaya Vihara did not take kindly to the idea of their again having to accommodate one of Anand-ji's non-monastic protégés, my elder brother in the Sangha asked me if I would mind putting Dinesh up at The Hermitage for a while. I did not mind, especially as Dr Kajiyama had left and I now had no one staying with me except my diminutive young cook-bearer Man Bahadur. I already knew a little about Dinesh. Apparently he had once worked for Anand-ji, had gone to teach Hindi in a remote part of rural Assam, and had there got into serious trouble about which he had written to Anand-ji and on account of which, I recollected, Anand-ji had been extremely worried. What the trouble was he soon told me. He had fallen in love with one of his pupils, and she with him, and they had entered into a liaison. Unfortunately for them, the people of the village where he was teaching were Tais, and moral standards were extremely strict, with the result that when the liaison was discovered the girl's brothers tried to kill him and he had to flee for his life. He did not even have time to say goodbye to his beautiful Mynah-bird, as he called her, Mynah being the girl's actual name, and had spent several days and nights hiding in the jungle before being able to make his way back to civilization, Kalimpong, and Anand-ji.

The episode had given him a nasty shock. At one stroke he had lost his job, his mistress, and very nearly his life. But he was of cheerful disposition, and naturally resilient, and though he shed tears when he told me his story, and continued to shed them whenever he thought of his beautiful Mynah-bird, not many weeks had passed before the tears were mingled with laughter at his own foolishness and eventually they ceased altogether. When Anand-ji was in Kalimpong, and he was often away attending the meetings of a wide variety of progressive organizations down in the plains, Dinesh usually spent much of the day at the Dharmodaya Vihara helping him. Otherwise he stayed at The Hermitage, where he passed his time either reading or playing ping-pong with our younger members, with several of whom, Sachin especially, he was soon on terms of friendship. When he had been with me for a month, and it had begun to look as though his stay was going to be prolonged indefinitely, it occurred to me that since he was, after all, a Hindi teacher, I might as well take advantage of his presence to improve my knowledge of that language. I had already made a start by practising my colloquial Hindi on him (he preferred practising his English on me), but I now wanted to study literary Hindi. The best way of doing this, we agreed, was for me to read a Hindi text with him and then translate it into English by myself, consulting him (and Bhargava's *Hindi–English Dictionary*) only when necessary. What better text could there be for me to read and translate than one of Anand-ji's writings? Eventually we chose his well-known *Bhikshu ke Patra* or 'Letters of a Buddhist Monk', a collection of essays on a variety of topics in epistolary form. This henceforth we read, and I translated, every morning straight after breakfast. From time to time Dinesh also read to me from a celebrated anthology of Urdu couplet poetry, reading first the Urdu originals and then the subjoined Hindi translations. Some of the couplets were so appealing that it was not long before I had learned them by heart. Many were, of course, on the subject of love (*ishq*). Anand-ji's 'Letters' proved to be less appealing. Mildly ironic in tone, it dealt with topics of general interest from the standpoint of a dilute rationalism only faintly tinged with Buddhism. The work was *patla*, Dinesh and I agreed; it was 'thin and weak', and after I had translated five essays we stopped reading it. If Anand-ji wanted to be known as the Voltaire of India, as he once told me he did, then *Bhikshu ke Patra* was not going to win him that particular laurel.

Since both Dinesh and I saw quite a lot of Anand-ji when he was in Kalimpong, and since we were reading one of his books together, it was only natural that his patron and my elder brother in the Sangha should be the subject of conversation between us. Dinesh had known Anand-ji for several years, and had a number of stories to tell about him, not all of them very creditable to the latter in his monastic capacity. One of his stories related to an incident that had taken place not long before he went to teach Hindi in Assam, and in which he himself had also been involved. Anand-ji had attended a meeting of the Association for the Advancement of the National Language at Indore with him and two other workers, and the four of them were travelling back to Wardha by the night train from Mhow. A few stations after Mhow the train suddenly stopped and was unable to proceed farther. Investigation revealed that owing to a serious mistake by the pointsman the engine had run into the siding. What was more, beyond the heap of sand there was a drop of about two hundred feet, so that had the engine not been stopped by the sand the whole train would have plunged to the river below. The incident had given Anand-ji quite a fright, Dinesh told me. He was morbidly afraid of death, and did not like to talk about it or to hear it mentioned. He was even reluctant to attend funerals, which as a monk he was sometimes obliged to do.

Here, then, was the explanation of why Anand-ji had asked me to give the funeral sermon at Bhutan House instead of giving it himself. He had asked me to give it because in a sermon of this kind it was impossible to avoid speaking about death and death was a subject that made him feel extremely uneasy. Either because Dinesh told Anand-ji that he had re-lated to me the story of their narrow escape from a watery grave, or because I myself happened to mention the incident when we were out walking, one day the subject of the fear of death came up between us, and Anand-ji told me about two similar incidents in which he had been involved. More than twenty years earlier, when he was studying in Ceylon, a train coming from behind had almost overtaken him as he was walking along the railway line one evening. Had he not leapt down on to the footpath at the last minute he would certainly have been killed. Four or five years later he made his first journey by air, flying from Bangkok to Rangoon. On its onward flight the plane on which he had travelled was struck by lightning and blew up in mid-air. These two incidents had given him a morbid fear of death, a fear which the third incident had served to exacerbate. Since my rationalistic friend seemed relieved to be able to talk about them, I suggested he should write an article describing the three occasions on which, as he believed, he had been 'about to enter the domain of Death'. This he eventually did, after a few reminders. Entitled 'On the Verge of Death', the article was published in the *Maha Bodhi*, the Maha Bodhi Society's Journal of International Buddhist Brotherhood, of whose editorial board I had in the meantime become a member.

While it was natural that Anand-ji should be the subject of conversation between Dinesh and me, and natural that Dinesh should regale me with stories about his patron, it was even more natural that the young Hindi teacher should tell me about himself. He was an Untouchable, or rather, untouchability having been officially outlawed, an ex-Untouchable. A native of the then Madhya Pradesh, he had been born into a very poor family (Untouchables were poor almost by definition), had received only a limited amount of education, had worked for Anand-ji when the latter was general secretary of the Association for the Advancement of the National Language, and had become a qualified teacher of Hindi. At one stage he had spent a couple of years in Bombay, that deceitful Mecca of the rural poor, making his living as an itinerant massage boy and in any other way that offered. It was as a result of hearing, in the course of that autumn, about Dinesh's experiences that I wrote the poem 'The Bodhisattva's Reply', with its vignettes of the prostitute and the massage boy, the exploited, robotic factory workers, and the despised early morning scavengers from the outcaste village. The story of Dinesh's life had, in fact, moved me deeply, and given me a better understanding of the plight of India's ex-Untouchables who, despite legislation, were still being treated with inhuman cruelty by their Caste Hindu compatriots and co-religionists. Three years later that understanding, for all its limitations, was to stand me in good stead when I came in contact with the newly converted ex-Untouchable Buddhists of Bombay and Nagpur and started working among them.

The fact that Dinesh spent much of the day at the Dharmodaya Vihara when Anand-ji was in Kalimpong, while Anand-ji himself often called at The Hermitage to take me for a walk and a talk, made for closer relations not just between Anand-ji and me but also between the two Buddhist establishments. Usually I did not go to the Dharmodaya Vihara. Before Anand-ji's appearance on the scene I had not set foot in the place for two years. My ten-month stay there had ended unpleasantly. Taking advantage of my absence in Sarnath, where I had gone to receive the higher ordination, the angry-looking Newar monk who had recently arrived from Kathmandu shut down YMBA activities at the Vihara, telling our members that the place did not belong to them and that they were not wanted there. *I* would be allowed to stay, he told me on my return, but I would have to pay him a hundred rupees a month for my room. This I could not do, and he therefore proceeded to act in such a manner as to force me out. Thus I had painful memories of my last days at the Dharmodaya Vihara, and not wishing to revive them usually did not go there. By the time Anand-ji started making the place his headquarters, however, these memories had lost much of their sting, and I could revisit the scene of my tribulations with comparative equanimity. Relations between the Dharmodaya Vihara and The Hermitage were therefore closer now. One result of this development was that I was asked to speak at the Vihara's Vaishakha celebrations, which were held the day after our own. Another was more surprising. Three months after the celebrations Aniruddha, the angry-looking Newar monk who had ousted me from the Dharmodaya Vihara, turned up at The Hermitage one morning and asked me to teach him English. If he did not quite remember how badly he had treated me, he must at least have had a vague recollection of his wanting a hundred rupees a month from me for my room, for he immediately added that his companion Mr Bhumiveda, who was staying with him at the Vihara and also wanted to study with me, would be paying tuition fees for them both.

For the next two months I taught the dour, choleric Newar monk and the plump, jolly, gold-toothed Thai layman almost daily, Aniruddha being the more painstaking of the two and Bhumiveda the brighter. At the end of that period Aniruddha had to discontinue his studies with me, as his presence was required in Lumbini. Bhumiveda continued to come. Not only did he continue to come. He asked me if in addition to teaching him English I would teach him Indian Philosophy, with the result that our lessons in English grammar and composition were from then on interspersed with discussions on Sankhya, Yoga, and the rest of the six (Hindu) classical systems. Bhumiveda was not interested in Buddhist philosophy. He was not even interested in Buddhism, though he had been born into a Buddhist family and treated Buddhist monks with all the deference that a well-brought-up Thai layman was expected to treat them with. Aniruddha had introduced him to me as a retired publicity officer, but as I got to know him better – and he was more communicative now that he came without Aniruddha – it transpired that he had been much more than that. He had in fact had quite a colourful career. Among other things he had been a surveyor, the superintendent of a jail, and the governor of a province. In this last capacity he had taken part in a *coup d'état*. He was one of those who had held a revolver to the head of the (unelected) prime minister and forced him to resign. (It was difficult to imagine Bhumiveda holding a revolver to anyone's head, but this is what he told me.) After the *coup d'état* he quarrelled with the prime minister's successor, whom he had helped to seize power, and was compelled to flee the country.

It was a familiar story. All over Buddhist South-east Asia politicians and others (not excluding monks) who were in trouble at home came to India on pilgrimage and lay low there until things had blown over and it was safe or politic to return. Doing the rounds of the holy places and making ceremonial food-offerings to the monks (if one was not a monk oneself) had the double advantage if earning merit and saving face. If one wished to promote a reputation for piety one might even 'take the robe' for a few weeks, not eating after midday or handling gold and silver, and under-going other hardships. Bhumiveda had certainly not taken the robe, but since he was officially on pilgrimage he may have dropped in at a holy place or two. He had met Aniruddha in Calcutta, at the Maha Bodhi Society's headquarters, Aniruddha had invited him up to Kalimpong, and now here he was, paying much more than a hundred rupees a month for a room at the Dharmodaya Vihara, studying English and Indian Philosophy with me, and having a very good time. He was something of a hedonist. Calling on him at his room one morning, Dinesh and I found him sitting on the floor in his *lungi* surrounded by a dozen or more Thai gourmet dishes he had prepared and looking for all the world like a lay version of the Laughing Buddha. Not that Kalimpong was able to satisfy all his fleshly wants. He had, I gathered, asked two or three of our younger members to show him where the town's brothels were, offering to pay for them too, and had been astonished by their embarrassment and astonished to learn that prostitution was virtually unknown in Kalimpong, at least among the Nepalese. What was wrong with the young men of the place, he wanted to know, and where on earth did they go in the evening?

If Bhumiveda wanted to study Indian Philosophy but not Buddhism or Buddhist philosophy, Bill Small wanted to study Buddhism but not Indian Philosophy. The latter was a tall, well built, fresh-faced young American from Shantiniketan who had arrived in Kalimpong at about the same time as Dinesh and was staying with Miss Barclay. He had not been with that lady for more than a month before the uncertainty, and withal the violence, of her temper became too much for him to bear. I therefore agreed to put him up at The Hermitage. This infuriated Miss Barclay, who in any case had been annoyed that I should go on teaching Bill after she had quarrelled with him. But I did not worry, as I was used to her ways and knew she would soon come round. Bill, for his part, now went in such terror of her that whenever she came to see me, which she quite frequently did, he kept well out of the way until she had gone. When he had been with me for less than a week, and I had given him a few more tutorials (he was writing a thesis on Buddhism for his MA) I received a visit from Father Eberhardt, who, not finding Bill at home, asked me to send him down to St Augustine's Priory as soon as possible. It was *very* urgent.

The following day Bill returned from the Priory white-faced and trembling. He would have to leave Kalimpong the next day. He had been very foolish. In his letters to his parents in America he had been highly critical of Pandit Nehru and of the policies of the Indian government. Now they had found out, and if he did not leave immediately, of his own accord, he would be ordered to leave and might not even be allowed to remain in India and finish his course at Shantiniketan. 'Get out right away, Bill!' Father Eberhardt had urged him. 'It's your *only* chance! They're *after* you!' The next day, therefore, the fresh-faced young American was gone. A couple of weeks later I told Joe what had happened. The lines of suspicion on the eccentric Canadian upasaka's gaunt features deepened. 'But how did Father Eberhardt know what was in Bill's letters?' he demanded after a pause. I had to admit I had not thought of that. Not long afterwards I heard that Joe had been seen paying one of his visits to Chandralok, the Central Intelligence Bureau's new regional headquarters, and sure enough, next time I saw him he had something to report. Father Eberhardt had an informant inside Chandralok, where, of course, all letters to and from foreign residents in Kalimpong were opened and read. The informant was a Catholic convert who whenever he visited the Priory, as he naturally did from time to time, passed on information to Father Eberhardt. *That* was how Father Eberhardt knew what was in Bill's letters. But why, I wondered, had the good father used his knowledge to scare Bill into leaving Kalimpong? Joe smiled superiorly. Bill was a Catholic by birth; he had visited the Priory a few times, and Father Eberhardt obviously feared that by studying Buddhism with me he was imperilling his immortal soul. There was never any question of his being ordered to leave Kalimpong on account of the foolish things he had written to his parents. The authorities were not as sensitive as all *that*. But this did not mean they were totally devoid of sensitivity. For one thing, they did not like foreign missionaries obtaining information through converts who worked for the Central Intelligence Bureau, and Father Eberhardt had been ordered to leave Kalimpong forthwith. As for the informant, *he* had disappeared.

What with Aniruddha and Bhumiveda, and Bill and the intellectual Narendra (who studied Western philosophy with me after Bill had left), besides two young Newar traders and a monk official from Tibet House, not to mention Sachin, during the latter part of the year I did quite a lot of teaching. I could have done much more. People of all ages and backgrounds would turn up at The Hermitage wanting me to take them on as pupils. Usually I had to refuse, either because they looked too dull to learn, or because we had no common language, or because I suspected them of thinking that if they studied English with an Englishman (it was English most of them wanted to study) they would acquire the language automatically, without having to make an effort themselves. One of those I refused was the round-faced young Newar nun from Kusinagar who had arrived in Kalimpong with Mahanam-ji and was staying with Gyan Jyoti and his family. Perhaps it was fortunate that I refused her. A month later she became very ill, and was found to be pregnant – not by Mahanam-ji, apparently, but by someone much higher up in the monastic hierarchy.

In between tutorials I wrote articles and poems, visited friends, and gave lectures and sermons, including funeral sermons. Funeral sermons in the plural not the singular, for towards the end of November there was another death and another funeral – not, indeed, of a personage as distinguished as Raja Dorji, but of someone who, to one person at least, was no less dear than Raja Dorji had been to his family. This was Miss Barclay's sixteen-year-old cat, whom she had brought with her from England. She had warned me the previous day that he was dying and that she would be bringing the body to The Hermitage for cremation. Now he was dead, and here was Miss Barclay coming up the path followed by Ang Tsering, the capable, cheerful Sherpa who had once worked for me and whom I had been sorry to lose. Ang Tsering bore a wooden box and in the box was the body of Miss Barclay's cat. We cremated it at the bottom of the garden, the whole business taking about two hours, since there was not much wood and the body burned very slowly. As the flames leapt up I chanted some Pali verses and spoke a few words about the deceased cat and about death and impermanence. Afterwards Miss Barclay went and did some shopping, returning from the bazaar an hour or two later to have lunch with Dinesh and me. She was less distressed by the death of her pet than I had expected. Perhaps she had been worried she might die before he did, and that after her death he would not be treated kindly or looked after properly. If that was the case, his dying in Kalimpong and being cremated with full Buddhist honours may well have come as a relief to her.

A few days after the death and cremation of Miss Barclay's cat I paid another visit to Darjeeling, once more staying at the Gandhamadan Vihara. The Burmese Maha Thera was no longer there, but the resident monk's kuti was not tenantless, being occupied (at least until my arrival) by a saffron-robed, though not shaven-headed, Miss Delannoy, now the *Anagarika* Dharmarakshita. I had last seen the anxious-looking, rather exigent Frenchwoman two or three months earlier when, having been ordained in Calcutta by a Bengali monk, she had spent a few days in Kalimpong and I had given her letters of introduction to the Burmese Maha Thera, Kali Kinker Barua, and P.T. Lama. Now she was comfortably installed at the Gandhamadan Vihara, was studying Madhyamika philosophy and Tibetan, and had already made a number of friends whom she wanted me to meet. Most of these friends were Hindus, and since like most Hindus they were convinced that the Buddha had *not* denied the existence of God and that Buddhism was in no way different from Hinduism, being in fact a part of it, meeting them involved me in more than one lengthy and rather inconclusive discussion. I also met a few of my own Hindu friends, one of whom was full of a Tantric yogi who had recently spent three weeks in the town, living at the cremation ground and using for his *asan* or seat the embalmed body of an eight-year-old girl. The main reason for my being in Darjeeling was to address a meeting organized by the Tamang Buddhist Association, and this I did on the day following my arrival, speaking on 'The Problem of Ahimsa' to an audience of more than a hundred people. The Anagarika also spoke, describing how she had become a Buddhist after seeing an image of the Buddha in the Khmer gallery of the Musée Guimet.

Darjeeling was not to be the last place I visited that year, nor the remotest. Early in December, when the poinsettia or 'Christmas red' was lifting its scarlet crowns by the wayside, Sachin and I left for Calcutta.

With us went Bill, who had come up to Kalimpong for a couple of days to collect the colourful bamboo-and-thread 'spirit traps', each of them four feet in diameter, that he had ordered from a Nyingma lama before his hasty departure from the town at the end of October. Sachin and I had been planning to visit Calcutta for some time. I had work with the Maha Bodhi Society, while he had friends and relatives to see. We would be 'out of station' for five or six weeks, and on the way to Calcutta would be calling at Shantiniketan.

Chapter Four

THE ABODE OF PEACE

THE OVERNIGHT JOURNEY FROM SILIGURI TO MANIHARI GHAT was not an enjoyable experience, especially if one's compartment happened to be crowded, as ours certainly was; but there was at least one compensation: the sight of the sun rising above the river as one crossed by paddle steamer from the northern to the southern bank of the Ganges to catch the connecting train a few miles downstream.

Sachin, Bill, and I had left Siliguri the previous evening, after making arrangements for the dispatch of the boxes containing Bill's 'spirit traps'. Dinesh saw us off. I felt a little uneasy at leaving him at The Hermitage with no companion save Man Bahadur, who in any case could not be relied on to spend much time at his place of work, since my young ex-Untouchable friend sometimes became depressed when he thought of the plight of his family in the plains and since, moreover, his Nepalese contemporaries did not always show him much consideration, one of them having in fact once struck him a blow that reduced him to tears. I therefore assured him that I would write to him regularly, and asked him to write to me. The inter-class compartment into which my two companions and I had managed to insert ourselves being so crowded, there was no question of our lying down for the night, at least not on the hard wooden seating, and Sachin and I therefore sat up throughout the journey while Bill, either more resourceful or less concerned about appearances, climbed up on to the luggage rack and stretched out there.

Though I had not had more than two hours' sleep, I felt not at all tired the following morning when, on our arrival at Manihari Ghat, we descended from the train and ploughed our way in semi-darkness through half a mile of soft, loose sand to the ferry, our red-shirted coolies preceding us with our luggage. As we embarked, the sun lifted his burning brow above the horizon and within minutes, as it seemed, there was a silver disc shining through the mist and lighting up the vast expanse of the river with a dull, leaden gleam. Half an hour later, when we were in midstream and out of sight of land, the silver disc, breaking free of the mist and the banks of low cloud, turned to a disc of burnished gold that glittered down at us from above the twin funnels of the ferry out of a sky immaculately blue. So brightly did it eventually glitter that it was no longer possible to look at it, and I turned away to gaze out over the waters of the Ganges, now jewel-bespangled, and to listen to the sound of the giant paddle-wheels churning their way through the turbid water. With four or five hundred other souls I was suspended between two mighty elements, those of water and air, a third element, fire, being represented by the sun that shone so fiercely upon us.

Hardly had we reached Sakaligali Ghat, after spending two hours on the ferry, than our ears were assaulted by a continuous hollow drumming sound so loud that it almost drowned the cries of passengers disembarking. The sound came from beneath our feet; it came from the lower deck of the ferry – came from the madly pounding feet of the hundreds of red-shirted figures who, as soon as the vessel came alongside, stampeded on board, swarmed up the stairways, and rushed to stake a claim to the luggage of the first, second, and inter-class passengers (third class passengers generally carried their own luggage), it being understood that the first coolie to lay hands on one's bundles and boxes had the right to be engaged to carry them. I did not always respect this convention, usually preferring to ignore the younger, more active coolies in favour of their older colleagues, who though slower were more reliable, and on this occasion too probably followed my rule. Be that as it may, we were soon off the ferry and into the train, which proved to be less crowded than the one in which we had spent the first part of our journey, so that we were able to watch the unfolding panorama of the Bengal countryside, with its lotus ponds, mud huts, and groves of coconut palms, from a position of comparative comfort. On our arrival at Bolpur, we took a broken-down old taxi to Shantiniketan, where Sachin and I were soon installed in the guest house.

Shantiniketan meant 'the Abode of Peace', and situated as it was in the heart of rural (West) Bengal the place certainly deserved the name. I had first heard that name in 1945 when, still in the army and stationed in Calcutta, I had been in the habit of spending as much of my off-duty time as I could at the Ramakrishna Mission Institute of Culture, where it was possible to meet some of the most distinguished members of the city's Bengali intelligentsia. When, having heard the name of the place two or three times, I enquired of my friend Kantaraj, the diminutive Rama-krishna Order swami who worked at the Institute, what sort of place Shantiniketan was, he mischievously replied that it was an educational institution where they turned boys into girls and girls into boys, meaning by this that the school's 'artistic' atmosphere had the effect of rendering the male students effeminate and the female ones mannish. During the next few years I continued to hear the name of Shantiniketan, the Abode of Peace, usually in connection with the fine arts or in a way that suggested it was a kind of Bengali counterpart to the British arts and crafts movement. Since my arrival in Kalimpong I had heard it more often than ever, mainly due to the presence in the town, during the summer months, of Pratima Devi, the niece and daughter-in-law of Rabindranath Tagore, the founder of Shantiniketan, who since the latter's death in 1941 had been mainly responsible for keeping alive the flame of his vision for the place and with whom I became quite well acquainted, she being prior to my removal to The Hermitage virtually my next-door neighbour. 'Oh you *must* visit Shantiniketan!' she had insisted, as though Shantiniketan was the very Mecca not only of Bengali but of world culture. My friends Lama Govinda and Li Gotami had sung the same siren song (they had come to know each other when he was a professor there and she a student), and it seemed I had no alternative but to visit the place sooner or later. Hence, my work with the Maha Bodhi Society calling for another visit to Calcutta, I had decided that this time I would spend a few days at Shantiniketan *en route*.

Started by Tagore at the turn of the century as an experimental school with five pupils and five teachers, Shantiniketan had developed into 'a centre of Indian culture, a seminary of Eastern studies, and a meeting place for the East and the West' (Krishna Kripalani), though without altogether losing its rural character and without growing too big for it to be possible for everybody to know everybody else. Visva-Bharati, or 'Universal India', as the great Bengali poet had called his miniature world university, included an art school and a music school, a technical institute and a handicrafts department, as well as a school of Sinology, all of which I visited in the course of the next few days and in all of which I met interesting people, both Indian and non-Indian. The first person I met after my arrival, however, apart from some young Bengali friends of Bill's, was Mme Combastet, the elderly, *soignée* Frenchwoman to whom I had given English lessons in Kalimpong earlier in the year. Other Western women might go around in saris and *shalwa-kameez*, but Mme Combastet stuck firmly to her Parisian fashions and looked, indeed, much more ready for a walk down the Champs-Elysées than for a stroll in rural Bengal. Despite her sartorial intransigence she was, it seemed, a popular, even an influential figure around the place, perhaps not least because she was in the habit (as I had noticed in Kalimpong) of assuring her Bengali friends that just as the French were the aristocrats of the West so the Bengalis were the aristocrats of the East. At any rate, she was influential enough to be able to suggest that before leaving Shantiniketan I should give a lecture. I should give it at Cheena Bhavan, as the school of Sinology was called – which on the penultimate day of my visit I did. Not surprisingly, I chose for my subject 'Buddhism and Art'.

Pratima Devi being then in residence at Uttarayan, the house in which Tagore himself had lived, I naturally lost no time in calling on her. The sweet, dignified old lady was delighted to see me in her beloved Shantiniketan, and as usual treated me with great kindness and consideration. Though it was as a poet and novelist that he was known to the world, having been awarded the Nobel Prize in Literature in 1913, towards the end of his long life Tagore had produced a series of extraordinary paintings and drawings; some of these were on display at Uttarayan, and when we had talked for a while Pratima Devi showed them to me, after which she took me for a stroll round the house's beautiful gardens. I also called on Dr and Mrs Liebenthal, who were then staying at Uttarayan, as well as on Professor and Mrs North, whom I had already met in Kalimpong, Professor North having in fact given a talk at The Hermitage on 'English Literature'. There were also visits to Cheena Bhavan, where I met Shantibhikshu Shastri and his wife, and Professor Tan Yun Shan. The first was a Buddhist, a scholar in Sanskrit and Tibetan, and a former bhikkhu. Not only was he a former bhikkhu. He was married to a former nun, and at the conclusion of our initial meeting he and Sujata invited me to have lunch with them a couple of days later. Both were very glad to see me and relieved to be able to talk about themselves without restraint. As I well knew, within the reformist Theravadin community to which they technically belonged (he was a Caste Hindu convert, she a Newar by birth) the position of a former bhikkhu or a former nun was a difficult one, and if the former bhikkhu and the former nun happened to be married to each other their position was doubly and trebly difficult. Shantibhikshu, who was very much the older of the two, was obviously not yet quite comfortable in his new role. Despite his layman's white shirt and dhoti, his manner was still very much that of the bachelor scholar, even of the scholar-monk. Sujata, on the other hand, had adjusted perfectly to the change, and was evidently overjoyed to be married. With her bobbed hair, short Western-style frock, and heavy make-up, she not only exuded satisfaction but was led to remark, in the course of our discussion, that there were others who were thinking of taking the step she and Shantibhikshu had taken. From what I knew of some of the younger Newar nuns I could well believe this to be the case, though I doubted if many of them would be able to find a former bhikkhu as highly qualified as Shantibhikshu and in as good a position to support them, therefore, as he was to support her. In India and Nepal, as in Sri Lanka, a former bhikkhu was unlikely to be as well off financially as a bhikkhu. Consequently few bhikkhus disrobed, even when they no longer had – if they had ever had – a real vocation for the monastic life.

Professor Tan Yun Shan wore the traditional black dress of the Chinese scholar, complete with black skullcap. He had been at Cheena Bhavan since its earliest days, having in fact been responsible for starting the school and being, even now, the moving spirit behind the place. He had started it with the support of General Chiang Kai-shek and his Kuomintang government. With the defeat of Chiang and the Nationalist forces by the Communists in 1949, and the former's withdrawal to Taiwan, Professor Tan had lost that support, and the nature of Cheena Bhavan's position in relation to the government of the People's Republic, the armies of which had recently invaded Buddhist Tibet, was unclear. Indeed, like that of many overseas Chinese, Professor Tan's own position was unclear, not to say ambiguous, it being rumoured that the new regime in Pekin wanted to replace Chiang Kai-shek's protégé with a nominee of their own. Naturally nothing was said of all this in the course of our meeting. Professor Tan showed me the Bhavan's collection of Chinese books, the centrepiece of which, at least in my eyes, was the Taisho edition of the Chinese Tripitaka, the one hundred thick, closely printed red volumes of which were said to contain more than 1,600 separate Buddhist texts, both canonical and extra-canonical. The following day I had tea with him, and he showed me his house and garden, which he evidently had tried to make as much like the traditional Chinese scholar's house and garden as Indian conditions permitted. Professor Tan had, it seemed, put down roots in the land of his adoption, and it was not going to be easy for China's new masters to dislodge him.

But interesting as I found the scholars of Shantiniketan, including some whose names I have forgotten, I found the artists and poets more interesting still. They were quite a mixed bunch. There was the famous sculptor Ramkinker, a stocky, grizzled figure in rumpled Western-style shirt and trousers whom I met at Kala Bhavan, the school of art, and with whom I talked at some length. Like many educated Bengalis, he was interested in Buddhism, at least to the extent that Buddhism was part of Indian culture, and I had already seen the figure of the meditating Buddha that he had created in the Kala Bhavan grounds. Considerably larger than life, its rough, 'unfinished' surface texture reminded me of that of some of Epstein's later work, especially his portrait busts. Ashok Raha, with whom I also talked at some length, was by vocation a Bengali poet and by profession a teacher of English literature. We talked mainly about Shelley, for whom he expressed great admiration. His admiration did not surprise me. I knew that most Indian *aficionados* of English poetry favoured the Romantics, Shelley in particular, and that the youthful Tagore himself had been hailed by his fellow Bengalis as the Bengali Shelley. While I certainly did not regard Shelley as the greatest of English poets, as some Indians did, I too admired and loved him, and my conversation with Ashok Raha, bringing back as it did memories of my ecstatic adolescent reading and re-reading of 'Adonais', 'Prometheus Unbound', and 'Epipsychidion', had the effect of reviving my interest in the poet and making me resolve that as soon as I reached Calcutta I would buy his poems and read them all again. Meanwhile, Ashok-da lent me his own copy of the Oxford edition of the complete poetical works, which he recommended as the best available, containing as it did Mary Shelley's notes and prefaces, so that late that night, while Sachin was out with Bill and his young friends, I had the satisfaction of renewing my acquaintance with the poet in the appropriately romantic surroundings of Shantiniketan.

Though at Shantiniketan, as elsewhere, Indian *aficionados* of English poetry tended to favour the Romantics, the Victorians were by no means neglected. Collecting Sachin from a meeting one afternoon, after fulfilling a couple of engagements of my own, I found some of Browning's poems being recited extremely well, with great feeling, without any of the mimetics which Bengalis seemed to think appropriate when reciting – or rather declaiming – poetry in their own language. Whether or not twentieth-century English poetry was neglected at Shantiniketan I did not stay long enough to find out. But I did meet a twentieth-century English – or rather a twentieth-century American – poet in the course of my visit. This was John Berry, who not surprisingly was a friend of Bill's and whom Bill, in fact, took me to see. The twentieth-century poet lived in a very un-twentieth-century mud hut, and with him, too, I had a long talk. He did not show me any of his poetry, but before Bill and I left he sang for our benefit, to the guitar, two songs that may have been of his own composition.

Besides artists and poets, during the five or six days Sachin and I spent in the Abode of Peace I also met, as though for good measure, a popular novelist. This was Annada Shanker Ray, a sophisticated figure in a dark Western-style suit who occupied, as it seemed, some kind of official position and who was the author of a number of satirical novels in Bengali. He was married, not surprisingly, to a Western woman, an American who, again not surprisingly, was a translator of Bengali fiction and poetry. The name of Leela Ray was in fact almost as well known as that of her husband, and the pair were the centre, in Shantiniketan at least, of a cosmopolitan literary circle consisting mainly of anglicized Bengalis and European and American expatriates, some of whom had, like themselves, married across the racial and cultural divide. Thus it was only natural that on the eve of my departure Leela Ray, who knew me as a contributor to the *Aryan Path* and other magazines, should give a tea party for me, a tea party at which I saw both people whom I had met already and people whom I had not met. It was on this occasion, I think, that Kshitish Roy, the translator of some of Tagore's poetry, whom I had not met before, invited me to contribute to the *Visva-Bharati Quarterly*, of which he was editor.

All too soon our visit to Shantiniketan was over, and after a hasty lunch Sachin and I were bowling along the road to Bolpur in cycle rickshaws to catch the Calcutta Mail, the very train from which we had descended less than a week earlier. Bill came with us to the station to see us off. Despite my having so many other people to see, the fresh-faced young American and I had managed to spend a fair amount of time together, discussing, among other things, Professor Burtt's comments on his thesis, which was now complete. He also took the opportunity of sharing some of his worries with me. One of these related to an incident which had taken place some weeks earlier and caused him considerable distress. Like most Westerners in Shantiniketan, he slept under a mosquito net. One night the mosquitoes were particularly numerous and persistent, and seeing how grievously his young servant, who slept on the floor of the same room, was being tormented by them, he democratically invited the boy to join him under the mosquito net, which the boy very thankfully did. Next morning a Bengali woman, happening to pass by, saw through the window a slim brown form emerging from beneath the mosquito net and from Bill's bed, with the result that within hours the news that the American student was sleeping with his young servant had spread through the campus. He had *not* slept with the boy, Bill assured me, almost with tears in his eyes, not in the sense that anything had actually *happened* between them, and I had no difficulty believing him. None the less, it was obvious that Bill had a decided liking for teenage boys and spent a good deal of time in their company, his particular favourite being Alok, a golden-skinned eighteen-year-old Adonis who seemed to be as fond of Bill as Bill was attached to him. Bill's greatest fear, now that his thesis was completed and he was due to return to America, was that something might happen to prevent Alok joining him in New York, as they had planned he should, there to finish his education. If *that* happened, he told me, as we sat side by side in the rickshaw on our way to Bolpur (Sachin was in another rickshaw with the bulk of our luggage) he did not know what he would do. He was *very* fond of Alok.... Whether he actually confessed to being in love with the young Bengali I do not remember, but after a long pause he sighed wearily and said, half to himself, 'I guess I must be homosexual.'

I did not know what to reply, if reply indeed was needed. The truth was that I knew little more about homosexuality than what I had gleaned, ten or twelve years ago, from the pages of Havelock Ellis's *The Psychology of Sex*, and in any case doubted, *pace* Freud, whether a strong emotional attraction to a member of one's own sex necessarily meant that one was sexually oriented in the same direction. Moreover, this was the first time that anyone had told me, in so many words, even that he 'must be' homosexual, and my silence was due as much to embarrassment as ignorance.

It was therefore in silence that Bill and I covered the rest of the distance to Bolpur, where we found Ashok-da waiting at the station and where, a few minutes later, Sachin and I said our goodbyes and boarded the train. On the first stage of our 300-mile rail journey, that from Siliguri to Manihari Ghat, I had passed the time talking to a friend of Sachin's who happened to get into the same compartment. Now, on the last stage of that journey, the time was shortened by a long conversation with a ticket-inspector who was interested in Buddhism, so that when, three and a half hours after our departure from Bolpur, the train clanked its way through the sordid northern suburbs of Calcutta and into Sealdah Station I was surprised to see that we were already there. The station was not a pretty sight. Encamped along the broad platforms, between the iron pillars, the stacks of wooden crates, and the refreshment kiosks, as well as outside in the station forecourt, were thousands, perhaps tens of thousands, of refugees from the former East Bengal, all living in conditions of the utmost wretchedness and degradation. Some of the earlier arrivals had contrived to build shelters out of gunny bags, flattened kerosene tins, and bits of cardboard, and from most of these, of which there must have been hundreds in the forecourt, there fluttered the red flag of Communism, Communist Party cadres having done more to relieve the sufferings of the refugees, apparently, than had the Congress state government, and being in fact very active among them. With the help of the young men from the Maha Bodhi Society office who had been sent to meet us, we pushed through the throng of passengers, both arriving and departing, hawkers, refugees, and beggars, and ten minutes later were being deposited outside the pink sandstone façade of the Sri Dharmarajika Vihara and the taxi driver was doing his best to overcharge me. As I usually did on such occasions, I left the tall, formidable *durwan* or gatekeeper to settle with him on my behalf and, followed by Sachin, made my way down the side of the Vihara to the three-storey building that was the Society's headquarters. Here we were greeted by Devapriya Valisinha, the general secretary of the Society, and others who were known to me, both monks and laymen, assigned our quarters (my old room on the second floor), and served very strong tea in cups of very thick white china. We then went out, on foot – out into the hustle and bustle that was Calcutta at five o'clock in the afternoon or, indeed, at almost any hour of the day or night.

After the sightseeing and socializing of Shantiniketan I would have been content to spend the evening quietly, perhaps with a book, but Sachin, who had not been to Calcutta before, was eager to see the bright lights of the big city. For him, as for so many young hillmen, Calcutta represented freedom, represented opportunity, represented excitement – represented, in short, Life with a capital L, and apart from New York (a distant, impossible dream) there was no place on earth that he, like them, was more desirous of seeing. Moreover, he was anxious to meet his relatives and since some of them lived in central Calcutta, a part of the city with which I was reasonably familiar, he wanted me to accompany him and help him locate the place. Having drunk our tea, out into the evening air we therefore went, cutting across College Square, with its crumbling statues of bygone dignitaries, into College Street, and going along College Street, past the butchers' stalls and the sweetmeat shops, as far as Wellington Square, famous venue of political meetings, where, turning right, we pursued our course down Dharamtala Street to the Esplanade and Chowringhee, all the while taking good care, whenever we were forced off the crowded pavement, to avoid the single-decker double tramcars that, every few minutes, came clanging and swaying along, all full and all with scores of passengers hanging on outside.

From Chowringhee we did not have very far to go to Hindustan Building, a solidly built, rather gloomy pile situated in the midst of dingy side streets. Sachin's relatives, who comprised two separate households occupying adjacent flats on the second floor, were delighted to see him and made me, too, very welcome. There were quite a lot of them, especially in the form of aunts and female cousins, besides several small children. In the course of the next few weeks I accompanied Sachin to Hindustan Buildings a number of times, and got to know the occupants of one flat quite well. Some of them, indeed, visited us at the Maha Bodhi Society, and one, an unmarried school teacher who was always referred to, even within the family, as Miss Singh, as though she was a school teacher even at home, became seriously interested in Buddhism and attended my lectures. During this first visit, however, they naturally were a little shy of me, Hari-didi bringing tea to me in the front room while Sachin was being entertained in the rooms behind. On our way back to the Maha Bodhi Society, two hours later, my companion and I looked into the bookshops in Dharamtala Street, these being still open, as were most shops. Not only were the shops open, the streets were full of people and there was plenty of noise. Even after I had gone to bed the roar of traffic, punctuated by the sound of human voices raised in anger or supplication, could still be heard, and it was a long time before I was able to sleep. If Shantiniketan was the Abode of Peace, I reflected as I lay there, surely Calcutta was the City of Dreadful Noise.

But Calcutta was not only the City of Dreadful Noise. It was also the city of palaces, most of them now in ruins, and the city of (mainly political) processions, of which there were said to be more than three hundred a year. It was the city of Kali and Saraswati, of Clive and Sirajah-daulah, of William Carey and Warren Hastings, of Thackeray and Macaulay, of Sri Ramakrishna and Swami Vivekananda, of the Tagores and the Mullicks. It was the city of Governor-Generals and Viceroys, of museums and learned societies, of the Victoria Memorial and the Ochterlony Monument, of the Hindu Mahasabha and the Muslim League, of students and workers. For me, of course, Calcutta was the city of Anagarika Dharmapala and the Maha Bodhi Society, with the Sri Dharmarajika Vihara and the headquarters building constituting, in my eyes, a tiny island of Buddhism in the midst of the vast ocean of Hinduism, an ocean in which there were only two or three other islands, each one tinier than that whereon I was encamped. Literally, and even, to an extent, metaphorically, my life in Calcutta centred on the Society. Attractive and interesting though the city might be, the Society was my base, and it was from this base that I went out and to which I returned.

Chapter Five

AMONG THE UNIVERSALISTS

MY CONNECTION WITH THE MAHA BODHI SOCIETY went back to the early months of 1947, when shortly after discharging myself from the army I stayed for a month or more at the headquarters building and helped with office work. The sun was setting on the Raj. Lord Mountbatten had just succeeded Lord Wavell as Viceroy, and the date for the handover of power to an independent India – and an independent Pakistan – was soon to be advanced to midnight of 14 August. During the war years the Society had kept a low profile, mainly on account of its pre-war links with Japan, but even though hostilities had now ceased the shabby, neglected headquarters building showed little sign of renewed religious activity. The Sinhalese bhikkhu-in-charge, who insisted on being styled His Holiness the High Priest, spent more time dabbling in municipal politics than in spreading the Dharma, so that eventually, disgusted with the worldly, unspiritual atmosphere of the place, I left Calcutta in the hope of finding less arid pastures elsewhere. Not surprisingly, I left with a decidedly negative impression of the Maha Bodhi Society.

This impression was reinforced two years later at Sarnath, the site of the Buddha's 'first sermon', when having spent the intervening period as a freelance wandering ascetic I asked the bhikkhus who ran the Society's centre there for ordination as a novice monk. My request was not only turned down with flimsy excuses that were no better than lies. I was treated with suspicion and hostility and made to feel that anyone who went barefoot and refrained from handling money, as I then did, must be out of his mind. None the less, a year and a half later those same bhikkhus were happily participating in my higher ordination, while I myself was staying, on my way to Sarnath from Kalimpong, as well as on the way back, at the Calcutta headquarters building. The fact was that the Maha Bodhi Society was effectively the only Buddhist organization in India, so that if one was in any way concerned with the revival of Buddhism in the land of its birth one could hardly avoid being involved with it. Moreover, Devapriya Valisinha, the general secretary of the Society, had recently returned to Calcutta from Ceylon, where he had spent the war years, and with his arrival on the scene the Society had begun to emerge from its state of suspended animation. Soon he and I were in correspondence, and I had not only organized the reception given by the Buddhists of Kalimpong to the sacred relics of Shariputra and Maudgalyayana, which Valisinha had recovered from the Victoria and Albert Museum, but had been invited to join the delegations accompanying the relics to Sikkim and Nepal. Finally, Valisinha had asked me to write a biographical sketch of Anagarika Dharmapala, the founder of the Maha Bodhi Society, for inclusion in the Diamond Jubilee Souvenir that he was planning to bring out, and during the autumn of the previous year I had spent several weeks with him in Calcutta for this purpose.

The writing of the biographical sketch brought about a change in my connection with the Society – indeed in my attitude towards it. Before writing the sketch I knew little more about Dharmapala than that he was a Sinhalese, that he had sought to wrest the Maha Bodhi Temple at Bodh-gaya, the site of the Buddha's Enlightenment, from Hindu ownership and control, and that besides reviving Sarnath as a centre of Buddhist pilgrimage he had succeeded in awakening interest in Buddhism among a section of the English-educated intelligentsia, especially in Calcutta. But as I went through his diaries, and read the articles he had written for early issues of the *Maha Bodhi Journal*, I came to realize that Dharmapala was not just an organizer and activist, as I hitherto had supposed, but also a yogi and ascetic with an intense inner life. I came to realize, too, that the Maha Bodhi Society I had encountered in 1947, and even later, bore little resemblance to the Maha Bodhi Society that had existed in Dharmapala's time and that could, with Valisinha's arrival on the scene, conceivably exist again. Moreover, I had observed, in the course of my two months at the headquarters building (the longest period I had yet spent there) that a covert and unacknowledged struggle for control of the Society was going on between Valisinha and his supporters on the one hand, and on the other Jinaratana, the High Priest, and the opportunist elements he had introduced into the Society, and even into its governing body, during Valisinha's prolonged absence in Ceylon. As Dharmapala's personal disciple and recognized successor, as well as general secretary for life, Valisinha was probably in the stronger position, but Jinaratana's resourcefulness and cunning were not to be underestimated. I therefore decided to throw my weight, such as it was, into the balance on the side of the *real* Maha Bodhi Society and give Valisinha whatever help and support I could.

The result was that on my return to Kalimpong the Young Men's Buddhist Association (India), which I had founded in 1950, became the Kalimpong branch of the Maha Bodhi Society, with me as bhikshu-in-charge, while the following autumn Valisinha wrote inviting me to move down to Calcutta and relieve him of the burden of editing the *Maha Bodhi Journal.* I was willing to relieve him of his burden. I was not willing to move down to Calcutta. Further correspondence ensued. In the end it was agreed that I should edit the monthly from Kalimpong, but that I should come down to Calcutta and bring out my first two numbers from there. This would enable Valisinha to hand over to me properly, besides enabling us to work out the logistics of producing a magazine that was being edited in a place three hundred miles away from the place where it was printed, published, and distributed. Thus it was that I came to be visiting Calcutta again, this time with Sachin, and again staying at the headquarters building, in the same corner room in which, a year earlier, I had written my biographical sketch.

My companion and I were not long in settling into a sort of routine. We had breakfast together, sometimes at a restaurant – the Society's standard breakfast of tea and two slices of toast being not always sufficiently substantial if one had been fasting since noon the previous day, as I at least had been – after which I saw Sachin on to a bus or tram and returned to the headquarters building. In the evening, if he was back in time from whichever of his relatives he had been visiting that day, we went out for a stroll, lingering over the second-hand bookstalls and finishing up, more often than not, in a restaurant where he could have a non-vegetarian meal and I a cup of very indifferent coffee. During the day I read, wrote letters, and worked on the proposals for the improvement of the *Maha Bodhi Journal* which, at Valisinha's suggestion, I had started drafting. Some days there was a puja or other religious ceremony to attend in the temple, as it was called, which occupied the first floor of the Sri Dharmarajika Vihara and was connected with the corresponding floor of the headquarters building by a little covered bridge. When I wanted a change from reading and writing I talked to the other occupants of the building, especially to my brother monks, most of whom I met in any case at our ante-meridian lunch, which in accordance with (Theravadin) custom we took separately from the laity.

Dhammaratana and Soratha, who both came from Ceylon, were already known to me, as was the Bengali monk Silabhadra. Dhammaratana's dark face always wore an apologetic smile. Quiet and studious by nature, and as sluggish in movement as he was slow of speech, he was a member of the editorial board of the *Maha Bodhi Journal* and sometimes helped with proof-reading. Though he had been a monk for twenty or more years, he was still technically a novice, and for reasons I never succeeded in fathoming steadfastly refused to take the higher ordination that would make him a bhikkhu. Soratha, who was much better known to me, was a very different kind of person. Bright-eyed and bustling, and so small that he was known as the Little Monk, he was as talkative as Dhammaratana was taciturn, a great reader of Sinhalese newspapers, and a science student at one of the local colleges. 'Does an amoeba have karma?' he had asked me, the first time we met, to which I replied, 'Does an amoeba have consciousness (*chetana*)?' and such exchanges had since become customary between us. I enjoyed his company more than I did that of the other monks, the more especially as he was a mine of information about Ceylon and Sinhalese Buddhism. Silabhadra, whom I knew only slightly, had taken the robe late in life after a career at the bar. Even now there was, I sometimes thought, more of the lawyer about him than the bhikkhu.

A monk I had not met before was Aniruddha, only son of wealthy, string-pulling Mrs Moonasinghe (a lady whose ambition it was to paint the Maha Bodhi Temple at Bodh-gaya bright yellow), and great-nephew of Anagarika Dharmapala. Though it was rumoured that he was being groomed to succeed Valisinha as general secretary, the tall, almost hulking young man showed no sign of harbouring any such aspirations or even of taking much interest in the affairs of the Society. Quiet and unassuming, he showed greater interest in making friends not just with me but also with Sachin, and more than once accompanied us to Hindustan Building, where he soon was so much at home with Sachin's aunts and female cousins that I started wondering if he was not better suited to family life than to monastic life. Perhaps it was a case of the mother seeking to realize her spiritual, or at least her socio-religious, ambitions through the son.

The only brother monk to whom I did *not* talk when I wanted a change from reading and writing, though I had known him longer than I had known anyone else in the building, was Jinaratana, the High Priest. Nor did he go out of his way to talk to me. The reappearance, as a member of the Monastic Order, of the same young Englishman who had been the

witness of some of his unmonklike, not to say un-Buddhist, behaviour
back in 1947, had given him a nasty jolt, and though I was careful not to
allude to the past, and though in the course of my previous visit much of
the awkwardness between us had been dispelled, he was still not quite
at ease with me. He may even have remembered telling me, on more than
one occasion, 'You'll see. Within two years I shall be general secretary of
the Society.' Whether he remembered or not, he was still only one of the
two joint secretaries (the other was bhikkhu-in-charge of the society's
Sarnath centre) and no nearer to the general secretaryship than he had
been six years earlier. If anything, he was further from it than ever.
Contrary to his expectations, Valisinha had returned; he had returned
and stayed, and during the twelve months that had elapsed since my last
visit Dharmapala's conscientious, hard-working disciple and successor,
besides strengthening his position relative to that of the aspiring High
Priest, had contrived to bring about certain changes in the Society –
changes that went some way towards making it a more truly Buddhist
organization. The biggest change was one whose significance was largely
symbolic. As I was already aware, six months earlier the Society had
acquired a new president. What was more, the new president was a
Buddhist.

That a Buddhist society should have a Buddhist president might seem
nothing out of the ordinary. Surely it was axiomatic that such a society –
especially one that had been founded expressly to revive Buddhism in
India, and whose journal had for masthead the Buddha's exhortation to
his disciples to go forth and preach the Dharma – would no more have a
non-Buddhist for president than a Christian religious body would have
a non-Christian at the helm of its affairs or a Muslim religious body a
non-Muslim. In the case of the Maha Bodhi Society it was apparently *not*
axiomatic. The three previous presidents of the Society, whose tenures
between them covered a period of nearly forty years, had all been Bengali
brahmins, the third being in fact the son of the first. Some Buddhists and
sympathizers with Buddhism outside the Society were surprised, even
outraged, by such a state of affairs. 'Why does your Maha Bodhi Society
have a Bengali brahmin for its president?' the ex-Untouchable leader Dr
Ambedkar had demanded, belligerently, in the course of our first meeting
only a year earlier. Himself an ex-Untouchable, Bhimrao Ramji Ambedkar had spent a lifetime fighting to liberate his people from the social,
economic, and religious disabilities imposed upon them by the Caste
Hindus, particularly the brahmins, and to him it was incredible that an
organization dedicated to spreading the teachings of the Compassionate

One should have a brahmin for its president. Adding insult to injury, from his point of view, was the fact that the Society's Bengali brahmin president, Syama Prasad Mookerjee, was also president of the Bharatiya Jana Sangh, a right-wing Hindu political party, and an old political opponent of his. I had therefore hastened to assure him that it was not *my* Maha Bodhi Society. Though happy to help the Society in whatever way I could (I had just written my biographical sketch of Anagarika Dharmapala), I did not actually belong to it, mainly on account of its having a brahmin for president and because its governing body was dominated by Caste Hindus who had no real interest in Buddhism. Moreover, some of the Buddhist members of the Society were as dissatisfied with the present state of affairs as he was and both they and I hoped that before long we would have an opportunity of doing something about it.

The opportunity had come sooner than I, or Ambedkar, or anyone else could have expected. In May Syama Prasad Mookerjee, who was opposed to the Congress government's policy in Jammu and Kashmir, entered the state without a permit, was arrested and held in custody, fell ill a month later, and died the day after being admitted to hospital. This dramatic development left the Maha Bodhi Society in need of a new president. There were two candidates. One was the *Maharaj Kumar*, or Crown Prince, of Sikkim, who was a Mahayana Buddhist. The other was Dr Sarvepalli Radhakrishnan, Vice-President of India and historian of Indian philosophy, who was a Telegu brahmin from Andhra. Canvassing was vigorous, with the Buddhist members of the governing body tending to support the Maharaj Kumar's candidature, while their Hindu colleagues tended to support that of Dr Radhakrishnan – partly because he was a Hindu, admittedly a very scholarly one, and partly on account of his occupying high political office. Valisinha was determined that the Maharaj Kumar should be elected, and to this end had recourse to a tactic which, though perfectly constitutional, had not been tried before and which no one would, in fact, have credited the normally shy, retiring little general secretary with possessing either the imagination to devise or the boldness to execute. The tactic was based on the fact that the bhikkhus working for and supported by the Society, of whom there were hardly more than a dozen in the whole of India, were *ipso facto* members of the governing body. Normally they did not attend its meetings. They did not attend them because they could not afford to do so on the pittance they received from the Society, and because the governing body, or rather its Hindu-dominated rump, the members of which all lived in Calcutta, refused to pay their travelling expenses. What Valisinha did was write to the bhikkhus urging them to attend the crucial meeting at which the new president was to be elected, and undertaking to meet their travelling expenses out of his own pocket (the exercise had cost him two thousand rupees, he told me with a rueful smile, and he would not be able to repeat it). Figures in varying shades of yellow and orange were therefore able to descend on Calcutta from Sarnath, Bombay, Delhi, Madras, and elsewhere, to attend the crucial meeting, and to vote for the Maharaj Kumar, with the result that – Buddhists being for once in the majority – the Society now had a president who was a Buddhist. The only yellow-robed figure not to vote for the Maharaj Kumar was Jinaratana.

Accustomed as they were to having things their own way, the Hindu members of the governing body, save for two or three non-Bengalis who were friends and supporters of Valisinha's, were shocked and dismayed by their failure to secure the election of Dr Radhakrishnan. They had been as determined to secure his election as Valisinha had been to secure that of the Maharaj Kumar. Such was their determination that, on getting wind of the little general secretary's tactics, they had not scrupled to spread scurrilous stories about the Maharaj Kumar in order to undermine support for his candidature. Alarmed, Valisinha had written to me asking if the stories were true, as Kalimpong was next door to Sikkim and I might be supposed to have my ear to the ground, and I had replied that to the best of my knowledge they were not. Support for the Maharaj Kumar's candidature thus remained firm, and to the shock and dismay of the Hindu members of the governing body he was elected. So shocked and dismayed had they been, that after the meeting they had rounded on the victorious Buddhists (so Valisinha told me) and accused them of narrow-mindedness, bigotry, and sectarianism in wanting to have a Buddhist as president of the Society.

Their reaction did not surprise me. Hindus were universalists. For them all religions were one, all paths led to the same goal, so that it was a matter of comparative indifference whether the head of a Buddhist organization happened to be a Buddhist or a Hindu. Indeed, as Hindus possessed, innately, a far deeper knowledge of Buddhism, or of any other religion, than its own professed adherents, it was actually better that a Buddhist organization should be headed by a Hindu than by a Buddhist. 'But Buddhism is in our *blood*,' Hindu friends would insist when I attempted to correct their misunderstandings of Buddhist doctrine, meaning that they had the ability to understand Buddhism without the necessity of actual study, simply by virtue of the fact that they had been born and brought up in India.

I was not a universalist. I did not believe that all religions were one, or that all paths led to the same goal, and I had therefore been heartily glad, six months earlier, to hear that it was the Maharaj Kumar of Sikkim, and not Dr Radhakrishnan, who had been elected president of the Maha Bodhi Society. Not that I had anything against his Bengali brahmin predecessors. All three were very distinguished men. One was an educationist, another the chief justice of Bengal, while the third, the Maharaj Kumar's immediate predecessor, was an educationist-cum-politician. But although they may have been prudent managers of the Society's finances, and have imparted to it a degree of acceptability among the Bengali intelligentsia, the fact that they were not themselves Buddhists meant that they were incapable of providing the spiritual leadership a Buddhist organization needed if it was to fulfil its function and be an effective vehicle for the dissemination of the Buddha's teaching. To what extent the Maharaj Kumar would be able to fulfil this function remained to be seen, but in the headquarters building, at least, a new spirit was already astir, and I felt happier to be living and working there than I had done the previous year. The only person in the building untouched by the new spirit was Jinaratana. He continued to lurk in the shadows, so to speak, ready to strike down any friend or supporter of Valisinha who was foolish enough to give him the opportunity (eventually one did). Though conscious of his dark, brooding presence at the edge of the bright space that had opened within the Society, I did not allow myself to be disturbed, and every day relieved Valisinha of a little more of the burden of editing the *Maha Bodhi Journal*.

I had relieved him of the greater part of it when my daily routine – and Sachin's – received an unwelcome interruption. Sachin was taken ill. At first it seemed to be nothing more serious than an attack of malaria, probably caught in Shantiniketan. Dr Soft, the Society's honorary physician, a septuagenarian Punjabi in the coarse white homespun of the orthodox Gandhian, whom I immediately called in, prescribed Comoquin tablets, as well as rest and liquid diet, and told me there was nothing to worry about. Three days later, however, Sachin's temperature having in the meantime fluctuated dramatically, his pulse was so low that Dr Soft started suspecting it might be either influenza or typhoid and changed the prescription accordingly. He also warned me that the patient had to be kept absolutely quiet. This was easier said than done. Not that Sachin himself was any problem. Like Good Deeds in the medieval morality play, he was 'sore bound' – not by his sins, indeed, but by sickness – and 'could not stir'. The problem was the various female cousins who sat on his bed talking to him for so long – sometimes for three or four hours at a stretch – that he was quite worn out. As they were relatives, I did not like to ask them to leave (they were quite impervious to hints), especially as I had not told Sachin how serious his condition might be and did not want him to know. Altogether it was a worrying time. All I could do for the sufferer, apart from taking his temperature and giving him his medicine every two hours, and soup at similar intervals, was to make him as comfortable as I could and keep Dr Soft informed about developments by telephone. In between I wrote letters and read proofs, leaving Sachin's bedside only to shop for him and, one evening, to give a lecture in the Society's lecture hall downstairs. This was the first of the weekly lectures Valisinha had asked me to give, and whether by accident or design the date of the lecture was 24 December, Christmas Eve, and my topic 'Buddhism and God'.

After more than a week in bed Sachin started to recover. He had not had typhoid, though he may have had influenza, and when his temperature and pulse had been normal for three days running I judged him well enough to get up and go for a stroll in College Square. Here we sat on a bench for half an hour, at the foot of a pedestal that had lost its statue, enjoying the winter sunshine and doing our best to ignore the unrestrained curiosity of the Bengali passers-by, some of whom stopped dead in their tracks in order to take a better look at us. A few days later, Dr Soft having pronounced him out of danger, my companion was again spending the greater part of his time visiting relatives, while I continued easing myself, as I thought, into the editorial chair of the *Maha Bodhi Journal*. I was no stranger to the pages of that publication. Articles, book reviews, and poems of mine had been appearing in the Society's 'Journal of International Buddhist Brotherhood', as it styled itself, for the last few years, and since July I had been contributing a monthly column entitled 'In the Light of the Dhamma' under the pseudonym of Himavantavasi. Himavantavasi, the 'Dweller in the Snowy Mountains' (the name had been found for me by Anand-ji), was a Buddhist hermit living in the Himalayas. He had no direct contact with the outside world, but reports of what was going on there, especially in the Buddhist part of it, somehow reached his ears from time to time and 'In the Light of the Dhamma' represented his reactions to what he heard.

It was the first time I had written under a pseudonym, and from a literary point of view, at least, the experience was an interesting one. Though the views to which I gave expression were very much my own, the manner in which I gave expression to them was not, in the sense that it was not quite the manner in which I would have expressed them had I been writing under my own name. 'Himavantavasi' was not so much a pseudonym as a mask. The mask represented a character, a character whom I had imagined but who was so real to me that whenever I sat down to write my column I became Himavantavasi. The mysterious 'Dweller in the Snowy Mountains' was an extension of my own personality, through whom I could say things in a way in which I could not otherwise have said them and through whom, therefore, I could experience myself in a way that I could not otherwise have done. Himavantavasi enabled me to be myself more fully.

Not that I wanted to 'be myself' in the subjective, individualistic sense of that phrase. What I wanted was to give expression to my views, views which I hoped were genuinely Buddhist, and to give expression to them in as many different ways as possible. I therefore intended to go on writing my column even as editor of the *Maha Bodhi Journal*. Indeed, as I settled myself more firmly into the editorial chair, in the last days of the old year and the first days of the new, I was planning to give Himavantavasi a stablemate. I was preparing to don another mask, the first-person-plural-using mask of 'the Editor', and to write each month one or more editorials. Through this mask, too, I would give expression to my views, but I would give expression to them not in the naïve manner of the 'Dweller in the Snowy Mountains' but in the weightier, more authoritative manner appropriate to the official organ of a society that was, after all, both the leading Buddhist organization in India and the best known Buddhist organization in the world. Hitherto there had been no editorials in the *Maha Bodhi Journal*. Yet there were numerous issues to which it ought to be drawing the attention of Buddhists both inside and outside India. Was not the ancient Buddhist site of Nagarjunakonda, in the newly created Andhra State, about to be totally submerged under a government irrigation scheme, despite the protests of historians and archaeologists? And had not Dr B.C. Roy, the chief minister, categorically refused to declare Vaishakha Purnima a public holiday in West Bengal, even though the Union authorities had recently declared it a central government holiday?

Hardly had my editorials on these issues been sent to the press, however, than I met with a serious disappointment. I would not be occupying the editorial chair of the *Maha Bodhi Journal* after all. In fact there was no editorial chair for anyone to occupy. Instead there was an editorial settee into which seven or eight persons, myself included, were to be squeezed. There was to be an *editorial board*. In theory there was

already an editorial board, and it was precisely because the other members of the board invariably left all the work to him that Valisinha wanted
me to relieve him of the burden of editing the Society's journal. None the
less, when the little general secretary proposed, at the governing body's
first monthly meeting of the year, that I should be formally appointed
editor, his proposal met with fierce opposition from the Hindu members,
and it was with the greatest difficulty that, aided by two or three friends
and supporters, he had got them to agree even to my being a member of
the newly constituted editorial board.

The reason for this opposition on the part of the Hindu members of the
governing body was not far to seek. I was critical of certain aspects of
Hinduism, particularly the caste system, and made no attempt to conceal
my views. This had led to their dubbing me anti-Hindu. *They* were of
course universalists, in whose eyes to be critical in any way of other
religions, with the possible exception of Islam, was to be intolerant, and
intolerance was the unforgivable sin. That I was anti-Hindu was a fact
that had been confirmed for them, a few months earlier, by a review I
wrote of a new translation of Tulsidas's *Ramacharitamanasa* – a review
Valisinha had published in the *Maha Bodhi Journal*. The sixteenth-century
Tulsidas, the 'Servant of the (Sacred) Basil', was a great poet; his retelling
of the story of the hero-king Rama, one of the *avataras* of the god Vishnu,
was a classic of Hindi literature, and the bible of the Hindi-speaking
people of (Hindu) northern India. But Tulsidas was also an orthodox
brahmin. His perfervidly devotional apostrophes to Vishnu-Rama were
mingled with repeated references to brahmins as the *bhudevas* or 'earthly
divinities'. A brahmin was to be worshipped, even though he possessed
all the vices, whereas a *shudra*, however virtuous, was to be despised.
Though conceding that the poem undoubtedly contained passages of
great artistic merit, I therefore described the work as a whole as 'sadly
marred by sectarian bias, devotional extravagance carried almost to the
point of frenzy, and social orthodoxy in its more repulsive form'. This
description did nothing to endear me to the Hindu members of the
governing body at the time and was now partly responsible for the
fierceness of their opposition to Valisinha's proposal.

Though disappointed that I was not, after all, to occupy the editorial
chair of the Society's journal, I was not discouraged. As Valisinha pointed
out, my position was no worse than his had been. I was a member of the
editorial board, the other board members (himself excepted) would take
little or no interest in the actual production of the magazine, though they
might criticize it afterwards, and I would be left to do all the work. I was

quite ready to do all the work, even though I would now be doing it not as editor but only as one member of an editorial team whose existence was confined to the front inside cover of the *Maha Bodhi Journal*. My only real worry was that the governing body might try to restrict my editorial freedom. Some of them, I knew, wanted to make sure I did not send articles direct to the press from Kalimpong, without them being seen and approved by one of themselves. But I was willing to take an optimistic view of the situation, and therefore continued to absorb myself more and more deeply in the work of implementing my plans for the improvement of the magazine.

I was not so deeply absorbed in the work, however, as to have no time for anything else. For pilgrims coming from the Buddhist countries of South-east Asia, Calcutta was the gateway to Bodh-gaya and the other holy places of northern India. The headquarters building was therefore a busy place, especially during the winter months, and it was inevitable that I should sometimes meet people. Among the people I met was U Thein Maung, the chief justice of Burma and a leading Buddhist of that country, to whom the Society subsequently gave a public reception. Devapriya-ji – as Valisinha was generally called by his friends and colleagues – also took me with him whenever he went to meet distinguished Buddhists who were passing through Calcutta but not staying at the headquarters building. In this way I met Jigme Dorji, whom I had last seen standing white-faced and horror-stricken beside his father's body, and the Maharani of Sikkim. The Maharani was, of course, the mother of the Maharaj Kumar of Sikkim, the Society's president. I had not met her before, but I had heard quite a lot about her, mainly from my old friend and supporter Marco Pallis, who was never tired of singing her praises as the most beautiful, intelligent, and vivacious woman one could possibly hope to meet, in Sikkim or anywhere else. That must have been some years ago. Now the Maharani was a stout, elderly woman of considerable charm but with only the remains of beauty. Her story was, I knew, a sad one. The mother of five children by the Maharaja, she had formed a connection with an incarnate lama from Tibet and, as a result, had given birth to a daughter, now nearly grown up. This had led to her banishment to a palace outside Gangtok, where she lived in seclusion, taking no part in public life. Though she was separated from the Maharaja, they were not divorced (he was said to be still quite fond of her), and she retained the title of Maharani. Was it my imagination, or did I not detect a hint of melancholy in her expression? She received us very graciously, but declined to visit the Society, probably on account of the equivocal nature of her position.

Dr Irene Bastow Hudson, MD, could never have been beautiful, and 'charm' and 'grace' were not the first words that sprang to mind in connection with her. Intellectual rather than intelligent, and despite her seventy-odd years possessed of demoniacal energy, she was a Canadian Buddhist-cum-Theosophist who had arrived in Kalimpong the previous summer with a letter of introduction from an old friend of mine in England. Though eccentric and opinionated, she was of a generous disposition (Joe, who had known her by reputation in Canada, maintained that she tried to buy people), and after her return to Canada had sent me two very welcome parcels of English classics (Spenser, Addison, Burns, and others), some volumes being school prizes she had won towards the end of the last century. She also agreed to finance the publication of a collection of my poems, the final proofs of which had already reached me from the Bombay publishing house that was bringing it out. Now she was back in Calcutta, and staying at the Grand Hotel, where I very soon had the opportunity of thanking her for her generosity. She had more or less decided to settle in Kalimpong, she told me over a cup of tea, and would go there as soon as her luggage had been cleared. Meanwhile, there was a lot she could do in Calcutta. For one thing, she could visit the headquarters of the Maha Bodhi Society. This she accordingly did the following afternoon, staying on for my weekly lecture, on 'Practical Buddhism for the Layman', and attending the *paritrana* or 'protection' ceremony that Aniruddha and I conducted in the temple afterwards.

Not that the elderly Canadian Buddhist-cum-Theosophist was the only Western visitor to the headquarters building that winter. Quite soon after my arrival I received visits from Dr Weintrob, a devotee of Anandamayi Ma who had spent three weeks at The Hermitage the previous year, and Mr Dameki, a Pole whom Anagarika Dharmarakshita (Miss Delannoy) had put in touch with me. How Dr Weintrob came to be staying at The Hermitage is something of a mystery. Probably he was simply escaping from the heat of the plains. Whatever the reason may have been, so intense was his devotion to the Bengali woman mystic that although he had intended to stay much longer in Kalimpong he announced, after only three weeks, that he was unable to bear the pain of separation from her and was returning to Benares forthwith. He was still in Benares, living at Anandamayi's ashram, and visiting Calcutta for a few days had heard that I was in the city. From the way he spoke it was clear that he was as devoted to Anandamayi as ever and, in fact, quite besotted with her. I could not but be reminded of my own contact with the 'Blissful Mother', more than five years earlier, when I had been shocked and disgusted by the scenes of hysterical devotion that were sometimes enacted in her presence. Mr Dameki, as I had gathered from the Anagarika's letter, was not a devotee but an intellectual, and we had a long conversation on Buddhism, yoga, and similar topics. The Society's most distinguished Western visitors during this period, however, were Professor and Mrs Franklin Edgerton, whom I showed round the temple with Devapriya-ji and Dr Soft. Professor Edgerton was the author of the newly published *Grammar and Dictionary of Buddhist Hybrid Sanskrit* and had recently delivered a series of lectures on 'Buddhist Hybrid Sanskrit Language and Literature' in Benares.

Among the people whom I met at the headquarters building, or who came to see me, was one who was neither a Buddhist pilgrim nor a Western visitor. This was Phani Bhusan Sanyal. I had met him at the Ramakrishna Mission Institute of Culture in 1945, when I was in the army and he a graduate student, and had sometimes accompanied him on his weekly visits to the shrine of Sri Ramakrishna's saintly consort, popularly known as the Holy Mother, to whom he was greatly devoted. Now I was a Buddhist monk and he a professor of Economics at a nearby Anglican missionary college and still unmarried. We had re-established contact shortly after my ordination as a bhikkhu, and he came to see me whenever I was in Calcutta, usually bearing a gift in the form of two or three slender green sticks of tuberose, of whose fragrance he knew I was particularly fond. A textbook example of an ectomorph, and light-skinned even for a Bengali brahmin, he invariably came dressed in a white shirt and dhoti (with, in winter, a dark *chadder* or shawl, elegantly draped) and wearing on his feet the black patent leather pumps of the *babu* or gentleman. In the course of my present visit to the city of Anagarika Dharmapala and the Maha Bodhi Society (as Calcutta was to me) or of Sri Ramakrishna and Swami Vivekananda (as it was to him) he came to see me not once but several times, the first time bearing not only sticks of tuberose but a copy of the Penguin selection of the prose of T.S. Eliot. If I happened to be free (Phani's visits were always unannounced) we went out book-hunting together, he being as great a lover of the printed page as I was and Calcutta being, for both of us, the city of bookshops. Among the bookshops to which he had introduced me, two or three years earlier, there was one that specialized – rather surprisingly, it being located in the depths of a department store – in Continental literature, and here I now bought translations of Baudelaire, Rimbaud, and Rilke.

Phani had also introduced me, two or three years earlier, to his widowed father, a retired judge of the Calcutta high court, taking me to meet him at what I assumed was the family's ancestral home. Conversation turned to the Ramakrishna Mission Institute of Culture, and to its secretary, Swami Nityaswarupananda. 'The fellow's no better than your Jinaratana,' observed the old man, who seemed to be as well acquainted with the affairs of the Maha Bodhi Society as he was with those of the Ramakrishna Mission. 'Has a car and a chauffeur and lady friends. Don't know what the Mission is coming to nowadays. Swamis are supposed to be *monks*.' These *obita dicta* were not very welcome to my spiritually-minded friend, who would much rather have talked about the *real* Ramakrishna Mission of Swami Vivekananda and the other direct disciples of Sri Ramakrishna than about its degenerate descendant, but out of respect for his father he remained silent. For my part, I was not surprised by the retired judge's remarks, though I had not realized that knowledge of Jinaratana's misdeeds was so widespread. In some respects Calcutta was a small place.

My connection with the Ramakrishna Mission went back a long way. It went back further than my connection with the Maha Bodhi Society. It went back, in fact, to the day when, as a nineteen-year-old soldier newly arrived in Colombo, I made my way along a road lined with flame-of-the-forest trees and knocked, not without apprehension, on the door of the local Ramakrishna ashram. The two swamis I met there were men of learning and spirituality and from them I imbibed, in the course of the seven months I spent in Ceylon, something of the spirit of Indian culture and something of their own enthusiasm for the spiritual life. So deep was the impression made on me by the two swamis, and by the literature I read under their guidance, that I kept up my connection with the Mission in Calcutta and Singapore, to which I was subsequently posted, as well as after my return to Calcutta. Indeed, on leaving the army at the beginning of 1947 I took refuge in the Ramakrishna Mission Institute of Culture, then located in Wellington Square, where I had met Phani more than a year earlier. Swami Nityaswarupananda wanted me to help edit the new edition of the Institute's three-volume *Cultural Heritage of India*, but after a month there was no sign of the work actually starting and I therefore left for Jinaratana and the Maha Bodhi Society.

I left with my faith in the Ramakrishna Mission considerably diminished. The Institute having been given a block of flats in Russa Road for its new premises, and the tenants having refused to move out before they had found alternative accommodation, Nityaswarupananda had ordered the novice in charge of the eviction proceedings to hire a gang of hooligans and drive the recalcitrant parties out by force, citing in justification of these brutal measures the *Bhagavad-gita*'s teaching of *nishkama karmayoga* or the yoga of disinterested action. The *Bhagavad-gita* was one of the texts I had studied in Colombo. I had studied it with the commentary of Shankara, the great non-dualist philosopher. The fact that its teaching was capable of being understood in such a way as to justify violence cast a new, lurid light not only on the Ramakrishna Mission but, also, on the nature of Hinduism; and though, in the course of my two years as a freelance wandering ascetic, I sometimes stayed at Ramakrishna ashrams, and indeed was made welcome there, my connection with the Mission gradually ceased to have any real meaning for me. Moreover, as my understanding of Buddhism deepened, and with it my experience of spiritual life, I came to realize that, in the words Anagarika Dharmapala wrote at the top of every page of his diary, 'The only refuge for him who aspires to true perfection is the Buddha alone.'

On one of my first visits to Calcutta after my ordination as a bhikkhu, however, I decided that I ought to acquaint the swamis I had known with the change in my condition, if only for old time's sake. Though some of them, I knew, had entertained hopes that I would become a swami and work for the Ramakrishna Mission, they at least would be pleased that I had renounced the world like themselves, albeit as a Buddhist monk. After all, they were universalists. They were universalists *par excellence*, Sri Ramakrishna having demonstrated the oneness of all religions by personally practising Hinduism, Islam, and Christianity in turn and discovering they led to the same goal. To see Nityaswarupananda, now installed in the Institute's new premises, I accordingly went. With me went Phani who, on our re-establishing contact, had warmly congratulated me on the step I had taken, at the same time gently reproaching me for my insistence that Buddhism was a separate religion from Hinduism. No congratulations were forthcoming from Nityaswarupananda. On seeing my yellow robe his face darkened. 'Why have you become a *Buddhist* monk?' he demanded, contemptuously. 'Hinduism is a great ocean, Buddhism only a tiny stream.' While all religions were one, some religions, it seemed, were more one than others.

Since then my contact with the Ramakrishna Mission had been limited to hearing its Kalimpong representative launch a virulent attack on Buddhism at a Buddha Jayanti meeting, and I had not expected to have any further dealings either with Nityaswarupananda or the Institute. This was not to be the case. When I had been three weeks in Calcutta, and was still seeing my first issue of the *Maha Bodhi Journal* through the press, I received a telephone call from Irene Ray, an Englishwoman who was married to a Bengali doctor and whom I had met in Kalimpong two or three years earlier. Irene was not only a devotee of the Ramakrishna Mission; she organized the Institute of Culture's weekly lectures, and edited its monthly Bulletin, and now she was telephoning to invite me to deliver next week's lecture. I accepted the invitation, and it was agreed I should speak on 'The Meaning of Buddhism and the Value of Art', a subject that had preoccupied me for some time, especially since my Shantiniketan lecture, and on which I had been doing some research in the Society's library. A few days later, therefore, I again met Nityaswarup-ananda, who appeared to have reconciled himself to seeing me in a yellow robe, and I delivered my lecture in the Institute's very modern auditorium to an audience of about two hundred people – considerably more than came to my lectures in the Society's old-fashioned and rather shabby hall.

The following day I was again at the Institute, this time attending a recital of devotional music by the famous Dilip Kumar Roy, a disciple of Sri Aurobindo. To my surprise I met Swami Siddhatmananda. He was one of the two swamis I had known in Colombo, and we had not seen each other for nearly ten years. Unlike Nityaswarupananda, he showed no sign of displeasure at my having become a Buddhist monk, and greeted me warmly. He was in Calcutta for an operation, he explained – for hydrocele. Afterwards my friend Kantaraj, who still worked at the Institute, was at pains to disabuse me of any wrong notions I might have as to the nature of the complaint. Hydrocele, he solemnly assured me, was an accumulation of semen in the testicles due to prolonged observance of strict chastity, and the purpose of the operation the swami would be undergoing was to drain off the accumulation.

My lecture on 'The Meaning of Buddhism and the Value of Art' having been greatly appreciated, Irene asked me to write it out in article form for publication in her Bulletin, which I gladly did. A speech I made shortly before my departure from Calcutta met with a much less favourable reception, and no one asked me to write it out for them. Speaking as the representative of Buddhism at the International Congress of the World Fellowship of Faiths, held in the Senate Hall of Calcutta University, the pillared neo-classical façade of which confronted the Ajanta-style façade of the Sri Dharmarajika Vihara from the other side of College Square, I emphasized that Buddhism rejected the idea of God and exhorted man to rely for deliverance on his own efforts. This emphasis of mine so upset His Holiness the Shankaracharya of Puri (not the amiable old gentleman with whom I was already acquainted but his much more orthodox rival), who was presiding over the session, that he spent a good part of his presidential address attempting to prove that Buddhists, even though they professed not to believe in God, really did believe in him, and that atheists and theists were bound for the same goal. For so long did he go on that people began leaving the hall in droves, and in the end, when he had been speaking for more than two hours, one of the organizers stepped up to the dais and removed the microphone. Far from being disconcerted by this high-handed treatment, His Holiness looked round the virtually empty hall with an air of triumph, as though he had succeeded in routing all opposition.

Subsequently I wrote for the *Maha Bodhi Journal* an editorial in which I protested against the attempt being made in some quarters to force Buddhism into a doctrinal framework repugnant to it. 'It is time Buddhists stopped allowing people of other religions to tell them what they "really" believe,' I declared. My comments referred not only to the Shankaracharya of Puri but to one of the speakers at the Sadharan Brahma Samaj's Fraternity of Faiths meeting, held a few days before the Parliament of Religions, which I also attended as representative of Buddhism. According to this speaker all religions believed in the Fatherhood of God and the Brotherhood of Man, and apart from the former belief the latter was unthinkable – a position I was obliged to controvert in my own address, declaring that though Buddhism denied the very existence of God its followers had exemplified the spirit of Brotherhood more fully than the adherents of other religions. In Calcutta I had indeed fallen among universalists.

But I was not to be among the universalists much longer. By the end of the third week of January Devapriya-ji and I had finalized our arrangements for the editing of the Society's journal over the next few months, that is, until my next visit to Calcutta; and after Sachin had spent a few more days visiting his relatives, and I had paid a few more visits to bookshops, my companion and I were again pushing our way through the throngs of people surrounding Sealdah Station – this time in the reverse direction. Devapriya-ji and one of the bhikkhus came to see us off, as did Miss Singh and other relatives of Sachin's and a number of friends. We left Calcutta with rather more luggage than we had brought. Both of us had presents for friends in Kalimpong, while I had some two dozen books that I had either been given or had bought, among them the Oxford edition of Shelley's complete poetical works. Above all, we had with us a very large and heavy box Anagarika Dharmarakshita had asked me to bring up to Kalimpong for her and which gave us a good deal of trouble on the way.

Chapter Six

ASSAM IDYLL

THE FIRST THING I HEARD on arriving at The Hermitage was that Miss Barclay had died that morning. As it was then three o'clock (we had reached Kalimpong later than expected owing to engine trouble on the way up from Siliguri) I went straight to the Manjula cottage, in the upper half of which Miss Barclay had established herself a few months earlier. What could have happened? Had Miss Barclay had a heart attack (in view of her violent temper this was not unlikely)? Or committed suicide? Or been murdered? So unexpected was the news of the elderly English-woman's death that speculations as to its possible cause preoccupied me to the exclusion, for the time being, of much in the way of an emotional reaction to the event.

Even when I was inside the four walls of the Manjula cottage, and standing in what had been Miss Barclay's sitting-room, it was some time before I was able to find out much about what had happened. The police were there, in the form of a Bengali sub-inspector and a Nepali sergeant, and the Maha Bodhi Society, as represented by Dawa, Joe, and Dinesh. There was also Mrs Perry, the proprietress of the Himalayan Hotel, and an Englishman whom I did not recognize but who appeared to be with Mrs Perry. On my way upstairs I had heard voices raised in heated argument and now, as I entered the room, all eyes were turned on me and several voices in unison demanded, 'Was Miss Barclay a Buddhist?' 'Why, yes,' I replied, as I sought to regain my breath, 'She was.' Dawa looked round the room in triumph, and could not forbear exclaiming, 'I told you so!' Mrs Perry managed to look both crestfallen and incredulous. At this point the Bengali sub-inspector interposed. 'Can you *prove* Miss Barclay was a Buddhist?' he asked. Again all eyes were turned on me, and I could almost hear the sudden intake of breath. Joe was clearly sceptical, and even Dawa looked a little anxious. Mrs Perry's face lit up with renewed hope, as did that of the unknown Englishman. 'Yes,' I replied composedly, 'I can.' The fact was that Miss Barclay had joined the Young Men's Buddhist Association (India), as the Kalimpong Branch of the Maha Bodhi Society then was, as an associate member, and in completing the membership application form, which she of course signed, had described herself as Buddhist by religion. 'That settles it, then,' said the sub-inspector briskly. 'Produce your proof at the *thana* and you can collect the body from the mortuary tomorrow morning.'

This was my first intimation that Miss Barclay's body was not still on the premises, as from the presence of so many people I had assumed. Indeed, from the circumstance that there were clearly two parties in the room, one Buddhist and one Christian, and that they appeared to have been vigorously disputing possession of Miss Barclay's body, one could almost have fancied that the body was lying there on the floor between them and that they had been fighting for it as literally as the Greeks and Trojans had fought for the body of Patroclus beneath the walls of Troy. But though Miss Barclay's body was not on the premises her belongings still were, and for these, when they had been packed in boxes and the boxes sealed, I had to give the police a receipt. While this work was in progress Mrs Perry left, taking with her the unknown Englishman, though not before she had introduced him to me and it had transpired that he was Dr David Snellgrove of the School of Oriental and African Studies in London, that he was a Tibetologist, and that he was staying at the Himalayan Hotel.

On our way back to The Hermitage Dawa and Dinesh told me what they knew of the circumstances of Miss Barclay's death, some of which I had already learned from the police. Apparently she had risen quite early, perhaps while it was still dark, had made her way down the outside staircase to the toilet, had missed her footing, had fallen, and in falling had struck her head against one of the cement pillars that supported the cottage's projecting upper storey. Her servant Ang Tsering, the Sherpa who had once worked for me, had found her body lying in the drain beside the veranda when he came in for work from the bazaar and had at once retraced his steps and informed the police. Within hours the news of the Englishwoman's death was all over Kalimpong. As soon as he heard it Dawa had hastened along to The Hermitage in the expectation, as he now told me, of my being back from my travels and either there or at the Manjula cottage. On learning from Man Bahadur that I was not yet back, and having waited for an hour, he decided to go to the Manjula cottage himself to find out what was happening. By the time he arrived

Miss Barclay's body had been removed, and Mrs Perry was claiming the right to take charge of her former guest's effects. She was also claiming the right to take possession of Miss Barclay's body after the autopsy. Miss Barclay had been a Christian, she told the police, and as a Christian herself she intended to make sure that Miss Barclay's body was given a proper Christian burial. Dawa naturally denied that Miss Barclay had been a Christian. Everybody knew she was a Buddhist, he declared, and the disciple of Venerable Sangharakshita. Mrs Perry countered by saying that having an interest in Buddhism was one thing, actually being a Buddhist quite another: Miss Barclay had only had an *interest* in Buddhism. This annoyed Dawa considerably, and the argument became quite heated. With the arrival of Joe and Dinesh it became more heated still, with Mrs Perry, vigorously supported by Dr Snellgrove (as he turned out to be), claiming Miss Barclay's body on behalf of the Christians, and Dawa, supported rather less vigorously by Joe and Dinesh, claiming it on behalf of the Buddhists. The police did not know what to think. It was at this point that I had arrived.

While the three of us were talking Sachin turned up with two other young Nepalis, one a cousin and one a friend. Not having got down when our car dropped me at the gate of The Hermitage, he had learned of Miss Barclay's death only after reaching home. Now he had come wanting to know if he could be of assistance. He and I having discussed the sad news, all six of us walked the mile or so up the road to Sachin's house, which was situated above the road, in the Scottish Mission compound. Here I met his father, Dr Ravi Singh, who besides being the popular 'Nepali doctor' of the Mission hospital was the local police surgeon. He had already performed the autopsy on Miss Barclay, he told me, in his usual friendly and cheerful manner. There was a slight bruise on the forehead, and there was no doubt that the poor lady had died of concussion, probably as the result of the fall. *Jyeo*, the body was in the dead house (as the tin shack that served as the hospital mortuary was called), and *jyeo*, *jyeo*, we could collect it in the morning, as the police had said.

At ten o'clock next morning, therefore, Miss Barclay's body was brought to The Hermitage in the back of a jeep. It was brought in a plain wooden coffin, the work of a carpenter in the bazaar who had stayed up half the night to have it ready in time. With the coffin came five lamas, as Tibetan monks were called, incorrectly, in Kalimpong, at least by non-Tibetophones. Dawa had brought them to see me soon after breakfast, and I had already discussed with them the arrangements for the funeral. Miss Barclay having been a student of Tibetan, it seemed appropriate that she should be sent on her way with at least minimal Tibetan Buddhist rites, especially as these were more colourful than anything I could manage on my own. Thus it was that five stalwart, red-robed figures were now manhandling the heavy coffin through the door and into the games room, where it was carefully lowered on to the ping-pong table, the trestles of which creaked beneath the weight. This having been done, they squatted in a row on the floor of the adjacent library and reading room, drew their texts and their *dorjes* and bells from the capacious bosoms of their robes, and started up a deep-throated, monotonous chant that, punctuated by the tinkling of bells and the occasional resounding clash of cymbals, continued for the next couple of hours. While this was going on people who had known Miss Barclay came with wreaths, bunches of flowers, and *khatas* to pay their last respects. Besides our own members there were Dr Roerich and Mrs Perry and, I was glad to see, several Church of Scotland missionaries, whom I made a point of welcoming and asking to come in, this being the first time any of them had visited The Hermitage and they were clearly unsure what they might encounter.

When the lamas had finished chanting and been served with three cups (or rather bowls) of tea in the traditional manner, the lid of the coffin was removed and Sachin, Dawa, Dinesh, and I gathered round to take our last look at Miss Barclay. Apart from a faint bruise on her right temple she looked as she usually did, though her features were set in what I thought was a rather stern expression. Before closing the lid I went into the sitting-room, where Mrs Perry and the missionaries were having tea (Dr Roerich had already left), and asked if anyone would like to come and take a last look at Miss Barclay. A shudder passed visibly through the group. 'Oh no!' quavered several voices, in tones of horror. 'Oh no thank you!' As our young members had not hesitated to look, and indeed were still crowded round the coffin for that purpose, this reluctance on the part of the missionaries was rather surprising. The lid of the coffin was therefore closed, the coffin itself loaded on to the jeep, and accompanied by me and the five lamas and as many of our members as could squeeze into the vehicle, and escorted by others walking behind, the Honourable Helena Beatrix Barclay set out on the last journey of her nine-and-fifty years.

It was a journey that soon became a triumphal progress. As we drove, almost at walking pace, through the High Street, pedestrians moved respectfully to one side and tradesmen came to the doors of their shops, many of them with flower garlands and *khatas* that they proceeded to place either on the bonnet of the jeep or on the projecting end of the coffin.

How pleased Miss Barclay would have been, I thought, to know how popular she was! Our destination was the Tibetan cremation ground up at Tirpai, a thousand or more feet above the bazaar. I had been there before, on my way to the Tharpa Chholing Gompa, and had enjoyed the cool air, the vibrant stillness of the place, and the uninterrupted view of the snows. There could hardly have been a more magnificent setting for a cremation. What I had not realized at the time was that men and women were cremated separately, on two different spots, and in different ways. Men were cremated lying on a kind of iron bedstead, whereas women were cremated standing within a stupa-like structure, and it was there-fore a few yards from the latter that our jeep eventually came to a halt.

What followed was not very pleasant. Having unloaded the coffin from the jeep, the lamas removed the lid, lifted out Miss Barclay's body, and proceeded to strip it, a clothed body being, as I knew, more difficult to burn. All this took place behind an improvised screen of white cloth, but as the screen was only breast high and I was standing on a slight elevation of the ground I could see everything that was being done, as could some of our young members, who in fact were peering round the edges of the screen. The lamas then hauled the startlingly white body up to the top of the stupa-like structure and lowered it inside. Or rather, they tried to lower it. Either because Miss Barclay was too stout or the funnel too narrow the body refused to go right in. Again and again the lamas lifted it and lowered it, but all to no avail. This was the most dreadful part of the proceedings. As the red-robed figures struggled with the body in the hot sun Miss Barclay's head lolled from side to side, and her long flaxen hair, which she had worn in neat braids round her head, cascaded over her shoulders and bosom. 'They're desecrating the temple of the Holy Ghost!' screamed a voice I recognized as being that of Mrs Bullock. 'I *told* you not to come!' shrieked Joe in reply. The Bullocks, as they were popularly known, were a missionary couple from China with whom Joe had recently become acquainted and who had persuaded him, against his better judgement, to take them with him to witness the cremation. Eventually, when they had lifted and lowered for ten or fifteen minutes, one of the lamas crawled inside the stupa-shaped structure and pulled on Miss Barclay's legs from below, the idea being to have the corpse straddle the iron bar traversing the middle section of the structure. His efforts proved successful, and Miss Barclay's head having disappeared from view the other lamas clambered down, willing hands thrust logs of wood in the four apertures at the structure's base, and at last all was ready for me, as chief mourner, to light the funeral pyre.

Soon clouds of smoke were billowing from the funnel of the kiln, as the stupa-shaped structure seemed to have become, and tongues of flame were darting forth. The lamas, seating themselves on the ground, again took out their texts and their *dorjes* and bells and embarked on another two-hour session of chanting, bell-ringing, and cymbal-clashing. By the time they finished the body had been reduced to ashes, and all that remained for those of us who were still there was to have a last cup of tea in Miss Barclay's memory and go home. My hand having been burned when I lit the funeral pyre, I stopped by at Sachin's house and had it dressed, after which Sachin and Dinesh accompanied me back to The Hermitage. Our talk, naturally, was of our departed friend. It was strange, mused Sachin at one point, that Miss Barclay should have died only two months after her beloved sixteen-year-old cat, who had travelled out from England with her in his own basket and occupied his own fully paid-up seat on the aeroplane.

But although Miss Barclay was no longer with us in the flesh the boxes in which her belongings had been sealed were still solidly present. What was more, they were still at the Manjula cottage. The morning after the funeral, therefore, I hired a jeep and with the help of Sachin, Dawa, and a few of our other members, as well as that of the faithful Ang Tsering, brought them down to The Hermitage and stored them in a back room. When Sachin came to see me the following day, shortly after lunch, he found me not my usual cheerful self, and under his concerned questioning I was eventually obliged to admit that I had been feeling depressed ever since the previous morning, when we had all gone up to Miss Barclay's old quarters and removed her belongings. What exactly it was that made me feel depressed I could not say. It was not simply the fact of Miss Barclay's being dead, though her death had saddened me, especially in view of the way it had happened. The feeling was definitely connected with the sight of the boxes, and of the things the police had thought it not worth the trouble of sealing up and which I had sorted out. It was as though Miss Barclay's belongings had been orphaned. More than that. It was as though they had been abandoned, and having now no common owner or protector, and therefore no purpose in common, could only separate and go their different ways. Part of the 'garden' on the upper floor of the Manjula cottage as they had been, with the disappearance of the Lady of the garden (albeit a less young and amiable one than Shelley's), they were sharers in the general dissolution of the place. They presented a picture of desolation. They evoked images of 'bare ruined choirs', both arboreal and monastic – images of towns reduced to rubble and cities where not one stone had been left standing upon another. It was this, or something like this, that lay at the back of my depression.

Whatever the explanation, the mood did not last, if only because there were many other matters to which I had to give my attention. There were letters to be written, including an urgent one to a bhikkhu in Assam about my forthcoming tour there, material for the February issue of the *Maha Bodhi Journal* to be edited and sent to Calcutta, and the enquiries of casual visitors to be dealt with. In any case, so far as Miss Barclay herself was concerned there was, I reflected, no real cause for depression on my part. Unfortunate though her death may have been, she had died a Buddhist. Not that her conversion to Buddhism had been merely formal (though I had received her into the Buddhist community in the traditional manner), as conversions of Hindus and Buddhists to missionary Christianity were apt to be in Kalimpong. She had become a Buddhist because she was convinced of the truth of the Buddha's teaching, and I had little doubt that it was owing to her contact with the Dharma that the last four or five months of her presence amongst us were the happiest period of what had been, by her own account, a life of singular unhappiness. The fact was a source of considerable satisfaction to me, as was the fact that I had borne with her outbursts of temper, her tantrums, and her angry tirades (of all of which I was the recipient, not the object), even though I was more than once sorely tempted to relieve myself of so burdensome a friendship by discouraging the exigent Englishwoman's almost daily visits to The Hermitage. I was heartily glad, moreover, that I was able to *prove* that Miss Barclay was a Buddhist and that we had been able, therefore, to give her a (Tibetan) Buddhist funeral – a funeral which had demonstrated her popularity with the local people and which on the whole had been, as our members and friends agreed, a great success.

The only person who did *not* think that Miss Barclay's funeral had been a success was Joe. When the Canadian upasaka came to see me a few days later he was in a bitterly critical mood. We had done everything we should not have done, and nothing we should have done. Worst of all, we had not consulted *him* about the arrangements. The funeral had been a complete and utter failure. Knowing that in his eyes nothing done without the benefit of his advice could be well done, and that he was in any case of a hypercritical nature, I did not take much notice of his tirade, and having regaled me, as he thought, with an account of how Mrs Bullock had flown to the telephone to tell her missionary friends all about the horrors of Buddhist funerals, he therefore soon turned from savaging our funeral arrangements to savaging Dinesh. It had been a great mistake

on my part, he declared with some vehemence, to leave the young
ex-Untouchable to look after The Hermitage while I was in Calcutta.
Though thanks to his own efforts (and Dawa's, he should in justice have
added) the full moon day celebrations and other activities had continued,
it had not been with any help from Dinesh. Why, he had not even
bothered to keep the place clean. All he had done was spend my money.
He had been grossly extravagant, and it was surprising that I wanted to
have anything more to do with such a feckless, unreliable, dishonest
creature.

As I listened to Joe's outburst I thought of the fable of the Fox and the
Grapes and smiled to myself. I knew more about what had been going
on in my absence than he appeared to realize. Anand-ji had spent a few
days in Calcutta during my sojourn there, both on his way to Nagpur
from Kalimpong and on his way back to Kalimpong from Nagpur, and
after his arrival from Nagpur had shown me a letter he had received from
Dinesh. Anagarika Dharmarakshita having arrived unexpectedly from
Darjeeling and taken it for granted that in my absence she was free to
occupy The Hermitage for a few days, he had gone to stay with Joe,
thinking it hardly proper for him to be living under the same roof as a
nun, or rather, for a nun to be living under the same roof as him. Out of
the frying pan into the fire! Joe had attempted to rape him, and he had
been obliged to take refuge in the Dharmodaya Vihara, even though
protégés of Anand-ji's were not particularly welcome there. These revelations did not surprise me, my elder brother in the Sangha having
already informed me, on his arrival from Kalimpong, that Joe had proposed to Dinesh that he should come and live with him, making the
proposal in such a way, as Anand-ji delicately put it, as to lower himself
in Dinesh's eyes. They did not surprise Sachin either, when he learned
about them. He had a revelation of his own to make. Joe had once tried
to persuade Dawa to spend the night with him, he told me. This I had
not known before, and I could well imagine the embarrassment the rather
strait-laced young Tibetan would have felt when the full significance of
the elderly upasaka's proposal dawned on him. Dinesh was far too
streetwise to be embarrassed even by an attempted rape, but the experience had none the less upset him, as he himself admitted to me on the
night of my return to Kalimpong. I had therefore arranged for him to
spend a week in Wardha with his family by way of consolation.

Naturally I did not let on to Joe that I knew what had really been going
on at The Hermitage – and elsewhere – in my absence, though I may have
protested against the notion that Dinesh had been extravagant. As I knew

only too well, he had not had the means of being extravagant, least of all at my expense. The truth was that I was going through a period of financial stringency, and the Kalimpong branch of the Maha Bodhi Society with me. This was due mainly to the fact that during the previous six-month period my only fee-paying student had been Mr Bhumiveda, and even his contributions had ceased when I went to Calcutta. What was to be done? One possibility was that we organize film shows in the Town Hall for the benefit of the branch's funds, which would at least have the effect of lessening the drain on my own resources. It was a possibility I had already explored in Calcutta, the famous film actor Raj Kapoor, whom I had met in Bombay two years earlier, having given me a letter of introduction to his distributors there and having agreed to our show-ing two of his films without payment of the usual charges. On my return to Kalimpong I therefore discussed the matter thoroughly with Dawa and the secretary of the Town Club, which was responsible for the letting of the Town Hall, and it was settled between us that the film shows would be held in the first week of April. Despite the desperate state of our finances it was not possible for us to hold them earlier, as I would be leaving for Assam in two weeks' time and we would need a full month for our preparations.

The next two weeks were very busy ones for me. Though Miss Barclay's funeral was over, there were letters to be written about her affairs, including a long one to Mrs Mitter, the owner of the Manjula cottage, who lived in Calcutta. There was also a memorial service to be arranged. This was held in the summer-house shrine at the end of the garden, and took the form of my chanting the *Mangala, Ratana,* and *Karaniyametta Suttas* and delivering a sermon on 'The Recollection of Death' to our assembled members and friends. Nor was I yet finished with Miss Barclay's boxes. Their contents had to be listed *in detail,* so I was informed one afternoon by two members of the West Bengal police, one of them the same sub-inspector who had asked me if I could prove Miss Barclay was a Buddhist. They and I, together with Sachin, who had been having lunch with me, therefore spent the next four hours listing Miss Barclay's be-longings separately, from the largest to the smallest, after which they were re-packed in the boxes and the boxes again sealed, this time with my own seal and the official seal of the West Bengal police. A few days later Anagarika Dharmarakshita arrived from Gangtok, the capital of Sikkim, having spent the last month visiting the tiny Himalayan princi-pality, and pitched her little tent on one of the terraces above The Hermitage. She was on her way back to Darjeeling, and stayed for only a few days, in the course of which we discussed the state of Buddhism in Sikkim and she showed me her books (the books that had made the large box I had brought up from Calcutta for her so heavy) and read aloud to me some extracts from Racine, thus giving me my first experience of the great French poet's sonorous alexandrines. After her departure I wrote up the Notes and News section of the February issue of the *Maha Bodhi Journal* (a task that naturally had to be left until the last minute), typed it, and sent it to Calcutta. This done, I was free to leave for Assam, and soon was once again dropping with dizzying rapidity down a succession of hairpin bends to Teesta Bridge and the plains.

With me in the car was Sachin's friend Hasta Bahadur Lama. Being unable to accompany me himself as he was attending college, and not wanting me to travel alone as I had been suffering from malaria and was not yet fully recovered, Sachin had arranged for the young Tamang to accompany me on this occasion. Though one of our members since the days of the Young Men's Buddhist Association (India), only in recent weeks had Hasta been much seen at The Hermitage, usually turning up there with Sachin, who had recently struck up a friendship with him. Some freak of heredity had distinguished him from the generality of Tamangs, certainly from the squat, bandy-legged specimens of the tribe I had seen at Longview. Relatively tall, and slim but well built, he was possessed of a copper-coloured skin, hair that was brown rather than black, a somewhat retroussé nose, and eyes that were, as the emperor Akbar's were said to have been, 'vibrant as the sea in sunshine'. Joe, who was apt to accost Hasta with cries of 'Oh you gorgeous creature!', much to the young man's embarrassment, professed to be quite overpowered by these eyes (or perhaps he actually was). By disposition Hasta was reserved and self-contained, with a distinct preference for sports rather than study, and though I did not know him very well I was glad of his company, the more especially as my illness had left me feeling rather depleted. Unfortunately the train, which we boarded at Siliguri, was so overcrowded that we could not find seats and eventually, when the time came to retire, had to spread our bedding on some boxes in the corridor. Unable to sleep, I passed an uncomfortable night, in the course of which I developed a slight temperature. In the morning we managed to get some breakfast in the dining car and at 10.30 reached Amingaon, where we had to detrain and cross the Brahmaputra.

I had crossed the Ganges on a number of occasions, but this was the first time I had crossed the Brahmaputra, and though we were probably crossing it at a point where it was comparatively narrow it seemed even broader than the Ganges, the Padma arm of which its main stream, the Jamuna, eventually joined. It was also the first time I had visited Assam, and I had to admit that I knew little more about this most north-easterly state of the Indian Union than that it was big and 'backward' (i.e. economically undeveloped), that it was thinly populated, with a high proportion of tribal people, many of whom had been converted to Christianity, that much of it was still covered with jungle, and that it produced tea and the famous straw-coloured tussore silk, shawls of which were hawked from door to door in cities all over India. I did, however, know that once it had been a centre of Buddhism, especially of Tantric Buddhism, and that even now it was a centre of Tantric Hinduism. At Kamakhya, in western Assam, there was a famous Kali temple, which marked the spot where the goddess's pudenda had fallen when she was dismembered by her wrathful consort Shiva. My old friend Buddha-rakshita had been there as a boy. The temple was situated at the top of a small hill, he told me, and pilgrims were given *prasad* not in the form of consecrated food, as was the custom elsewhere, but in the form of a piece of white cloth with red stains on it – the goddess's menstrual rag. During our wandering days he had in fact been eager that we should visit the place together. But if Tantric Hinduism had survived in Assam, Tantric Buddhism had not. Buddhism had not survived there in any form. Though there were said to be forty or fifty thousand Buddhists in the state, the majority of them were comparatively recent immigrants of Thai or Bengali stock who were followers of Theravadin Buddhism in its Thai form in the case of the Tais (as they were called, apparently to distinguish them from the Thais of Thailand) and in its Burmese form in the case of the Bengalis. It was in order to establish personal contact with these isolated Buddhists that I was visiting Assam, many of them having come to know of me through *Stepping-Stones*, our monthly journal of Himalayan religion, culture, and education, which thanks to the vigorous colportage of a brother disciple of mine had circulated widely in the state during the twenty months of its existence.

The crossing of the Brahmaputra having taken little more than twenty minutes, we disembarked at Pandu to find our connection waiting at the platform and were able to secure seats without much difficulty. Securing food was another matter. There was nothing to be had at the tiny rural stations along the way, and it was only on our arrival at Lumding Junction in the evening that Hasta, at least, was able to eat. I then slept for a couple of hours, having been too tired during the day and perhaps too out of sorts to pay much attention to the scenes through which we were passing.

Some time after midnight we reached Mariyani, where Venerable Dharmawansa and a novice, together with four or five lay supporters, were waiting to meet us. Buddharakshita and I had known the young monk when we were ourselves still laymen, the three of us having lived together for a few weeks at the Maha Bodhi Orphanage in Calcutta during the 1947 Hindu-Muslim riots, and I had met him once or twice since receiving my higher ordination. It was he who had made arrangements for my tour, and sent me my travelling expenses, and it was he who now whisked Hasta and me away by jeep to the little town of Jorhat and to the Jorhat Buddha Vihara, which we reached about an hour later. The Vihara had been built by a small group of, mainly, Bengali Buddhists, and with some of these I talked for a while before going to bed at three o'clock, having been travelling for more than thirty-six hours and having had only two hours' sleep.

In the morning I felt unwell, but it was *Magha Purnima*, the February–March full moon day, people were already turning up at the Vihara, and as soon as I had forced down a morsel of breakfast I was obliged to devote myself to them. At 10.30, by which time the place was full, I inaugurated the day's celebrations by hoisting the five-coloured flag and giving a speech on its significance. The five colours represented the six colours of the Buddha's halo, I explained, the sixth colour, which was indescribable, being represented by the five colours in combination. As for the colours of the halo themselves, *they* represented the five principal elements of the Buddha's physical body in their refined, transmuted form. The Buddha's attainment of Enlightenment had changed the watery content of his body into blue light, his bones into white light, his blood into crimson light, his flesh into orange light, and his marrow into yellow light, while his body as a whole had been changed into a light of a colour for which there was no earthly name. The gross had been changed into the subtle, matter into pure radiance. Thus the Buddhist flag was a symbol of the transformation of un-Enlightened into Enlightened humanity – a transformation that could be brought about by following the Path taught by the Buddha. Though it had been designed, in its present form, by Col. Olcott, the co-founder of the Theosophical Society, the World Fellowship of Buddhists had recently adopted the five-coloured flag as the international Buddhist flag, so that it now was not only a symbol of the transformation of the individual Buddhist but a symbol, also, of the unity of all followers of the Buddha, and I was therefore glad to have had the privilege of hoisting it on the present occasion.

Hardly had I finished speaking than there arrived from a nearby temple a ragged little procession of monks, novices, and men and women devotees escorting a stupa-shaped reliquary containing, so I was told, bone relics of the Buddha. The reliquary, which was evidently of local workmanship, was adorned with large imitation cabochons of red and green glass, and borne by the oldest of the monks, who proceeded to deposit it on the image table in the Vihara's shrine-room where, its lid having been removed, the relics inside were exposed to view and a short puja conducted of which they were the focal point. The sight of the procession and the reliquary, but especially of the reliquary, with its gaudy imitation cabochons, affected me strangely. It was as though I was witnessing the arrival not of a concrete, visible reminder of the Master's life and teaching, as Buddha-relics were supposed to be, so much as that of the local fetish or ju-ju. The Bengali Buddhist laity were, it seemed, little better than fetish-worshippers, and their religion was in effect a species of fetishism, with the monks as the custodians of the fetish. Theravadin Buddhism had degenerated in their hands from a universal into an ethnic religion, or at least into a religion that incorporated a strong ethnic element. Not that I was in principle opposed to a universal religion like Buddhism incorporating an element of this kind. It was a question of proportion, and the sight of the procession and the reliquary had given me the impression that the pious supporters of the Jorhat Buddha Vihara and of the neighbouring temple had not got the proportion right. The impression did not, however, prevent me from joining in the puja – which I quite enjoyed – along with the other monks. After the puja came the *bhojana-dana* or ceremonial food-offering. About a hundred people came forward, one by one, to drop a few spoonfuls of rice or curry into my bowl (as the custom was, I was carrying this with me), but I was unable to eat anything solid and took only a little soup and some fruit.

In the afternoon the Vihara was the scene of a well attended public meeting. Held under the presidency of a member of the State Assembly, it started at two o'clock and did not finish until a good three hours later. The principal item on the programme was my own speech which, the requirements of health coinciding with the dictates of tradition, I delivered sitting down. It was Magha Purnima, I reminded my audience. We were commemorating the day on which 1,230 monks of varying spiritual attainments spontaneously came together in order to pay their respects to the Buddha. On that occasion the Buddha uttered what was probably the best known verse in the entire Pali Canon. 'Cease to do evil,' he declared. 'Learn to do good. Purify the mind. *This* is the teaching of the

Enlightened Ones.' Ceasing to do evil corresponded to the practice of ethics, the first stage of the path leading to nirvana. Learning to do good corresponded to the development of mental concentration, the second stage, while purifying the mind – purifying it of the stain of spiritual ignorance, the greatest of all stains – corresponded to the development of wisdom, the third and final stage. Having explained each stage in some detail, I turned to the question of Buddhist education, pointing out that it was the duty of Buddhist parents to bring up their children in the knowledge and practice of the Dharma. In conclusion, I congratulated the Buddhists of Jorhat on the fact that, though few in number, they had succeeded in building a vihara and appealed for the establishment of a Buddhist college of the traditional type. As usual, I spoke vigorously and with feeling, with the result that I started running a temperature and after the meeting had to lie down. None the less I continued to have visitors. Most of them were English-educated Hindus who, while sympathetic to the Buddha's teaching as they understood it, had no interest in the rather ethnic Buddhism of their Bengali Buddhist neighbours and who normally would not have set foot inside the Vihara. Naturally they had a lot of questions to ask the English monk (for as such Dharmawansa had been careful to advertise me), and it was several hours before I was free. By this time I had developed a severe headache and my temperature had risen. After taking some tomato juice and fruit I therefore retired for the night and took no further part in the celebrations, which continued until quite late and concluded with the ordination of two teenage boys as novices.

While I was dealing with the questions of my English-educated visitors Hasta was being subjected to a friendly interrogation by some of the more curious of the Vihara's lay supporters. Was he a Buddhist, they wanted to know. Yes, he was a Buddhist. Was he a follower of the Theravada? No, he was not a follower of the Theravada. What was he, then? He was a follower of the Mahayana. The Mahayana! What was that? But Hasta had reached the limits of his knowledge, and had to admit, as he told me afterwards, that he did not know what the Mahayana was and that they would have to ask me. Though the lay supporters may well have attributed the young Tamang's replies to modesty rather than to ignorance, there was no doubt that Hasta was woefully ill-informed about his own religion, and I could not but hope that having been made aware of this he would in future be more regular in his attendance at The Hermitage where, if I did not have much to say about the Mahayana, I certainly had a lot to say about the fundamental principles of the Dharma and about the application of those principles to one's daily life.

Though the Jorhat Buddha Vihara had been built mainly by Bengali Buddhists, it was in fact the Tais who made up the greater part of the Buddhist population of Assam. They apparently had migrated from Thailand several generations – even several centuries – ago, and unlike their Bengali co-religionists, who were more urbanized, lived in isolated villages of their own and engaged in agriculture. There were two of these Tai villages only fifteen miles from Jorhat, Dharmawansa informed me, and he had arranged for me to visit them. Accompanied by Dharma-wansa himself, as well as by Hasta and several of the Vihara's lay supporters, including the young man who had translated my speeches the previous day and whose services would again be required, I accordingly set out by station-wagon to meet the Tai Buddhists and observe their way of life. I did not set out until some time after lunch, the doctor having warned me that there was congestion at the back of the lungs and that if I did not take rest pneumonia might develop.

On my arrival at Balijan, the first of the two villages, I was given an extremely cordial reception by the monks, novices, and lay people of the place and conducted to the vihara, the steeply pitched roof of which was reminiscent of Thai rather than Indian architecture. Here I talked, and discoursed on the Dharma, for about three hours uninterruptedly, for such was the atmosphere of devotion by which I was surrounded, and so great was the evident eagerness for religious instruction on everyone's part, that despite my continuing temperature I had no alternative but to rise to the occasion and give of my best. From Balijan our little party, escorted by the villagers and by boys carrying five-coloured Buddhist flags, proceeded on foot to Nasyam, the second of the two villages, where we were to spend the night. Here too I was kept busy talking and discoursing on the Dharma (the Tais seemed to have an insatiable appe-tite for sermons), and it was past midnight when I got to bed. I did not get to bed, however, before having some unexpected visitors. I was lying down, but still discoursing, when word was brought me that three sahibs had arrived at the vihara and were asking to see me. The three sahibs turned out to be Swale Ryan, the ex-army man who had helped me found the Young Men's Buddhist Association, and two planters from the tea estate nearby where he was now working. He had heard I was in the neighbourhood, he announced in his usual hail-fellow-well-met fashion, and had dropped in to say hallo. As it was late, the visitors did not stay long. He would send a jeep for me the day after next, Swale promised before they left, as he wanted to show me round the estate. Only when I was on my own, and free to go to bed at last, did I realize that despite the exertions of the day I was not feeling tired. On the contrary, I felt quite buoyant.

The following morning, by special request of the villagers, I gave a talk on the differences between Buddhism and Christianity. Buddhism was a non-theistic religion, I explained, whereas Christianity was theistic. Buddhists meditated, whereas Christians prayed. The Buddhist monk was a teacher and exemplar, whereas the Christian priest was an inter-mediary between God and man. In Buddhism one gained Enlightenment by means of one's personal efforts, whereas in Christianity one was saved through the merits of a redeemer. Buddhism emphasized wisdom and compassion, whereas Christianity emphasized faith. For Buddhists the Buddha was an Enlightened human being, whereas for Christians Christ was the incarnate son of God. These simple antitheses depicted the differences between the two religions much too starkly, of course, but they had to be depicted starkly if they were to be made clear to the villagers, who apparently had been troubled by the preaching of the missionaries; and in any case I had only an hour or two in which to comply with their request and make, moreover, a definite impression on their minds. When the talk had been given, and the Refuges and Precepts administered, I and the rest of the party left for Jorhat, this time travelling not by station-wagon but by bullock cart. Though the sleek white bul-locks stepped out with a will, so that the unsprung wooden vehicle, with its iron-bound wooden wheels, bumped and rattled its way along the deeply rutted track at a reasonable speed, it took us more than an hour to reach the road where we were to catch the bus. Either because we had been misinformed about the time of its arrival, or because it was behind schedule, the bus did not turn up for nearly three hours. As we were waiting, two Sinhalese Buddhists who were working as mechanics in a nearby tea estate came and spoke to me, while an aged brahmin, on learning than I was a Buddhist, did his best to convince me that the Buddha was the ninth incarnation of the god Vishnu.

Back at the Jorhat Buddha Vihara, which we reached at about three o'clock, I found that I again had a temperature and therefore lay down. The rest of the day passed quietly. I had a lengthy discussion on Buddh-ism with a friend of my translator, and talked with Dharmawansa, and that was about all. Like the translator himself, the friend belonged to a community that had migrated from Thailand long before the Tais but which unlike the Tais had in the course of centuries become more or less completely Hinduized. As for Dharmawansa, though hailing from Bihar he belonged, as far as I knew, to the Bengali Buddhist community. At the time when Buddharakshita and I lived with him he was invariably quiet and composed, walking with a grave, dignified gait, his eyes modestly downcast, and was so meek as not to resent the thrashing Buddharakshita once gave him. In fact he became meeker than ever. He was still quiet and composed, and still walked with a grave, dignified gait, but now that he was older, and moreover incumbent of the Jorhat Buddha Vihara, he was, I thought, not quite so meek as before. At any rate, he was quietly assertive in his dealings with the Vihara's lay supporters and besides having organized my tour was at pains to take me wherever there was something worth seeing and wherever he thought my presence might do some good. Thus it was that, the morning after our return from Nasyam, he took me to see the Jorhat Technical Training Institute, where we were shown round by the foreman and where I gave a short address to the students. The jeep not turning up to take me to the tea estate as Swale had promised, the rest of that day, too, passed quietly. As it happened, this was just as well. I had a high temperature, and pains in the head, all the afternoon and evening, and went to bed early.

The community to which my translator and his friend belonged was not the only immigrant community to have been Hinduized. As I discovered the next morning, when Dharmawansa and I, together with Hasta and two novices, were given a ceremonial food-offering at the house of a lay supporter of the Vihara, the Bengali Buddhists of Assam had been Hinduized too, though to a much lesser degree and probably even before they entered the region. When I had given the family the Refuges and Precepts, and they had ceremonially offered food, our host, a Mr Barua, indicated that before Dharmawansa and the others fell to I should offer a portion of the food to the images in the domestic shrine behind my head. There were two images, one of the Buddha, the other of Lakshmi, the Hindu goddess of wealth. Without saying anything, I put the image of Lakshmi carefully to one side, and made the offerings to the image of the Buddha only. Probably Mr Barua was not surprised by my action. He must have known that the monks of his religion never worshipped the Hindu gods and goddesses, though the laity sometimes did, even if they were not supposed to. This was the first time I had seen a Hindu deity installed beside the Buddha in a Bengali Buddhist domestic shrine, and it was not to be the last. Hinduism being so very much the dominant religion in India, it was not easy for the Buddhist laity to withstand the constant pressure to Hinduize, and I could readily understand how, in the absence of a monastic order, those whose Buddhism consisted in little more than making offerings to the monks were in the long run bound to succumb to that pressure altogether.

Having returned to the Vihara from the Barua house, I made ready to leave Jorhat on the next stage of my tour. Catching the bus from Jorhat to Mariyani Junction, Hasta and I, accompanied by Dharmawansa and my translator, caught the train from Mariyani Junction to the village of Dishenpani. It was extremely hot, and the train rather crowded, so that by the time we reached our destination two hours later, at about three o'clock in the afternoon, Dharmawansa and my translator were hardly less exhausted than were the two visitors from Kalimpong. At the station our little party was met by some lay supporters and taken by car to Dishenpani Vihara, where we were welcomed by Venerable Nanda-wansa, the incumbent, and others, and where I talked for a while with a group of high school students. I was not feeling at all well, however. Besides having a high temperature, I felt weak in all my limbs, and after taking a dose of medicine went straight to bed. Fortunately I woke feeling somewhat better, and after eating a little breakfast gave a sermon for the benefit of the assembled lay supporters and administered the Refuges and Precepts. We then left Dishenpani for Chalapathar.

The two villages being both situated on the banks of the Brahmaputra, we made the journey by country boat. This was the most idyllic part of my whole tour. Although it was already quite hot, there was a coolness coming from the river, which together with the breeze created by the vessel's motion made the trip an extremely pleasant one. As we approached the village we were met by boys with gongs, and before long were being welcomed ashore by the assembled populace and escorted to the vihara amidst scenes of great enthusiasm. The name of the Tai village of Chalapathar was already familiar to me. It was the village where Dinesh had taught, where he had entered into a liaison with one of his pupils, and where he had been in danger of losing his life at the hands of the girl's brothers when the relationship was discovered. On our way to the vihara, which was situated about a mile from the river, I therefore looked about me with interest. It was as though we were in Thailand rather than India. Not only were the simple thatched houses raised on stilts. In both complexion and cast of feature the villagers were distinctly Mongoloid, while their costume was characteristic of South-east Asia rather than of the Indian subcontinent, the men being uniformly clad in white shirts and sarongs and the women and girls, no less uniformly, in tight-fitting white blouses and black sarongs. All looked healthy and happy, and I was conscious of the presence of a brighter, cleaner atmosphere than that which usually prevailed in the country's Hindu villages, sunk as the latter so often were in apathy and gloom. It was also noticeable that the inhabitants of Chalapathar, lively and expressive though they were, at the same time comported themselves in a disciplined and orderly fashion, so that it was not difficult for me to believe that their moral standards were indeed strict, as Dinesh had discovered to his cost. At the vihara I naturally had to deliver a sermon and administer the Refuges and Precepts, after which there came the usual ceremonial food-offering. Out of complaisance to our hosts I tried to eat, but could manage no more than a little soup and half a slice of toast. Indeed, my temperature having shot up I was obliged to lie down for a while, rising only to hear a group of evidently well-trained children recite devotional verses not just in Pali but also in Sanskrit.

Our departure from Chalapathar was even more spectacular than our arrival. At least mine was so. Not wanting me to exert myself unnecessarily, the villagers made a seat for me in the village woodcart, and with the women pulling in front and the girls pushing behind I was conveyed in triumph as far as the railway line. Why the men did not lend a hand was not clear. Perhaps the woodcart was female property. Or perhaps the women and girls were simply more devotionally inclined and more eager to 'make merit'. Be that as it may, they pulled and pushed with a will, to the accompaniment of a good deal of laughter. It was, in fact, a very jolly occasion, with the men shouting encouragement and the women and girls chattering among themselves like so many magpies. Looking down at the happy faces surrounding the cart, and at the array of dazzling white blouses and shiny-black sarongs, I thought I had rarely beheld a more charming sight. Was Dinesh's Mynah-bird, as he called her, one of the merry throng, or had she been married off to prevent her getting into further mischief and gone to live in another village? Whichever may have been the case, it was more than likely that she was already beginning to forget her erstwhile lover, even as he had already begun to forget her. At the railway line I dismounted from the cart, the villagers paid their last respects to the two yellow robes, and our little party – still four in number – started walking along the track in single file to Safarai Station. Here we caught the train to Tinsukhia Junction, which we reached two or three hours later, at about 7.30 in the evening, after a quite comfortable journey. From Tinsukhia Junction it took us only an hour to get to Digboi, where we were met by a Bengali lay supporter, another Mr Barua, and where, having been driven to this gentleman's residence, I spent several hours in discussion with him and other lay supporters before finally retiring for the night.

Digboi was to be the farthest point of my tour. I had originally intended to go as far as Sadiya, which was only a hundred or so miles from the easternmost extremity of India, where it bordered on both Burma and China, but though my temperature was normal I was still not eating, and moreover had developed a troublesome cough, and mindful of the warning I had been given by the doctor in Jorhat I therefore decided to go no farther and, in fact, to return to Kalimpong forthwith. I did not leave Digboi without seeing something of the little town, which was an important centre of the Indian oil industry and expanding rapidly. The following morning, after breakfast, a friend of my translator's came and took us for a drive round the oilfields, where the derricks towered black against a smoke-obscured sky and the smell of oil filled the air. Indeed, the whole town was grimy with oil. It was as though a black blight had fallen upon the green face of the earth and was spreading in all directions. If this was what economic development meant then I, for one, preferred that Assam should remain 'backward'. In the afternoon, having administered the Refuges and Precepts to our host and his family, I talked with some of the lay supporters who had come to pay their respects to me and my brother monk. There were only a few Buddhists in the town, they told me, most of them being from Chittagong in East Bengal, which now that it was part of (East) Pakistan was not the healthiest place in the world for a follower of the Enlightened One to be.

The train arriving nearly two hours late, our little party did not leave Digboi until eight o'clock that night. At Tinsukhia Junction, where we had to change, we managed to secure seats, and after sleeping, on and off, for a few hours, finally woke at four o'clock to find we had reached Mariyani. Here Dharmawansa and my translator got down, leaving Hasta and me to continue our journey without them. In the course of the day the compartment gradually became very crowded, so that I was not sorry when, at about five o'clock in the afternoon, we reached Pandu and had to detrain in order to cross the Brahmaputra. At Amingaon, on the other side, we secured seats only with difficulty, and for the whole of the rest of the journey the train was crowded to an uncomfortable degree. When night fell, Hasta climbed on to the luggage rack and slept there, while I curled up on the seat below. At half-past seven we reached Siliguri, and less than an hour later, having breakfasted in the station restaurant, we were seated in the Landrover and heading for the hills.

On our arrival at The Hermitage, soon after midday, I took a little stew, and having rested and read some *Spectator* essays went to see Sachin, who was overjoyed that I was back and gave me a bottle of cough mixture. Next day I was well enough to take a proper (rice) meal, my first for nearly two weeks, and started going through my mail, putting together the March issue of the *Maha Bodhi Journal*, and writing letters. Almost the first letter I wrote was to Venerable Dharmawansa, thanks to whom I had been able to make my tour. I was glad to have seen something of Assam, and to have made personal contact with the Buddhists of the state. In particular, I was glad to have had an opportunity of visiting the Tai Buddhist villages, and observing the way of life of the people there. Despite my poor health the tour had been, on the whole, quite idyllic, and my only real regret, as I looked back, was that I had not been able to stay longer or go farther.

SELLING TICKETS – AND THANGKAS

GOLD MIGHT OR MIGHT NOT BE DESERVING of the opprobrious epithets heaped on it by moralizing poets, and money might or might not be the root of all evil, but abstention from handling gold and silver was certainly one of the precepts taken by the *shramanera* or novice monk at the time of his ordination. I had been ordained as a shramanera at Kusinara in May 1949, and on my arrival in Kalimpong nearly a year later was still observing the precept strictly, not touching money in any form, even though I knew that the majority of shramaneras and bhikshus honoured the precept more in the breach than the observance. For my first six months in the town I continued to observe the precept, relying on my alms-bowl for food and on the generosity of friends and lay supporters for whatever else I needed. At the end of this period I found myself in a quandary. I had either personally to accept some money that had been collected for my support during the rainy season, when it would be difficult for me to go out on my morning alms-round, or risk exposing the well-meaning person who had collected it to the charge of retaining it for his own benefit. In the end I decided, most reluctantly, to accept it, and allowed the grubby currency notes and tarnished coins to be counted into my hand. Subsequently I found myself having to raise funds for the Young Men's Buddhist Association (India), as I still had to do for the Kalimpong branch of the Maha Bodhi Society, and in this way came to be more involved with money than I had been for many years.

According to a celebrated Mahayana treatise, the possession of gold and silver allowed a monk to be more useful to others and to help them. Very likely it did, but I was inclined to regard the argument as a rationalization and to wish that I, for one, could have helped people through my Buddhist work *without* the necessity of handling gold and silver, or rather, of having anything to do with money. One of the circumstances that had made my Assam tour so idyllic was the fact that, our tickets for the journey once purchased, I could simply forget about money. Whether I was with the Bengali Buddhists or the Tai Buddhists, food, clothing, shelter, and medicine (the four basic necessities for which the monk was dependent on the lay community) were all provided, and for the time being, at least, I needed nothing more. It was like being on the open road, as I had been during my years as a wandering ascetic, when equipped with my bowl and my robe as a bird with its two wings (the traditional simile) I was free to fly whithersoever I wished.

Now the idyll was over. I was back at The Hermitage, and into my role as bhikshu-in-charge of the Kalimpong branch of the Maha Bodhi Society. My wings were again folded, and like Baudelaire's albatross (I had read the French poet a lot during the past few months) I had been obliged to exchange freedom for captivity. According to Baudelaire, the Poet was in the same predicament as the albatross. Exiled on the ground, he was unable to walk because of his great wings. The Monk, or at any rate the Mystic, was also in that predicament, I thought, for at times circumstances forced him, too, to let his wings drag at his sides, as it were, or at least to fold them. But regardless of whether or not *my* wings were folded, or whether I even possessed wings at all, I had to walk as best I could. There was a lot to be done now that I was back in Kalimpong. Not only was there mail to be opened, an issue of the *Maha Bodhi Journal* to be put together, and letters to be written (to say nothing of a regular meditation practice to be kept up). There were also visitors to be seen, Sachin to be helped in his studies, the branch's monthly accounts to be made up, and copies of some of my more recent poems to be dispatched to the editor of the *Illustrated Weekly of India*. Most pressing of all, there were arrangements for the holding of the film shows to be finalized – the film shows which would, I hoped, place the finances of the Kalimpong branch of the Maha Bodhi Society on a more secure footing and lessen the drain on my own resources.

At the time of Raj Kapoor's agreeing that we could show two of his films without payment of the usual charges I was going through a period of financial stringency, and the Kalimpong branch with me. Since my return from Calcutta the stringency had increased, the expenses of Miss Barclay's funeral having swallowed up whatever money I had, and though I could expect to be reimbursed from her estate, this was going to take a long time (in the end it took a year), and meanwhile I had to continue subsidizing the branch's activities and supporting myself and my few dependants. By the time I left for Assam the state of my own, and the branch's, finances was indeed desperate, and two weeks later it was more desperate still. Within days of my being back in Kalimpong I was confronted by the fact that I had, literally, no money, and no prospect of having any until the arrival of the next instalment of the grant which, on the recommendation of my teacher Kashyap-ji, I was receiving from a wealthy Hindu philanthropist. News that the English Buddhist monk was in financial difficulties was not long in getting around, and even reached Darjeeling. Anagarika Dharmarakshita sent me a cheque for a hundred rupees by way of a loan, at the same time taking it upon herself to advise me regarding the kind of life I ought, as a Buddhist monk, to be leading. 'Those who give help cannot refrain from offering advice,' I confided to my diary. Next day I wrote to her returning the cheque, explaining that to accept a loan would only render my position more difficult later on. I also made it clear that I wanted no advice on spiritual matters. Later in the week, when I was still without any money, Sachin turned up one morning with thirty rupees he had borrowed for me from his father. Touched by his thoughtfulness, for I had said nothing to him about my difficulties, I accepted the loan – partly because it was a small one and therefore easily repayable, and partly because it came unaccompanied by any advice.

Before my departure for Assam it had been settled that our film shows would be held in the first week of April. The cruellest month – in India cruellest because hottest – was now almost upon us, and after talking with Dawa, the secretary, I therefore called a committee meeting in order to assign responsibility for such matters as the printing of tickets and the putting up of posters. In the course of discussion it transpired that we would need to borrow or hire a ciné projector. Sachin volunteered the information that a friend of a friend of ours in Darjeeling owned one, or had access to one, and two days later, therefore, only a fortnight after my return from Assam, I found myself once more seated in a Landrover and once more dropping down a succession of hairpin bends to Teesta Bridge and, this time, not the plains but an even longer succession of even more acute hairpin bends *up* to ever-misty Ghoom, eight thousand feet above sea level, and thence along the ridge and down a few hundred feet to the Queen of the Hill Stations. As we approached the town I saw on the hillside the pink and white and red of the beautiful flowering trees, at this time of year at their best.

The friend to whom Sachin had alluded was Omiya, the popular Bengali proprietor of a small watch-repair shop on Mackenzie Road. *His* friend was Tilak Prasad, a Nepalese who taught at one of the local colleges and whom I already knew slightly. Both young men were Hindus by birth, English-educated, and quite Westernized in their out-look, but whereas Omiya, who was the elder of the two, was still very much a bachelor, Tilak was already married and the father of a child. Contrary to my expectation, Omiya was not in his shop when I called there after breakfast the following morning (normally he was to be found nowhere else during business hours), but eventually I tracked him down and arranged to meet him and Tilak Prasad at the latter's place that afternoon. Yes, he had access to a ciné projector, Tilak was able to assure me a few hours later, over a cup of tea. The college had one, and he was confident of being able to borrow it for us. It would take him a little while, however, to arrange matters with the principal. I therefore decided to stay in Darjeeling three more days. This would enable me to see a few people, as well as to make quite sure that Tilak was, in fact, able to borrow the ciné projector for us and that I would not have to look for one elsewhere.

One of the people I wanted to see was Dr Hudson, who had decided, in the end, to settle in Darjeeling rather than Kalimpong, at least for the time being, and whom I found comfortably installed in a pleasant bun-galow with a cook-bearer and an *ayah*. She seemed pleased to see me, perhaps because she was in need of someone to talk to (her servants understood her English, apparently, no better than she did their Nepali). At any rate, she talked uninterruptedly for six hours, mostly about Buddhism and Theosophy, and I was able to get away only after prom-ising to have tea with her the following day. Tea with her at four o'clock the following day I accordingly had, trying not to intervene when mis-communication between the irate mistress, with her two words of Hindi, and the puzzled servants, with their broken English, became too acute. This time Dr Hudson held forth on the subject of radiaesthesia, about which she seemed to know a good deal, and soon had me performing, in this connection, various experiments with her crystal pendulum – experi-ments which I found quite interesting. We also discussed meditation. Before eventually allowing me to depart she insisted on giving me a viaticum in the form of a (homoeopathic) dose of arsenic, the pendulum having indicated a deficiency of that substance.

From crystal pendulum to diamond sceptre – the 'diamond sceptre of the lamas', as it was sometimes called – was perhaps only a short step, at least from the Jungian point of view. Short step or not, early next morning I was making my way to Aloobari Gompa (Aloobari, or 'Potato Field', was a small settlement too far from Darjeeling to be called a suburb and too near to be called a village), where one might reasonably expect to find

the acknowledged symbol of the Vajrayana, and even of Tibetan Buddhism itself, very much in evidence. On my arrival at the *gompa*, which was
a temple rather than a monastery, I was welcomed by the head lama and
his assistant, as well as by Dorje Bhutia, an English-educated young man
of the locality who, as his surname indicated, was a 'Darjeeling-born'
Tibetan. Situated on the quiet hillside, away from any habitations, the
unpretentious, white-washed building was a peaceful place. It was also
very well maintained, even though the locality was not, to all appearances, a prosperous one. What was more, the *lhakhang* or 'house of
divinities', as the Tibetans called it, besides being richly decorated was
dominated by a giant sedent image of Padmasambhava. Though not so
big as the one in the Tamang Gompa, in the heart of the bazaar, the sight
of which had affected me so profoundly four years earlier, it was no less
impressive. The light that came through the doorway revealed the same
'diamond sceptre' and skull cup, the one held in his right hand, the other
cradled in his left, the same red cloak, the same trident-tipped staff resting
in the crook of his arm, the same 'lotus hat' with the vulture feather, the
same moustached face, the same 'wrathful smile'.

As it happened, I had received that very week a review copy of *The
Tibetan Book of the Great Liberation*, the beautifully illustrated fourth volume in Dr Y.W. Evans-Wentz's famous Oxford Tibetan Series, and in fact
had brought it with me to Darjeeling so that I could go on reading it.
Among other riches, the volume contained 'An Epitome of the Life and
Teachings of Tibet's Great *Guru* Padma-Sambhava', based on excerpts
rendered into English by the late Sardar Bahadur Laden La, Darjeeling's
most famous son, assisted by Lama Sonam Senge. Though the mysterious
and inspiring figure of Guru Rimpoche – the Precious Guru – was
imprinted so vividly on my consciousness, during the four years that had
elapsed since my experience in the Tamang Gompa I had been able to
find out no more about the facts of his life than was already known to me
from scholarly histories of Buddhism. With biographical fact in the
ordinary sense, however, the Laden La/Evans-Wentz 'Epitome' was little
concerned. Its eighty-odd pages were replete with marvels and miracles,
some of them quite bizarre. As I subsequently observed when reviewing
the volume as a whole for the *Aryan Path*:

> While the present Epitome is of very great anthropological
> interest, one cannot help regretting that it was not possible for
> the first comprehensive account in English of the great Guru's
> career to have presented him in a more balanced and, we think,

in a truer way as a thinker and saint rather than as a 'Culture
Hero' and thaumaturgist. Though the text translated in the next
section [i.e. the 'Yoga of Knowing the Mind'] does enable us to
gain a more complete picture of his personality, those who have
been fascinated by the spiritual authenticity of the *Life of Milarepa*
[an earlier volume in the Oxford Tibetan Series] will, we are
afraid, be deeply disappointed by the Epitome of Padma-
Sambhava's Biography.

After all, various books were ascribed to the great Guru, and from these
Lama Govinda, at least, had got a vastly different impression of him, an
impression, namely, that he was – as my good friend had recently written
to me, in words I took the liberty of quoting in my review – 'a very sane
and profound thinker, a great saint, and a powerful personality, who
impressed the people around him so deeply that in their urge to convey
his greatness to posterity, they had to take resort to the superhuman and
to the miraculous.' I was also critical of Evans-Wentz's tendency, in some
of his elaborate annotations, to assimilate Buddhist to Hindu teachings,
as well as of Carl Gustav Jung's identification, in the 'Psychological
Commentary' that constituted the Foreword to the volume, of the One
Mind of the 'Yoga of Knowing the Mind' with the Unconscious of modern
psychology. None the less, I was grateful for *The Tibetan Book of the Great
Liberation*, and read it with avidity. If it failed to enlighten me as to the
historical biography of Padmasambhava, it certainly made me better
acquainted with his *symbolical* biography, and more vividly aware of
Padmasambhava the myth, as distinct from Padmasambhava the man.
So well had I become acquainted, by the time of my visit to the Aloobari
Gompa, with the symbolical biography of the great Guru, that I was able
to explain to the two lamas and Dorje Bhutia the significance of episodes
of which they had not even heard. Dorje Bhutia, in particular, was greatly
excited by these explanations, and on my happening to mention the
source of my information insisted on coming to see me that same day in
order to inspect for himself the wonderful book in which the secrets of
his religion were revealed. At four o'clock in the afternoon, therefore, as
arranged, the young Darjeeling-born Tibetan arrived on my doorstep,
and I had the satisfaction of showing him my copy of *The Tibetan Book of
the Great Liberation* and allowing him to go through its pages.

I was staying, as nowadays was my custom when visiting Darjeeling,
at the Gandhamadan Vihara, the Bengali Buddhist centre on the steep
hillside below Chota Khagjhora, a rather insalubrious locality on the

main road into town. There was still no resident bhikshu, nor any likelihood of there being one, the monks of the Bengali Buddhist Association, of which the Vihara was a branch, not being very keen, by all accounts, on living in a place as cold as Darjeeling could be and ministering to its tiny Theravadin community. But if there was no resident bhikshu there was at least a resident nun, in the person of Anagarika Dharmarakshita, who was occupying not, indeed, the wooden kuti reserved for members of the monastic order, but one of the row of pukka guest rooms immediately adjacent. On my arrival at Chota Khagjhora from Kalimpong she was not at home, but we met that evening, after I had been out and about all day, and though the hour was late, and I was tired, she insisted on telling me all about her latest troubles and difficulties. I listened without saying very much, for though not unsympathetic I knew the aggrieved Anagarika well enough, by this time, to be aware that she had a tendency to compound her difficulties, such as they were, by her own tactless and aggressive behaviour. This tendency was well illustrated by an unpleasant incident which occurred that very evening. While we were talking (or rather, while she was talking and I listening), an elderly Bengali Buddhist who was a permanent occupant of one of the guest rooms came back from work the worse for drink and proceeded to create a disturbance. Out rushed the Anagarika, her face scarlet, and quivering with indignation, and upbraided the offender severely, reminding him that the place was a vihara and that he should behave accordingly. The elderly Bengali was not disposed to take this lying down, and retaliated with a torrent of coarse abuse. No doubt he should not have been drinking, nor have created a disturbance in what was supposedly a monastery, but the Anagarika should have known better than to scold a man while he was under the influence of alcohol and better, moreover, than to scold him so harshly.

The Anagarika was far from seeing matters in this light, and when, the following afternoon, we visited a leading lay supporter of the Vihara, a Dr Barua, in order to discuss Buddhist activities in the area, she complained bitterly to him and his wife about the way in which the drunken Bengali had spoken to her. As she saw it, she had simply acted to protect the sanctity of the Vihara and been insulted for her pains. If the Bengali Buddhists of Darjeeling had any regard at all for their religion, or for those who *did* observe its precepts, they would not allow one of the guest rooms at their religious centre to be polluted by the presence of a drunkard but would throw him out immediately! Excessive though the Anagarika's reaction the previous evening may have been she did, of course, have a point. As I had noticed on my previous visits, two or three of the guest rooms were occupied, permanently as it seemed, by some rather disreputable-looking Bengalis, presumably Buddhists, who took no part in the religious activities of the place, minimal as these were, and who appeared to have turned their corner of the premises into what was virtually a drinking and gambling den. Two days later, therefore, when Kali Kinker Barua, the secretary of the Vihara, gave me a ceremonial food-offering at his house, as he always did at least once whenever I was in Darjeeling, I raised the matter with him. The situation down at Chota Khagjhora was not very satisfactory, he admitted. But what was he do ? He could hardly ask the occupants of the guest rooms to leave. The rent they paid was the Vihara's only regular source of income. There was no *dana* worth mentioning. There was no *dana* because there were no activities, and there were no activities because there was no resident bhikshu. To all this there was little I could say, especially as I knew that Kali Kumar was a devout (Theravadin) Buddhist who had the interests of the Vihara very much at heart. Like the Kalimpong branch of the Maha Bodhi Society, the Darjeeling branch of the Bengal Buddhist Association suffered from lack of adequate financial support. Kali Kumar had solved the problem by letting some of the guest rooms, albeit to the wrong sort of people. I was trying to solve it, at least temporarily, by holding benefit film shows. We were both in the same boat.

What with having tea with Dr Hudson, visiting the Aloobari Gompa, and spending time with the Anagarika and my Bengali Buddhist hosts, besides seeing various other people I knew, my additional days in Darjeeling were fully occupied. Omiya and Tilak I met several times after our initial coalescence, and eventually Tilak was able to inform me that he had arranged matters with the principal and that Omiya would be bringing the ciné projector to Kalimpong in good time for our first performance. I was now free to leave Darjeeling, which I did straight after breakfast the following morning. I was not able to bid the Queen of the Hill Stations farewell, however, without having been obliged to hear more about the Anagarika's troubles and difficulties. Her recital of these had in fact culminated, the day before, in her telling me that she felt depressed and homesick and shedding a few tears. But deliverance was at hand. Scarcely had she finished wiping her eyes and blowing her nose than there descended on the Vihara, enquiring for her, a French married couple. They were Theosophists, it transpired. Like Dr Hudson, the husband seemed to know a lot about radiaesthesia, and he in fact soon offered to 'give some energy' to me as my vibrations were weak. Radiaesthesia seemed to be catching on in the West, I reflected, at least in Theosophical circles. The arrival of her two compatriots was a tonic to the Anagarika, and before the visit was over she had arranged to take them to Ghoom the following morning – the morning of my departure – and show them the famous Ghoom monastery. I was therefore able to leave her in a state of excitement as extreme as that of her previous depression. My own feeling, as I left Darjeeling behind me, was predominantly one of relief. Now that I had succeeded in borrowing a ciné projector there was no reason why the selling of tickets, and other preparations for the film shows, should not go ahead. Apart from our having to pick up two police constables and their prisoner, an unkempt Nyingma lama, the journey passed without incident, and I was back at The Hermitage in time for lunch. After lunch, it being a full moon day, I decorated the shrine in readiness for the evening puja and sermon. Not many people attended, but I gave what I thought was a good sermon, on 'Who is a Buddhist?' Joe was among those present, but after the meeting he became involved – rather inappropriately, I thought – in a long political discussion with a Bengali Hindu friend of mine.

Politics was, in fact, difficult to get away from, at least politics in the sense of having dealings with the local administration and the police. Film shows were entertainment. As such they were liable to entertainment tax. If we were to be exempted from having to pay this, on the grounds that our shows were for charity, then we would have to obtain an exemption certificate. I therefore saw both the Deputy Commissioner, who was in Kalimpong on tour, and the Sub-Divisional Officer, they being, apparently, the authorities concerned. I also dispatched Dawa to the thana, as the police had some (undefined) role in the business. With both Dutt-Majumdar and the youthful Bengali SDO I not only talked about the film shows, and found out just what was involved in obtaining the exemption certificate, but had a lengthy discussion regarding Christian missionaries and what was to be done about their undesirable methods of conversion, a delicate question I had already raised with Dutt-Majumdar when we met at Longview. In the SDO's case, I also discussed Miss Barclay's affairs and explored the possibility of Vaishakha Purnima, the anniversary of the Buddha's Enlightenment, being declared a public holiday throughout the sub-division. With politics, or at any rate its administrative *avataras*, out of the way, Dawa and I were able to meet the secretary of the Town Club and finalize the details of our bookings, and as the third week of March was succeeded by the fourth, preparations for the film shows started gathering momentum. Posters went up in the bazaar. Tickets were given to members and friends to sell from door to door. Volunteers were briefed on their duties at the Town Hall on the three nights of the film shows. Finally, to make assurance doubly sure, Dinesh was sent to Siliguri to check whether the precious cylinders had, in fact, been dispatched to us from there by ropeway.

While these preparations were in progress I was also having to carry on with my usual work. There were letters to be written, the *Maha Bodhi Journal* to be edited, and callers to be dealt with – not to mention my having to see to the day-to-day running of The Hermitage. There was also Sachin to be taught. Since my return from Darjeeling we had embarked on an intensive study of Shelley's shorter poems, such as 'When passion's trance is overpassed', 'To Jane: the keen stars were twinkling', and 'When the lamp is shattered'. As tended to happen when we studied poetry together, we were both sometimes left, at the end of a session, in a mood bordering on the ecstatic. There was also teaching of a more prosaic type to be done. Since my return from Darjeeling I had acquired two new pupils. One of these was the youngest of Sachin's three (younger) sisters; the other, Lobsang Phuntsok Lhalungpa, the young Tibetan aristocrat to whom Thubden Tendzin (Marco Pallis) had introduced me four years earlier and who had recently moved, with his wife and small son, into the Manjula cottage flat formerly occupied by Miss Barclay. Meera was twelve or thirteen and, like her brothers and sisters, strikingly good-looking. If Sheila, the eldest sister, could be described as handsome, and Beena, the middle one, as beautiful, Meera could best be described as extremely pretty. Though she seemed to enjoy her lessons with me she was not very bright, and was much more interested in new saris and the precise arrangement of her kiss curl than in her school books. That I had been asked to teach her (actually, to give her practice in English conversation whenever I happened to be at the Singh bungalow) was indicative of the increased closeness of my relations with the whole family. Sachin having spoken very warmly of the way in which I had looked after him in Calcutta during his illness, I was in fact for both his parents and his siblings now more *amicus familiae* than ever.

Lobsang Phuntsok was the son of the Nechung Oracle, the oracle consulted by the Tibetan government, and had been educated in Lhasa as a monk-officer. When I first met him he was still a monk-officer. Since then he had reverted to lay status and married, though whether he continued to be in the service of the Tibetan government was unclear. There was no doubt, however, that he was of a scholarly disposition and highly intelligent. Intelligence beamed from the broad, flat face, which often wore a look of amusement, and twinkled in the small, slit eyes. Mrs Lobsang – Darjeeling-born and half Bhutanese – was as beautiful as her husband was handsome. Among Tibetans, at least, she was reputed to be the most beautiful woman in the district, being even more beautiful than Princess Pema Tsedeun, the eldest daughter of the Maharaja of Sikkim, now past her prime. Unfortunately she had the habit of screwing up her eyes every few minutes, which rather detracted from the impression she made. Despite being such a belle, she was of a friendly, obliging disposition, and though I had met her only once or twice I had no hesitation in giving her two or three books of tickets and asking her to sell them. As it happened, she sold more tickets for us than anyone else did, selling them mostly to Tibetan government officers who, I suspected, bought them more because they wanted to please her than because they wanted to support the work of the Kalimpong branch of the Maha Bodhi Society.

The week of the film shows was now, in fact, upon us. The cylinder containing the films had been collected from the ropeway station. Omiya had brought the ciné projector from Darjeeling, and on the morning of 3 April, immediately after breakfast, with Dawa and three or four volunteers, I conveyed the equipment by jeep to the Town Hall, where we spent the rest of the morning making the shabby, run-down old place as presentable as we could. With so much depending on the reliability of the projector, I took the precaution of getting Mr King, a Nationalist Chinese who had worked as an electrician in Lhasa, to come and check that it was functioning properly. He having assured me that it was functioning perfectly, and that I had nothing to worry about, I went home for lunch, returning to our temporary cinema an hour later. There was still much to be done, and the volunteers and I were kept busy right up to the time the doors opened. Despite all our efforts, however, the performance was a flop. Only seven tickets were sold, which meant that even allowing for the fact that a number of people had bought tickets in advance but not bothered to come, our first film show was a decided failure. Drastic action would have to be taken. Next morning I gave Mrs Lobsang more tickets to sell, and myself spent the remainder of the morning, and most of the afternoon, selling tickets from house to house and shop to shop in the bazaar. The result was that our second show was a success. The first performance (there were two performances this time) was very well attended, possibly because it was Sunday, though attendance at the second was less good. There being two performances, the show ended very late, and I did not get to bed until 2.00 a.m.

Most of the people attending the shows were Tibetans, of both sexes and all ages, and including a generous sprinkling of shaven heads and red robes. As I already knew, Tibetans were great cinema-goers, and few were the sturdy exiles from the Land of Snows who did not see every film that was screened at the town's (then) one and only 'bioscope'. As I also knew, the Tibetans were particularly fond of violent films. Thus it was not surprising that their favourite genre should have been the Western, in which there was a clearly defined conflict, in which plenty of blows and shots were exchanged, and which ended with dead bodies lying on the ground. If they had had the patience to wait for the last act, the Tibetans would probably have enjoyed *Hamlet*. Which genre – or genres – the two Raj Kapoor films represented I did not know, as I refrained from actually seeing them. They were certainly not Westerns, and in all probability contained little or no fighting. Some of the Tibetan members of the audience may, therefore, have been disappointed. One of them undoubtedly was, though whether because of the lack of violence or for some other reason was unclear. As I stood beside the door, waiting for the end of the performance, a burly figure strode out in disgust, loudly declaring that it was the worst film he had ever seen.

Despite this unfavourable verdict on the part of at least one of our patrons, I did not allow myself to be discouraged but did whatever I could to ensure the success of our third and last film show. As this did not take place until Wednesday, I had two clear days in which to boost the sale of tickets. On the Wednesday afternoon, however, when two volunteers had spent the morning giving the show extra publicity in the bazaar, Mr King discovered that the projector's exciter bulb had fused. Having failed to obtain a replacement either in the bazaar or at the Chinese School, I decided, as a last resort, to try Dr Graham's Homes. The Homes was, of course, a Christian missionary institution, and I had already tried, with no very great success, to sell tickets there, on the principle that if Christians could ask Buddhists and Hindus to support their work (as they frequently did) then there was no reason why Buddhists and Hindus should not ask Christians to support *theirs*. Mr Duncan, the whey-faced, tight-lipped superintendent of the Homes, obviously did not believe in such mutuality, and frostily told me, 'We do not approve of your activities,' though eventually he did agree, with the greatest reluctance, to accept a few tickets and even to put up a notice about them. Rubicund Mr Muir, the headmaster of the Homes' school, and his deputy Mr Ross, were more co-operative. They did not have a spare exciter bulb, but they did have a projector, and this they agreed to lend us. Back with it I therefore sped to The Hermitage, where the volunteers were waiting to take our equipment to the Town Hall and where I quickly finalized arrangements for the evening's show.

As if the fusing of the exciter bulb was not trouble enough, I also had to deal, that afternoon, with the problem of the Anagarika. The volatile Frenchwoman had arrived with her two French friends soon after my own return from Darjeeling, the friends had stayed for two days, putting up at the Himalayan Hotel, and she had shown them the sights of Kalimpong and taken them to see Joe and Dr Roerich. On their departure for Calcutta, after I had conducted a special puja for them in the shrine, she was again thrown on her own resources, which meant that she took to spending more time at The Hermitage than was either convenient or desirable. She also took to handing me a written 'confession' after the evening puja, sometimes staying on to explain or discuss it. As I was planning to leave for Calcutta in the middle of the month, in order to see the Vaishakha number of the *Maha Bodhi Journal* through the press, and did not want her moving in to The Hermitage during my absence, as she had done before, I took the precaution of making arrangements for her to stay at Tirpai. When I tried to speak to her about these arrangements, however, after the volunteers had left for the Town Hall with our equipment, she burst into tears and wept bitterly for half an hour. I was therefore obliged to spend another half hour, and more, reminding her that the monastic life had its difficulties, and that she could not always have what she wanted, with the result that I was later leaving The Hermitage than I had intended.

On arriving at the Town Hall I found the place nearly full, and people still turning up. But if fortune, that fickle goddess, had decided to favour us that evening, she soon changed her mind. Despite our combined efforts, we could not get the Homes' projector working, and at the end of three hours were forced to admit defeat. By this time the audience had become restive, even vociferous, and having made what excuses we could we had to send people home with the promise that there would be a (free) show the following evening. When they had gone we again tested the projector and eventually, at about eleven o'clock, managed to get it working. That night I did not sleep until the early hours. 'Very trying day with innumerable disappointments and luck apparently dead against us,' I noted in my diary, adding, 'But we must carry on.' In the immediate context, carrying on meant putting on a film show that very evening (the evening of Thursday, as it now was), and putting on a film show meant finding a new exciter bulb, for it was obvious we could not rely on the

Homes' projector and would have to fall back on Tilak's. No exciter bulb being obtainable in Kalimpong, finding a new one meant making a trip to Darjeeling. In the morning I therefore caught the nine o'clock Land-rover, reaching my destination in the record time of less than two hours. After scouring all the radio and electrical shops in the town without success, meeting many friends on the way, I eventually located the bulb I wanted with a friend of Tilak's. As I, too, was a friend of Tilak's, and as this naturally made me *his* friend, and he mine, he was happy to let me borrow it, and I was back in Kalimpong, the elusive exciter bulb safe in my shoulder bag, a couple of hours before the film show was due to begin.

This time fortune smiled on us the whole evening. The Town Hall was full, the projector gave no trouble, and the audience seemed to be satisfied. As I walked up and down outside, in the dark, waiting for the performance to finish, I felt relieved that we had been able to keep our promise, relieved that the film shows had proved not wholly unsuccess-ful, and relieved (I had to admit) that the last performance would soon be over and that I would soon be seeing the last of our present audience, at least in their cinema-going capacity. But had it really been worth it? Had all the trouble and worry been justified? In any case, I was a monk; I was trying to lead a spiritual life; yet here I was, organizing film shows, selling tickets in the bazaar, and running from place to place in search of exciter bulbs. Why was I doing this? True, the work of the Kalimpong branch of the Maha Bodhi Society had to be carried on, and its finances therefore placed on a secure footing, but was this really a sufficient reason for my becoming so deeply involved in what were, undeniably, worldly activities, and what was the significance of such involvement for my own spiritual life? Was I being (or trying to be) a good bodhisattva, engaging in worldly activities for the benefit, ultimately, of other people, or was I simply being a bad monk, allowing myself to be distracted from my true vocation of self-purification?

Whichever it may have been (and the two were not necessarily anti-thetical), the end of the film shows did not mean the end of the work connected with them. Films and projectors had to be returned, chairs in the Town Hall restored to their former positions, money collected from Mrs Lobsang and others, and full details of ticket sales submitted to the DC, the SDO and the police in connection with our application for exemption from entertainment tax. There were also the accounts of the film shows to be made up, and the extent to which the Maha Bodhi Society's Kalimpong branch had benefited from them ascertained.

Unfortunately, it had not benefited as much as I had hoped it would – certainly not enough to place its finances on a secure footing even for a short period. This did not altogether surprise me. The sluggishness of ticket sales prior to the shows, and the piling up of unlooked-for expenses, had forewarned me that such would probably be the case and I had already taken action accordingly. The action had been drastic. I had sold the only objects of any monetary worth I possessed: my *thangkas*. These thangkas, a set of three depicting the Sixteen Arahants travelling by sea to China on the backs of various monsters, had been a farewell present from Marco Pallis, and hence possessed a sentimental as well as a religious value for me, so that I was extremely loth to part with them. But part with them I did: in the circumstances, I had no choice. Fortunately I did not have to do the actual selling myself. Joe happening to mention that he thought he could sell them for me, I handed them over to him, and a few days later he brought me six hundred rupees. Neither then nor afterwards did he tell me to whom he had sold the thangkas, only assuring me that he had sold them, as I had stipulated, to someone who would treat them with proper respect. However, I knew that Prince Peter, for whom Joe had recently started working, currently had the Italian Ambassador staying with him, and drew my own conclusions.

Six hundred rupees was not a great sum, but together with what we had made from the film shows it would cover the branch's expenditure for the next few months. I could therefore prepare for my journey to Calcutta with a light heart, without having to worry about the immediate future of our work. Whether because the strain of organizing the film shows was now over, or for some other reason, during the week that preceded my departure lightheartedness was indeed the dominant mood among The Hermitage's little band of youthful habitués. Certainly it was the mood when Sachin and Dawa and I, together with half a dozen others, spent the day picnicking at Durpin, at the south-eastern end of the ridge on which Kalimpong was situated. Rain had recently fallen, and the haze being finer than usual we could see, four thousand feet below, and bathed in the golden sunlight, a vast expanse of level countryside stretching away into the distance for forty or fifty miles, as it seemed, before finally merging with the overarching blue of the sky.

This picnic was not my only outing that week. One afternoon I had tea at Tirpai with Geshe Wangyal, a Mongolian monk who was a friend of Marco Pallis's and had been his guest in England in the thirties. The Geshe, or 'Doctor of Buddhist Divinity', as some translated the title, was planning to leave Kalimpong. In fact he was planning not only to leave

Kalimpong but to emigrate to America and teach Tibetan there in an institute of higher learning. I had no such plans. I was happy in Kalimpong, and whatever the difficulties I would stay there and work for the good of Buddhism as my teacher had directed.

Chapter Eight

Proof-Reading at 110°F

The Sri Gauranga Press was situated down a narrow lane behind the headquarters building. They were reputed to be one of the best printers in Calcutta, and the Maha Bodhi Society had dealt with them for many years. During the two and a half weeks for which I was in the City of Dreadful Heat, as it now also was, seeing the Vaishakha number of the *Maha Bodhi Journal* through the final stages of its production, many a half hour did I spend in the Press's dark, cramped little front office checking last-minute corrections and signing print orders on the completed formes.

Most of my time, however, was spent in my room on the second floor of the headquarters building, whither there came to me, in rapid succession, first the galleys and then the proofs, brought while the ink was still wet by the Sri Gauranga Press's black-fingered printer's devil. The galleys took the form of narrow strips of paper, often as much as eight or ten feet in length, on which was a single, continuous column of type. If there were more than forty or fifty misprints on a strip (the compositors did not know English, or knew very little), I sent it back with the misprints corrected and called for a second galley. Sometimes I had to call for a third. Otherwise – or when galley misprints had been reduced to no more than six or eight – the corrected matter came back to me in page-proof form and set up in the Journal's traditional double columns. First page proofs did not often contain more than half a dozen misprints, so that I was usually able to give the print order on the second page proof, whether at the Press or in my own room, it being my practice to give this only after I had seen a perfectly clean proof. The Press, I had already learned, could not always be trusted, good as they were, to carry out my final corrections before printing (time was money) or, even if they did carry them out, not to make any fresh mistakes in the process. Since the Vaishakha number comprised more than a dozen formes (there were eight pages to a forme), and since I was often reading the page proofs of earlier formes and galleys of later ones at the same time, my little table in front of the barred window was usually covered with proofs of different kinds, at their various stages of progress, the long strips of the galleys hanging over the edge of the table and trailing across the floor.

If the proofs came from the Sri Gauranga Press with the ink still wet, they often went back damp with my perspiration, which fell in great drops on to the paper from my forehead and soaked it from the palms of my hands and the underside of my wrists and forearms. On my arrival in the city, which I reached in mid-afternoon, the weather had been very sultry, with a hot wind blowing. Since then the wind had subsided, but it continued to be sultry, and before many days had passed the thermometer was standing at 110°F. In Calcutta, it seemed, April was indeed the cruellest month, even if it was cruel, here, for reasons different from those which the author of the famous line proceeded to allege. I sat at my proof-covered table wearing only my inner robe (a sort of waist-cloth), the coarse cotton of which adhered uncomfortably to the seat of my chair and felt disagreeably tight about my middle. Every now and then I had recourse to the earthenware water pot that stood in the corner by the door, or, more occasionally, sent out one of the Society's bare-legged servants to a nearby tea stall for tea. Before lunch I doused myself, Indian style, in the bathroom on the opposite corner of the inner veranda, but ten minutes later I would be as hot and sticky as ever. On days when the heat was particularly trying I took a second bath in the afternoon, and even a third one in the evening. Great as the temptation might be, however, one had to be careful not to take too many baths, as this tended to deplete the skin's natural oils, with the result that one came out in an unsightly and rather painful rash. Since it was so hot I had little or no appetite, and found the Society's meagre breakfast of two slices of toast and its insubstantial, ante-meridian lunch (for the monks) of rice and curry, supplemented by the occasional tiny pot of sweet curds, more than sufficient for my needs. Night brought but scant relief. The atmosphere was close; I slept heavily, almost as though I had been drugged, and woke to the grey dawn light with a feeling of the oppressiveness of existence – a feeling that weighed not only on my eyelids but almost on my soul. By six o'clock, however, having meditated a little and had breakfast, I was seated at my table getting on with the work for which I had come to Calcutta at this, the very time of year I would least have wished to be there.

That work had started long before my arrival in the City of Dreadful Heat. For two months and more I had been collecting articles for the Vaishakha number, reading them, corresponding with their respective authors, and preparing the articles themselves for the press. Now they were all passing through my hands in proof form and I was reading them once again, perhaps even more closely than before. As befitted the avowedly international character of the Journal, indeed of the Maha Bodhi Society itself, the authors of the articles were of seven or eight different nationalities, belonged to both the East and the West, and represented – in the case of the Buddhist contributors – both the Theravadin and the Mahayana traditions. The authors of no fewer than five of the articles had previously been contributors to *Stepping-Stones*, my own minuscule journal of Himalayan religion, culture, and education; after its demise I continued to be in contact with them, and on my appointment to the editorial board had succeeded in enlisting them as contributors to the bigger and better known *Maha Bodhi*, then in its sixty-third year of publication. Perhaps the most prominent member of the group was Lama Govinda, with whose interpretation of Buddhism I was very much in agreement and who was now a personal friend. The lama, who had known Anagarika Dharmapala, and been actively associated with the Society in the early thirties, had of course contributed to its journal before; but disagreements having arisen between him and Devapriya Valisinha he ceased contributing and in fact virtually severed his connection with the Society. One of the disagreements between him and Devapriya-ji was of a personal nature, relating to Govinda's style, or distinguishing title. At first, at the time of his association with the Society, the future lama had styled himself Brahmachari Govinda, as he had done previously in Ceylon. Subsequently, however, he began styling himself first Anagarika Brahmachari Govinda, then Anagarika B. Govinda, and finally, after his initiation into Tibetan Buddhism and his marriage to Li Gotami, Lama Anagarika Govinda. Devapriyji had strongly objected to this latest development. How could a married man call himself an anagarika, he wanted to know. An anagarika was by definition homeless, and hence wifeless; he was one who, without being a bhikkhu, gave up all domestic ties and civic responsibilities in order to devote his life to the Dharma – as Anagarika Dharmapala had done. For Govinda to go on calling himself an anagarika after his marriage was highly improper. It was an insult to the memory of the Society's revered founder, who had been a *real* anagarika. Devapriya-ji, who as Dharmapala's personal disciple and chosen successor cherished his memory deeply, had therefore refused to print Govinda's articles in the *Maha Bodhi Journal* as being by Lama *Anagarika* Govinda (he had once, I believe blue-pencilled the offending title), with the result that Govinda had ceased to submit articles.

As the friend of both parties, as well as editor of the Journal, I naturally was anxious to bring the disagreement to an end and for Govinda to become as regular a contributor to the *Maha Bodhi* as he had been to *Stepping-Stones*. Since neither the German lama nor the Sinhalese upasaka would yield, a compromise had to be found. Devapriya-ji's insistence that Govinda was *not* an anagarika, and that he therefore could not be so styled in the pages of the official organ of the leading Buddhist society in India, had somehow to be reconciled with Govinda's claim (in his correspondence with me) that the dropping of 'Anagarika' from his title would seriously affect his interest in the copyright of *all* his writings. My solution to the dilemma was that contributions by Govinda should appear in the *Maha Bodhi* as being by 'Lama A. Govinda'. This solution having proved acceptable to both parties (I had arrived at it earlier in the year), I had already been able to print Govinda's poem 'The Buddha's Seat', and now had an article from him for publication in the Vaishakha number.

The article was entitled 'The Buddha as the Ideal of the Perfect Man and the Embodiment of the Dharma'. 'That the Buddha lived as a man among men,' the lama wrote, 'gives us the courage to follow him. That as a man he succeeded in overcoming the man within him, gives us the certainty that we also can overcome ourselves, that we also can overcome our human limitations and liberate ourselves from the shackles of death and rebirth.' But though the Buddha was a man in the general sense of the word, he was not *only* a man, but something more, something that reached out into the timeless and infinite, where concepts like 'man' and 'not-man' lost their meaning. Buddhahood, the lama insisted, was in fact transcendental, and this 'transcendental' nature was in no way in conflict with the humanness of the Buddha. Being transcendental, the Buddha's nature was, in the words of the *Prajnaparamita Sutra*, 'inconceivable' and only to be 'hinted at' in symbols. It was not to be communicated by creating a plastic image of the Buddha in the conventional-realistic style of Greek portraiture, an attempt which had resulted in 'the pathetic failure of Gandhara art' which, though of great interest to the archaeologist and art historian, was entirely devoid of religious inspiration and depth of feeling for the supramundane greatness of the *Tathagata*. In Govinda's opinion it was fortunate that Gandharan statuary had died as quickly as it had come into existence and been soon superseded by a new wave of spiritual art, in which the symbolic value replaced the naturalistic tendency in the representation of the ideal form of Buddhahood. As with the visible representation of the Enlightened One, so with the treatment of the Buddha's life story. What was important to the Buddha's followers were not the material facts and their occurrence in time or chronological sequence, but the Buddha's spiritual quest, the development of his spiritual career, the psychological facts and inner experiences that led to his Enlightenment and the formulation of his teachings. 'These inner experiences were subsequently concretized into external occurrences in the description of the Buddha's life, and gave rise to the most beautiful and profoundly true symbolism of art and poetry which carried the eternal message of the Buddha into the farthest corners of the world and did more for the propagation of Buddhism than the learned treatises of philosophers and scholars.'

The transcendental also featured in an article on 'Conditions and the Unconditioned' by Edward Conze, another of the five contributors to the Vaishakha number who had previously been contributors to *Stepping-Stones*. An object, Dr Conze pointed out, was swallowed up by the conditions which governed its presentation, and could not be separated from them. The same held good when we regarded a thing not as a datum but as a process or *event*, and considered the conditions which produced it. An investigation of conditions was of central importance for the Buddhist scheme of meditations, undermining as it did our belief in the fixity and ultimate validity of the sense-given distinctions between things around us. Buddhists meditated on conditions in order to win salvation from all conditioned things, with a wish to reject them in so far as they were conditioned, thereby winning through to the Unconditioned.

In the articles by the three other members of the group the transcendental featured only by implication. Dr George Roerich wrote on 'Vanaratna – the Last of the Great Panditas', basing himself on the Tibetan *Blue Annals*, which he was then translating, while Marco Pallis wrote on 'Some Aspects of Buddhist Education' and HRH Prince Peter of Greece and Denmark on 'Buddhism and the Japanese Character'. Marco Pallis made, *inter alia*, much the same point with regard to the representation of the Buddha in art that Lama Govinda had made. Latterly there had appeared in the Buddhist world, he complained, a good many cheap prints showing episodes in the life of the Victorious One and other pious subjects, which had been copied, as far as style was concerned, from the 'naturalistic' atrocities which nowadays passed for religious art in

Europe, and these were tending to replace the traditional models. It was forgotten that these models were the work of inspired craftsmen, who knew how to give form to the symbolical aspect of the thing they portrayed: the naturalistic image for its part stopped short at the perfunctory reproduction of surfaces. 'The true Buddhist iconography therefore is accurate in an "essential" sense, which no "photographic" image can ever be, and that is why it is able to evoke in the beholder those genuine intellections, but for which piety would rapidly degenerate into mere sentimentality, as it has done elsewhere.' In view of the current Zen boom in America, echoes of which had reached me even in Kalimpong, Prince Peter's observations on the relation between Buddhism, particularly in its Zen form, and the Japanese character, were of special interest. A psychologist and anthropologist who had recently visited Japan, he believed that in that country the techniques of mysticism had been adopted without the mysticism. The average Japanese, endowed as he apparently was with an unusually liberal dose of fierce aggression which had, at all times, to be kept in check, looked upon the Buddhist teachings mainly as efficient precepts of self-discipline, of self-training in perfection, as the means by which one might obtain 'expertness' which causes a man to be completely absorbed in the tasks he has undertaken, eliminating the 'observing self' and giving him total dedication during action. Such training culminated in a supreme release from conflict, from the ever-present watchfulness of that which we in the West called our conscience. 'And that is where the special aspect of the Japanese character reveals itself. The everyday conflict between one's own terrific aggression and one's social obligations is so great with the Japanese that, in order to free themselves from it, they seek the techniques if not the meaning of Buddhism.' This gave their conception of the Dharma a very special, national distortion, at which one could not help wondering.

Articles by former contributors to *Stepping-Stones* were, of course, in the minority, though it was noticeable that they were of a more substantial character than the rest. Prominent among the latter were D.T. Devendra's 'Where a Hero King was Born', an account of the excavation of a twelfth-century stupa in Ceylon, and Christmas Humphreys's 'The Menace of Belief', in which the founder of the Buddhist Society, London, 'speaking with thirty years of experience in the Western Buddhist field', declared that one of the great attractions of Buddhism was that it lacked the warlike voice of authority. 'No one School of Buddhism has the monopoly of the Dhamma, and woe betide the School or nation which claims it.' Most of the remaining articles were very short, being in effect little more than expressions, on the part of well known Buddhists like Alexandra David-Neël and U Maung Maung Ji, and scholars like Dr Pachow and Dr Anukul Chandra Banerjee, of goodwill towards the Society and its work. The rest of the Vaishakha number was made up of the Journal's regular features, such as book reviews, the Notes and News section, and an editorial, as well as the 'messages' from sundry presidents and prime ministers to which the Society seemed to attach so much importance and with which I could willingly have dispensed.

The editorial, which as usual was from my pen, was headed simply 'Buddha Gaya'. But I was not concerned only to recall the Figure beneath the Bodhi-tree, radiant and victorious in the early morning sun, or even to remind readers of the fact that, after sixty years of agitation, the Buddhists of India still had less than half a share in the management of their own holiest shrine, and the millions of Buddhists in Ceylon, Burma, Siam, Cambodia, China, Japan, Tibet, and Nepal no share at all. I was concerned with the fact that, according to reports appearing in the press, Bodh-gaya was 'shortly to assume further importance in the eyes of the world' by having a *Samanvaya Mandir*, or centre for religious, cultural, and racial synthesis, built there by Acharya Vinoba Bhave, the veteran follower of Mahatma Gandhi, whose movement for the voluntary donation of land had recently attracted a good deal of attention and support. The attainment of Enlightenment by the Buddha, I commented, apparently did not suffice. Bodh-gaya would now be given full importance by having a Samanvaya Mandir built there by Sri Bhave. It was as though one should think to increase the importance of the Himalayas by building a sand-castle on their lower slopes. Not only was the importance of Bodh-gaya to be enhanced; the teachings of the Buddha were, it appeared, to be improved upon. '*Vedanta* and *Ahimsa* (teachings of the Lord Buddha) were inter-linked,' the press had reported the Acharya as saying, 'one could not exist without the other. Particularly *Ahimsa*, non-violence, could never have [a] solid basis without the foundation of Vedanta', for '*Satya* (Truth) was revealed in all its glory only in Vedanta.' That Sri Bhave's ideas were not without powerful backing was evinced by the fact that the digging of the well which would mark the centre of the Samanavaya Mandir had been inaugurated by the president of India, while the prime minister had made a donation toward the cost of sinking the well. The abbot of the Shaivite monastery at Bodh-gaya, whose predecessor had opposed by all means, fair and foul, the transfer of the Maha Bodhi Temple to Buddhist hands, had donated five *bighas* of land to the institution – a circumstance which must surely have aroused the worst suspicions of any Buddhist who had even the slightest knowledge of events in Bodh-gaya during the last sixty years. I concluded by wondering what would be the reaction of the Muslim world, or of the Roman Catholics, in similar circumstances, and asking what answer the Buddhist world was going to make to the challenge now being made to the very existence of Bodh-gaya as a centre for the dissemination of pure Buddhist religion and culture.

When I wrote my editorial I was not aware that the press reports about Acharya Vinoba Bhave and his Samanvaya Mandir were all by-lined not from Bodh-gaya but from Sarvodayapuri. Overnight Bodh-gaya, which had borne that name for centuries, had become Sarvodayapuri – the City of Sarvodaya! Bhikkhu Silabhadra, one of the vice-presidents of the Society and a member of the editorial board, accordingly wrote to the editor of the *Hindustan Standard*, a leading English daily, protesting against the innovation; but his letter was not published, and I therefore inserted it at the back of the Vaishakha number, together with a note to the effect that we were printing it there for the information of our readers, as well as to show how difficult it was for the Buddhist point of view to find expression in a certain section of the press.

Besides the actual proof-reading, seeing the Vaishakha number of the *Maha Bodhi Journal* through the press meant commissioning an artist to produce a special cover, which he did to a design of my own, choosing the illustrations (this involved a visit to the Indian Museum in Chowringhee), and finding fillers for the blank spaces at the end of some articles. Finding fillers was less easy than one might have thought, but in the case of the present (double) issue of the Journal I was fortunate, having just come across a copy of *The Path of Light*, L.D. Barnett's (incomplete) English rendering of Shantideva's *Bodhicharyavatara*, a work I subsequently characterized as 'one of the brightest gems in the thickly studded tiara of Mahayana Buddhist literature.' So delighted was I with this work, and so inspired by the combination of ecstatic devotion and penetrating insight with which the author celebrated the incomparable Bodhisattva Ideal, that I could not forbear sprinkling the pages of the Vaishakha number liberally with quotations from it on such topics as the Thought of Enlightenment (as the translator called the *bodhichitta*) and the different *paramitas*, the 'perfections' or 'transcendental virtues'. All this – reading proofs, commissioning a cover, choosing illustrations, and finding fillers – I had to do quite singlehanded, sitting at my desk in front of the barred window, in my room on the second floor of the headquarters building, with the perspiration trickling down my body and dripping from my forehead. Devapriya-ji was not in Calcutta. He was in Japan, or at least was on his way there, having left Calcutta by steamer a few weeks earlier in order to attend the Pan-Pacific Buddhist Conference that was to be held in Tokyo. With him he had taken a portion of Buddha-relics and two Bodhi-tree saplings for presentation to the Buddhists of Japan. If he ever happened to think of me sweltering over the proofs of the Vaishakha number in his stead he must have smiled to himself, and may even have recollected his comment to me the previous year, when the Society's predominantly Hindu governing body, having refused to accept his proposal that I should be formally appointed editor of the *Maha Bodhi Journal*, reluctantly agreed to my becoming a member of the seven- or eight-man editorial board. I remembered his words very well. Himself excepted, he had said, the other board members would take little or no interest in the actual production of the magazine, though they might criticize it afterwards, and I would be left to do all the work. So far no criticism had been forthcoming from that quarter, but in other respects the little general secretary's prediction had proved accurate, and now that he was in Japan and I in Calcutta, seeing the Vaishakha number through the press, it was proving more accurate than ever.

Devapriya-ji's was not the only familiar face missing from the head-quarters building. Soratha, the Little Monk, was also away, so that there was no question of my being able to relieve the tedium of proof-reading by indulging in the lively verbal exchanges that had become customary between us. He and our common friend Venerable Sangharatana, the voluble and eccentric bhikkhu-in-charge of the Society's important Sarnath branch, had gone to Ceylon. With them had gone Anagarika P. Sugatananda (Francis Story), the English-born director of the rather grandly named Burma World Buddhist Mission, whom I had happened to meet on one of my earlier visits to Calcutta. I naturally had welcomed the opportunity of exchanging ideas with a fellow Western Buddhist, but the meeting turned out to be a great disappointment to me, as perhaps it was to him too. Sugatananda, who was a few years older than me and had like me served in the army, was a rationalistic neo-Theravadin, and his constant scoffing and sneering at the supposedly degenerate Maha-yana was so little to my taste that I felt no inclination to pursue the contact any further. He indeed struck me as being a good example of a middle-class Englishman of the superior, supercilious type which had helped make the very name of 'Englishman' obnoxious to people in so many parts of the world, and I wondered how my two warm-hearted Sinhalese friends were faring in his company now that the three of them were travelling together in Ceylon.

But if Devapriya-ji and Soratha were missing from the headquarters building, Jinaratana, the High Priest, most certainly was not. In the absence of Devapriya-ji, who as general secretary ranked as his administrative, though not his religious, superior, his polished pate and yellow silken robe were more in evidence than ever, and even when he himself was not to be seen his harsh, discordant tones could be heard coming from some other part of the building as he gave orders, berated the servants, or greeted visitors of the more well-to-do sort. Since I could not in honesty regard him as being other than a bad monk, a bad Buddhist, and even, in certain respects, a bad man, and since he was aware of this, and aware of at least some of the reasons for my attitude, relations between us, though less awkward than they had been, were neither close nor cordial. For my part, I felt unable either to respect him as someone senior to me and more developed spiritually, on the one hand, or, on the other, to tell him what I really thought of his arrogance, his worldly way of life, and his wholesale hypocrisy. He, for his part, probably felt equally unable either to treat me as a junior monk or to be as open as he was (in their own language) with the other Sinhalese monks, for most of whom a bhikkhu was a bhikkhu and the question of his being a good or a bad one hardly arose, though of course appearances had to be kept up in front of the laity. With Devapriya-ji and Soratha away, however, and me seeing the Vaishakha number through the press, we were thrown more into each other's company than usual; relations between us improved, and we somehow arrived at a *modus vivendi*, possibly as a result of our several times discussing the finances of the Journal, of which Jinaratana was managing editor, with a seat on the editorial board and responsibility for subscriptions, advertisements, and dispatch and distribution. That relations between us had improved, and a *modus vivendi* arrived at, was both a source of satisfaction to me and a source of uneasiness. It was a source of satisfaction to me because it pained me to be on anything less than friendly terms with a brother monk, or fellow Buddhist, even a bad one, but a source of uneasiness inasmuch as I feared that in being on better terms with him I might in fact be condoning, or appearing to condone, certain (unsavoury) aspects of his behaviour, thus compromising, if not actually betraying, the very ideals I was pledged to uphold.

Though Jinaratana and I saw more of each other than usual, the self-styled High Priest was far from being my only source of company. I spent an evening or two with Sachin's relatives in Hindustan Building, attended a tea party in Park Street in the flat of Marguerite Allen, a friend of Irene Ray's, who was also present, where we discussed Tantric Buddhism and Sri Aurobindo's poetry (of which I did not have a very high opinion), and went for walks in the vicinity of College Square with Jayadev, another young ex-Untouchable protégé of Anand-ji's, who had once worked for him in Wardha and was now at a loose end. There were also meetings with old friends like Venerable Amritananda, the young-looking secretary of the *Dharmodaya Sabha* in Nepal, Dr Kajiyama, who was still studying with Kashyap-ji at Nalanda, and Phani Sanyal, who took me on another visit to his father, with whom I had a long discussion on the place of grace in Buddhism, as well as exchanges with a Bengali student on Communism and Socialism and with a Tamil student from Ceylon on Buddhism and Tamil literature. The greater part of my time, however, I spent in my room, with little company other than that of the black-fingered printer's devil who, three or four times a day, brought me a fresh batch of proofs and took away those I had corrected. Though the Sri Gauranga Press worked quickly, they did not work quickly enough for my liking. Not only did I want to get away from the heat of Calcutta; I was also anxious to be back in Kalimpong in good time to prepare for our Vaishakha Purnima celebrations. I therefore fixed the date of my departure and gave them an ultimatum: either send me the remaining proofs by 5 May, while I was still in Calcutta, or be forced to post them to me in Kalimpong after that date – which of course meant that the printing would take more time and cost them more money.

The final page-proofs therefore came flooding in, with the result that my deadline was met, though not without my having had to proof-read right up to within half an hour of my departure from the headquarters building. Jinaratana came to the station and saw me off, as did Jayadev. With me in the reserved second-class compartment were Phani and his small nephew, my universalist friend having decided that he and his young relative would benefit from spending a few weeks in the comparative cool of the hills. Jayadev wanted to come too, but I already had one protégé of Anand-ji's staying with me at The Hermitage and did not really want another, the more especially as Dinesh had been misbehaving of late and I was expecting that after my arrival in Kalimpong I would probably have to ask him to leave.

Chapter Nine

SURVEYING BUDDHISM

THE ADAGE THAT 'ONE THING LEADS TO ANOTHER' may be seen as a homelier version of the basic Buddhist principle of *pratitya-samutpada* or conditioned co-production, the principle that phenomena come into existence not by chance, or as a result of the decree of fate, but in dependence on a certain complex of causes and conditions. It was an adage that was certainly exemplified in the case of the circumstances that led to my being in Bangalore in the summer of 1954 and there delivering, under the auspices of the Indian Institute of Culture, the lectures which subsequently appeared in book form as *A Survey of Buddhism*.

The catena of these circumstances stretched back to the early months of 1947, when I was staying at the Ramakrishna Mission Institute of Culture in Calcutta and happened to come across a dusty pile of back numbers of the *Aryan Path*, a monthly magazine published from Bombay. Containing as it did articles on both Eastern and Western religion and culture I found the magazine of great interest and spent many a happy hour working my way through the pile. During my wandering days I read it whenever I chanced to light upon a copy, whether at an ashram or in someone's home, and after my arrival in Kalimpong not only arranged to receive it in exchange for *Stepping-Stones* but started contributing articles, poems, and book reviews. These contributions led to an exchange of letters with the editor, Sophia Wadia, who turned out to be connected with the Ananda Vihara, Bombay, and to have helped with the production of Dr N.K. Bhagwat's edition and English translation of the *Dhammapada*, a copy of which I had bought in Delhi within weeks of my arrival in India and had carried around with me ever since. Sophia Wadia was in fact a Theosophist and sympathetic to Buddhism, as was her husband B.P. Wadia, who wrote in the *Aryan Path* under the Buddhistic pseudonym of 'Shravaka'. They were not, however, Adyar Theosophists.

They belonged to a branch of the Theosophical movement that repudiated as aberrations the Hinduizing and Christianizing tendencies of Annie Besant and C.W. Leadbeater and sought to return to the 'original' Theosophy of Mme Blavatsky, which they believed to be closer to Buddhism. Such being the case, it was not surprising that they should be anxious to see a knowledge of Buddhism flourishing in India, and not surprising that they should want to have a series of lectures on Buddhism at the Institute they had established in Bangalore. This was where I came in. At the beginning of the year Sophia Wadia had sounded me out as to the possibility of my paying a visit to the Garden City, I had responded positively, further letters had been exchanged, and eventually B.P. Wadia had formally invited me to give four lectures at the Institute during the first half of July. The last two days of June therefore saw me travelling down the east coast of the subcontinent in the Calcutta-Madras Mail.

Soratha came with me to Howrah Station and saw me off, as did the scholarly Saddhatissa, who was studying for his BA at the Benares Hindu University and who four years earlier had been present at my bhikkhu ordination in Sarnath. I had spent little more than a week in Calcutta, and had barely had time to see the July issue of the *Maha Bodhi* through the press or listen to Soratha's accounts of how he and Sangharatana had fared in Ceylon with Anagarika Sugatananda. They had not fared very well, the Little Monk admitted ruefully, pursing his lips and shaking his head at the recollection of what he and his brother monk had had to endure. The Anagarika undoubtedly possessed a good knowledge of the Dhamma, and was an excellent speaker, and the speeches he had delivered at twenty or more different parts of the island – speeches which he and Sangaratana had translated – had been received with great enthusiasm, but he possessed a foul temper, was extremely exigent, and quarrelled with almost everyone with whom he had any dealings. A hundred times a day he and Sangharatana had exclaimed to each other, 'If only we were travelling with Sangharakshita and translating for *him* instead of for Sugatananda!' As it happened, this could well have been the case. Only a few months earlier the Maha Bodhi Society of Ceylon had proposed that I should write a full-length biography of Anagarika Dharmapala and invited me to spend a few months at their Colombo headquarters for that purpose. Had I accepted the proposal (and so far I had not actually rejected it) I could have been leaving for Ceylon that afternoon instead of for Bangalore, and Soratha, instead of coming to the station to see me off, could have been accompanying me.

With me in the second-class sleeping compartment, in which I had a reserved berth, were three other passengers, all of them South Indians. Two were middle-aged businessmen, the third a Catholic priest. It was my experience that even travellers *not* occupying the more democratic third-class and inter-class carriages usually were not slow to enter into conversation, especially if their journey was going to be a long one, but on this occasion my friendly overtures met with little success. Neither of the two businessmen knew much Hindi (I knew only a few words of Tamil), while the priest was obviously wary of speaking to an Englishman who very evidently was not a Christian and might, for all he knew, actually be the Devil in disguise. I therefore took out Gide's *The Immoralist*, which I had bought a few days previously, and soon was absorbed in 'Michel's adventure', as the author called his hero's story of his self-discovery, of the growth in him of a confused consciousness of untouched treasures somewhere lying covered up, hidden, 'smothered by culture and decency and morality', of the terrible cost of freedom, and of the burden that freedom itself could be. So absorbed was I in the story that I did not sleep that night until – long after the occupants of the other berths had switched off their lights – I had turned the last page of the book.

Whether because of my having spent the previous evening absorbed in *The Immoralist*, or on account of a difference in the air (we were not far from the coast), or simply because I had slept particularly well, when I awoke in the morning my mood was one of exhilaration. It was a mood that was enhanced by my enjoyment of the lyricism of certain passages in Gide's *Fruits of the Earth*, which I had bought at the same time as *The Immoralist* and into which, after an early breakfast, I started dipping. But though I enjoyed the French writer's lyricism, as a whole his prose style was too stilted and self-conscious – I had almost said too affected – for my taste, nor did I like his constant references to the Deity or appreciate the curious mixture, in *Later Fruits of the Earth*, of the Gospels and Communism. For all his avowed hedonism, and his protestations that he called nature God, he struck me as being in some ways a very Christian – even a very Protestant – sort of writer, and after a while I laid the book aside and spent the rest of the morning looking out of the window. At every station at which the train stopped – and there were many stops – it was wonderful to see what a variety of things was being sold by the hawkers who marched up and down the platform crying their wares. There were cakes, biscuits, fruits, books and magazines in half a dozen languages (and half a dozen scripts), brightly painted toys, and fried delicacies hot and crisp from the pan, as well as lunches which came packeted in a plantain leaf and with each individual item, even the liquid ones, neatly wrapped in its own separate segment of rubbery green. One such lunch I bought. It cost me only a rupee and two annas, and was the best meal I had tasted for a long time. What a difference there was, I reflected, between the stations on the Calcutta–Madras line and those on the Calcutta–Siliguri one, on which there were relatively few stations and where it was sometimes impossible to get so much as a cup of tea!

Nor was it only the stations, and the catering arrangements, that were different. The landscape, too, had changed, especially now that we had entered Madras State. Gone was the dense green vegetation, so rank and so profuse, of Bengal and Orissa – vegetation out of which there protruded, every few miles, the cluster of thatched huts that denoted a village. In its stead was a predominance of scrub and bare soil with, here and there, a line of areca palms silhouetted against the sky. We were in another climatic region, another culture, even another world, one that differed from the world of northern India in so many ways, and which I had not seen for more than five years. Already Calcutta, and even the foothills of the Himalayas where I now lived and worked, seemed very far away, and as the warm afternoon wore on I found myself reviewing my activities over the last two months, from my return to Kalimpong after editing the Vaishakha number of the *Maha Bodhi* to my arrival in Calcutta the previous week, almost as though they had been those of another person. May and June had been comparatively uneventful. I had continued to teach Sachin, Meera, and Lobsang Phuntsok, and to spend time with visitors; the Kalimpong branch of the Maha Bodhi Society had celebrated Vaishakha Purnima, both with a religious function at The Hermitage and a public meeting at the Town Hall; Dinesh had left in a huff, after being told he must either mend his ways or find somewhere else to stay; and Sachin and I had spent a week in Darjeeling and Kurseong, in each of which places I lectured and conferred with local Buddhists, besides spending a night at Longview, where I renewed acquaintance with Dutt-Majumdar, the Deputy Commissioner, who with the District Superintendent of Police was then investigating a disturbance in a neighbouring tea estate.

But uneventful though May and June had been, there was one circumstance that was perhaps of greater significance, in the light of subsequent developments, than I realized at the time. This was the fact that prominent among the four or five local Buddhists whom I invited to address the Vaishakha meeting at the Town Hall was the red-robed figure of Dhardo Rimpoche, the Gelug incarnate lama who lived in the Old Bhutan

Palace at Eleventh Mile. We had met the previous year, when I went to see him in connection with a dispute that had arisen in Bodh-gaya between him, as abbot of the Tibetan monastery there, and the monk in charge of the adjacent Maha Bodhi Rest House, and I had come away from the interview not only convinced that he was the innocent party but deeply impressed by his patent goodwill, candour, and integrity. It was no surprise to me, therefore, that when I took Phani to see him, a few days before the Town Hall meeting, my spiritually-minded Bengali friend should have been equally impressed and have commented in the warmest terms on the Rimpoche's serene, friendly, and unassuming behaviour. As this was Phani's first experience of Tibetan Buddhism – and Tibetan Buddhists – I was delighted that his impression was such a positive one. His impression of Christianity, at least in its missionary form, was rather less positive. As we passed through Dr Graham's Homes one morning, on our way to a picnic at Dailo, I was mocked and jeered at over the wall of their cottage by a group of teenage Christian boys who evidently regarded a Buddhist monk as an interloper and an enemy. Usually I ignored such manifestations of intolerance, but on the present occasion I swept in through the gate, closely followed by Phani, the boys scattering in terror as I did so with cries of 'He's coming in!' Inside the cottage I found the house mother, as she was called, and severely upbraided her for not teaching her charges to show more respect for the representatives of other religions. The wretched woman stammered a half-apology, though she was not personally to blame for what was in fact still the ethos of the whole institution, despite Independence, and later on I sent Mr Duncan, the Superintendent of the Homes, a formal letter of complaint.

Recalling the incident that warm afternoon, as I reviewed my activities over the last two months, I wondered, not for the first time, what it was that made people intolerant of beliefs and practices other than their own and whether some religions were not intolerant by their very nature. Christianity appeared to fall within this category. All its major historical forms had on occasion proscribed and persecuted, even tortured and burned alive at the stake, and it was not surprising that the missionaries – inheritors as they were of this grim tradition, and surrounded as they believed themselves to be by the forces of darkness – should be narrow-minded and intolerant.... Christianity was said to have taken firm root in South India. Were the missionaries of Madras, I wondered, as intolerant as those of Kalimpong...?

Madras! After I had spent a second night in the train, here we were at Madras Central, and here was Venerable Jinananda waiting on the platform to welcome me and whisk me off to the Maha Bodhi centre in Kennett Lane for breakfast. Though quite large, the building in which I partook of that meal was old and inconvenient, and I noticed that there was no shrine-room. Like several other Maha Bodhi centres, the place was in fact not so much a temple or a monastery as a caravanserai for Sinhalese pilgrims on their way to the holy places of northern India. The bhikkhu-in-charge looked after the pilgrims, made merit for them by accepting their offerings ('making merit' was the principal object of a pilgrimage for old-fashioned Buddhists), and in his spare time he did what he could to propagate the Dharma among the more educated portion of the predominantly Hindu population. On the whole it was not a very inspiring life for a well-meaning monk, as Jinananda seemed to be, and in the afternoon, after I had written a few letters, he was glad to accompany me to the Ramakrishna Math at Mylapore, the brahmin quarter of the city. Here I met Swami Kailashananda, the Math's rather saturnine president. I had met him in the same place seven years earlier, within days of my going forth 'from home into the homeless life', and when I was still rather conscious of my shaven head and saffron robes. On that occasion he had seemed dubious of the wisdom of the step I had just taken, but now, no doubt realizing that I had persevered in my chosen way of life, he welcomed me as cordially as his rather aloof temperament permitted and we had a very friendly conversation. Back in Kennett Lane, having found the city's leading English bookshop closed, I talked to a young monk who was studying at one of the local colleges, then left to catch the overnight train to Bangalore, Jinananda accompanying me to the station and seeing me off.

Bangalore was one of the pleasantest cities in India. From the fact that its central area abounded in beautifully laid-out parks and gardens, some of which dated from the Moghul period, it was known as the Garden City. In 1949 I had spent several weeks there, on my way back to northern India and, I hoped, formal monastic ordination, and I thought I knew the city, but as the car that had met me at the station made its way through the busy streets to the Wadias' residence on a tree-lined avenue in a quiet suburb I failed to recognize a single landmark. Either Bangalore had changed a lot, as had so many Indian cities in the years following Independence, or I had seen less of it than I supposed. The residence in question was a substantial, Western-style building. As if to emphasize the owners' link with Buddhism it was called Maitri Bhavan, which could be rendered as 'the Abode of Loving-Kindness', *maitri* or loving-kindness being the first of the four *brahma-viharas* or 'sublime (mental) states' to be developed, in meditation, by the Buddhist. B.P. Wadia was there to welcome me. We had not met before, but on one of my visits to Bombay I had been taken to Flora Fountain to hear him speak on Theosophy, and had a vivid memory of a packed hall and a powerful lecture that obviously impressed the audience deeply. In appearance he had not changed much since then. As his 'surname' indicated, he was by birth a Parsee (in fact, a member of the wealthy Bombay shipping family), but he was taller and bulkier than the average member of his community and wore, moreover, a beard which, together with his benign look and confident bearing, served to give him an appearance of almost regal dignity. After we had talked for a while, he escorted me to the Institute and there installed me in the guest room. For the rest of the morning I was left to my own devices, so that I was able to look at the extensive and well-equipped library, next to which the guest room was conveniently situated, and write a few letters. It was then time for lunch. This I had at Maitri Bhavan with B.P. Wadia, after which the car returned me to the Institute, where I rested and wrote more letters and where I received a visit from Dr and Mrs Doraiswamy, who it seemed were responsible for the day-to-day running of things. The former, as I already knew, and as he was not slow to remind me, was a cousin of my friend R.A. Padmanathan, the hospitable manager of Longview.

That evening I met Sophia Wadia, with whom I had been so long in correspondence. Younger than her husband, who must have been well over sixty, and the shorter by a head, she had a broad forehead, an earnest expression, and a resonant contralto voice that at times seemed too big for her frame, and she was dressed entirely in white, almost like a priestess. Annie Besant, as I remembered reading somewhere, had also dressed entirely in white, even her shoes being of that colour, so that it was possible for a brahmin admirer to style her, on account of her erudition and eloquence, as Sarva-shukla-Saraswati or 'the All-White Saraswati', Saraswati being the popular Hindu goddess of education and learning. There was no doubt that Sophia Wadia could also be so styled, at least as far as her appearance went. Whether she was comparable to the legendary Annie Besant in point of erudition and eloquence was another matter. Soon I had an opportunity of judging for myself, or at least of forming an initial impression. Maitri Bhavan, where we met, besides being the residence of the Wadias when they were in Bangalore, was the local centre, apparently, of the United Lodge of Theosophists, the branch of the Theosophical movement to which the couple belonged, and it so happened that there was to be a study class that evening. I was invited to sit in on this class, which was led by Sophia Wadia and was on a section of Robert Crosbie's *The Friendly Philosopher*. The name of Robert Crosbie was new to me. As I discovered later, he was an American Theosophist, under whose guidance and inspiration the United Lodge of Theosophists had been formed in 1909 in Los Angeles, California. He had worked closely with W.Q. Judge, joint founder with Mme Blavatsky and Col. Olcott of the Theosophical Society in 1875, and in the ULT his and Judge's writings were prized next only to the more voluminous but less immediately accessible output of Mme Blavatsky. Though I found *The Friendly Philosopher*, or rather the section of it chosen for study that evening, rather pedestrian, from her comments on the text, as well as from her replies to questions, it was obvious that Sophia Wadia had a thorough knowledge of the principles of Theosophy and could explain them clearly. I noticed, however, that the dozen or so members of the class stood very much in awe of her, as they did of her husband, and that on account, presumably, of her French extraction she was addressed, deferentially, as 'Madame'.

As my lectures were not due to begin for three or four days I was able to take advantage of the library, and to read works to which I did not have access in Kalimpong or even in Calcutta. The Institute's library was, in fact, the best I had encountered since my time at Benares Hindu University with Kashyap-ji, when my kind teacher had allowed me to use his ticket to the university library, and contained many rare and valuable items collected by B.P. Wadia in the course of his travels in the West. Besides immersing myself in such authorities on Buddhism as Suzuki and E.J. Thomas, I dipped quite extensively into Oscar Wilde, W.B. Yeats, and 'Æ' (George William Russell). A discovery of particular interest was *Literature and Occult Tradition* by Denis Saurat, an author of whom I had not heard before. There were also letters to write and members of the Institute to see, among the latter being S.K. Ramachandra Rao, with whom I had corresponded a couple of years previously and who was deeply interested in Buddhism. The two people of whom I saw most were, naturally, B.P. and Sophia Wadia, with whom I had lunch every day at Maitri Bhavan and, more often than not, a lengthy discussion. Most of our discussions centred on Buddhism, especially in its relation to the teachings of Mme Blavatsky, and although I sometimes disagreed with my host and hostess I could not but admire the purity of their devotion to Theosophy and the sincerity with which they strove to apply its principles in their own lives. Lunch may have been served in some style, with a butler and other servants in attendance, but it was simple to the point of being spartan and the meal was always preceded by a reading from a religious text and a few minutes of silent recollection. On one occasion we discussed the missionary threat, and Roman Catholic dogmatism, about which both husband and wife felt very much as I did, and Sophia Wadia related how, when she was on a lecture tour in Argentina (she seemed to have South American connections), she had been given police protection as the authorities had received information that the Jesuits might try to poison her. In the evening there was usually a function of some kind to attend, either at Maitri Bhavan or at the Institute. Thus I heard my white-robed hostess give an address on 'After Death – What?' at the former venue, while at the latter, a speaker having failed to turn up, two members of the Bangalore intelligentsia, M.K. Venkata Rao and K. Guru Dutt, gave brilliant extemporaneous talks on the philosophy of George Santayana. As the talented duo were not unrepresentative of the kind of audience I would shortly be addressing, I was thankful that I had prepared my lectures with even more than my usual care.

In a way I had been preparing the lectures for some months, at least in my own mind. It might even be said I had been preparing them for some years, in fact ever since I awoke to the fact that I was a Buddhist, and that between them they constituted a summation of all I had learned about Buddhism during the intervening period, whether from books, from my teachers, from discussions with friends (and foes, i.e. foes of the Dharma), and from my own independent reflection and meditative experience. B.P. Wadia's invitation indeed came at exactly the right moment for me, as well as at the right moment for the movement of Buddhist revival in modern India, then on the eve of experiencing a dramatic quantum leap, and presented me with both an opportunity and a challenge. With an opportunity, inasmuch as I would be communicating the Dharma to a predominantly Hindu audience which, cultured and intelligent though it might be, possessed for the most part only a superficial or a distorted understanding of the Buddha's teaching; with a challenge, inasmuch as I would be able to take full advantage of that opportunity only if I stood back and asked myself how I really saw Buddhism and what it really meant to me.

Work on the preparation of the lectures in the more specific sense had started only a month earlier, when B.P. Wadia wrote asking me to draw up a prospectus for distribution as part of the Institute's publicity. This entailed finding a title for each lecture, and therewith determining what material it should contain, as well as finding a title for the whole series, which eventually I decided to call 'A Survey of Buddhism: Its Doctrines and Methods Through the Ages' – with acknowledgements, as to the subtitle, to the excellent volume of Buddhist texts that had just appeared under the editorship of Dr Conze. For a lecture (as distinct from a sermon of the traditional type, which I delivered extemporaneously) I was in the habit of making a few notes, covering in most cases only a page or two. On this occasion, however, I made several pages of notes for each lecture, for my view, like that of Observation in the opening lines of Dr Johnson's famous poem, was going to be an extensive one, and I would be survey- ing not, indeed, 'mankind, from China to Peru', but Buddhism, from the Theravada to Zen and Shin. Moreover, I would be surveying it not only in its breadth but in its depth, which meant seeing it in its deeper interconnections, both within itself and in relation to the Dharma-life of the individual Buddhist. This called for a tremendous intellectual and spiritual effort on my part, an effort that the putting together of the notes, concentrative of my energies as this was, helped me to make. The notes for most of the lectures had already been written. In fact I had only the notes for the fourth lecture to write, those for the first three having been assembled during my week or so in Calcutta, which was why I could spend my first few days in Bangalore taking advantage of the library, seeing people, and attending functions at Maitri Bhavan and the Institute.

I started giving the series on Tuesday 6 July, four days after my arrival, when I spoke on 'The Buddha and Buddhism'. I spoke to a full hall, and under the chairmanship of Sophia Wadia, who after saying a few words of gracious introduction read my poem 'Taking Refuge in the Buddha'. The audience being quite new to me, I fumbled for the first few minutes getting the 'feel' of it, so to speak, but once I had done this – and for me, getting the feel of an audience was a process so tangible as to be almost physical – I very quickly got into my stride and with the help of my notes spoke fluently for more than an hour and a half. In speaking about the Buddha I was concerned not so much to recount the story of his life, complete with legendary embellishments, as to place that life within its traditional cosmological context and, by so doing, to reveal in what the Buddha's greatness and role truly consisted. Similarly, in speaking of Buddhism, in the sense of the Original Doctrine, I did not want to dwell on specific ethical and spiritual teachings, important as those teachings undoubtedly were, so much as to lay bare the philosophical principle underlying them – the principle, that is to say, of universal conditionality, in its two modes, the 'cyclical' and the 'spiral'. In particular, I wanted to show that the Buddhist nirvana was not synonymous with a state of annihilation, as the Hindu critics of Buddhism believed, any more than the path leading to that nirvana consisted solely in the eradication of negative mental states. My second lecture, which followed two days later, was devoted to 'Hinayana and Mahayana'. In it I insisted on the 'transcendental unity' of all forms of Buddhism, traced the rise of the Mahayana, and dealt with some of the more important of its distinctive tenets. I was also at pains to emphasize the purely instrumental nature of the Dharma.

In between the giving of these two lectures I continued to see people and to attend functions at Maitri Bhavan and the Institute, besides going for a drive with the Doraiswamys' son, who showed me the famous Lal Bagh, with its centuries-old trees, and took me into the city centre. Mrs Doraiswamy, his mother, for her part showed me round the Cosmopolitan Home, the student hostel the Wadias had built next door to the Institute and where there was a devotional meeting once a week led by B.P. Wadia. She was an Englishwoman by birth, and I was glad to find that she shared my own views regarding Christian missionaries. The Institute and the Bangalore ULT had, in fact, several English and Dutch members, some of whom were married to Indians. As in Singapore, where I had first encountered Theosophists, in 1946, it was heartening to see people of different races and different national and religious backgrounds (the Institute even had a few Christian and Muslim members) associating on terms of friendship. Though I might not agree with some of the teachings of Theosophy, I was certainly full of admiration for the way in which individual Theosophists, both Adyar and non-Adyar, sought to practise the principle of Universal Brotherhood, the first of the three declared Objects of the parent Theosophical Society.

The next two lectures, which I gave on 12 and 14 July, were firmly based on the two previous ones. Having dealt with some of the more important of the Mahayana's distinctive tenets in my second lecture, I proceeded, in my third, on 'The Schools of the Mahayana', to deal in turn with the scriptures, teachers, and treatises of the Madhyamikavada, of Devotional Buddhism, of the Yogachara, and of Tantric Buddhism. Each school, I declared, had developed a specific aspect of Buddhism, and far from their being mutually exclusive the Mahayana itself could be understood only if they were viewed in their totality as complementary aspects of the Dharma. The fourth and last lecture in the series was dedicated to 'The Bodhisattva Ideal'. After describing the place of the Bodhisattva Ideal in Buddhist thought, and dealing with popular interpretations, I outlined the Bodhisattva doctrine as presented in authoritative texts. I then gave an account – an account afterwards described as 'glowing' – of the Six Paramitas or 'Perfections' and the Ten Stages of the Bodhisattva's career, and concluded by trying to communicate to my audience something of my own enthusiasm for the spiritual life as exemplified by the glorious Bodhisattva Ideal. Despite having notes to make, in between my third and fourth lectures I found time for two encounters of an ecumenical nature. The first of these was with the Jain Community. At their invitation, I visited their temple, where they gave me a formal reception, complete with tea party and speeches of welcome, and where I spoke of my contacts with Jainism and on the Jain doctrine of *anekantavada*. My second such encounter, which was of a more intimate character, was with a bright-eyed, gnome-like Roman Catholic priest named Father Monchanin, one of the founders of the first 'Christian ashram', with whom I had a two-hour-long conversation on Buddhism, especially the Madhyamikavada, the Vedanta, and comparative mysticism.

After the conclusion of the fourth lecture, and therewith the completion of my survey, the Wadias and I left for Maitri Bhavan, where fourteen or fifteen leading members and friends of the Institute later joined us for an informal celebration. Both B.P. and Sophia Wadia were highly pleased with the lectures, the former having asked me, after I had given my first lecture, to write them out for publication in book form. Indeed, from what I heard that evening I gathered the series had attracted a good deal of attention, and even been something of an event in the cultural and religious life of Bangalore. This did not surprise me. Throughout the series the hall, comfortably full at first, had become more tightly packed with each lecture, while the audience, greatly augmented though it was, had grown ever more attentive, and more concentrated. Thus by the time I gave the last lecture I had a very large – and appreciative – audience indeed, such as the Institute apparently had not seen before. It was an audience, moreover, with which I had succeeded in establishing a definite rapport. As I spoke, and they listened, time almost stood still, and it was as though we were transported to another world. To what extent they felt this I could not tell, but I certainly felt it very strongly, and whether on account of their receptivity, or on account of my own enthusiasm for the Dharma, or both, at the end of one lecture, in particular, I found myself in a very exalted state of consciousness.

That time should almost stand still was not without its disadvantages, even though the audience and I might be transported to another world. The Wadias, contrary to the usual Indian practice, were great sticklers for punctuality and keeping to schedule, and before the commencement of the series I was warned that I should on no account exceed my allotted sixty, or at the very most seventy-five, minutes, as this could seriously disrupt whatever other events might have been planned of the rest of the evening. Unfortunately, my first lecture exceeded even the more generous allotment by a full fifteen minutes, and subsequent lectures exceeded it by as much as half an hour or more. The fact was that I had so much material, and found that material so inspiring, that it was hardly possible for me to keep to the prescribed limit without doing a serious injustice to my subject and perhaps even to myself. Moreover, though Sophia Wadia kept glancing meaningfully at the clock when my time was up, as did her successors in the chair, it was clear the audience did not want me to stop, and both then and subsequently I ignored the signals and carried on. Each time this little drama between the speaker and the chair was enacted, smiles of amusement appeared on people's faces. Evidently they were by no means adverse to seeing protocol flung to the winds and the proceedings conducted in a manner that was more in accordance with Indian cultural traditions. As for my host and hostess, in the goodness of their hearts they refrained from taking me to task for my intransigence, though it was obvious that they ran the Institute and the ULT as very tight ships and were not accustomed to having their wishes disregarded.

Having made the notes for three of my lectures in Calcutta, I did not have much to do by way of preparation in Bangalore. None the less, during the week in which I was engaged in surveying Buddhism I had thought it best to avoid distractions as much as I could and stay close to base, my base being the double one of the Institute and Maitri Bhavan. Now, however, the lectures were over, and I was able to see more people and go out and about more. As the second city of a predominantly Kannada-speaking area that had once been under Muslim rule, Bangalore was a tolerant, cosmopolitan place, with a polyglot citizenry that included people from most parts of India and of many different faiths. Among those who came to see me, or whose hospitality I accepted, there were Bengalis and Kashmiris, Tamilians and Mysoreans, devotees of Swami Ramdas and disciples of Ramana Maharshi, followers of the Lingayat sect, Vishishtadvaitavada pandits, Muslims, Christians, and Jains – but not a single Buddhist, though after my first lecture a local man had come up to me and introduced himself and his wife as Buddhists. Most of those who came did so out of curiosity or to 'talk religion' in the platitudinous, pseudo-intellectual sort of way that was so common in India (I once observed that Hindus, in particular, discussed religion much as the English discussed the weather), or even to beg me, as one elderly Tamil brahmin repeatedly did, to teach them some 'Tantric rites'. A few there were, however, whose interest was of a more serious nature. They included two young men, one of them a student, with whom I had several worthwhile discussions and to whom, at their earnest request, I explained the *anapana-sati* or 'respiration-mindfulness' practice. Not that I usually taught meditation, or even thought of myself as a 'meditation teacher'. Though I now had been meditating for a number of years, my principal concern was still to deepen my own practice, and while I had no objection to explaining *anapana-sati* to the occasional sincere individual, it was to be many years before I started teaching meditation on a regular basis or to more than one person at a time.

The fact that I saw more people and went out and about more, during my last few days in the Garden City, did not mean that I neglected my base. If anything, I had more to do with it than ever. To begin with, the lectures having created intense interest among the local intelligentsia, many of whom declared that it was the first time they had been given a complete and coherent picture of Buddhism, B.P. Wadia made arrangements for a special Question and Answer Meeting. At this meeting, which was held under the chairmanship of his white-robed coadjutrix, I answered more than sixty written questions on the philosophy, history, literature, and spiritual practices of Buddhism. B.P. Wadia also arranged for me to give, under his own chairmanship, a lecture on *The Voice of the Silence*, the devotional treatise compiled and translated by Mme Blavatsky, allegedly from Tibetan Buddhist sources. I was quite fond of this little work, which I knew to be immensely popular with all Theosophists, though in view of some of its terminology I found it difficult to regard it as being *in toto* an authentically Buddhist composition. Besides making these two additional appearances at the Institute, I gave several informal talks for the benefit of the occupants of the Cosmopolitan Home, B.P. Wadia apparently thinking that the students to whom he stood *in loco parentis* could not have too much of a good thing in the way of moral and religious instruction from visiting holy men of whatever persuasion. On other occasions I carried my base, as represented by the Wadias, with me when I went out – or my base carried me. Thus my host and hostess and I were guests at a lunch given by the Ghataks and spent a musical evening with the Lalkakas. Among the other guests at the lunch were Svetoslav Roerich, the younger brother of George Roerich, and his wife Devika Rani, the famous film actress, both of whom I had met a few weeks earlier in Kalimpong at a tea-party given by Mrs Tagore in honour of Dr and

Mrs Liebenthal's fortieth wedding anniversary. I was seated opposite Devika Rani and we talked about her mother, a niece (or perhaps it was a grand-niece) of Tagore, whom I had known in Kasauli and who in fact was one of the last people to whom I spoke before going forth 'from home into the homeless life' in August 1947.

At the Lalkakas' the Wadias and I were the only guests. Major Lalkaka had served in the British – not the Indian – army, and though no longer wearing the Queen's uniform was very pro-British. He was also very pro-Western. So extremely pro-Western was he that he and his wife had not been content to adopt the language and social customs of their (former) rulers. They had gone so far as to adopt their religion too. Both were converts to (Roman Catholic) Christianity, and I noticed that running round the pointed arch of every doorframe in their comfortable, European-style bungalow there was a text from the Vulgate, neatly executed in Gothic script and in the original Latin. Despite such apparent signs of orthodoxy, the kind and hospitable Lalkakas were not in the least bigoted, as converts to Roman Catholicism so often were, and I concluded that their Christianity was a matter of culture rather than of religion in the strict sense. Major Lalkaka was in fact a great lover of Western classical music, and in the course of the evening he played some of his favourite Bach and Mozart records for us on the gramophone. In my teens I had been passionately fond of classical music, and had listened to it (on the radio) as much as I could. During my years in India I had been able to hear it only in odd snatches, and by accident, and in any case there was a rule prohibiting members of the Theravadin monastic order from listening to music. As the ultra-orthodox Narada Thera had once remarked to Lama Govinda, in my hearing, a Buddhist monk was not allowed to appreciate beauty – and classical music was certainly beautiful. Yet though I had been so fond of classical music in the past, and had listened to it so much, I did not miss it now, and never felt I was being deprived of something essential to my emotional wellbeing. I could therefore enjoy Major Lalkaka's Bach and Mozart without wanting to prolong or repeat the experience, and even when, on my departure, he presented me with two boxes of records, my only thought – apart from gratitude to him for his generosity – was that since I did not possess a gramophone I would have to give them to somebody who did. Perhaps Joe would like them.

Less harmonious than the musical evening at the Lalkakas', in principle at least, was the situation I encountered when Sophia Wadia and I, on the afternoon of my last day in Bangalore, went to see the vihara that was being built at Gandhinagar, in the older, western quarter of the city. It was being built by the Maha Bodhi Society of Ceylon, and was nearing completion, and we were shown round the place by A.R.S. Chari, the retired judge of the Bangalore High Court who had presided at my lecture on 'Hinayana and Mahayana'. Mr Chari, I gathered, was in overall charge of the building project. He was also chairman of the vihara committee. Or rather, he was chairman of one of the two committees then contending in the courts for control of the vihara. The dispute had been going on for some time, as a paper drawn up by the retired judge informed me, and had become quite complicated. Whether by accident or by design, the leading member of the other committee, one Ramaswami, was on the premises at the very time Sophia Wadia and I were being shown round, and later that day he came to see me at the Institute.

It did not take me long to get to the root of the problem. The root of the problem, as so often was the case in South India, was the deep-seated antagonism between brahmins and non-brahmins. Chari was a brahmin, Ramaswami a non-brahmin. Chari's committee consisted of brahmins and other Caste Hindus, Ramaswami's of members of the Scheduled Castes. Several of these latter were, it seemed, followers of Dr Ambedkar, who for years had been telling the Scheduled Castes peoples that there would be no improvement in their lot so long as they remained within the Hindu fold and that they would have to change their religion. Only recently there had been rumours to the effect that the Scheduled Castes leader was about to embrace Buddhism, together with his followers, and several of the questions handed in at my Question and Answer meeting had related to this burning topic. From the nature of the questions it was fairly obvious that the Caste Hindus were opposed to any change of religion on the part of the Scheduled Castes peoples, and I was left with the impression that should Ambedkar and his followers ever take the drastic step of giving up Hinduism for Buddhism they could expect little sympathy or understanding from that quarter. Much as Caste Hindus might appreciate Buddhism, to them it was only a branch of Hinduism, and they saw no need for anyone born a Hindu to 'convert' to it as though it was a separate religion like Christianity or Islam. In their eyes Ambedkar was simply a politician, and his periodic threats of mass defections from Hinduism were no more than a political stunt.

Scheduled Castes South Indians like Ramaswami saw things differently. For them Ambedkar's threats were seriously meant and conversion to Buddhism was a real option. Caste Hindu insistence that Buddhism was not a separate religion but only a branch of Hinduism was intended, so they believed, to make it impossible for the Scheduled Castes peoples to escape from Hinduism and, therefore, from Caste Hindu tyranny and exploitation. Chari's involvement in the affairs of the Bangalore branch of the Maha Bodhi Society had a similar purpose. He and his brahmin and other Caste Hindu friends knew that a revival of Buddhism was inevitable and they wanted to be in a position to contain it. According to no less an authority than Swami Vivekananda, Hinduism had killed Buddhism with a loving embrace, and it would no doubt try to repeat the performance if its hated rival ever came back to life.

Thus the root of the conflict between the two vihara committees was not even just a conflict between brahmins and non-brahmins, or between Caste Hindus and members of the Scheduled Castes. It was a conflict, also, between different attitudes towards Buddhism, even different ideologies. If those conflicts were not resolved, or even if they were, what would be the future of the vihara? What would be the future of Buddhism in Bangalore?

Chapter Ten

BUDDHISM AND THE NAGPUR BAR

DHARMA CHAKRA DAY WAS THE SECOND MOST IMPORTANT FESTIVAL in the Buddhist year. It was the day on which the Buddha, two months after his attainment of Enlightenment, 'set in motion the Wheel of the Law' or, less poetically speaking, started communicating the Truth he had discovered. Like Vaishakha Purnima, Dharma Chakra Day was a lunar festival, falling on the full moon day of the month *Shravana*, corresponding to June–July of the Western calendar. This year it had fallen on Thursday 15 July, the day of my lecture on *The Voice of the Silence*. Arriving at Madras Central three days later, however, on the morning of Sunday 18 July, I found that the Madras centre of the Maha Bodhi Society had yet to celebrate the festival. Whether because a Sunday was more convenient than a weekday, or because I would then be in the City, the celebration had been postponed to that afternoon. There would be a public meeting at five o'clock, Venerable Jinananda informed me, after we had exchanged greetings. It would be held at Kennett Lane, there would be three speakers, and I would be presiding over the function.

At five o'clock I therefore took my place on the stage that had been set up in the courtyard, Jinananda administered the Refuges and Precepts to the hundred or so people – some of them Buddhists – who had assembled for the occasion, and the meeting proper began. The three speakers were all from South India, and all addressed the audience in excellent English, a circumstance that reminded me of the region's proud boast that although the English language might be forgotten in England it would never be forgotten in Mylapore. The second, and principal, speaker was R. Jayachandram, whom I had known when he was a boy in Travancore and who now was Lecturer in Philosophy at the Vivekananda College, one of the city's more prestigious educational institutions. We had renewed our acquaintanceship prior to the meeting, and reminisced about the time, six or seven years earlier, when he was a student and I one of the two long-haired, long-bearded wandering ascetics then staying at the haunted ashram on the outskirts of the little town of Muvattupuzha. Some of my Buddhism had perhaps rubbed off on him. His lecture, which I was required to announce as being on 'The Life of the Buddha is not the story of an *avatara*, but the story of a man's true emancipation', was not only very well delivered, in a highly poetical style, but also imbued with the speaker's strong feeling for the person of the Enlightened One, a feeling especially in evidence when he was describing the Buddha-to-be's disillusionment with mundane existence, his departure from home, and his early struggles for light. So vividly did Jayachandram describe these events, and to such a degree did he empathize with what he believed were the youthful Siddhartha's thoughts and feelings at the time, that he seemed to have been almost an eyewitness – or even to be speaking from personal experience. If he now and again departed from strict historical accuracy, or showed rather too marked a tendency to sentimentalize the figure of the Buddha, no one appeared to mind, or even to notice, and when he sat down it was to warm applause.

One person there was who did not join in the applause. This was the third and last speaker. As the rather cumbrous title of Jayachandram's address had made clear, the young college lecturer did not believe the Buddha to be an *avatara* or 'descent' of the god Vishnu, and he in fact had more than once been at pains to remind his audience that the founder of Buddhism was a human being who had attained Enlightenment by his own human exertions. His successor at the microphone, who from his 'surname' I knew to be a brahmin, was of a different opinion. The Buddha *was* an *avatara* of Vishnu, he insisted. He insisted on the point so vehemently, and criticized Jayachandram in such unreasonable terms, that the latter could not forbear retorting, and had I not intervened to restore order the stage might well have been the scene of an unseemly altercation. Rain in any case had started to fall, as if to cool hot tempers, and I proceeded to deliver my presidential address, in the course of which I underlined the principal points made by Jayachandram and spoke at some length on the danger of Christian missions, the avowed object of which was to destroy the religious and cultural traditions of India. By the time I finished it was raining heavily, and we were forced to retreat indoors. Here I talked with some of the South Indian Buddhists who had attended the meeting, as well as with two Italian travellers who had come to ask my advice about extending their visas. One of the Italians was eager to visit Tibet, but I assured him that with the Chinese Red Army occupying the country this was impossible.

At ten the next morning I gave a lecture at the Vivekananda College, which as its name suggested had connections with the Ramakrishna Mission, Swami Vivekananda, after whom the college was named, having been the founder of the Mission. The lecture was attended by about a thousand people, mostly students, and after five or ten minutes of Vedic chanting I spoke, by special request, on 'The Differences Between the Principles of Buddhism and Hinduism'. Who asked me to speak on this topic, which was obviously a controversial one (though a Hindu speaker would probably have denied that there was any difference between the two religions), I no longer remember, but whoever it was I had taken the request seriously, perhaps even as a challenge, and had sat up late the previous night writing my notes. After pointing out that both Hinduism and Buddhism were to be viewed against the wider background of Indian spiritual tradition, I went on to give a systematic – if somewhat black and white – account of the more important philosophical and ethical differences between them. This took me the best part of an hour, and paved the way for a vigorous attack on the caste system and on orthodox Brahminism, the exclusiveness and bigotry of which I not only condemned in the roundest terms but contrasted with the spirit of universality and compassion shown by the Buddha. The attack came as a severe shock to the brahminical part of the audience, and the principal of the college, who was in the chair, and who was himself a brahmin, did not know what to say. Many of the students, however, were clearly pleased, and even some of the more orthodox remarked that the Buddhist point of view, though different from that of Brahminism, was deserving of careful study.

The remainder of the day was divided between poetry and philosophy, the former being represented by one Krishnamurti, the poet-proprietor of an arts and crafts emporium, who already had presented me with his latest book of (English) poems, entitled *The Cloth of Gold*, and the latter by Jayachandram, with whom I spent the evening discussing Buddhism and other topics of common interest. In the morning, straight after breakfast, I went to see Dr Natarajan, the scholarly successor of the famous Narayan Guru, who as Jayachandram had informed me was then staying in the city. I had met Dr Natarajan – or Nataraja Guru, as he was also called – once before, in Travancore. Circumstances had permitted only the briefest of exchanges, and on the present occasion, too, the interview had to be a short one, as I was seeing him on my way to the station and had a train to catch. There was time, however, for him to tell me about the radical new interpretation (and translation) of the *Bhagavad-gita* on which he was then working and had, in fact, been working on for a number of years. At Madras Central I located my berth, bought a volume of English essays at the station bookstall, said goodbye to Jinananda, and settled myself for the journey. Punctually at 9.15 whistles blew, doors were slammed, and I was on my way – not to Calcutta but to Nagpur.

Nagpur, 500 miles from Madras, and situated at the exact geographical centre of India, was the capital of Madhya Pradesh. Though it lay on the main line between Bombay and Calcutta, and though I had passed through it several times, I knew little more about it than that it was the orange-growing capital of India and the headquarters of the Rashtriya Sevak Sangh or National Service Association, an ultra-nationalist, right-wing Hindu organization one of whose members had assassinated Mahatma Gandhi. In recent months I had become more aware of the place's existence. Venerable Silabhadra, one of my colleagues on the editorial board of the *Maha Bodhi*, had lectured there on 'Buddha and Buddhism' at the invitation of the local Ramakrishna Ashram, then celebrating its Silver Jubilee, and I had been in correspondence with A.R. Kulkarni, the Secretary of the Buddha Society, Nagpur, who was a supporter of the Maha Bodhi Society and an occasional contributor to its journal. Either Kulkarni suggested I might like to visit Nagpur, or I suggested the Buddha Society might like to invite me. Whichever it was, a visit had been arranged, and I now was making a grand detour and returning to Calcutta from Madras by way of Nagpur. During the whole day only three other persons entered the compartment, and I spent the time immersed in my volume of essays. At ten o'clock in the evening, as we were passing through Hyderabad State, a group of three Muslims got in for an hour. It was a rather unusual group, consisting of a well-built police inspector, a handsome young man, and a very pretty boy. Soon the police inspector was arguing politics with a Tamil brahmin who already occupied one of the berths, while his two companions, who may not have understood English, sat quietly beside him. Twelve hours later the train reached Nagpur.

Kulkarni was waiting for me on the crowded platform. A middle-aged man of medium height, he was simply clad in a white *kurta* and *dhoti*, and was shaven-headed, though without the crown lock that denoted the orthodox Hindu. As I later discovered, he saw himself as a Hindu follower of the Buddha rather than as a Buddhist, which explained why the organization of which he was secretary, and of which he was indeed the founder and moving spirit, was a Buddha society and not a Buddhist society. A taxi conveyed us to his residence in Dharampeth, which as its name indicated was or had once been a brahmin locality, where I met his doctor brother and his two teenage nephews. The women remained in the background, cooking and washing clothes and drawing water from the well in the yard. After we had discussed the condition of Buddhism in Nagpur (it was not good), and I had had lunch and written a letter to Kalimpong, he took me with him to see various people who would, he thought, be interested in arranging lectures. We did not meet with much success. The registrar of the University, a UP brahmin, did not respond at all favourably to my host's suggestion that I should deliver a lecture in the Convocation Hall. Indeed, it was my impression that the forthright-ness of Kulkarni's approach, and the bluntness of his manner, which made a suggestion seem very much like an order, rather disconcerted him, not to say annoyed him. The fact was that Kulkarni was by birth a Maharashtrian brahmin, and Maharashtrian brahmins, as I had yet to learn, were renowned for their harshness and militancy – though the Deshastha brahmins, of whom Kulkarni was one, were much less harsh and militant than the Chitpavans. At the Ramakrishna Ashram, which we visited next and where we met the two resident swamis, one young and one old, we fared hardly better than we had done at the University. While Young Swami was interested in my giving a lecture there, Old Swami very clearly was not – perhaps because they had already had a lecture on Buddhism that year, or because Silabhadra's lecture had not been to his liking. In the end it was agreed that if it was possible for them to arrange a lecture they would let us know. With the Theosophists we were more fortunate. A Bengali follower of Mme Blavatsky assured us that there would be no difficulty in arranging for me to speak at the local TS lodge, and promised to ask the lodge secretary to get in touch with us. The rest of the afternoon, as well as most of the evening, was spent visiting first the Buddha Society's library and reading room, then a temple where an image of the Buddha had been installed, and finally the headquarters of the State Congress. By the time we returned to Dharampeth I was feeling rather tired. Kulkarni, despite his fifty-odd years, was still full of energy, and bustled about preparing 'English tea' for me.

The following morning it became apparent that our labours of the previous day had not been in vain. From breakfast time until well after midday there was a constant flow of visitors, several of whom either wanted to arrange lectures or had already done so. The Principal of the

Science College had arranged one for that very evening, the secretary of
the TS lodge wanted to arrange one for the following Saturday (it was
then Thursday), while a *brahmachari* or novice from the Ramakrishna
Ashram came with an invitation to speak there the following Sunday.
Young Swami had somehow managed to persuade Old Swami! The
result was that for that and the next three days I was kept busy preparing
and giving what seemed an uninterrupted stream of lectures and ad-
dresses. Kulkarni, who was a lawyer by training, kept a faithful record
of them all, and an article from his pen entitled 'Bhikshu Sangharakshita's
Lecture Tour in Nagpur' eventually appeared in the *Maha Bodhi* and
elsewhere. Many of the details of where I spoke, to whom, and what I
said, had vanished from my recollection even before the article appeared.
On the other hand, incidents of which he made no mention, and of which
he probably was quite unaware, were indelibly impressed on my mind.
Biography and memoirs supplement and correct each other, especially
when the biographer writes about the memoirist from personal knowledge. Concerned as it was with my public activities rather than with my
private ones, Kulkarni's article naturally began with my visit to the
Buddha Society's library and reading room.

> On the very first day of his arrival Rev. Bhikshu Sangharakshita
> paid a visit to the Library of the Buddha Society, Nagpur, which
> is located in Sitabaldi in the magnificent building of Dada Saheb
> Dhanwale, known as Dhanwale Chamber. After this the revered
> Bhikshu paid a visit to the Siddhartha Bhagyodaya Library
> located in the Vithal Rukmini Deosthan Temple, Sitabaldi,
> Nagpur. The revered Bhikshu was immensely pleased to notice
> the beautiful image of the Buddha installed in the temple in the
> heart of the Nagpur city. The revered Bhikshu then paid a visit to
> the Abhyankar Congress House and attended the mass common
> prayer conducted therein. Sri A.R. Kulkarni recited *Trisarana* and
> *Panchasila* and the revered Bhikshu made a short speech
> explaining their meaning. The audience was spellbound when
> the Bhikshu was delivering his sermon.

Dhanwale Chamber may or may not have been a magnificent building,
but the hundred or so Hindi, Marathi, and English volumes, some of
them on Buddhism, that formed the Society's library, certainly could not
be considered a magnificent collection. Running the library was, however, the Society's one permanent activity, and apart from Kulkarni's
occasional lectures it had for some years past been virtually the only sign

of Buddhist activity in Nagpur. More interesting to me was the image of
the Buddha in the neighbouring Siddhartha Bhagyodaya Library. It was
more interesting not on account of its beauty but because, as Kulkarni's
article failed to mention, it had been installed there by the Scheduled
Caste followers of Dr Ambedkar. How it came to be installed there,
especially as the library was located in a Hindu temple, I was unable to
discover. Whatever the explanation may have been, in view of the
momentous change that was to take place in the lives of Ambedkar's
followers only two years later, in that very city, it could be said that
coming events were casting their shadow before.

> On the second day, i.e. on July 22nd, the revered Bhikshu gave a
> lecture in the Science College Hostel on 'Buddhism and the
> Modern World' under the presidentship of Dr Krishnamurti,
> Principal, Science College, Nagpur. In his opening address Dr
> Krishnamurti pointed out how Buddhism was the purified form
> of Hinduism. The learned Bhikshu told the science students how
> Buddhism inculcated a scientific attitude in man. Buddhism
> never believed in accepting anything on trust. 'Come and see for
> yourself' is the motto of Buddhism. It was for this reason the
> most rationalistic religion on earth. The learned Bhikshu aptly
> pointed out that there was never any conflict between Buddhism
> and science. The lecture had an abiding effect on the students
> who actually declared their faith in Buddhism by saying
> *Buddham Saranam Gacchami.*

As my lecture lasted for an hour and a half, Kulkarni's account of it was
not even a summary. Probably I was at pains to rebut Krishnamurti's
assertion that Buddhism was a purified form of Hinduism, but I no doubt
did this gently, as the Principal of the Science College was a friendly,
likeable man, and I had no wish to injure his feelings. The attitude
inculcated in man by Buddhism was, of course, 'scientific' only in the
wider sense of its being objective, as I must have explained. Similarly,
Buddhism's 'Come and see' meant not that it was rationalistic (a word I
never used in this connection) but that it was rational – a very different
thing. As for the dozens of students who, at the conclusion of my lecture,
thronged round me with joyful shouts of *'Buddham saranam gacchami*! I
go for refuge to the Buddha!' – they were members of the Scheduled
Castes, and followers of Dr Ambedkar. Once again, coming events were
casting their shadow before.

On July 23rd the revered Bhikshu delivered a learned discourse on 'Buddhism' in the Nagpur Mahavidyalaya under the auspices of the Philosophical Society of the College and under the presidentship of Prof. Ramnathan, Vice-Principal of the College. Earlier the revered Bhikshu had delivered a discourse on the *Dharma Chakra* under the auspices of the Harijan Sewa Sangh. The occasion was the mass spinning programme organized by the Sarvodaya workers of Nagpur to commemorate the eighty-sixth birthday of Mahatma Gandhi. The function was attended by Sri R.K. Patil, ex-Minister, Sri Rauka, Sri Wazalwar and other eminent Sarvodaya workers. The whole audience was highly impressed by the learned and illuminating discourse delivered by the revered Bhikshu. After questions and answers the function terminated. Sri R.K. Patil was also presented in the evening function held in the Nagpur Mahavidyalaya.

The fifty-odd Sarvodaya workers taking part in the mass spinning programme were the biggest collection of freaks and eccentrics I had seen for a long time. Old rather than young, and clad, or half clad, in coarse white homespun, they were wild-eyed, long-haired and, in some cases, long-bearded. Some tried to carry on hand-spinning when they stood up to address the audience. Others spoke with the most extraordinary gestures, at times touching the ground with one hand while simultaneously shooting the other towards the ceiling. The most sensible-looking person present was a local mill-owner in a white Gandhi cap who sat silent and impassive, and without a *charka*, to one side. The Sarvodaya workers were all disciples of Vinoba Bhave, whose proposal to enhance the importance of Bodh-gaya by building there a temple of his own I had recently ridiculed in the *Maha Bodhi*. Gandhi's economic ideals, of which Bhave was the principal inheritor and custodian, appealed to me strongly (the Mahatma's *Hind Swaraj* was one of the first books I read after my arrival in India), but if those ideals depended for their implementation on Bhave's Sarvodaya movement, as represented by the present collection of crackpots, then I for one could not see them transforming Indian society.

On July 24th the learned Bhikshu delivered at 5 p.m. a lecture on 'Buddhism the Gospel of Action' in the Hislop College, Nagpur, under the auspices of the Philosophical Society of that College. Sri Padye, Professor of Philosophy, presided. The learned lecturer pointed out in the course of his stirring lecture how Buddhism

was essentially a religion of action. This lecture created a
favourable impression on the younger generation who mostly
attended it. Immediately after this lecture was over the revered
Bhikshu delivered at 6.30 at the Theosophical Lodge, Dhantoli, a
lecture on 'Buddhism and Theosophy'. The learned Bhikshu
pointed out the many common points between Buddhism and
Theosophy and laid particular emphasis on the universal
brotherhood of man which was an essential feature both of
Theosophy and Buddhism. The Theosophical Lodge was packed
to its full capacity and the entire audience was listening to the
discourse with rapt attention. The simple but easy flowing style
of the learned Bhikshu created a deep impression on the
audience and they thought they were listening to something
which they had not witnessed before. In fact the revered
Bhikshu's lectures had created a sensation in Nagpur.

The Hislop College lecture was delivered at the invitation of the students
themselves, two of whom had come only that very morning to ask me to
address them. Buddhism was a religion of action, but not of activism. It
was a religion of action in that it recognized the law of karma, the law in
accordance with which impure actions of body, speech, and mind were
followed by suffering, and pure ones by happiness. Thus Buddhism was
a religion of ethics. Meditation consisted, essentially, in an uninterrupted
succession of ethically pure mental actions (or skilful volitions), that is,
in an uninterrupted succession of mental actions free from greed, hatred,
and delusion.

On the morning of July 25th the revered Bhikshu went to the
village of Bahadma at a distance of about 7 miles from Nagpur, to
witness the anti-Untouchability campaign launched by Sri
Rauka-ji and others. On this occasion the revered Bhikshu
delivered a speech before the villagers in English which was
rendered into Marathi by Sri A.R. Kulkarni. In the course of his
very simple but convincing speech the revered Bhikshu laid
emphasis on unity in life and pointed out how disunity amongst
them may lead to their ruin.

For the last mile of the journey we had to walk, threading our way
between the paddy fields along the narrow raised paths. On our arrival
in the village we had breakfast with Sri Rauka-ji and other members of
the Harijan Sewa Sangh in an Untouchable hut. (*Harijans,* or Children of

God, was Mahatma Gandhi's name for the Untouchables, but many of them rejected the designation as a condescending euphemism.) While we were having breakfast I had an experience that affected me more strongly than anything else I saw or heard during my visit to Nagpur. We were seated directly on the beaten earth floor of the hut. In front of each of us was a *thali* and beside the *thali* a brass tumbler. On picking up the tumbler beside my own *thali*, and raising it to my lips, I found the water in it so thick with ochre-coloured clay as to be opaque. What was the reason, I asked. Apologetically, our host explained that Untouchables were not allowed to draw water from the village well. They were therefore obliged to take it from the river, which at that time of year was naturally very turbid. Not allowed to draw water from the village well! Not even during the rainy season! Those few simple words, spoken quietly and without bitterness, seemed to sum up all the wrongs the Untouchables had suffered, down the ages, at the hands of the Caste Hindus. They haunted me for months afterwards, and I never forgot them.

> At 4 p.m. the revered Bhikshu recited the Mangala Sutta at the residence of Dr D.R. Kulkarni in the true Buddhist style and explained its meaning in English which was rendered into Marathi by Sri A.R. Kulkarni. This was a sort of private informal function attended by the members of Dr Kulkarni's family and his personal friends, viz., Rao Bahadur D.K. Mohoin and Sri M.Y. and Mrs Koli and others.

Besides his two sons, Dr Kulkarni's family consisted of his wife and a grown-up daughter who was at medical college. The previous day the two women, together with the elderly maidservant and a little girl who may or may not have been a relation, had been formally presented to me. Dressed in their best saris, bejewelled, and with flowers in their hair, they had come forward one by one, had silently touched my feet, and then had withdrawn. During the whole course of my stay they did not address a single word to me, any more than I did to them, but they were very much aware of my presence in the house, as I well knew, and did their best to meet, and even anticipate, my material needs. With Dr Kulkarni and his sons I naturally had more contact, as I also had, to an even greater degree, with the indefatigable brother of the one and uncle of the others. More than once did I sit on the flat roof of the house with the doctor and his elder son, Krishna, discussing Buddhism, until long past midnight. My discussions with Kulkarni usually took place during the intervals between lectures, especially when the two of us were travelling by car or cycle rickshaw to the next venue, or when we were waiting for a bus. In the course of these discussions I learned, bit by bit, of the circumstances that had led him, a Deshastha brahmin by birth and a lawyer by profession, to declare himself a follower of the Buddha and to dedicate his life to the task of making India 'Buddha-minded'. It was an interesting story, and began twenty years earlier in the Nagpur High Court.

A Hindu monk from the Punjab had come and taken up residence in a deserted Shiva temple in Nagpur. The monk belonged to the Mahanubhava sect, the members of which worshipped not Shiva but Vishnu, particularly in his *avatara* as Krishna, the preacher of the *Bhagavad-gita* and lover of the *gopis* or cowherd maidens. After taking up residence in the temple, the Mahanubhava monk installed there an image of Krishna, as a result of which the Krishna temple, as it now was, became a popular place of worship for the local Hindus. At this point a Sanatani or 'orthodox' monk who as a follower of the non-dualist philosopher Shankara was a worshipper of Shiva, filed a civil suit against the Mahanubhava monk, contending that the temple had been built by his guru and that on the latter's death he, the plaintiff, was its rightful owner. He further contended that the temple was a Sanatani temple and that the Mahanubhava monk, not being a Sanatani Hindu, had no right to reside there and no right to manage the place as he was doing. Kulkarni appeared in the case for the defendant. He had already appeared for him in the criminal case that had preceded the civil suit and which the Sanatani monk, then also the plaintiff, had lost. This case did not really form part of Kulkarni's story, and I in fact learned about it only much later, on one of my subsequent visits to Nagpur. In the civil suit there were three questions to be determined. What was a Hindu? Were Mahanubhavas Hindus? What was the difference between a Hindu and a Sanatani Hindu? Under cross-examination the plaintiff defined a Hindu as one who believed in the authority of the Vedas; admitted that the Mahanubhavas were Hindus; and averred that a Sanatani Hindu was one who, on the authority of the Vedas, believed – as the Mahanubhavas did *not* – in the caste system and untouchability. In support of his contention that the Mahanubhavas, though Hindus, were not Sanatani Hindus, he called as witnesses a number of brahmin pandits, the most eminent of whom Kulkarni cross-examined at some length. From this pandit he elicited statements to the effect that the caste system was based on birth, not on merit, that Tukaram, the famous poet-saint of Maharashtra, despite his spiritual attainments was to be classed as a Shudra (which he was by birth), not as a brahmin, and that the Buddha was not an authority on religion.

These uncompromising statements shocked and distressed Kulkarni, the more especially as they represented the considered opinion of a brahmin pandit well versed in the Hindu scriptures. He realized that in orthodox Hinduism there was no place for social justice, and that the very people who were supposed to teach the principles of true religion were themselves ignorant of those principles. The only remedy for such a state of affairs, he concluded, was the Buddha. Only the Buddha could remove the evils of caste, untouchability, and communalism from the present-day Indian society. With the help of friends and well-wishers he therefore founded in Nagpur, in 1944, a Buddha Society, with himself as Secretary. As I discovered later, the principal supporters of the little organization were all Maharashtrian brahmins and all members of the legal profession. Between Buddhism and the Nagpur bar there seemed to be a definite connection. There was also a connection between Buddhism and the Nagpur bench, the President of the Society being a judge of the Nagpur High Court. The connection between Buddhism and the Nagpur bar, at least, was not a new one. Both then and in the course of my subsequent visits to Nagpur, Kulkarni was wont to reminisce not only about the Mahanubhava case but about some of his other experiences as a lawyer. In particular he reminisced about the legal giants, both British and Indian, who had dominated the Nagpur High Court in the days of the Raj. Prominent among these legendary figures was Sir Hari Singh Gour, about whose forensic battles Kulkarni had many a story to tell and whom he as a young lawyer had evidently much admired. The name of Sir Hari Singh Gour was not unknown to me. He was the author of *Spirit of Buddhism*, a substantial and scholarly work on the life, teaching, and influence of the Buddha that had been published soon after my birth and which, as a teenager who recently had realized he was a Buddhist, I had devoured back in the early forties.

Two years after the founding of the Buddha Society Kulkarni experienced a further shock. In order to popularize the Buddha and make the people of India Buddha-minded, as he put it, he had started celebrating Buddha Jayanti every year on the Vaishakha Purnima (significantly, it had not been celebrated in Nagpur before), and in 1946 invited Tukloji Maharaj, the well-known musician-saint of Maharashtra, to sing *bhajans* or devotional songs on the thrice-sacred day. Tukloji Maharaj being extremely popular, and his bhajans greatly appreciated, the function was a huge success. 20,000 people attended. Afterwards, however, as the crowd dispersed, Kulkarni heard several people asking, 'Who is this Buddha whose Jayanti is being celebrated today?' These enquiries shocked and distressed him even more than the brahmin pandit's uncompromising statements had done two years earlier. That the Buddha, who was the glory of India, should be unknown in the land of his birth, was intolerable. It was a stigma on the fair name of India. The stigma must be removed. Who would remove it? *He* would undertake to do so. A few weeks later he therefore gave up his practice as a lawyer and became a homeless beggar for the sake of the Dharma. When he came to this part of the story Kulkarni was so overcome that he shed a few tears, as he would do on future occasions when he related it to me, and I saw that he was a man not only of iron determination but of powerful emotions. Having given up his practice he paraded the streets of Nagpur every morning reciting the Refuges and Precepts, distributing pamphlets, and calling out, 'O noble sons of Bharat, arise, awake! Remove the thorn of misery and be happy! Destroy casteism, destroy communalism, destroy untouchability, destroy Brahminism! Preach the Dharma of humanity! Love mankind and glorify the Buddha!' Though he had kept this up for several years, even extending his activities beyond Nagpur, the noble sons of Bharat had so far shown little sign of responding to his appeal. The Buddha Society had not grown, being still confined more or less to a handful of brahmin lawyers. But Kulkarni was not disheartened. He still wanted to make the people of India Buddha-minded, and was overjoyed that I was visiting Nagpur and that my lectures were proving a success.

At 7.30 p.m. the learned Bhikshu delivered his last lecture at the Shivananda Hall of the Ramakrishna Mission. The subject of this lecture was 'The Spiritual Path in Buddhism'. By this time the revered Bhikshu's fame had spread far and wide in Nagpur and therefore this lecture attracted a large audience. In fact the entire Shivananda Hall was packed to the full. The audience was easily about 300 and was a distinguished one which included many prominent persons. The meeting was presided over by Swami Bhaskeshwarananda. The revered Bhikshu in the course of his lecture pointed out how spirituality was of the essence of Buddhism, and how there could be no progress in spirituality unless we laid stress on ethics and on renunciation. An emphasis on the *Panchasila* was the right emphasis in life. The learned Bhikshu further pointed out that the regular practice of meditation was indispensable to the higher life, and that nirvana could be attained only by the complete elimination of the concept of ego. The learned president in the course of his presidential speech profusely praised the lecturer and underlined the need for renunciation and meditation. After the lecture was over there was a rush towards the revered Bhikshu as everybody wanted to have a look at the young English monk.

People seemed to be struck as much by the speaker's youth as by the fact that he was a Westerner, as indeed had been the case in Bangalore. Not that I was really so very young. I was in my twenty-eighth year, though being shaven-headed probably made me look younger than I actually was. In India religious knowledge tended to be associated with age, notwithstanding the fact that youthful – even sixteen-year-old – gurus were not unknown to tradition.

In fact many institutions in Nagpur wanted to arrange the lecture of the learned Bhikshu but they were disappointed as the Bhikshu had no time. The revered Bhikshu left Nagpur by Calcutta Mail on July 26th.

I had no time because there was an issue of the *Maha Bodhi* waiting to be brought out. Otherwise I would gladly have stayed longer in Nagpur. Not only could I then have given more lectures; I could also have spent more time with my host and his family and got to know them better. Short though my stay beneath their hospitable roof had been, there was already a good deal of warmth between us, and when the time came for us to say our goodbyes, soon after breakfast, they were all subdued and sad. Krishna and his brother Raja, particularly, were quite affected. Krishna was so affected, in fact, that he did not come to the station, and I was seen off by the two elder Kulkarnis and Raja. Rather unusually, the compartment in which I had a reserved berth, and where the three of them sat and talked with me until the train's departure, was otherwise unoccupied, so that for the early part of my journey I was able to sit back and think my own thoughts without fear of interruption. The visit had been a memorable one. I felt moved by all the devotion I had encountered, and wondered what I had done to deserve it. In the course of the day only two or three people got into the compartment, with one of whom, the Punjabi manager of a Birla concern, I had a little conversation before sleeping. The following morning, having enjoyed a good night's rest, I talked with some of the passengers who had joined us during the hours of darkness, including a young Bengali who turned out to be the nephew of someone I knew and an MP from Orissa who was deeply interested in Tantric Buddhism. Thus the time passed pleasantly, so that when the train reached Howrah Station I hardly noticed that we were three hours late. Soon I had crossed the mighty cantilevered span of Howrah Bridge and was making my way through the congested streets of Burrabazaar to College Square and the Maha Bodhi Society.

Within hours of my arrival at the headquarters building I received a nasty shock. While I was away a meeting of the editorial board of the *Maha Bodhi* had been held, and at this meeting, as a copy of the minutes informed me, decisions had been taken which were plainly designed to check me in my work for the Journal and make it virtually impossible, in fact, for me to carry on. These treacherous and underhand proceedings angered me considerably. I flatly told Silabhadra, who was the prime mover in the business, that I proposed to take no notice of the editorial board's decisions and asked Jinaratana to call a special meeting of the board. I then made up the August issue and the following morning, after heated exchanges with my two yellow-robed colleagues (the third, the pacific Dharmaratana, was either away or remained in his room), began sending it to the press as usual, without going through all the channels I was now supposed to go through and without first obtaining the approval of all the people whose approval I was now supposed to obtain. The special meeting, held a week later, was a stormy affair, but despite Silabhadra's determined opposition I carried the day, and with the rather lukewarm support of Dr Kalidas Nag, the chairman of the board, and Dr Nalinaksha Dutt, managed to have the decisions previously taken rescinded. What with proof-reading and counteracting the machinations of Silabhadra and Jinaratana (at one stage they even tried to intercept my letters to members of the governing body), the time between my arrival and the holding of the special meeting was a busy one, so that with the exception of Soratha, who lived on the premises, I could see little of my Calcutta friends. After the special meeting, however, I was able to see more of them, especially Phani Sanyal and his father and Sachin's relations at Hindustan Building. I was even able to pay a visit to the Kamalalaya book department, where I bought a copy of Gide's *If It Die*.... None the less, the atmosphere at the headquarters building was such that I had no wish to stay longer than was absolutely necessary and accordingly left Calcutta after spending little more than a week there. Soratha, who had sympathized with me throughout, and who had written about my difficulties to Devapriya-ji, then still in Japan, accompanied me to Sealdah Station and saw me off.

During the daytime I talked with a Baptist missionary, and pointed out in very strong terms the shortcomings of the Christian missions. In the evening we crossed the Ganges, and from the upper deck of the paddle steamer I watched the rose-red disc of the sun drop with increasing rapidity beneath the grey horizon. That night it was very warm and my berth so infested with bedbugs I was unable to sleep. Between Siliguri and Teesta Bridge there were some forty landslides. Once I had to transship, scrambling knee-deep in mud along the mountainside for about thirty yards, with a sheer drop to the swollen waters of the river far below. At midday I reached Kalimpong – and The Hermitage. Hasta arrived soon afterwards with a companion, then Sachin's cousin Durga, whom I had recently started teaching, then Sachin himself with a big bundle of mail, and finally Anand-ji. I was relieved to be back and overjoyed to be once again surrounded by friends.

BRICKBATS – AND A BOUQUET

IN THE NOTES AND NEWS SECTION of the August issue of the *Maha Bodhi Journal* there appeared an item that was of more than usual interest to me. It was headed 'Non-Theravada Articles in the Journal' and had been written not by me but by Dr Nalinaksha Dutt, who had joined the editorial board a few months earlier. He had written it as a result of a letter that had been received from Joseph Alles, the editor of the *Buddhist World*, a fortnightly paper published in Colombo, complaining that the Journal was publishing articles by Mahayana Buddhists, a practice Mr Alles seemed to think was not only an innovation but contrary to everything for which the Maha Bodhi Society and its Journal were supposed to stand. As I was, effectively, the editor of the *Maha Bodhi*, the letter was obviously aimed at me and was not, in fact, the first brickbat to have been hurled in my direction by the occupants of that citadel of supposed Buddhist orthodoxy, Theravadin Ceylon. Indeed, it was not the first brickbat to have been hurled in my direction by the band of militant 'fundamentalist' Theravadins who were responsible for conducting the *Buddhist World*. They had been deeply upset, even outraged, by my appointment to the editorial board of what they insisted on regarding as a purely Theravadin publication, and had lost no time in attacking the appointment in the pages of their fortnightly, which of course meant attacking me. Joseph Alles's letter represented a continuation of the campaign.

The *Buddhist World*'s attack on me and my appointment, which was couched in that paper's usual intemperate style, was entitled 'Thus Are We Misled' and was by Dhamma Mamaka, a pseudonym that concealed the identity of the wife of the founder and first editor of the paper, Major-General Tun Hla Oung. This article of hers was a good example of the kind of attitude that was, and unfortunately still is, characteristic of certain representatives of the modern Theravada (as distinct from the Theravada of the Pali Canon), and as Western readers of *A Survey of Buddhism* – as my Bangalore lectures became – and other writings of mine may have wondered whether my portrayal of the narrowness and big-otry of these people did not contain an element of exaggeration I repro-duce Dhamma Mamaka's article here in full, together with a few comments. The article appeared in the *Buddhist World* of 28 April 1954, and was featured on the front page.

> Thus are we misled
>
> By Dhamma Mamaka
>
> The *Mahabodhi*, Vol 62, no 2 announces an improvement in its editorial board consequent on the appointment of a Mahayanist Bhikshu (not Bhikkhu) as one of its senior members, despite his *vas*. What improvement, we are entitled to ask, could be expected from association with one having vetulyan ideas? Is it not an insult to the memory of its revered Founder and the numerous Theravadins who have supported and maintained this journal for the past 62 years to publish in its pages articles by avowedly Mahayanist contributors? It will be observed that all the four articles in this issue are by Mahayanists!

'Vetulyan' meant heretical, the Vetulyavada being a quasi-Mahayanist, possibly Tantric, movement in early Sinhalese Buddhism that had been forcibly suppressed by the dominant Theravada and whose name was regarded, by modern Theravadins like Dhamma Mamaka, as synony-mous with every kind of doctrinal error and moral depravity. As for my having been appointed as one of the senior members of the *Maha Bodhi*'s editorial board 'despite my *vas*', i.e. despite my *vassavasa* or 'rains-resi-dence', it was not clear what the writer meant by this objection. Did she mean despite the fact that, having received the higher ordination in 1950, I had observed the rains-residence only thrice, and was therefore a very junior monk, or did she mean despite the fact that for the duration of the rains-residence, which lasted for three months, a monk was not allowed to travel? In either case her objection was beside the point. My being a junior rather than a senior monk did not disqualify me from appointment to the editorial board, any more than my having been appointed to that body in January was really incompatible with my observing the vassa-vasa later in the year.

The columnist 'Himavantavasi' hides under his pseudonym the Mahayanist ideas of the Editor of this journal. Four columns of his article 'In the Light of the Dhamma' have been devoted for the benefit of one of his staunch supporters, who, as 'a sincere European Buddhist' makes the preposterous suggestion to turn the wheel of the Norm backwards. He actually dares to insult, and the columnist-editor apparently approves, the readers by asserting that the 'current Theravadin system that makes the present [year] 2497 is incorrect'. He had even gone to the extent of insulting the Burmese who are sparing no pains to make the Sixth Buddhist Council the great success it undoubtedly would be.

The 'Sincere European Buddhist' happened to be G.F. Allen (ex-Bhikshu Y. Siri Nyana), the scholarly author of *The Buddha's Philosophy*. He was not a supporter of mine, staunch or otherwise, but simply a regular reader of the *Maha Bodhi* who had written to me in my editorial capacity. His 'preposterous suggestion', which according to Dhamma Mamaka amounted to a turning of the Wheel of the Norm backwards, related to the chronology of the Pali Canon. Inasmuch as such traditional stories as that in which Lord Buddha is said to have taught Abhidhamma to his departed mother in Tushita heaven and returned to earth to expound it to mankind, and that the Tipitaka was rehearsed at the First Council held a few months after the *parinibbana*, were not fact but legend, and inasmuch as there was in existence a copious library of scholastic research into the chronology of the Pali Canon, contributed over the last half-century by the finest scholars of Buddhism of both the East and West, did not the approaching Sixth Council offer an admirable opportunity for the best brains of the Buddhist world to face that vitally important subject in a rational and scientific manner, and work out an acceptable detailed chronology of the Three Pitakas? My well-meaning correspondent, who was himself a (liberal) Theravadin, ventured to offer two further suggestions for the Council's agenda: that a uniform system of referencing the Pali canonical quotations be introduced, and that the Council agree upon a chronology of dates for the Buddhist era, the current system that made the year 2497 being incorrect.

Why this last suggestion should be regarded as an insult to the readers of the *Maha Bodhi* was unclear, unless the *Buddhist World*'s fiery contributor was under the impression that the Journal's readership was made up entirely of orthodox Theravadins, and unless she believed, likewise, that the Theravada was incapable of being mistaken in its chronology. It was also unclear in what the insult to the Burmese consisted. In fact it was unclear whether it was the Sincere European Buddhist who had insulted them or his friend the columnist-editor, the writer's rage apparently having affected her ability to write coherently. But probably it was the columnist-editor. Earlier in the year I had upset some of the more conservative Burmese Theravadins by pointing out that the Burmese pronunciation of Pali was incorrect, as well as by suggesting, in an editorial, that the money being spent on building new shrines and gilding old ones should be devoted, instead, to propagating the teachings of the Buddha. For the latter offence the Australian-born editor of *The Light of the Dhamma*, the official organ of the Union of Burma Buddha Sasana Council, threatened me with rebirth as a dwarf, while the *Buddhist World* attacked me on both counts in the most vitriolic terms. To these attacks I responded with two light-hearted squibs in my Himavantavasi column and, more seriously, with an editorial on 'Controversy' in which, after referring to the Buddha's warning against 'wordy warfare', I quoted at length from Addison's *Spectator* essay 'Modes of Disputing'. The *Buddhist World*, I observed, had discovered a mode of disputing unknown to Addison, which we might call 'arguing by abuse'.

> Whoever disagrees with its narrow, dogmatic and intolerant
> views is at once attacked in the vilest and most virulent
> language. 'Heretic', 'pseudo-Buddhist' and 'Devadatta' are
> among the milder epithets with which it favours anyone whose
> ideas do not coincide in every particular with its own. The
> leading Buddhist layman of Ceylon, who has done more for the
> revival of Buddhism than any other Sinhalese since Anagarika
> Dharmapala (who, by the way, had to face similar attacks even
> on his death-bed), is assailed with accusations so wild and abuse
> so gross that one wonders how the paper concerned can venture
> to describe itself as Buddhist. Of course it is not difficult for
> ill-nature to disguise itself as zeal for religion, or dogmatism to
> pose as 'saddha'. In fact the paper's official description of its
> mud-slinging policy is 'radiating Metta'.

But regardless of whether my response to their attacks was light-hearted or serious, it saddened me that I should be the object of abuse by fellow Buddhists. When I confided my feelings to Anand-ji, however, my cynical and worldly-minded elder brother in the Order only laughed. 'If they want to make you famous why should you worry?' he wanted to know. But I preferred not to be made famous by such means.

> The 'Sincere European Buddhist' has asked his friend the columnist-editor to 'see your way to making the suggestion in the columns of the M.B. Journal, i.e. the premier and eldest mouthpiece of *our* (the italics are ours) Buddhist world – providing, of course, that you agree as to its importance – it might bear fruit.' We understand the agreement between these two friends. That is why so much space has been allowed in this journal. It will certainly bear fruit – the rotten fruit which should never have found a place in this journal. We would ask 'Himavantavasi' to disclose the name of his friend, the 'Sincere European Buddhist' or, is he ashamed or afraid to divulge it? 'Himavantavasi' and people of his ilk would do well to bear in mind that the *Mahabodhi* is a purely Theravada publication, supported and maintained by Theravadins all these long years, and that anti-Theravadin views should not be allowed to sully its pages.

I did not disclose the name of my alleged friend, the Sincere European Buddhist, as I did not wish to embroil him in my own disagreements with the *Buddhist World*. Had I disclosed it, Dhamma Mamaka might well have received a shock, G.F. Allen having spent several years in India and Ceylon as a monk and been highly regarded in Theravadin circles. His reference to 'our Buddhist world', to which Dhamma Mamaka took such exception, was simply an innocent acknowledgement of the fact that all Buddhists were members of a single ecumene. It did not represent a laying claim to the Buddhist world on behalf of the Mahayanists, as Dhamma Mamaka seems to have thought. Whether the Maha Bodhi Society was a Theravadin organization, and its journal a purely Theravadin publication, was the principal point addressed in Dr Dutt's Notes and News item on 'Non-Theravada Articles in the Journal', as shortly will transpire.

> It would, perhaps, interest readers to know what the editor of *The Western Buddhist* says about *Maha Bodhi*. Here it is: 'We value highly the encouragement given by many Buddhist periodicals, especially the most friendly welcome accorded us in the pages of *Maha Bodhi* at the pen of Ven. Himavantavasi. We should do our utmost to justify the welcome support of the Ven. Bhikkhu and to

fulfil the prophecies he makes about us.' The Ven. Bhikshu is also
a preacher of the western order!

The *Western Buddhist* was the organ of the Western Buddhist Order,
founded about two years earlier by Robert Stuart Clifton, an American
Buddhist, and its editor was Jack Austin, the young English bank clerk
who was one of my most faithful correspondents. Though I did not agree
with all Clifton's ideas, and had not been too pleased at my involuntary
co-option into his Order, I had, as Himavantavasi, indeed given the
Order's little journal a warm welcome on its first appearance. Dhamma
Mamaka evidently thought that this fact would interest her readers as
constituting further evidence, if such were needed, of my Mahayana
proclivities, the Western Buddhist Order being admittedly based on the
Far Eastern (Mahayana) Sangha of Japan, for which and other shortcomings it had already been more than once castigated in the pages of
the *Buddhist World*. She concluded her article by recurring to the theme
that it was an insult to the memory of Anagarika Dharmapala that
Mahayanists should be allowed to control the *Maha Bodhi*.

> The Maha Bodhi Society of India must realize that it is an insult
> to the memory of its reverend Founder and its numerous
> supporters in all parts of the Theravada world to allow
> Mahayanists to control this valued Journal, and that the sooner
> they can get the 'Rakshita' to 'change his spots' the better it
> would be if its continuance is to be ensured for many, many years
> to come. This is the earnest wish of Theravadins. Otherwise, its
> knell would be sounded sooner or later, sooner perhaps than
> later. If this were to happen, it would indeed be a tragedy, and a
> success for the Bhikshu!

I did not change my spots, or at least did not change them in the way
Dhamma Mamaka had in mind, and continued to edit the *Maha Bodhi
Journal* and – *pace* her despicable suggestion that I was out to destroy it –
managed to ensure its continuance as the leading English-language
Buddhist journal until my final return to the West twelve years later. The
history of the *Maha Bodhi Journal* thereafter was one of steady decline.
With 'Mahayanists' no longer in control, its knell indeed sounded, and
eventually it ceased publication.

But in 1954 all that was in the distant future. Though the August Notes
and News section's item on 'Non-Theravada Articles in the Journal' had
been written as a result of Joseph Alles's letter, it in fact made no mention

of that letter. Instead it took issue with Dhamma Mamaka's article in the *Buddhist World*. The truth of the matter was that the nature of Alles's letter had at first been seriously misunderstood, and the action which, as I discovered on my return to Calcutta from Nagpur, had been taken by the editorial board in order to restrict me in my work for the Journal, had been taken on the basis of the misunderstanding. The letter had been received, apparently, by Silabhadra. At any rate, it was Silabhadra who had placed it before a meeting of the Governing Body, and Silabhadra who had informed the meeting that it was a complaint about the editorials that had been appearing in the Society's journal, editorials which were, as was well known, written by me. The result was that, without those present having actually read the letter for themselves, a resolution was passed upholding Alles's complaint and, by implication, criticizing me for writing the editorials. Armed with this resolution, Silabhadra was able to persuade the editorial board to pass a resolution of its own restricting me in my work for the Journal and making me, in effect, a tool in the hands of himself and the other members of the board. But Joseph Alles's letter did not so much as mention my editorials, as I ascertained from a perusal of the minutes of the Governing Body's meeting, to which a copy of the letter was attached. His complaint was that the *Maha Bodhi Journal* was publishing articles by Mahayana Buddhists, so that the resolution passed by the Governing Body was entirely beside the point. I therefore went to see Keshub Chandra Gupta, one of the Vice-Presidents of the Society, under whose chairmanship the Governing Body meeting at which this resolution was passed had been held.

Keshub Babu was a tall, dark-complexioned, saturnine Bengali in late middle age whom I had seen a few times at Society functions but with whom I was personally unacquainted. Besides being a prominent member of the Calcutta Bar, he was connected with several educational institutions, and was a regular contributor to leading Indian dailies and monthlies, both English and Bengali. He was, of course, a Hindu, though not a brahmin, and I was not sure how sympathetic a hearing he would give to my representations, it being well known that I was no less critical of orthodox Hinduism than I was of fundamentalist Theravada. I need not have worried. As I proceeded with my story Keshub Babu's heavy eyebrows elevated themselves in astonishment and he listened with increasing interest. The Governing Body had not understood the nature of Mr Alles's letter, I explained, nor grasped its implications. Mr Alles had not complained about my editorials, as Silabhadra had led it to believe. His complaint was that the *Maha Bodhi Journal* was publishing

articles by Mahayana Buddhists, which he seemed to regard as an innovation. The point to be decided by the Governing Body was, therefore,
*whether articles by Mahayanists, or contributions dealing with Mahayana
Buddhism, were to be excluded from the Journal or not.* In deciding this point
it would have to bear in mind that neither the Society nor its Journal were
limited to any sect of Buddhism: both were international and inter-
sectarian. Many members of the Society, including the President, were
Mahayanists. It would also have to bear in mind that articles by Mahayanists, and articles dealing with Mahayana Buddhism, had appeared in
the Journal ever since its inception. The Founder himself had written
several appreciative articles on Mahayana Buddhism, including one in
the first issue of the Journal (May 1892), and we were certainly not being
unfaithful to his memory by continuing the practice of publishing such
articles. The Governing Body might also like to take note of the fact, of
which it had evidently been unaware (though Silabhadra had been well
aware of it), that Mr Alles happened to be the editor of the *Buddhist World*,
a fortnightly paper published from Colombo that was well known for the
violence and virulence of its attacks on Mahayana Buddhism. In view of
these considerations, I concluded, the Governing Body should pass a
fresh resolution, to the effect that a reply be sent to Mr Alles – preferably
over the signature of himself as chairman of the meeting – informing him
that the Society and its Journal were not limited to any sect of Buddhism,
and that as the Journal had published articles on Mahayana Buddhism
(including some by the Founder himself) from the very beginning, his
complaint on this score could not be entertained.

Experienced criminal lawyer that he was, it was not difficult for Keshub
Babu to see the force of my arguments. Neither was it difficult for him to
see that Silabhadra had acted in a less than straightforward manner. He
therefore told me that he agreed with me on all points and that if I would
write to him officially he would raise the matter at the next meeting of
the Governing Body. Business thus having been dispatched to our mutual
satisfaction, we turned to other topics, and spent the rest of the evening
discussing Buddhism and literature.

My next step was to have the decisions that the editorial board had
taken in my absence rescinded. This I did at the special meeting of the
board that I had asked Jinaratana to convene, though I did not manage
to do it without coming into violent conflict with Silabhadra, who was
determined that the decisions should not be rescinded and who seemed,
in fact, to share Joseph Alles's – and Dhamma Mamaka's – conviction that
the *Maha Bodhi Journal* was a purely Theravadin publication. In the course

of our rather heated exchange I confronted him with the deception he had practised on the Governing Body, as well as on the editorial board itself, and took him severely to task for his treacherous and underhand behaviour. My language was rather strong, perhaps stronger than it should have been to such an old man (Silabhadra was more than twice my age, and was to die the following year), but I was outraged that one who did so little for the Journal should seek to obstruct my own efforts on its behalf and exasperated, moreover, by the obstinacy with which he continued to maintain his position even when it had been shown to be without foundation.

The result of my meeting with Keshub Chandra Gupta, and of my having the editorial board's decisions rescinded, was that I was able to leave Calcutta for Kalimpong secure in the knowledge that I was still the *de facto* editor of the Journal and free to operate without the restrictions Silabhadra had sought to impose on me. A few days after my return Sachin brought me, along with the rest of the mail, my copies of the August issue of the *Maha Bodhi*, in which there appeared, as the second item in the Notes and News section, Dr Dutt's 'Non-Theravada Articles in the Journal'.

My scholarly colleague did not express himself as forcibly as I might have done, but he expressed himself forcibly enough, his contribution being in fact based upon an editorial on 'Our Policy' that I had sent Keshub Babu – along with the official letter for which he had asked – but which had not been used. Moreover, though he had given me only lukewarm support at the special meeting of the editorial board, soft-spoken, bespectacled Dr Dutt was, I knew, very much of my own way of thinking with regard to the *Maha Bodhi Journal*. When I saw him in his room at the University, where he was Head of the Department of Pali, the day after the meeting, he indeed went so far as to characterize Silabhadra's attitude as narrow-minded and bigoted. Thus it did not surprise me that although the item of which he was author could have been more forcibly written, he should have struck, in his opening paragraph, a sufficiently stern and decisive note.

A recent pseudonymous article published in the *Buddhist World* (28 April 1954) of Colombo, he declared, had dragged in the name of the Society's founder Anagarika Dharmapala without giving sufficient thought to the magnanimity of his outlook expressed in the early issues of the *Maha Bodhi Journal* in these words:

> The Society representing Buddhism in general, not only single
> aspects of it, shall preserve absolute neutrality with respect to the
> doctrines and dogmas taught by sections and sects among the
> Buddhists. It is not lawful for anybody, whether a member or not,
> to attempt to make it responsible, as a body, for his own views.
> Membership being open to all, whether professed Buddhists or
> not, the Society is bound to guarantee them their rights as
> neutrals. It will be equally ready to publish expositions of all
> Buddhist sects, but without committing itself to any one.

Dharmapala's outlook had indeed been a magnanimous one, as I well
knew, from having written about the Anagarika's life two years earlier,
and the noble statement cited by Dr Dutt served to make it clear, once
and for all, whether or not the Society and its Journal were the exclusive
property of the Theravadins. Dr Dutt also drew attention to the fact that
the writer of 'Thus Are We Misled' had even shut 'his' eyes to the cover
of the Journal in which it was clearly stated that 'the Maha Bodhi is a
monthly Journal of International Buddhist Brotherhood'. He then proceeded to show that out of the four articles complained of as being by
Mahayanists three established nothing but Theravadin points of view,
while the fourth paper was a descriptive one, giving information about
later Buddhism which, the editors considered, should be made known to
the Theravadin Buddhists. As regards the particular exception that had
been taken to the remarks of a 'Sincere European Buddhist' who had
attached more value to the results of critical scholarship than to orthodox
beliefs, such views admittedly might not appeal to all Buddhists but there
were Ceylonese scholars like Prof. Malalasekera and others who adhered
to the former views. (Dr Dutt was evidently unaware that along with
Christmas Humphreys, Robert Stuart Clifton, and me, G.P. Malalasekara
was one of the *Buddhist World*'s principal *bêtes noires*, and that it was
constantly attacking him.) Finally, though probably upset by the names
of the contributors, the writer of 'Thus Are We Misled' should, on the
contrary, have appreciated that so many foreigners had been attracted to
Buddhism and had studied the Pali texts in order to find out what
Buddhism really was.

Thus my scholarly colleague. Though disappointed that my editorial
on 'Our Policy' had not been used, I could see that it was better that
Dhamma Mamaka's allegations should be refuted in the Notes and News
section of the Journal rather than in an editorial, which would have given
the *Buddhist World* more importance than it deserved. In any case, my

policy of printing articles by Buddhists of *all* persuasions had been amply vindicated, and the brickbats hurled at me from Theravadin Ceylon had fallen short of their mark.

But if brickbats were sometimes hurled in my direction I was also the recipient of the occasional bouquet. Not long after my return to Kalimpong there arrived at The Hermitage a copy of *The Mysorean*, self-described as 'a National Weekly with an International Outlook'. It contained an article by M.A. Venkata Rao, a literary member of the Indian Institute of Culture to whom, on my departure from Bangalore, I had presented a complete set of *Stepping-Stones*. Clearly the gift had not been wasted. The article, which was entitled 'Poison – But Also Nectar', bore the sub-title 'When East meets West the fruit is sometimes of uncommon value', and it was about me. Bhikshu Sangharakshita's lectures at the Indian Institute of Culture that year had shown him as a scholarly student of Buddhist lore with a remarkable gift for clear and attractive exposition, the writer was so good as to declare. But the puzzle remained as to why attraction towards ancient Buddhist teachings should have led a young Britisher to burn his boats and become a bhikshu. Were not specialization, assimilation, and even exposition possible without accepting *sannyas* and formal monasticism and binding oneself to the limitations of historical dogmatical schools? Whatever the answer to that question, a glimpse into the discourses and poems contained in the twenty numbers of *Stepping-Stones* revealed, in the writer's opinion, 'a singularly attractive personality. One gets the impression that here we have one of the romances of the inner life of our times.' Though the meeting of East and West had generated much poison it had also brought forth nectar (as in the puranic story of the churning of the ocean by gods and asuras), the nectar of immortality.

Not that the bhikshu's case was unique. A whole series of earnest and inspired Westerners, touched by something deep and unfathomable in Eastern tradition, had devoted themselves heart and soul to the service of the Asian peoples. Such, in India, had been Sister Nivedita, C.F. Andrews, and Miraben, and such now were Sri Krishna Prem and Father Verrier Elwin. What, then, made this British youngster come to India at the early age of nineteen at the height of the war of world powers (1944), casting out the pride of race and empire? And what sustained his resolve and carried him into the fold of Buddhist monasticism, in this age of secularism? Venkata Rao thought *Stepping-Stones* revealed much of the answer.

The young bhikshu (he is now 29) is a poet and has a genuinely aesthetic temperament. His discourses and poems show a perfect and attractive fusion of poetic and spiritual strains. The appeal of beauty in life and nature overflows naturally into the sense of the transcendental. We find here a variant of the new kind of priest, preacher or interpreter of spiritual things, of which there is a great need everywhere. For the bhikshu has approached the Buddhist scriptures, not as an orientalist or unattached scholar but as a thirsty soul seeking the water of everlasting life. And the little magazine is full of the appealing result.

Though I had certainly not achieved a perfect fusion of the poetic and spiritual strains of my own nature, I could appreciate that there was a need for a new kind of priest, preacher, or interpreter of spiritual things, and it was interesting that my Bangalore friend should see me as a variant of such a figure. Lama Govinda, I knew, believed that religion and poetry – indeed religion and all forms of art – were closely connected. In his Introduction to *The Veil of Stars*, my little (as yet unpublished) volume of poetic aphorisms, he had expressed his belief that 'It was the poet in Sangharakshita that led him to the religious life, and it was the path of renunciation that enabled him to see the world in a wider and truer perspective, which is the hall-mark of genuine poetry.' He had also gone on to quote the words of Novalis: 'Poets and priests were one in the beginning, and only later times have separated them. The real poet, however, has always remained priest, just as the real priest has always remained poet.' In my essay 'The Religion of Art', written the previous year, I had affirmed my belief that art and religion overlapped, and that just as there was in religion a constituent that was aesthetic, so there was also in art a constituent that was religious. The essay indeed concluded with the declaration that the Religion of Art, as I called it, was peculiarly fitted to produce a kind of character, a type of spiritual personality, which would be the living embodiment of the fact that Religion and Art were in essence one, and that Beauty was not merely Truth, but Goodness as well. Not that I thought of my own character or personality as constitut-ing such an embodiment. I still saw myself as simply a monk who wrote poetry, even though there were moments when aesthetic experience and spiritual experience seemed to coincide. Perhaps I needed to redefine my identity.

Be that as it may, having given a thumb-nail sketch of the young bhikshu's temperament Venkata Rao turned to Kalimpong, the place where he had settled, which he described at some length and in the most grandiloquent terms. Situated on a foothill of the Himalayan range, within sight of Kanchenjunga peak (which bore an unearthly purity and splendour when the clouds lifted), with the deep and narrow river flowing and turning upon itself, skirting deep gorges between hills, covered with evergreen forests of sal and deodar, hills whose tops dotted the horizon all round, leading up on the north to the ice-clad Himalayan peaks in mid-sky, as it were, with houses peeping through foliage round the slopes of the hills at all levels, and the central road becoming the market road at the Tenth Mile – Kalimpong was a dream of restful and various beauty, wrapped in translucent, lambent radiance all its own. Beyond the Himalayas lay the mysterious land of Buddhist Tibet, 'fabled still to contain teachers of primeval wisdom.' From Tibet, via one of my poems, it was not difficult for the writer to make the transition to reincarnation and karma, and from these to some of the topics with which I had dealt in my discourses, as he called my articles, from the 'stepping-stones' of right conduct, meditation, and wisdom, to the Bodhisattva Ideal, and from the simple life to the nature of Buddhahood. Unfortunately, Venkata Rao's appreciation of my having worked out for myself 'an appealing form of Mahayana Buddhism through which a positive spiritual idealism gleams forth, not in technicalities but in terms of thought and feeling while seeking out the higher values of life' was vitiated, for me, by his typically Hindu insistence on seeing this as constituting a return, by an alternative route, to Upanishadic idealism. None the less I was pleased with the article. It really was a bouquet, even if among the flowers there was a weed or two. I particularly appreciated the writer's pointing out the way in which the sights and sounds of Kalimpong, besides forming a natural background to my thoughts, provided much of the symbolism and imagery of the 'discourses' and poems. And of course I appreciated his quoting from three of my poems, even if his attribution to 'Messengers from Tibet' of a 'certain eerie lilt recalling Yeats and Walter de la Mare' rather puzzled me.

My poems were very much in my mind at the time. Forty-five of them, most of which had been contributed originally to various magazines, had recently been brought out by a Bombay publishing house under the title *Messengers from Tibet and Other Poems*, and notices had already begun to appear. The *Illustrated Weekly of India*, in an unsigned review that was probably by the English-born editor, Mr Mandy, characterized this my first publication in book form as 'a pleasant volume, mainly religious and descriptive in tone'. The idiom was conservative and the rhythm mellifluent; there was no great depth of thought behind the imagery, which was purely factual for the most part, as for example in 'Mountain Mist', from which the reviewer proceeded to quote. 'A poet of gentle sentiments and wistful longings, Bhikshu Sangharakshita consistently employs straight rhymes, of a studiously correct and simple nature, and one feels that had he resorted occasionally to well-contrived assonance, the result would have been more effective.' I was best, the reviewer thought, in my shorter lyrics, some of which had 'a strong flavour of the work of Walter de la Mare.' Miss I.B. Horner, the distinguished translator of the *Vinaya-Pitaka*, reviewing the collection in the *Maha Bodhi*, concentrated on the fact that the author of 'these charming and happy poems', as she called them, was deeply in the debt and under the spell of India, that 'great and beautiful land, with her kindliness, patience and age-old wisdom, the birthplace of "the Lord of Compassion"', that 'Void-born Compassion diamond-hard and petal-tender' to which I appealed in 'Invocation'. Several of the poems, she pointed out, had India, 'with her snowy mountains, her rivers, plains and villages, her flowers, her sunshine, mists and rain as the fount and as the symbols of man's adventures as he strives and aspires to fulfil the spiritual growth for which the Teaching of the Buddha provides a Way, a Track of "sunward-mounting golden stages".' She also drew attention to the fact that the poems were 'happy' because their inspiration stemmed from Buddhism, and in Buddhism there was nothing sad, dismal, or depressing.

Having a book published, it has been said, is one of the all-time most satisfying experiences. A good part of the satisfaction lies in presenting copies to one's friends. One of the first recipients of *Messengers from Tibet* was Clare Cameron, the pixie-like former editor of the Buddhist Society's journal *The Middle Way*. The volume was in fact dedicated to her. Ten years earlier I had shown her the best of my youthful verses and she had given me, in the course of a walk in Kensington Gardens, the benefit of some very sound criticism for which I was still grateful. Recipients of the volume nearer home included Sachin, Dawa, the Anagarika, Joe, and, of course, Dr Hudson (still settled comfortably in Darjeeling), who had defrayed the cost of publication. When I handed Joe his copy the hypercritical upasaka could not forbear heaving a small brickbat of his own in my direction. Glaring through his spectacles at the cream-coloured little volume as though it was something the cat had brought in, he professed himself extremely disappointed. Why, for the generous sum Dr Hudson had given me he had expected to see a handsome *dee* luxe edition, printed on the best hand-made paper, lavishly illustrated by a well-known

Bombay artist, and with beautifully designed endpapers and a watered silk marker! But there it was. I had done things in my own way, as I always did. I had not consulted anybody, least of all him, with the result that the publishers had swindled me and Dr Hudson's money had been wasted.

Joe's outburst momentarily confounded me. Dr Hudson had given me seven hundred and fifty rupees, this being what the publishers had asked for bringing out my poems, and from what I knew of printing and binding costs in Calcutta their demand was not unreasonable. None the less I was sufficiently disturbed to write to Sophia Wadia, in whose *Aryan Path* a brief notice of *Messengers from Tibet* had appeared, asking her if she thought I had been swindled. Her reply was unequivocal. Seven hundred and fifty rupees was not a great deal of money, and I could rest assured that the book had been produced to as high a standard as could be expected for that sum. Joe remained unconvinced, and not only refused to retract his brickbat but before long was assuring Dr Hudson that it was useless for anyone to give me money as I was totally impractical and always wasted it.

Brickbats and bouquets were, it seemed, an integral part of mundane existence. Sometimes there were more of the former, sometimes more of the latter, but one never experienced the one without sooner or later experiencing the other. The wisest course was to treat them as one should, according to Kipling's famous poem, treat those two impostors Triumph and Disaster, that is, 'just the same', or else be, in the words of the *Mangala Sutta*, one of those 'whose mind does not shake' when touched by the 'eight worldly conditions' of pleasure and pain, gain and loss, praise and blame, fame and infamy. Not that the wisest course was necessarily the easiest, especially to someone as sensitive as I was to people's emotional reactions to me and as liable, moreover, to fluctuations of mood – fluctuations which, more often than not, found expression only in my poetry. Nevertheless, conscious of the need to develop equanimity I did my best to be neither cast down by Dhamma Mamaka's (and Joe's) brickbats nor elated by Venkata Rao's bouquet, and carried on with my work for Buddhism and the local people. As usual, this included the giving of a good deal of personal tuition. After my return to Kalimpong I had resumed teaching Sachin and Meera (the latter at her home, whenever I happened to be visiting there) and had started teaching Durga, Sachin's sixteen-year-old cousin, History and English Literature. Sweet-natured but inclined to be taciturn, Durga lived near Sixth Mile, and in the evening, after giving him his lessons, I sometimes walked a mile or two down the road with him, instead of going up the road to Sachin's place.

I also started teaching the Anagarika, or Thupten Chhokyi as she now was, having been ordained as a *shramaneri* or novice nun by Dhardo Rimpoche that summer. In her case the lessons were meant to serve the double purpose of helping her improve her English and deepen her knowledge of Buddhism (not to mention satisfying her chronic need for attention), but they did not continue for long, as after a few weeks the ever-restless Frenchwoman decided she would be better off back in Darjeeling.

I was not sorry to see her go, for though intellectually stimulating she was extremely demanding, and had taken to complaining about the Rimpoche's supposed lack of interest in her in a way I did not like. Besides, I had not forgotten B.P. Wadia's request that I should write out my Bangalore lectures for publication in book form and wanted to set to work as soon as possible. This was not proving easy to arrange. Not that giving tuition was the only thing that took up my time. There were meetings to be organized, letters to be written (usually I wrote several a day), and visitors to be received, as well as the *Maha Bodhi Journal* to be edited. Eventually, however, on the last day of August, I seated myself at the rickety gate-legged table that served me as a desk, spread out my lecture notes, and started writing. 'The importance of Right Motive, of a correct attitude of mind, is emphasized more strongly in Buddhism than in any other form of traditional teaching,' I wrote. Work on the first chapter of *A Survey of Buddhism* had begun! Two hours later, having filled several foolscap sheets, I put down my pen and walked out into the garden. Despite the rain, the sun was shining brilliantly. Looking up into the sky, I saw a rainbow. According to Tibetan Buddhist belief the appearance of a rainbow was an auspicious sign. Double and triple rainbows had spanned my path when, almost exactly seven years ago, I had 'gone forth' from home into the homeless life. *This* was a single rainbow. None the less, I hoped its appearance was auspicious and that, now I had started writing the *Survey*, I would be able to get on with the work without too many interruptions.

Chapter Twelve

CRAIGSIDE

IN A LONG AUTOBIOGRAPHICAL POEM written in 1949, when I was staying
with Kashyap-ji in Benares, I had described myself as roaming, after the
havoc wrought by war,

> Without a friend, without a home,
> For many a year, with unquiet breast,
> Perplexed between the East and West.

In this there undoubtedly was an element of hyperbole. I was perplexed
between East and West only in the sense that, notwithstanding Venkata
Rao's eulogy, I had not yet succeeded in integrating the East as represented by Buddhism, with the West, as represented by English (and
European) literature, and in particular by English poetry. Though a keen
student of the Pali Canon and the great Mahayana sutras, of Shantideva
and Ashvaghosha, I was still an avid reader of Shakespeare and Milton,
Wordsworth and Shelley, besides a host of lesser names. My spiritual life
seemed to derive nourishment from both streams of inspiration. Though
I had not roamed entirely friendless (had not Buddharakshita shared my
life for two years and more?) since my departure from England ten years
earlier I had certainly been without a home. Indeed, for the last seven
years, ever since the be-rainbowed day on which I had 'gone forth' from
home into homelessness, I had been formally pledged to being without
one. None the less, from the time of my arrival in Kalimpong I had led a
comparatively settled life. After six months as the (eventually unwanted)
guest of the Dharmodaya Vihara and six months as the guest of the exiled
Prince and Princess of Burma, I had moved into The Hermitage, where I
had now lived for more than three years and which had become the
centre of my activities. But if I was in any danger of forgetting that the
semi-derelict frame building was *not* my home, and that I was in reality

a homeless wanderer, I was soon to be given a sharp reminder of the true state of affairs. In the middle of October, when I had been working on the first chapter of the *Survey* for no more than six weeks, I received a curt message from the landlord. The Hermitage was going to be pulled down and rebuilt, and we would have to vacate the place.

Whether the landlord ever intended to rebuild, or whether he simply wanted us out so that he could accommodate some of the drivers of his expanding fleet of taxis and buses, I never discovered. There was certainly no rebuilding during my remaining years in Kalimpong, nor was it long after my departure before wild-looking men who may well have been drivers were to be seen occupying my old abode with their families. Whatever the landlord's real reason for giving us notice may have been, the fact was that I had to find fresh accommodation for myself and the Kalimpong branch of the Maha Bodhi Society. Fortunately this did not take me long, nor did we have to go very far. Jutting from the hillside on the other side of the road, directly opposite The Hermitage, there was a spur, and strung out along this spur, at increasingly lower levels, there were three bungalows. At the base of the spur, immediately below the road, stood Glengarry, the biggest of the three, which was surrounded by tall privet hedges and occupied by Mrs Hamilton, the elderly, grim-faced Anglo-Indian widow with whom I sometimes had morning coffee. On the far end of the spur stood an anonymous bungalow that was occupied, during the summer months, by a Bengali family from the plains. In between the two, but nearer Glengarry, whose well kept privet hedges towered like a green wall above its red rooftiles, stood Craigside, a modest pukka building with a generous expanse of front lawn and a few rose-bushes. Craigside was occupied by cheery, pipe-smoking Major Cummins, the retired commander of a Gurkha regiment, who strode about the town in khaki shirt and shorts and was much saluted by Nepalese ex-servicemen and others. We were not unacquainted; each occasionally dropped in on the other for a cup of tea, and soon after my return from Calcutta I had borrowed his gramophone in order to play some of Captain Lalkaka's records. On my returning the device he told me that he would be moving to Darjeeling shortly, as he wanted to be nearer some of his old comrades-in-arms. At the time the information meant little or nothing to me, but on receiving our landlord's message I remembered it and at once went to see Major Cummins, who not only confirmed that he was moving to Darjeeling shortly, in fact that very month, but also gave me the address of his Marwari landlord. The upshot was that by the end of October Major Cummins had moved out of Craigside and I had moved in.

The business of moving did not take long. Apart from pictures and crockery, which with Major Cummins's agreement I had sent down separately a couple of days earlier, my worldly goods comprised little more than robes and bedding, a few aluminium cooking pots, several dozen bundles of *Stepping-Stones*, a typewriter, and the handsome glass-fronted bookcase I had recently had made for my growing collection of books. All the same, they filled the back of the jeep I had hired for the occasion, and as we negotiated the track leading to my new abode I could not but reflect, somewhat ruefully, that whereas I had arrived in Kalimpong with no more baggage than I could carry myself I now had fifteen or twenty times that amount. If one stayed very long in one place, it seemed, possessions had a way of multiplying, which was probably why the Buddha not only had restricted the personal belongings of his monk followers to just eight items but had exhorted them, moreover, to spend the greater part of the year wandering from village to village and town to town. That eventually the majority of them settled permanently in one spot, there to enjoy the use of corporate monastic property, was another story, and one with which I would be concerned in the second chapter of the *Survey*. But although my worldly goods now filled a jeep, they at least did not include any furniture, other than the glass-fronted bookcase. The Hermitage having been let to us furnished, that is to say, equipped with a table and chairs and two or three wooden bed-platforms, I had not needed to acquire any furniture. The same was the case with Craigside, which was also let furnished. The only difference was that the furniture in my new quarters was of a better kind, the table being a real dining-room table and the beds real beds, with springs and mattresses such as I had not seen for years and with which I could well have dispensed. Better or not better, the furniture was soon re-arranged, and within a few hours of their being unloaded my belongings had been distributed among the various rooms.

There were three principal rooms in the bungalow, which was L-shaped and flanked by an outhouse containing three much smaller rooms, the middle one of which was the kitchen. In the biggest room, which occupied the body of the L, I installed on a table beneath the casement window at the far end our three Buddha images, one standing and two sedent, thus transforming the apartment into our new – and much more spacious – shrine-room. This meant that we would be unable to have a games room, as there was no other room in the bungalow capable of accommodating our full-size ping-pong table. Not that I regretted the loss of the games room. On the contrary, I had for some time past been wanting to phase out our recreational activities, which in any case were a legacy from our earlier days as the YMBA, and to lay greater emphasis on the more specifically religious activities that were appropriate to our position as a branch of the Maha Bodhi Society. One of the results of our moving from The Hermitage to Craigside was that this could happen quite naturally, rather than it being the result of a definite decision on my part. Far from regretting that we now had no games room, I therefore did not even regret our having had to leave The Hermitage, despite the associations the place had come to have for me. In some ways I was even glad to leave. For the last few months relations with the angry-looking driver who, with his large family, occupied the tiny cottage at the far end of the garden, had not been very happy. On my return from Calcutta he complained that during my absence our members had torn up a number of letters that had arrived for him, a charge the latter all vigorously denied. Moreover, for the last eight or nine months he had refused to pay his share of our joint electricity bill (the cottage was supplied by an extension from The Hermitage, and the account was rendered in my name), alleging that the responsibility for paying it rested with the landlord, who was also his employer. The landlord apparently did not recognize any such responsibility, and if I was not to continue paying for the driver's electricity I had either to disconnect the extension or deduct his share of the bill from our rent each month, neither of which courses I was keen to pursue. The landlord's announcement that The Hermitage was to be pulled down and rebuilt, which served to resolve the impasse, therefore came as something of a relief. My only real regret at our leaving The Hermitage was for the loss of the garden up and down the gravel path of which I had so often walked, either thinking about my next lecture or composing a poem, or simply listening to the bird calls and enjoying the silent companionship of the flowering trees and shrubs. If The Hermitage was pulled down and rebuilt the garden would, I hoped, be spared.

But man is an adaptable creature. Within a matter of days I had ceased to regret the loss of the garden, or even to think about it very much, and had begun to feel as though I – and the Kalimpong branch of the Maha Bodhi Society – had been at Craigside for years. This feeling was due partly to the fact that my personal routine continued virtually unchanged, as did the rhythm of our more public activities. On the very day after we moved in there was a dana party. It was arranged by Dr Hudson, who a few weeks earlier had left Darjeeling to live a mile or so down the road at a house called Winston (there was another nearby called Churchill). According to her, the dana party was a traditional Buddhist institution, and she had come to know about it during a visit to Burma. In a letter sent out over her signature, our members and friends were invited to come and see our new premises (I had to type the letters, Dr Hudson's typewriter having broken down) and to bring with them gifts in cash or in kind. Not many people actually turned up, though a number sent gifts of one kind or another, from small sums of money to household items. Among those who did come were our two most generous donors, the fascinating Princess Pema Tsedeun ('Coo-Coo La'), the eldest daughter of the Maharaja of Sikkim, and her husband Mr Pheunkhang. Though I knew Princess Pema Tsedeun fairly well, I think it was the first time I had met her husband, who had probably been away in Lhasa. Pheunkhang-se or Pheunkhang Junior, as he was known, his father being still alive, was a pink-cheeked, affable young Tibetan nobleman, the descendant of the families of *two* previous Dalai Lamas, who some years later, when we were near neighbours, became quite a close friend. The day after the dana party I resumed work on the *Survey*, and a week after that we celebrated the full moon day in our new shrine-room with an inaugural puja at which I spoke on the Buddha's famous 'Song of Victory'.

Thus the days and weeks went by, and as autumn gave way to winter I was able to become more and more deeply involved in my writing. Sometimes I wrote sitting out on the little veranda, from which I could look up at the increasingly clear blue of the sky and at the dazzling whiteness of the ever more frequently visible snows. Not that I was never interrupted, even in the mornings, when I was supposedly incommunicado. More often than not, the interruptions took the form of visitors, both expected and unexpected. One of my earliest visitors was Vilasak, a novice monk from the Dharmodaya Vihara who had no money for necessaries and whom I promised to help. Another was Dr Ravi Singh, Sachin's cheerful and good-natured father, who came with Mrs Singh and Meera to see the new premises. There was also a visit, one fine morning towards the end of the month, from tall, white-haired Mrs Barnet, a widow who lived with her unmarried elder sister in a big house not far from Joe. According to the woman-wary upasaka, she wanted to marry him and was always giving him opportunities of proposing to her. However, their *tête-à-têtes* were invariably interrupted by the flirtatious, girlishly-attired elder sister, who also had her eye on Joe and who, to Mrs

Barnet's annoyance and Joe's relief, would come flouncing in at the critical moment.

My own acquaintance with the husband-hungry widow was much slighter, being more or less limited to the occasion when, two years earlier, she had invited me to lunch and shown me some black kittens for whom she was anxious to find good homes. When I enquired whether they were male or female she replied that she would have to ask the servants, as 'they always know about such things'. On the present occasion she had come not to dispose of unwanted kittens but to ask me if I would speak to Dr Hudson about renting her house. Like other United Kingdom citizens left high and dry by the retreating tide of the Raj she was worried about her future in an independent India, especially as a feme sole with a penniless sister to support, and wanted to let or sell her house and move to England. Eventually, Dr Hudson being already suited, she sold out to a local businessman, said goodbye to Kalimpong and her hopes of marrying Joe, and went to live in the Home Counties. Soon Joe was being inundated with heart-rending letters of complaint. England was unbelievably expensive. She and her sister were living in a top floor back room with no amenities and had to do all their own work, even to the extent of carrying buckets of water up three flights of stairs. Bitterly did she regret giving up her big house, her beautiful garden, and her band of devoted servants.

Mrs Barnet was an unexpected visitor. Around the middle of December I had a whole cluster of visitors whose arrival was not only expected but even, in the case of one of them, eagerly anticipated. This especially welcome visitor was Dhardo Rimpoche, who came accompanied by Lobsang Phuntsok. Like me, the Rimpoche had moved since our first meeting the previous year. He had moved, a few months earlier, from Sherpa Building at Tirpai, where he occupied a flat above the ground floor one formerly occupied by Joe, to the Old Bhutan Palace at Eleventh Mile. The Old Bhutan Palace, so called to distinguish it from Bhutan House farther up the road, which had been built in the thirties, was a large, two-storey wooden structure in the traditional Bhutanese style of architecture. Once it must have been a magnificent sight. Now, though still impressive on account of its size and noble proportions, it was so shabby and in such a state of disrepair as to resemble the ruined mansion so graphically described in the *White Lotus Sutra*'s 'Parable of the Burning House'. Dhardo Rimpoche lived in a suite of rooms on the first floor, where I had seen him the previous week and invited him to visit Craigside and give us his blessing. In two of the big downstairs rooms classes in Tibetan had been started, it being the Rimpoche's ambition to establish a school where Tibetan boys and girls could study both the Dharma and modern subjects through the medium of their own language, instead of being obliged, as so many of them were, to attend Christian missionary schools where non-Buddhist and even anti-Buddhist values were inculcated. Soon after his arrival at Craigside Dhardo Rimpoche was joined by Geshe Wangyal, who had not yet left for America and whom I had also invited. With the assistance of the Geshe and his personal attendant, a rather dour-looking monk who had been with him for many years, he then performed the traditional Tibetan ceremony of purification and blessing, after which he and Lobsang Phuntsok discussed with me their plans for a Tibetan school. I was already familiar with those plans. They were part of a bigger plan, for the creation of an Indo-Tibetan Buddhist Cultural Institute, also to be located, for the time being at least, at the Old Bhutan Palace. In fact I had already agreed, at Lobsang's request, to draw up the rules of the Institute. During the weeks that followed his and the Rimpoche's visit, the young ex-monk officer was a frequent visitor to Craigside, with the result that I not only became better acquainted with their plans for the Institute but agreed to give a fortnightly lecture under its auspices. I also promised to help him write the chapter on Tibetan Buddhism he had undertaken to contribute to a book on the Path of the Buddha that was being brought out by an American publisher.

My most frequent visitor during this period, however, apart from my regular students, was Thupten Chhokyi, who having changed her mind about being better off back in Darjeeling was now again in Kalimpong. Restless as ever, she was staying up at Tirpai in someone's outhouse, and was hoping to be able to move into a cave she had discovered in the hillside just above the village, by the side of the track leading to Dailo. Meanwhile, she spent a good part of each day at Craigside, arriving as soon as it was light and joining me in my puja and meditation. In the week or so following my removal to the new premises she had a reason for being so much in evidence there, having taken on the responsibility for arranging the shrine-room and sewing the maroon silk hangings. This task she accomplished with her usual energy, and on the whole I was pleased with the result, even though there were perhaps rather too many frills and furbelows for some tastes. Unfortunately, the fact that she had worked so hard on the shrine-room led to her developing a proprietary attitude towards it and even towards Craigside. Sometimes I thought she was developing a proprietary attitude towards me. She certainly resented my spending so many hours a week teaching Sachin, Durga, and my other students, an activity she frankly regarded as being a sheer waste of time, especially as it meant I had less time to spare for her and her problems than I might otherwise have had. For Durga, in particular, she appeared to feel something akin to hatred, and would dart in his direction, whenever she saw me giving him a lesson, venomous glances that gave meaning to the expression 'if looks could kill'. Durga, for his part, remained unperturbed by the Frenchwoman's hostility, only remarking once, after she had gone, that he could not imagine anyone less like a Buddhist nun, who was supposed to be the very embodiment of gentleness and compassion.

Poor Ani-la (as the Tibetans called her, Ani-la or 'Reverend Auntie' being the customary way of referring to, or addressing, a female monastic), she was her own worst enemy! Though loud in her demands for help, especially for help with her Tibetan studies, and bitter in her complaints when that help was not forthcoming, she invariably acted in such a way as to frustrate the efforts of those who were trying to help her. At her request, Dhardo Rimpoche had arranged for her to read a Tibetan text with his dour-looking personal attendant. She soon tired of this, however, the text being of a simple, devotional character, and began plying the monk with questions about the Madhyamika philosophy, a subject which he had not studied and which she, in any case, did not know Tibetan nearly well enough to be able to discuss properly. Moreover, she was in the habit, when having her lesson, of sitting as close to him as possible, sometimes squeezing herself up against him and even leaning so far across him as to be almost sitting in his lap. Such behaviour he, as a monk, found extremely embarrassing. So embarrassing did he find it that he eventually begged the Rimpoche to relieve him of the responsibility of teaching such a pupil. This the Rimpoche had no alternative but to do, with the result that Ani-la became more than ever convinced that Dhardo Rimpoche was not really interested in her and had no desire to help her.

She could not have been more wrong. During the last two or three months, ever since the discontinuance of her lessons with Gelong Lobsang, as the dour-looking personal attendant was called, Dhardo Rimpoche and Lobsang Phuntsok had more than once jointly consulted me, with every sign of concern, about the reason for the terrible mental states into which she tended to fall and what the three of us could do to help her become a better and happier person. So far we had been unable to come to any definite conclusion. But if our consultations brought no immediate benefit to Ani-la, they at least had the effect of strengthening the ties between Dhardo Rimpoche and Lobsang Phuntsok, on the one hand, and me on the other, and now that I was co-operating with them in their plans for a school and a cultural institute those ties were becoming stronger still. Not that Ani-la was left entirely without help. Somehow I found myself acting as an intermediary between her and the Rimpoche, especially when she wanted to communicate something which, she was convinced, he would not understand unless it was accompanied by detailed explanations from me. Once I was in the uncomfortable position of having to ascertain from him whether a certain activity, in certain circumstances, did or did not amount to (female) masturbation and, therefore, to a breach of the Vinaya or monastic code. Not that I felt particularly uncomfortable discussing such matters with the Rimpoche himself, but Ani-la was so anxious that he should understand the exact nature of her question that she insisted on communicating to me facts about the anatomy and physiology of the human female that I had no wish to hear and in fact found distasteful. Thereafter I was careful to steer the conversation away from sexual topics, which she seemed more eager to discuss than a nun ought to have been, though I continued to act as her intermediary with Dhardo Rimpoche. I also found myself acting, not long after the move to Craigside, as her unofficial meditation instructor. Since she found the mantra-recitation and deity-visualization practices into which the Rimpoche had initiated her too difficult, or at least not to her liking, I taught her the rudiments of the *anapana-sati* or 'respiration-mindfulness' practice, at the same time pointing out that this did not make me her teacher and that I was not assuming any responsibility for her spiritual progress. She was Dhardo Rimpoche's disciple, I firmly reminded her, and whatever help I was able to give her was given in my capacity as friend and fellow Buddhist.

Towards the end of December, when despite visitors I had managed to write at least two or three foolscap pages of the *Survey* virtually every day for the past six weeks, I paid a short visit to Darjeeling. It was my third or fourth visit that year, and the second since my return from Calcutta and since my starting work on the first chapter of the *Survey* at the end of August. This time I was accompanied by Durga, who was currently in disgrace for having failed his yearly examinations and with whom his father, the municipality's gnome-like head fitter, was so angry that he very nearly refused to allow him to make the trip, relenting only at the last minute as a result of Sachin's intercession on his young cousin's behalf.

In Darjeeling I stayed at Chota Khagjhora, at the Gandhamadan Vihara, whose Bengali Buddhist supporters treated me with their usual hospitality. On my previous visit, which had taken place in September, when I had been working on the *Survey* for only six weeks, I had stayed in Bhutia Busti, the 'Tibetan' settlement on the hillside below the Chowrasta, on the other side of the town. My stay there had lasted two weeks, and I had been the guest of the local Young Men's Buddhist Association. The Bhutia Busti YMBA, as it was known, had no connection with its now defunct Kalimpong counterpart. It had been founded about twenty-five years earlier by Bhikkhu Jinorasa, a Sikkimese monk of noble family who had received ordination in Ceylon. After his death in 1931 the association's religious activities had come to an end, except for the celebration of Vaishakha Purnima, and it was in the hope of my being able to revive these that I had agreed to stay in Bhutia Busti that autumn, at the YMBA's spacious but run-down premises. Besides giving a public lecture on the Three Refuges and Five Precepts, and presiding at the Mahatma Gandhi birth anniversary celebrations, during my stay there I took every opportunity of pointing out to the people of the locality, many of whom were Buddhists, the need for taking a more active interest in the Dharma. I also spent time with Dr Hudson, then still living in Darjeeling, who pressed Theosophical literature on me, showed me the manuscript of her book on blood (not to be published, lest the information in it be used for purposes of black magic), and reminisced at great length, and to her own evident satisfaction, about her various record-breaking achievements in the early years of the century. On my happening to remark, in all seriousness, that she seemed to have had a wide experience of life, and to know a great deal, her craggy features lit up with a smile of amusement at my having only just woken up to the fact and she replied, with a complacent chuckle, 'Oh, I know *everything*!'

My most vivid memory of those two weeks, however, was of the weather. It was bitterly cold, much colder than in Kalimpong, which was only four thousand feet above sea level to Darjeeling's eight thousand, and I shivered in the mornings as I sat in my unheated room at the YMBA trying, with frozen fingers, to write a few more pages of the *Survey*. But there were compensations. If it was cold, it was also clear, and I had only to step outside to see piled up against the intensely blue sky, bigger and whiter than they were when seen from Kalimpong, the jagged sunlit masses of the eternal snows.

On the occasion of my present visit to the town, the fact that I was staying at Chota Khagjhora did not prevent me keeping up my contact with Bhutia Busti and its Young Men's Buddhist Association. Indeed, one of the reasons for my being in Darjeeling again so soon was that the secretary of the association, a Nepalese Hindu sympathetic to Buddhism, had invited me to preside at the annual prize-giving ceremony of the YMBA primary school. The function took place the morning following my arrival. After the pupils of the school had given a variety performance, Ani-la, who had left Kalimpong before me, distributed the prizes, and I gave an address on the importance of dana or giving, explaining it in the traditional manner as the giving of material things, of education, and of the Dharma. In the course of my two remaining days in Darjeeling I received a visit from two leading mountaineers, one a Tamang and one a Sherpa (*not* the famous Tenzing Norgay), with whom I had an interesting exchange about mountaineering and Buddhism. I also went to see Mankazi Lama, a Newar Buddhist who had confined himself to a tiny room for puja and meditation. Something about him must have impressed me. That night I dreamed that the two of us were in Gangtok and that he was giving me mantras. The morning after this dream I left for Kurseong, still accompanied by Durga, who had spent much of his time in Darjeeling learning to ride. In Kurseong, to which we travelled by the toy train, taking three freezing hours to cover a distance – as the crow flies – of about twenty miles, I presided at another prize-giving ceremony and gave, under the auspices of the Young Tamang Buddhist Association, a lecture on the Bodhisattva Ideal. From Kurseong it was only an hour, by jeep, to Longview, where Durga continued his riding lessons and where Padmanathan took me to view the site of a new temple he was planning to build.

Soon after my return to Kalimpong I received a visit from Anand-ji. He did not come alone. With him came Dinesh and Jayadev, now transformed into Naginda and Sumedha and wearing, rather shamefacedly I thought, the yellow robes of the Theravadin *samanera* or novice monk, Anand-ji having just ordained them. The ordinations came as a complete surprise to me, neither of the young men having shown the slightest interest in the monastic life, and I could only assume that my none-too-scrupulous elder brother in the Order had ordained them simply as a means of enabling himself to keep them with him at the Dharmodaya Vihara. There were also visits from Ani-la, who had returned to Kalimpong before me. It did not take me long to realize that trouble was brewing. The first time she came she was extremely angry with me for going out without waiting for Lobsang Phuntsok, who had arranged to see me but was late; the second time she left in a huff, without staying for lunch as she usually did when she came in the morning, and the third time she handed me a note and her keys and went away without speaking. Understanding from this last action that she was thinking of committing suicide I called her back, as she no doubt knew I would, and did my best to reason with her. 'Like summer tempests came her tears', though unlike the subject of Tennyson's poem she wept not for a real loss but out of self-pity and because of the frustration of her unreasonable demands. In the end, having talked with her for an hour or more, I succeeded in bringing her a little to her senses, and as it was by that time quite late allowed her to stay the night in Man Bahadur's room in the outhouse.

But if I had thought that my talking with her had produced more than a transient effect on Ani-la I was soon made to realize my mistake. A few days later there occurred an incident that illustrated, all too clearly, the recalcitrant nature of the material with which I had to deal. Dr Hudson, having noticed that the little table at which I worked stood on the cold cement floor, had brought me a small woollen rug and had herself spread it beneath my feet. Soon after her departure, when my lower extremities were beginning to feel pleasantly warm, Ani-la arrived. Her sharp, darting eyes immediately saw the rug. 'That's *much* too good for your feet!' she exclaimed, in shocked tones. 'Its proper place is in the shrine-room.' Whereupon she whipped it from beneath my feet and without further ado bustled with it into the apartment in question. Thinking the matter not worth arguing about, I said nothing and went on writing. Next time Dr Hudson came to see me she naturally wanted to know where her rug had gone. When I explained what had happened she was extremely annoyed, not so much with me for my weakness (as she saw it) in allowing Ani-la to have her own way as with the French nun for having had the temerity to interfere with *her* arrangements. Marching into the shrine-room, she retrieved the rug, replaced it beneath my feet, and sternly told me that it was on no account to be used for any other purpose than the one for which she had expressly given it. When Ani-la saw the rug again beneath my feet she became quite hysterical, crying, 'Oh the beautiful rug! You will spoil it! It must go into the shrine!' and attempted to take it from me. This time, however, I was firm with her and did not allow her to have her own way, with the result that she wept all through lunch and left Craigside looking crushed and miserable.

Chapter Thirteen

Two Funeral Pyres

People taking up the spiritual life tend to fall into one or other of two categories. There are those who are drawn to the Unconditioned because they are disgusted with the conditioned, and there are those who lose interest in the conditioned because they are enamoured of the Unconditioned. The former, one might say, are pushed from behind by the sheer painfulness of mundane existence, whereas the latter are pulled from in front by the sheer beauty and attractiveness of the transcendental. So far as I could tell, I belonged more to the second than the first category, my overall experience of life having been positive rather than negative. One of the main reasons for the painfulness of mundane existence is that it involves separation, especially separation by death, from those who are near and dear to us. Though I had been geographically separated from my parents and my sister, as well as from my English Buddhist friends, for more than ten years, the circumstance of my having as yet suffered no serious bereavement meant that, while I knew I would die one day, the fact was not fully real to me. With the sudden death of Miss Barclay a year ago, however, it had assumed greater reality, the elderly English-woman having been a friend of sorts, despite all the trouble she gave me; and with the loss, during my first few months at Craigside, of two more members of my circle of friends and acquaintances in Kalimpong, it assumed greater reality still.

The first to go was Miss Rao's mother. Miss Rao was the tiny, fantastic-ally dressed South Indian woman who from time to time came and poured out her woes to me, usually at great length and when I was busy. Often she could be heard coming in the distance, as it was her practice to start talking long before she actually reached my door and to continue talking, on her arrival, without pausing for breath and as though I had been listening to her all the time. She invariably addressed me not as

'Bhante', as everybody else did (except, of course, my seniors in monastic ordination), but as 'Swamiji', which was the mode of address for Hindu renunciants. Bedaubed, bedizened little Miss Rao was in fact a universalist of the deepest dye, though from instinct rather than from intellectual conviction. For her there was no difference between Buddhism and Hinduism, all religions being one or, what amounted to the same thing, nothing but different forms of Hinduism. It was therefore not surprising that besides addressing me as Swamiji she should have done her best, over the years, to make me look like a Hindu renunciant and my abode like a Hindu temple or ashram. At different times she presented me with sealed copper pots of holy Ganges water, a yellow silk 'Benares shawl' stamped in red with the name of Rama, a pair of wooden sandals, and a string of brass mango leaves. While I had no objection to hanging the string of brass mango leaves above my door, I drew the line at installing the pots of holy Ganges water in the shrine-room and at wearing the yellow silk shawl or the wooden sandals – particularly at wearing the wooden sandals. It was not simply that they were very uncomfortable (there was a peg to be gripped between ones's great toe and its neighbour), or that it was generally the more orthodox Hindu renunciants who wore them. The black-maned, crimson-clad Bengali *tantrik* who lived at Eighth Mile sported a pair, creating a tremendous clatter with them as he walked up the road on market days, and I had no wish to resemble him in that or any other respect. Not that my reluctance to be Hinduized seemed to bother Miss Rao, if indeed she was aware of it at all (I sometimes thought that the Hinduization of Buddhist India had been as much the work of the Miss Raos of the time as of the Vedantic philosophers). She continued to inundate me with details of her financial difficulties, her brother's misbehaviour, and her differences with her landlady, and indeed to treat me as a combination of Roman Catholic father confessor and Hindu family priest. Thus it was that I had learned from her that autumn, when I was still living at The Hermitage, that her seventy-year-old mother was seriously ill. Would I mind going to see her?

Naturally I did not mind. During the next few weeks I went to see Mrs Rao a number of times, at first visiting her in the flat she and her daughter occupied in the High Street and then, her illness having taken a turn for the worse, in a private room at the Charteris Hospital, where she was attended by Dr Singh. Each time I saw her she seemed to have grown thinner and weaker, and her refined, aristocratic features – so different from those of poor Miss Rao – more transparent to the tiny flame that still flickered within. She made no complaint, her only anxiety being about her two children. But eventually even that anxiety received its quietus, and one morning, as I was about to have breakfast, I heard that Mrs Rao had died. I at once went to the hospital, where I consoled Miss Rao and her brother as best I could and gave instructions to the Nepalese Christian nurses about the laying out of the body. Returning to Craigside, I then sent Dawa up to Tirpai to inform the lamas of the Tharpa Chholing Gompa of Mrs Rao's death and invite four or five of them to take part in the funeral. Normally, funeral arrangements were made by the older male members of the deceased's family, or at least (in the case of Hindus) by his or her caste-fellows, and had Mrs Rao died in South India this is undoubtedly what would have happened. In Kalimpong the Raos had neither relations nor caste-fellows, so that had I not taken on the responsibility for making the necessary arrangements, as the distraught brother and sister both begged me to do, the old brahmin lady would probably not have had a proper funeral and her remains, in all likelihood, would have been unceremoniously disposed of by the hospital authorities.

As it was, at three o'clock that afternoon there issued from the hospital compound, where a small crowd had gathered to see Mrs Rao off on her last journey, a cortège consisting of a lorry and two or three other vehicles. In the back of the lorry with the coffin were Miss Rao's brother, the lamas in their red robes and yellow ceremonial headgear, and as many of our members and friends as were able to squeeze themselves in. Miss Rao had of course to be left behind, it not being the custom for women to be present at a cremation. She was in any case still hysterical with grief, and before we set out I asked Beena, the most good-natured of Sachin's three sisters, to look after her. From the hospital the little procession slowly made its way through the High Street down to Craigside, where the lamas and others were given tea, and then, rather less slowly, from Craigside down to the River Teesta. The cortège having halted a few hundred yards short of Teesta Bridge, the coffin was manhandled down the narrow, zigzag track that led from the road to a stretch of white sand lying within a bend of the river. Here a shallow trench was dug, a row of stones placed on either side of the trench, and wood from the nearby bazaar laid, in alternate lengthwise and crosswise layers, on top of the stones to a height of two or three feet. Mrs Rao's body was then taken out of its coffin and lowered on to the pyre, more layers of wood were added, kerosene was sprinkled, and finally Miss Rao's brother, as next of kin and chief mourner, thrusting a lighted torch in among the wood set the whole structure on fire.

Soon a ruddy blaze was illuminating the foreshore and the faces of the twelve or fifteen people who, in little groups, sat watching the flames leap up and the smoke billow forth. At first very little was said, but as time passed everyone relaxed, and there was a distinct change in the atmosphere. Voices again rang out, cups of tea appeared, and there was the occasional burst of laughter. Even Miss Rao's brother, who sat next to me, seemed to be affected by the general change of mood, At any rate, he now had a more cheerful look, and we exchanged a few commonplace remarks. I had not really met him before, though I had seen him once or twice, but I had heard a lot about him from Miss Rao, according to whom he was the worst of sons and brothers, a drunkard, a wastrel, and an inveterate frequenter of bad company. In appearance he was admittedly not very prepossessing, being as thin and black, though not as saucer-eyed, as the *pretas* or hungry ghosts I had once seen at the haunted ashram at Muvattupuzha. But he seemed inoffensive and well-meaning, and was evidently grateful for the help he had received in connection with his mother's funeral, and in any case I had always taken Miss Rao's denunciations of her sibling with a grain of salt.

By this time night had fallen, the stars had come out above the Darjeeling hills, and the pyre was beginning to burn low. There could hardly have been a more beautiful setting for a cremation, or one that was more appropriate, and I could understand the poetry of the old Indian custom of committing a body to the flames on the bank of a river, where the four elements to which it was being returned were all present in some of their sublimest forms. On the occasion of Mrs Rao's cremation we had all round us the steep, tree-clad slopes of the Himalayan foothills; between the foothills wound the river, glassily sliding down to join the Brahmaputra, and on the hither bank of the river stood the pyre, its last plumes of smoke slowly dissolving into the air. Even the fifth element, that of ether or space, was present, being represented by the dark blue inverted bowl of the sky, now 'thick inlaid with patines of bright gold'. As I watched, a shower of golden sparks flew up from the pyre, so that for a moment I was unable to tell which were the sparks and which the stars.

The following morning I arranged for Miss Rao to spend a couple of weeks at the Singh family's bungalow, where she would have the company of Sachin's mother and sisters. This, I thought, would be better for her than going back to the cheerless flat in Chung Building, where she would be on her own most of the time, it being unlikely that she would want to see much of her brother, though he did not seem to have the same animosity towards her that she had towards him. In the event Miss Rao stayed with the Singh family for more than a month, and the arrangement worked quite well, at least at the beginning. As she recovered from the shock of her mother's illness and death, however, some of the more bizarre features of her character and behaviour started reasserting themselves. In particular she made herself ridiculous by addressing Sheila, the oldest of Sachin's sisters, as *'Didi'* or 'Elder Sister', just as Meera and Beena did, even though that college-going young lady was little more than half her own age. What was worse, at least from my point of view, was that she managed to convince herself that her mother had on her deathbed entrusted the responsibility for looking after her to *me* and that I had accepted the responsibility. This was sheer fantasy, but it was a fantasy that gave her an excuse for visiting me several times a week, even several times a day, in order to consult me about even the most trivial matters. Eventually, Sachin's mother having warned me that the frequency of her visits to Craigside might give rise to misunderstanding on the part of 'uneducated people', I wrote and asked her not to come more than once or twice a month as I wanted to devote more time to the writing of the *Survey*. To her credit, she accepted the situation with a good grace and cut down on her visits, so that I was able to help and advise her, when she did come to see me, without laying myself open to the kind of misunderstanding to which Mrs Singh had referred.

Before all this happened I had, however, suffered the loss of the second member of my circle of friends and acquaintances to die during this period. Having just had breakfast, I was about to settle down to my morning's work on the *Survey* when Anand-ji came to tell me that Burma Raja had died the previous night. The news affected me much more deeply than the news of Mrs Rao's death had done. Burma Raja, as he was popularly known, was Prince K.M. Latthakin of Burma, the nephew and son-in-law of ex-King Thibaw. I had been his guest for six months before moving to The Hermitage. In fact he had come to my rescue at one of the most difficult and painful times in my life, when the choleric Newar monk in charge of the Dharmodaya Vihara was trying to oust me from my room there and I had nowhere else to go. He and the Princess had treated me with great kindness during my stay with them and Burma Raja himself had become, indeed, a good friend. After my removal to The Hermitage we still kept in touch. I went to see them from time to time, though less and less frequently, and very occasionally Burma Raja came to see me. For the last few months there had been no contact between us. I had not even known that Burma Raja was ill. The news of his death therefore came as quite a shock, and I at once set out for Panorama with Anand-ji.

During my stay with them Burma Raja and the Princess, together with their adopted son and their maidservant, had occupied the upper bungalow, or Panorama proper, and I had occupied the lower bungalow, or guest cottage, which stood on a lower level, in its own compound. Separating the two compounds there was a hedge, in which Burma Raja had made a hole so that he could come and see me – as he did nearly every morning – without having to go round to the front entrance. Since my last visit he and his little family evidently had shifted from the upper to the lower building. On our arrival Anand-ji and I found the Princess sitting out in the sun, in the little garden beside the guest cottage, smoking a cigar and having her long grey hair combed by the maidservant. She seemed quite unperturbed by Burma Raja's death, but was obviously glad to see me and indicated, in her quaint mixture of Hindi and Nepali, which sounded like gibberish to anyone who did not know her, that I would find Raja Sahib inside the cottage. Inside the cottage I indeed found him. I found him in the little room I had used as a bedroom. My old friend's face was so purple as to be almost black, his jaw had collapsed, and his wispy white hair, normally concealed beneath an imposing turban, lay scattered across the pillows. He looked as though he had died after a long and debilitating illness.

Within minutes I had dispatched notes to my lawyer friend Madan Kumar Pradhan, who was Vice-Chairman of the Municipality, and to the Second Officer of Kalimpong, informing them of Burma Raja's death and asking for their co-operation in making arrangements for his funeral. The Government of India had, I knew, inherited from its imperial predecessor a certain undefined responsibility for him and the Princess, and in fact paid them a modest monthly allowance, the Burmese Government having refused to pay them anything unless they returned to Burma, which Burma Raja steadfastly refused to do. He was safer in India, he declared. While I was writing my notes people started arriving, some of them with bunches of flowers and *khatas*, but it was not possible for them to pay their last respects as the body had not been laid out. After I had talked with Alaungyi, Burma Raja's adopted son, and with the maidservant, both of whom were evidently quite upset, I accompanied Anand-ji back to the Dharmodaya Vihara. On the way we met Madan Babu, who had received my note and was now hastening to Panorama. Money would have to be found for the funeral expenses, I told him, as according to Alaungyi the Princess was in debt, as she usually was, and there were only a few rupees at the bungalow. Madan Babu promised to see what he could do, and having left Anand-ji at the Dharmodaya Vihara I went home.

My lawyer friend was as good as his word. Soon after lunch, when I was typing an urgent letter to Devapriya-ji, he arrived at Craigside with the two thousand rupees he had drawn from the Kalimpong Treasury, as well as with Anand-ji, whom he had collected on the way, and the three of us set out for Panorama. By this time quite a number of people had gathered outside the guest cottage, as well as in the lane that led to the Panorama compound. Many of them were known to me, at least by sight, and now that money was available I asked some of these to help with preparations for the funeral. One of the first things to be done was to send to the Tharpa Chholing Gompa for four lamas. No sooner had the burly, red-robed figures clambered out of the jeep, however, than difficulties arose. The Princess, who so far had shown no interest in the proceedings, seemed to take a dislike to them and refused to allow them to touch Burma Raja's body, insisting that it should be prepared for cremation by me and only by me. Eventually Madan Babu and I succeeded in convincing her that it would be impossible for me to do what was required singlehanded, and she grudgingly allowed the lamas access to the body, on the strict understanding that I would remain in the room with them all the time and personally supervise everything they did. The Princess's reluctance was due not so much to the fact that the lamas were followers of Tibetan Buddhism, whereas she was a Theravadin, as to the fact that they were complete strangers and she was by nature suspicious almost to the point of paranoia.

Even with the help of four lamas the task of preparing Burma Raja's body for cremation was not an easy one. Nor was it a pleasant one. The old man could not have been properly cared for during the last few days of his life, and may even have died *before* the previous night. On removing the coverlet we found his sheets and nightshirt soaked in urine and faeces and stuck together in a solid mass that could not be separated from the body. Used as they were to such work, the four lamas were horrified by the sight, as I also was. There was no question of Burma Raja being laid out in the usual fashion. While Anand-ji remained in the background, looking very sick, we arranged the body as best we could, wrapped it, sheets and all, in the coverlet, and laid it in the coffin. The coffin was then loaded on to one of the waiting vehicles and the cortège – a rather more impressive one than had accompanied Mrs Rao's body – started moving up the lane and on to the road. As it left the Panorama compound Burma

Raja's maidservant burst into tears. The Princess, however, remained unconcerned. Or rather, she was concerned about only one thing. As Anand-ji and I were about to board the vehicle with the coffin, she drew me aside and hissed vehemently in my ear, 'Raja Sahib must be cremated with sandalwood logs. Nothing but sandalwood logs. Members of the Burmese royal family cannot be cremated with anything else.'

On the cortège's arrival at the Tibetan cremation ground at Tirpai the vehicle containing the coffin came to a halt, not near the stupa-like structure in which Miss Barclay had been cremated but in front of the iron bedstead, as it seemed to be, lying on which those of the nobler sex were cremated. It did not take long to build a pyre, plenty of wood being available from the stall inside the entrance. There was no question of our cremating Burma Raja with sandalwood logs, which would have cost a fortune, though one or two Marwaris had bought packets of sandalwood powder. When the pyre was complete Alaungyi set it alight, and Anand-ji and I chanted Pali *suttas* and other verses appropriate to the occasion. *Sic transit gloria mundi*, I thought, as I watched the flames leap up, except that Burma Raja had not experienced much *gloria* in his life, despite having been born into a royal family. But if he had not experienced much *gloria* neither had he experienced much hardship. Judging by the tenor of some of his remarks to me, the happiest time of his life had been the years before the war, when the Raj paid him and the Princess a generous monthly allowance (generous in comparison with what the Government of India subsequently paid them) and when he had been a leading figure in the social life of Kalimpong, taking part in everything from tennis parties to tiger hunts.

As the evening was growing cold, it being mid-January, I left early, without waiting for Burma Raja's funeral pyre to burn itself out, and having had a hot drink at Sachin's place made my way back to Craigside. Ani-la was chanting in the shrine-room. When she came out I talked to her for a while, then finished typing my letter to Devapriya-ji and attended to *Maha Bodhi Journal* work until it was time to go to bed.

A few days later came offerings from the Princess. Obviously I should go to see her; but I was busy, and kept putting the visit off, until one day I heard that she had left the Panorama guest cottage, together with Alaungyi and the maidservant, and gone to stay in an outlying village. She was living in a hut, and subsisting on greens from the garden. Though I made extensive enquiries, no one could tell me the name of the village or in which direction it lay, and I had no further news of her until I learned that she had moved to Calcutta. She was living with her sister, and

Alaungyi was working in the Burmese consulate as a clerk. Though I never saw her again, this was not the end of my connection with the strange old woman. Two years later I found myself standing inside the very 'hut' in which she had spent her last days in Kalimpong, and the building thereafter came to occupy an important place in my life.

Chapter Fourteen

THE UNACCEPTABLE FACE OF COMMUNISM

WHEN I WENT FORTH FROM HOME into the homeless life, on 18 August 1947, it was with the intention of renouncing the world in the fullest and most literal sense. For me *pravrajya* or 'going forth' meant giving up family ties, social position, and national and racial identity, as well as mundane interests and activities of every kind. It meant giving up pleasure and possessions, and whatever else might serve to aggrandize the ego or enhance the sense of separative selfhood. The only thing from which I did not go forth that day – not because I refused to go forth from it but because the idea of so doing did not occur to me – was my mother tongue, English, to which I was in fact (unconsciously) quite attached. Since then it had been borne in upon me that it was less easy to achieve a full and literal renunciation of the world than I, in my youthful enthusiasm, had imagined, and that the reasons for this were not merely subjective but also solidly objective. Because I had no identity papers and refused to declare my nationality, saying that as a renunciant I had none, I had not been allowed to enter Buddhist Ceylon, and because I had no money, as I was trying to observe the precept of not handling gold and silver, I had been refused ordination by the time-serving Theravadin monks of Sarnath. Eventually I had been obliged to make concessions. In Kalimpong I admitted to being English, though without going into details, and not only handled gold and silver, in the form of specie and bank-notes, but engaged in at least some of the transactions of which this was an inseparable part.

But concessions were one thing, abandonment of principle quite another. Believing as I did that 'going forth' was of the essence of the spiritual life, I tried not to think of myself as an Englishman, did my best not to utilize whatever money came my way for the gratification of personal desires, and abstained as much as I could from mundane interests and activities. Thus I abstained from reading newspapers and from discussing politics, though at times it was difficult for me to stop my ears against Joe's violent denunciation of all the works and ways of Prime Minister Winston Churchill and President Dwight Eisenhower or even to refrain from questioning some of his wilder assertions. Largely because I did not read the newspapers I had little sense of what was going on in the wider world, or even in India. I lived for meditation and study, for my students, and for the work for the good of Buddhism that my teacher Kashyap-ji, before his departure from Kalimpong, had enjoined upon me. Nevertheless I was vaguely aware of vast events looming on the horizon. I was aware that in the West World War II had been succeeded by the Cold War between the Soviet Union and Eastern Europe on the one hand and the United States and Western Europe on the other, and that in the East Tibet had been occupied by the forces of Communist China and its religion and culture ruthlessly suppressed. I was aware that the aim of Marxian Communism was world domination.

Unlike many others of my generation I had no sympathy with Communism, either as a philosophy or as a programme for social change, and no sympathy with its adherents as such. Why this should have been so I find it difficult to say. My lack of sympathy was instinctive rather than being the reasoned result of study and reflection. It was as though I sensed in Communism a threat to everything I held most dear, whether in the realm of ideas, the field of poetry and the fine arts, or the domain of ethics and spiritual life. Communism was the negation of truth, of beauty, of goodness. Not that I knew very much about Marxian Communism, factually speaking. As a fifteen-year-old evacuee in Barnstaple, during the war, I had read *Das Kapital*. Why I read it I do not know, except that in those days I read everything on which I could lay my hands, but for me there was no Marxist equivalent of a 'road to Damascus' experience and I was not converted to the faith. A year or two later, having returned home towards the end of the Blitz, I discovered a left-wing bookshop near Tooting Broadway (probably it was the only bookshop in the whole of south-west London) and after a certain amount of hesitation bought and read Lenin's *The State and Revolution*, which was more interesting than *Das Kapital* as well as being much shorter. At about the same time one of my colleagues at County Hall, where I was working, lent me a copy of David Guest's *Dialectical Materialism*. This colleague was himself a Communist, but if he had expected David Guest to succeed where Marx and Lenin had failed he was disappointed and I remained unconverted. When I returned the book to him it was with the remark that in my opinion it was not Hegel (in whom I was then deep) who was standing on his head, as the author alleged, but Marx, it being axiomatic for Marxist thought that Marx had found Hegel upside-down and had restored him to his feet, that is, had given his idealism a materialist interpretation. Not long afterwards my colleague received his calling-up papers and our discussions came to an end. Before the time came for my own induction into the armed forces he was back in the department and doing his old job – minus both legs and on crutches.

The war was inflicting its terrible casualties, in both Europe and the Far East, and on service personnel and civilians alike. During those days I *did* read the newspapers, as well as listen to the wireless (as many people still called the radio), and though the full horror of what was happening was sometimes concealed from us we were aware that what was happening was dreadful beyond imagination. In particular we were aware, in the winter of 1942–43, of the long-drawn-out battle for Stalingrad and of the sufferings of the Russian people as they endured, then resisted, and finally routed, the forces of invading Nazi Germany. With others in Britain I rejoiced at their victory and mourned their great losses, nor could I hear the soulful, not to say sentimental, popular ballad 'Russian Rose' (as I think it was called), with its promise of new life for the heroic Russian people, without the tears coming into my eyes and a lump rising in my throat. It was the Russian people who were victorious, not the Communists. Russia was not Trotsky and Lenin, Stalin and Beria. Russia was Pushkin, Lermontov, Gogol, Turgenev, Chekhov, Tolstoy, and Dostoevsky. In the very month that I had read *Das Kapital* I had also read *The Brothers Karamazov*, and there is no doubt which of them had made the deeper impression on me.

It was the same in the case of China. To me it was not the Chinese people who had invaded Tibet so much as the Chinese Red Army. China was not Mao Tse-tung and the *Little Red Book*. China was Confucius and Lao-tzu, Wei Lang and Chi-i, Li T'ai-po and Tu Fu, as well as the great painters of landscapes and of flowers. I therefore felt for China and the Chinese people the same love that I felt for Russia and the Russian people, so that when, towards the end of February, the two young Nepalese organizers came with an invitation to speak at the inaugural meeting of the Kalimpong branch of the Indo-Chinese Friendship Society I was happy to accept, the more especially as the meeting was to be held under the presidentship of Anand-ji. Not that I accepted without having ascertained the exact nature of the gathering. Relations between democratic India and totalitarian China were then at their most cordial; on all sides the mantra *Hindi-Chini Bhai Bhai,* or 'Indians and Chinese are Brothers', could be heard. In these circumstances it was unlikely that a body whose objective was the promotion of friendship between the two Asian giants would not have at least a quasi-political agenda, and neither as a Buddhist monk nor as a foreign national residing in a sensitive border area did I wish to get involved in politics. I could take part in the meeting, I therefore informed the two young men, only if it was completely non-political. This would certainly be the case, they both hastened to assure me: the meeting was to be a purely cultural affair, without the least trace of politics; and Anand-ji, when I met him a few days later, gave me a similar assurance.

The afternoon of the first Sunday in March accordingly saw me leaving Craigside for the Town Hall soon after lunch. I did not really need to leave so early, but knowing Anand-ji's dilatory, dawdling ways it was my intention to call for him *en route* and make sure he was not late for the meeting. On entering the upstairs room he occupied at the Dharmodaya Vihara I found he was not alone. With him was Arun Karki, one of the young men who had invited me to speak at the inaugural meeting. This in itself was not surprising. What was surprising was that the two of them were engaged in finalizing the wording of some three dozen resolutions and that these resolutions, which were to be passed at the meeting, were each and every one of them strongly condemnatory of the policies and actions of the United States in this or that part of the world. Under cross-examination Arun Karki eventually admitted that the real purpose of the inaugural meeting was political, and that the Indo-Chinese Friendship Society was in fact a political organization, whereupon I told him that it would be impossible for me to attend. Anand-ji did his honeyed best to persuade me to change my mind, but I was not to be moved by his specious pleadings, and having reminded them that the meeting was at two o'clock and that they had five minutes in which to get to the Town Hall I left the building and made my way back to Craigside.

As I walked down the road I experienced a variety of emotions. I was annoyed that the young organizers should have attempted to gain my support for their society by deliberately misleading me as to its true nature, and annoyed that Anand-ji should (apparently) have seconded them in the attempt. At the same time I was relieved that their machinations had not succeeded, for had I spoken at the meeting (no doubt *before* the resolutions were read out) I would have been placed in a very awkward, indeed a quite false, position. To have supported the resolutions, if only by my silence, would have given the impression that I was anti-American and pro-Communist, while to have objected to them would have given the impression that I was pro-American and anti-Communist. In either case I would have become involved in politics, or at least have appeared to have become involved in them, which in a place like Kalimpong amounted to much the same thing.

My predominant emotion, however, as I made my way back to Craigside that afternoon, was one of satisfaction, almost of elation. I was glad I had not yielded to Anand-ji's pleas not to leave him in the lurch, or accepted his absurd suggestion that, as a compromise, I should sit with him on the platform but not actually speak. The knowledge that I had done what I believed to be right, regardless of possible untoward consequences, indeed had the effect of giving me an increased sense of energy and purpose. It was as though my refusal to take part in the inaugural meeting, after discovering its true nature, constituted an affirmation of my status as a moral agent and of the fact that in the last analysis, and irrespective of circumstances, the responsibility for my life and actions was mine and mine alone.

What explanation Anand-ji gave for my absence from the meeting I never really knew. According to one account he said I was unwell. According to another he joked about my having changed my mind at the last minute for unexplained reasons no doubt connected with the poetic temperament. Whatever he may have said, the fact that I had not attended the meeting was the subject of a good deal of comment and speculation in the town, especially as I had been billed as the principal speaker. So much was this the case that I decided, a few days afterwards, to make my position clear. What better way was there of doing this than through the medium of the local press? The press existed, after all, to keep its readers informed about matters of public interest. I accordingly wrote a letter to the *Himalayan Times*, the town's English-language weekly newspaper, describing exactly what had happened, and dispatched it to the editor with a covering note requesting him to publish it as soon as possible. He did not publish it, either that week or any other. If my experience with the Indo-Chinese Friendship Society gave me a glimpse of the unacceptable face of Communism (not that there was necessarily an acceptable face behind the unacceptable one), then my experience with the *Himalayan Times* gave me a glimpse of the unacceptable face of the press. As was to be increasingly borne in upon me in the years to come, newspapers and magazines, no less than Communist front organizations, had their own agendas, and the dissemination of truth did not always feature among them. Perhaps it was a measure of the extent to which I had 'gone forth' from the world and its ways – a measure of my ignorance of *real life*, Joe would have said – that it had not occurred to me that the organizers of a public meeting might want to mislead and deceive me or that the editor of a local newspaper might be unwilling to give space to a statement of the facts on a matter of public interest, especially when that statement clarified a confusion.

My refusal to speak at the inaugural meeting of the Indo-Chinese Friendship Society, or even to support Anand-ji with my silent presence on the platform, made no difference to my relations with my opportunistic elder brother in the Order, as I knew would be the case. There was little that he did not regard with good-humoured cynicism, least of all the objections and reservations of his eccentric, over-idealistic young friend who, he was convinced (to the extent that he could be convinced of anything), was inclined to take his Buddhism far too seriously and to be much too rigid in his attitude towards such things as bending the truth a little in the interests of a good cause. A glimpse of just how cynical Anand-ji really was had been vouchsafed me only a few weeks earlier. Happening to call at Craigside one morning, and having entered my room without my noticing, he had looked over my shoulder to see what I was writing. I must have been working on the *Survey*, for I had written, that very moment, something about ethics, meditation, and wisdom being the means to the realization of nirvana. 'Why are you wasting your time on that old-fashioned stuff?' a sneering, contemptuous voice behind me wanted to know. The unfeeling words pierced me to the quick. It was as though Mara himself had released a poisoned arrow from his bow. However, out of respect for Anand-ji's seniority I made no attempt to justify myself, and welcomed the unexpected visitor in my usual fashion.

His characterization of ethics, meditation, and wisdom – the three great stages of the Buddhist spiritual path – as old-fashioned was no momentary aberration. For him 'old-fashioned' meant 'not to be taken seriously', even as 'new', 'modern', 'up-to-date', and 'advanced' meant 'to be taken seriously' – though not *too* seriously. As I already knew, Anand-ji was at least as much a progressivist as he was a Buddhist. Or rather, he was a Buddhist only to the extent that Buddhism could be seen as 'progressive', that is, seen as a rationalistic, scientific, and iconoclastic system that was in keeping with the times and in line with the latest contemporary thought. It was thus possible for him to give his support to a Communist front organization, and even to help draft anti-American resolutions, without feeling that this was in any way incompatible with his role as a Buddhist monk. At the same time, he was not so very much a Communist as to want actually to identify himself with Communism, or to risk a breach with me on its account. For my own part, I considered it no business of mine to correct one who had spent more than twenty years in the robes, and in any case, Anand-ji always treated me with so much friendliness, and evaded my attempts to draw him into serious discussion with such an engaging mixture of adroitness and good humour, that notwithstanding our differences of temperament and outlook I found it impossible to quarrel with him or even to get him to acknowledge any real divergence of opinion between us. Our first meeting after the Sunday afternoon debacle therefore passed off quite amicably. Anand-ji asked me to help him edit *Lumbini*, an English-language magazine devoted to the Buddha's birthplace that Gyan Jyoti wanted to bring out, and I agreed to do so. We also discussed, on this and several other occasions that month, his and Gyan Jyoti's plans for an evening college at the Dharmodaya Vihara. Most of these discussions took place in Anand-ji's room. He was usually writing when I called, but occasionally I found him talking with a visitor or two, and an exchange that took place between him and a Newar devotee served to open my eyes to another side of his character, though without making it any easier for me to comprehend him.

In the vicinity of Tenth Mile, behind a row of open-fronted shops, stood half a dozen tumbledown wooden shacks. I knew these shacks well, having included them in my alms-round in my early days in Kalimpong, when first with Kashyap-ji, then on my own, I had followed the time-honoured practice of relying for my one meal of the day on my begging-bowl. They were inhabited by poor but devout Newars, and it was between Anand-ji and one of these good folk, the supporter of a wife and five or six children, that the exchange in question took place. Cap clasped respectfully to his chest with both hands, the Newar, a grey-haired, shabbily dressed man of about forty, was kneeling in front of Anand-ji and regarding him with an expression of intense devotion. My elder brother in the Order, for his part, sat on the edge of his bed and appeared to be contemplating one of his sandals, which was broken. For a while nothing was said. Anand-ji then mused, as though speaking to himself, 'Well, it's broken. I won't be able to wear *these* sandals again.... But how will a poor bhikkhu like me get a new pair, I wonder?' Whereupon the fish swallowed the bait. 'I'll get you a new pair, Bhante, if you permit me,' breathed the devotee, his eyes shining. But Anand-ji was too experienced an angler to pull on the line straight away. 'Well,' he sighed, 'it would be nice if somebody bought me a pair. Otherwise ...' This was permission enough for his interlocutor who, having made a triple prostration, left for the bazaar, returning half an hour later with a pair of sandals which he then presented, with another triple prostration, to a smiling Anand-ji. I was shocked. The sandals must have cost twelve rupees, and the Newar, a silversmith who was nearly always out of work, did not make more than forty-five or fifty rupees a month, whereas Anand-ji received a pension of two hundred and fifty rupees a month from the Association for the Advancement of the National Language, whose General Secretary he had been for many years. Having glimpsed the unacceptable face of Communism, and the unacceptable face of the press, was I now being vouchsafed a glimpse of the unacceptable face of Theravadin monasticism? But while shocked, again out of respect for Anand-ji's seniority I said nothing, though I wondered for how much longer I would be able to remain silent. Anand-ji was not only a Buddhist. He was also a progressivist, and as such highly critical of any exploitation of the poor by the rich. Did he not realize that by representing himself as a poor bhikkhu who did not know where his next pair of sandals was coming from he was guilty of falsehood and guilty of taking advantage, moreover, of the faith of a poverty-stricken Buddhist layman? I myself, knowing the straitened circumstances of the Newar and his family, did not even accept their invitations to bhojana-danas or ceremonial food-offerings, which I somehow managed to do without hurting their feelings. Yet here was the comparatively wealthy Anand-ji angling for a pair of sandals which, as he must have known, the donor could ill afford to give him. Had he, then, no heart, either as a Buddhist or as a progressivist?

But if I said nothing about the incident to Anand-ji, I could not help unburdening myself to Naginda, who knew his preceptor a good deal better than I did. The young ex-Untouchable had long since got over his resentment at the undue strictness, as he saw it, with which I treated him, and since his ordination had been to see me a number of times, usually in order to borrow money. Anand-ji was not exactly tightfisted, he explained. It was not that he bought nothing that he could get another to buy for him, or that he never spent money on anyone. But his generosity was certainly selective. If you were one of his favourites, as Sumedha was, he could be very generous, but if you were not a member of that select band, as he himself was not, you got little or nothing. That was why he was always coming to me for money, Naginda added with a laugh. Anand-ji must have allowed the Newar to buy him the sandals so that he would have more money to spend on Sumedha, Gunakar, and Co., the second of whom, who was studying in Darjeeling, as I well knew, was costing Anand-ji quite a bit in college fees and pocket money. All the same, he agreed, it was wrong of his preceptor to have manoeuvred the Newar into buying the sandals for him, especially when he had two thousand rupees in his account with the Kalimpong branch of the Central Bank. How did he know this? Anand-ji had sent him to collect his pass book and on the way back to the vihara he had taken a peep inside and seen the amount.

Though Naginda's disclosure made Anand-ji's exchange with the Newar devotee seem even more shocking, I was as far as ever from comprehending my many-sided elder brother in the Order. No doubt he was deceitful and manipulative, besides being a thorough cynic, and no doubt he did not scruple to exploit those who were less astute, or more principled, than he was himself. Yet he also possessed many admirable qualities. He was good-tempered, approachable, and without a trace of the arrogance and self-importance that characterized so many Theravadin bhikkhus. Moreover, he lived simply, without caring for fine robes or rich repasts, and he did not eat in the evening – though he always took a glass of hot milk before going to bed, which strictly speaking was against the Vinaya. Like me, but unlike the vast majority of our yellow-robed brethren in Ceylon, Burma, and Thailand, he was a vegetarian, probably as much because of early cultural conditioning (he had been born into a brahmin family) as out of religious conviction. A 'progressive' journalist rather than a writer on Buddhism, he had contributed to the revival of Buddhism in India by translating the *Anguttara-Nikaya* or 'Book of the Numerical Sayings' into Hindi and was now engaged in translating the entire Jataka Book.

Thus Bhadant Anand Kausalyayan, politician, Buddhist monk, journalist, and translator, champion of the national language and scourge of Hindu reactionaries, was a complex figure, and as such difficult of comprehension. Though he once had told me it was his ambition to be known as the Voltaire of India, there seemed to be no master principle, no dominant theme, no overriding motive – no *jiban-debata*, or 'life-god', in Tagore's language – which could be regarded as reconciling the different, even contradictory, sides of his character, and giving unity of purpose to his various activities. He was certainly not aiming at the attainment of Enlightenment in this life, but neither was he wholly bent on professional success, whether political, journalistic, or even religious. There were occasions when I thought he did not really believe in anything, and simply wanted to pass the time in as amusing a fashion as possible, even if this meant his having to stir up a hornet's nest or two.

Because I found Anand-ji difficult to comprehend I was not always sure how I should conduct myself towards him. I could hardly treat him as my monastic superior in the real sense, with all that this involved in the way of receptivity on my part and responsibility on his. Indeed, it was not always easy for me to regard him as a Buddhist. At the same time, there was no question of my being able to treat him simply as a politician or a 'progressive' journalist, or even as an ordinary fellow monk. I therefore compromised, outwardly showing him all the formal respect and deference due to a senior member of the Order, but inwardly keeping my thoughts to myself, except when circumstances obliged me to reveal them by my actions, as had been the case that Sunday afternoon at the Dharmodaya Vihara when I had glimpsed the unacceptable face of Communism.

Chapter Fifteen

A Life in the Day of the English Monk

Ani-la, otherwise known as the French Nun, had received her shramaneri ordination from Dhardo Rimpoche in May the previous year. News of the event was not long in reaching the ears of the three elderly ladies who ran Les Amis du Bouddhisme, the Gallic counterpart of Christmas Humphreys's London Buddhist Society, for soon afterwards I received a letter from G. Constant Lounsbery, the American-born president, asking me for what was, in effect, a progress report on the former Dominique Delannoy. Miss Lounsbery was clearly troubled. She was troubled by Ani-la's periodic changes of tack, from Sanskrit to Indian Archaeology, from Indian Archaeology to Vedanta, and from Vedanta to Tibetan Buddhism and the Madhyamika, and troubled above all by her recent ordination. What would happen, it seemed she was wondering, if the tempestuous nun were to return to France? What would be her position vis-à-vis Les Amis du Bouddhisme and what effect would her presence have on the tiny French Buddhist movement? I did my best to reassure my correspondent. Since her ordination Ani-la had definitely been more settled, I wrote, and in her red Tibetan robes, with shaved head, she was now a calm and dignified figure.

Unfortunately she did not stay settled for long, and more often than not she was neither calm nor dignified. Perhaps her most serious lapse from grace was when, some months after her ordination, she became so enraged with the driver of a Landrover who had let her down that she struck him a blow in the face with her fist, knocking out two or three of his teeth and causing the blood to flow. The incident occurred in Darjeeling, where she was then staying. She was of course overwhelmed with shame and remorse and wrote me a penitent letter the same day. While admitting that she had lost all self-control she at the same time pleaded extenuating circumstances and begged me to be careful how I treated her (this was a constant theme of hers), as in her present state she was sensitive to rejection and capable of killing herself for a trifle. If Dhardo Rimpoche and I were as clever as her (Catholic) Christian director had been, she concluded, we would 'make a docile sheep of this savage masculine compressed nature'. Dhardo Rimpoche certainly never succeeded in reducing Ani-la to a state of ovine docility, and I was able to do little better. For all her theatrical self-abasement and protestations of humility and submissiveness, neither before nor after her encounter with the Landrover driver (to whom she made amends with an apology and a tin of fifty cigarettes) was she really amenable to control or discipline – not even when performing the little penances which, at her insistence, I imposed on her from time to time. It was as though she was willing to be directed, but only on condition that she could tell the director exactly how he was to direct her. Perhaps the cleverness of her Christian director had consisted in his allowing her to think he was directing her in the way she wished to be directed when in reality he was doing no such thing. Be that as it may, the fact that I had been firm with her over the incident of the rug, which took place three or four weeks after her assault on the driver, and had not allowed her to have her own way, certainly did not mean that she had become more manageable or less liable to outbursts of temper or fits of sullen uncommunicativeness. Before long there was a crisis. The immediate cause was some remarks she made in front of Sachin and Miss Rao. The remarks were so unkind and so sarcastic, and showed her to be in such a state of rebellion against everything to which she was supposedly committed as a Buddhist and a nun that I at once wrote and handed to her a severe letter about her spiritual condition, it being customary between us to communicate in this fashion when we had anything of importance to say, as Ani-la felt she was at a disadvantage when it came to communicating orally in a language not her own. The letter had the effect of reducing her to a truly dreadful state of despair and self-accusation, and I was obliged to spend more than an hour dealing with the emotional frustration that underlay the unkindness and sarcasm of her remarks and restoring her to something like normality. Sachin and I then walked up the road with her as far as his house (Miss Rao had already left), from where a subdued French nun continued her journey up the hill back to Tirpai alone.

All's well that ends well, even if it is well only for the time being. As a result of Ani-la's crisis I took the initiative and consulted with Dhardo Rimpoche and Lobsang Phuntsok about what could be done to help her. This time our consultations bore fruit. Ani-la obviously needed help with her Tibetan studies and in her spiritual life, as well as needing, perhaps, more structured conditions under which to pursue both the one and the other. With the Rimpoche's approval, Lobsang undertook to give her Tibetan lessons four or five times a week. He would give them at Craigside, where she came practically every day, and where he himself had in any case started coming of an afternoon in connection with the article on Tibetan Buddhism he was writing and I revising. For my part, I undertook to conduct for Ani-la's especial benefit a regular evening session of puja, readings from the scriptures, and meditation. These arrangements, we hoped, would enable our unruly French nun to do greater justice to her vocation and to be more at peace with herself. When the plan was communicated to her, the object of our consultations responded, initially, with gratitude and enthusiasm, and Lobsang and I lost no time putting it into operation. For me this meant a few changes in my existing routine, but I did not mind. Though there were times when Ani-la's irrational behaviour exasperated me, I knew her sufferings were none the less real for being largely self-inflicted, and therefore sympathized with her and was glad to be doing something to help. She was a strange woman, I reflected, as I looked out suitable readings for the first of our evening sessions. What did she really want (Freud's famous question with regard to all women!) and just why did she sometimes become so very upset? It was to be hoped that as she developed, under the influence of the new arrangements, into a better and happier person, answers to these questions would be forthcoming. Meanwhile, the concluding words of her letter provided me with a clue to at least part of her nature, and I would do well to bear them in mind in my future dealings with her, including those that were to be conducted, in the case of our evening sessions, in a formally religious context and with the sanction of her official guru.

Savage, masculine, and compressed were the terms she had used to characterize that nature of hers, and no doubt she knew herself well enough for them to be of significance. She was certainly *savage* in the (dictionary) sense of being 'wild; untamed', at times 'ferocious in temper', and in certain respects 'crude', though not – paradoxically – 'uncivilized'. Notwithstanding my having described her, to Miss Lounsbery, shortly after her ordination, as being a calm and dignified figure, her overall appearance tended to be expressive of the more savage side of her nature. A common friend, a cultivated European woman, was years later to aver that Ani-la had the physique of a French peasant and looked as though she had been made to do heavy farm work and produce lots of babies. Of medium height, and sturdily built, she had a red bulldog face that was capable of turning scarlet with indignation, rage, or sardonic mirth, and from which there looked out two blue-grey eyes that either blazed or glittered. Possessing as she did a peasant-like physique, it was not surprising that she should have been at home with animals. More than once, at the Gandhamadan Vihara in Darjeeling, I had found her sitting on the floor amidst her pots and pans surrounded by stray dogs and cats she had taken in and whom she allowed to push their noses into the very plate from which she was eating. Every now and then she would suddenly catch up one of the cats and press it to her capacious bosom, at the same time smothering it with kisses and squeezing it so tightly that the wretched creature struggled to escape. Brisk and decisive in her movements, except when overcome by feelings of despondency or despair, she was always 'on the go' and had a positive mania for rearranging things.

Masculine was for her more or less synonymous with 'intellectual', and having as she did a high opinion of intellect she naturally entertained a low opinion of women, whom she considered insufficiently endowed with that faculty. Members of her own sex, with few exceptions, she in fact regarded almost with contempt and thought talking to them a waste of time. Whether or not she was 'masculine' in the more accepted sense of the term (and certainly she had a few hairs on her chin) there was little doubt that hers was a highly intellectual nature. A former professor of Philosophy and Literature, she had become a Buddhist for reasons that were metaphysical rather than religious in the narrower, more emotional sense of the term. Disillusioned with Catholic theology and mysticism, as well as with the Advaita Vedanta, she had found in Buddhism alone, especially as represented by the Madhyamika of Nagarjuna, the non-substantialism she had come to regard as constituting the true doctrine of liberation. My own reasons for becoming a Buddhist were less clear-cut, and less metaphysical. Nevertheless the exigent Frenchwoman and I had a lot in common intellectually, and I always enjoyed our discussions, at least when they related to Buddhism. She enjoyed them too, when she was in the right mood and not preoccupied with her personal difficulties. Once she went so far as to declare that with the possible exception of Dr Roerich (who was in her bad books, having refused to teach her Tibetan) I was the only person in Kalimpong who was her intellectual equal and the only person, therefore, with whom she could have a worthwhile exchange of ideas. As Kalimpong was a small place, this was not really much of a compliment. With her high, sometimes impossibly high, intellectual and academic standards, Ani-la naturally was an extremely critical person and very difficult to please. When she *was* pleased, however, she could praise lavishly, even excessively, her favourite term of approbation being 'formidable'. Thus Dr A.C. Banerjee, with whom she had studied in Calcutta, was a formidable Sanskrit scholar and Paul Mus's magnum opus *Borobudur*, a formidable study of Indian Buddhism.

Probably it was to the lack of opportunities for intellectual exchange, among other things, that Ani-la was referring when she characterized her nature as *compressed*. It was compressed in the sense that her intellectual and emotional energies were squeezed into a space that was much too small for them. They had no proper outlet, no adequate means of expression. Hence she felt frustrated, dissatisfied, restless. She was even 'compressed' linguistically, in that her command of English, let alone Hindi or Tibetan, did not allow her to express her thoughts and feelings as fully or as freely as she would have liked. It was noticeable that her spirits soared when she had someone to talk to in her own language, even if it was only Aryadeva, the Darjeeling-based French samanera, of whose mental capacities she did not have a high opinion. An intensely patriotic person, with a strong feeling for the French language and French culture, she evidently was no less ill at ease outside her native milieu than was the fish in the *Dhammapada* simile out of its watery home. Sometimes I thought that her real ambition was to spend half a lifetime working on a truly stupendous piece of original Indological research and then, when it was finished, return in triumph to her own country. Having delivered before the Academy or the Sorbonne a formidably brilliant allocution on the extent and significance of her discoveries she would declare, amid tumultuous applause, that her humble efforts had all been for the glory of France.

This, then, was the person for whose benefit I had undertaken to conduct a regular evening session of puja, readings from the scriptures, and meditation, and for whom I was having, therefore, to make a few changes in my existing routine. Once those changes had been made, and the evening session incorporated into the structure of my day, the new routine remained virtually unchanged for several months, until my departure for Calcutta towards the end of March. So little did it change during this period, and so much was each day like every other, that to describe one day was to describe them all. In fact to describe one day was to describe my life at that time, so that a visiting journalist could well have written not of a day in the life of the English monk, or Imji Gelong as the Tibetans called me, but of a life in his day.

That day began before dawn, as people's day usually did in India. After a cup of tea I performed puja in the shrine-room, reciting (in Pali) the Salutation to the Three Jewels, the verses for offering flowers, incense, and lighted lamps or candles, and verses invoking the blessings of the *devas* or shining ones. Sometimes I also recited such texts as the *Mangala* or 'Auspicious Signs' *Sutta* and the *Ratana* or 'Jewel' *Sutta*. All this took ten or fifteen minutes, after which I meditated for an hour, concentrating my mind by means of the *anapana-sati* or 'respiration-mindfulness' practice, and becoming absorbed, on some days at least, in the lower *dhyanas* or superconscious states. After puja and meditation came breakfast, which consisted of tea and buttered toast (without jam) and for which I was joined by Sachin. Examination time was approaching, and my young friend was staying with me so that he could revise subjects in which he was weak without being disturbed by siblings or visiting friends. On some days I helped him, after breakfast, with his revision. Otherwise I was at my writing table by eight o'clock, or earlier, and there remained, with Dr Hudson's rug beneath my feet, until it was time for lunch. Usually I wrote three or four foolscap pages, occasionally two or even only one. Besides the actual business of writing, there were quotations to be selected and references checked. At my request Marco Pallis had sent me, from London, several dozen volumes of important texts and studies that I did not have in my own small library, and which were indispensable. Thus for three or four hours I was totally immersed in the serene, radiant, and majestic world of the Dharma, or perhaps I should say 'of the Doctrine' (as distinct from the Method), for had I not also been immersed in that world, in a different kind of way, when performing puja and meditating?

Lunch was at twelve o'clock or even later. Strictly speaking, as a bhikkhu I was supposed to finish eating by noon, but for the last year or so I had been observing the *vikala-bhojana* or 'untimely meals' rule in the spirit rather than in the letter. Not that I thought the letter unimportant or that I was in the least disposed to disregard it completely. Spirit and letter were closely connected, the latter being ideally an expression of the former and its observance, therefore, a means to the observance of the former. I had been shocked and disgusted, however, by the extreme formalism of many Theravadin bhikkhus, whose strict observance of the letter of the *vikala-bhojana* rule was accompanied by a total disregard of its spirit, and had no wish to risk becoming one of that company. For me the principle behind the rule was *moderation in eating*, and there was no necessary connection between this and the particular hour at which one ate. Lunch was therefore at twelve o'clock or even later and for this meal, too, I was joined by Sachin. Our simple rice and vegetable curry repast was prepared and served by my new cook-bearer Padam Bahadur, a cheerful, competent thirty-year-old who at times struck me as being a Nepalese version of Sam Weller, Mr Pickwick's quick-witted Cockney servant.

After lunch I gave Aniruddha and his companion Luparatna, Gyan Jyoti's cashier, a lesson in English grammar and composition. I had taught the Newar monk before, when his companion had been the hedonistic Mr Bhumiveda, and now that he was again back in Kalimpong he was continuing his studies with me. By this time relations between us were quite cordial, despite their having got off to such an unpropitious start five years earlier, and I had the impression that he had a better opinion of me than he had of Anand-ji, for some of whose ways he at times expressed strong disapproval. Aniruddha and Luparatna having departed, it was time for me to teach Durga and his school friend Mitra Kumar, a strapping young Hindu Newar whose family ran an orchid-growing business down at Seventh Mile. Sometimes I taught them Geography and Indian Administration, sometimes Civics and English Poetry. Occasionally they were joined by Lalit Shamsher, another of Durga's friends, who was also Mitra's cousin. The rest of the afternoon was spent writing letters, or editing the *Maha Bodhi Journal* (including writing the editorial and Himavantavasi's column), and making up accounts.

At half-past five or six o'clock I took my place in the shrine-room, Ani-la sitting opposite me on the other side of the image table. She had arrived an hour or two earlier, and Lobsang had given her a Tibetan lesson while I was occupied with my students. After we had performed puja (the same Pali puja that I performed in the morning) I read aloud a lengthy extract from a Theravadin or Mahayana canonical text, the idea being that we should listen as receptively as possible and allow every syllable of the *Buddhavachana* or Word of the Buddha (as these texts were, according to tradition) to sink into the depths of our consciousness. This was the first time I had experimented with reading (as distinct from chanting) the Buddhist scriptures in a liturgical context, and I soon discovered it to be a highly effective spiritual practice. A 'reading from the scriptures' always formed part of our full moon day pujas, but as people's attention span was limited the text chosen was short and the impression it produced therefore correspondingly slight. From receptive listening to the Buddhavachana the transition to meditation was an easy and natural one. At least it was comparatively easy and natural for me. For Ani-la meditation was the least enjoyable part of the evening. Though not unused to the cross-legged posture, she was extremely restless, and could not sit still even for a minute. What kind of mental state she was in at such times I did not like to think. None the less I gave her further instruction in the 'respiration-mindfulness' practice, and did my best to clear up her various doubts and difficulties, though I took good care to do this only after we had finished meditating. Had I attempted to clear them up before we started we probably would not have got started at all, for Ani-la's doubts and difficulties were hydra-headed, and no sooner was one cleared up than two more appeared in its place.

That I found the transition from receptive listening to the Buddhavachana to meditation easy and natural did not mean that I necessarily found meditation itself easy. Though I had been meditating, fairly regularly, for seven or eight years, I still had to cope with wandering thoughts, with negative emotions, and, sometimes, with the sheer disinclination to sit down on the folded towel that served me as an *asana*, to close my eyes, to watch my breath, and to calm and concentrate my mind. There were even periods of complete dryness, when for days on end I would be unable to concentrate properly and when Mara whispered in my ear that nature had not meant me for a yogi and I had better stick to books. Yet there also came, every now and then and sometimes when least expected, experiences that not only encouraged me to carry on meditating but pointed to the possibility that, eventually, Enlightenment would be attained. My whole body, especially the forehead, might be pervaded by an indescribable feeling of refreshment. Or I might 'see' the Buddha. Or the *kundalini* might start bubbling in the *manipura-chakra*. Or I might have a strong sense of the impermanence of all conditioned things. Whatever the experience, and however much it was welcome (and sometimes it was very welcome indeed), I told myself it was only a signpost, not the goal, and that I must press on. During the period of my evening sessions with Ani-la these experiences came to me more frequently than usual, especially experiences of *vipassana* or 'insight' into – or, more literally, 'clear vision' of – the true nature of existence. This was probably due to the fact that I was meditating twice a day instead of once, and that when I meditated for the second time it was after performing puja and listening to the Buddhavachana. By traditional Buddhist standards, two hours of meditation a day represented a very modest achievement, but I had no doubt that in combination with other spiritual practices, and with the support of an ethical life, it really did conduce to progress towards Enlightenment.

The end of my session with Ani-la did not mean the end of my day. Sachin was waiting for me, and together we walked up the road and through the brightly lit High Street to his house. Here I gave Meera her lesson while he had his (non-vegetarian) evening meal, after which we returned to Craigside. Neither of us burned any midnight oil, but the lights were on in our respective rooms until quite late, as he did more revision and I concluded my day in the company of Rilke or Dostoevsky.

Yet though my routine, during the first three months of the year, changed so little that a journalist could well have written a life in the day of the English monk, that routine was by no means unpunctuated by interruptions. These interruptions usually took the form of casual visitors, either local people who were passing by and called to pay their respects, or sightseers staying at the Himalayan Hotel, or Darjeeling friends who were in Kalimpong for a day or two and wanted to see me. If I was writing or teaching I dismissed them as soon as I decently could – unless, of course, it was someone like Anand-ji, who could not be disposed of so easily. Otherwise, if I was free, I talked to them about the Dharma, about the Maha Bodhi Society, and (especially if they were Buddhists) about the need to revive Buddhism in India and spread the teachings of the Buddha as widely as possible. Thus the days passed, each one much the same as every other, until my work for the *Maha Bodhi Journal* required me to go down to Calcutta. Sachin went with me. His examinations were over, and as he was confident of passing he wanted to look into the possibility of his joining one of the Calcutta colleges. Having said goodbye to the friends who had gathered at Craigside to see us off, we left Kalimpong on a cold, wet afternoon in the third week of March, and within twenty-four hours of catching the evening train at Siliguri were in hot, sticky, noisy, overcrowded, insalubrious Calcutta and unfastening our bedding rolls in my old room in the Maha Bodhi Society's headquarters building.

This time no nasty shock awaited me. Far from trying to check me in my work for the Journal, as they had done the previous year, Silabhadra and Jinaratana received me almost with open arms and behaved as though we had always been on the best of terms. Their change of attitude was not entirely disinterested. As my friend Soratha, the Little Monk, soon privately informed me, they had been guilty of a serious dereliction of duty for which Devapriya-ji (now again out on tour) had taken the pair of them, Jinaratana especially, severely to task, and as a result of which they were in the Governing Body's bad books and very much on the defensive. The dereliction related to the licence under which copies of the

Maha Bodhi were dispatched to the Journal's subscribers all over the world at a special reduced postal rate. This licence had to be renewed each year and the responsibility for its renewal rested with Jinaratana, as Managing Editor, and to a lesser degree with Silabhadra. This year they had omitted to renew it, with the result that the Post Office had refused to accept copies of the February issue at the reduced rate. The cost of dispatching them at the standard rate being prohibitive, they had not been dispatched at all and were still piled up on the floor of Jinaratana's office awaiting a solution to the problem.

One of my first tasks after my arrival, therefore, was to accompany Jinaratana to the General Post Office and there lend him, for a space of two hours, my moral support as he pleaded, argued, and expostulated with various officials. The situation was even worse than had appeared. Not only did the Journal's licence have to be renewed each year. It had to be renewed within a certain time and each issue had to be posted by a specific date in the month in which it was brought out. Moreover, there had to be twelve issues a year, neither more nor less, which meant that there could be no Vaishakha double number as in previous years. Somehow it was all sorted out, at least to an extent, and Jinaratana returned to his office to arrange for the copies of the February issue lying there to be dispatched at last and I to my room to start tackling the backlog of press work. The February issue having not gone out, the articles for the March issue had not been sent to the printers. These I now had to see through the press, as well as edit and proof-read the April and May issues – all within the space of three weeks. The May *Maha Bodhi* was, of course, the Journal's Vaishakha number. Though not a double number this year, it was sufficiently substantial in content, including as it did articles by Dr Conze and Lama Govinda, among others, as well as an extract from the second chapter of the *Survey* entitled 'The Transcendental Unity of Buddhism', and an editorial on 'The Reign of Law'. There was also a special cover, designed by a Shantiniketan-trained Bengali artist, and a black-and-white frontispiece. The latter was an art photograph of a seventh-century bronze head of Shakyamuni from the Nara Museum. 'The gentle eyes, the powerful lines of the nose, and the benevolent expression of the face impart to this head a deeply religious feeling', the museum's guidebook observed. 'It is one of the finest creations of the earliest period (7th and 8th centuries) in which Buddhist culture first permeated all Japan.'

My efforts on behalf of the Society's journal did not go unnoticed, or even unappreciated, and at a meeting of the editorial board held when I was nearly half-way through my stay its chairman, silver-haired and silver-tongued Dr Kalidas Nag, presented me with a small (verbal) bouquet. Under my editorship the *Maha Bodhi* had improved enormously, he declared, in his customary charming manner, and he and his colleagues – in fact all the Society's members – were deeply grateful to me for what I had done. The contrast between the present harmonious occasion and the stormy meeting that had taken place last time I was in Calcutta was striking, and I hoped it was indicative of a change of heart on the part of some of my colleagues.

The fact that I had to bring out three issues of the *Maha Bodhi* in as many weeks meant that I spent the greater part of the day (not excluding the evening) in my room, at a table strewn with galleys and page proofs, and had little time to spare for other things. Nevertheless I took part in some of the functions organized by the Society, even speaking at one and presiding over another, and delivered three lectures in the Society's hall, including one on 'The Recollection of Death' which I gave just after recovering from a bout of fever. The biggest and in its own way most successful of the functions held at this time was the public reception given to the ex-King of Cambodia, Prince Norodom Sihanouk Varma, in his capacity as leader of the Goodwill Delegation to India, which was attended by members of the Diplomatic Corps, Ministers of the West Bengal Government, prominent citizens of Calcutta, and other distinguished guests. On me, for one, the ex-King did not make a very favourable impression. A podgy figure in a white tunic and dark Cambodian-style sarong, he had crafty eyes and a suspicious expression that indicated, I thought, an unfriendly and deeply mistrustful nature.

Besides taking part in functions organized by the Society I talked with visitors to the headquarters building, lunched at the Grand Hotel with Dr Hudson, then on her way back to Kalimpong from Sarnath, visited the Sikh Cultural Centre and the Sri Aurobindo Centre, had my usual discussions with Phani Sanyal, and on two or three occasions accompanied Sachin to Hindustan Building to see his relations. There were also meetings with two highly regarded members of the Theravadin monastic order, one of whom was from Cambodia, the other from Ceylon. Venerable Veera Dhammawara, the Cambodian monk, had founded near New Delhi a vihara where he not only taught the Dharma but practised naturopathy for the benefit of the local people. Though more or less settled in India, he maintained links with his native land, and was said to be an adviser to the ex-King, whom he in fact had accompanied to the Maha Bodhi Society's reception. Venerable Ananda Maitreya, the

Sinhalese monk, was a scholar, preacher, and educationist who was well known even outside Ceylon. Though both were very much my seniors (Ananda Maitreya had been ordained years before I was born), neither of them showed the least disposition to treat me otherwise than as an equal and I soon had the satisfaction of discovering that they were well-informed, open-minded men who were Buddhists first and Theravadins afterwards. Ananda Maitreya even displayed a knowledge of the Mahayana, indeed a positive sympathy with it, that in my experience was rare among Theravadins.

My most enjoyable meeting, however, was with my old friend Buddharakshita, the companion of my wandering days, who was passing through Calcutta on his way back to Burma. We had not met since 1949, when he left for Ceylon and I went to stay with Jagdish Kashyap at the Benares Hindu University. Letters had passed between us from time to time, and from his I had gathered that he was not having an easy time in the Copper-Coloured Island. The irresistible force that was Sinhalese Theravadin Buddhism had collided with the immoveable object that was brahminical cultural conditioning (my friend had been born into a Bengali brahmin family), and there had been an explosion. The explosion had blown him to Burma, where he had studied on a government scholarship, had learned Burmese, and was now serving as interpreter and liaison officer between the Burmese authorities and the Indian bhikkhus attending the so-called Sixth Buddhist Council. This Council, which was the brainchild of the Burmese Prime Minister, U Nu, was being held near Rangoon in a specially constructed artificial cave. Proceedings had begun in 1954 and were due to come to a close in 1956, the year of the 2,500th anniversary of Buddhism.

Buddharakshita was full of praise for the Burmese laity but rather critical of the monks, at least in certain respects. U Nu had made arrangements for the 2,500 bhikkhus attending the Council to be offered vegetarian, rather than non-vegetarian, food each day, judging this to be more in accordance with the nature of the occasion. The Burmese bhikkhus, who were very much in the majority, strongly objected. Unless they were given meat and fish, a delegation told him, they would withdraw from the Council *en masse*. U Nu had no alternative but to capitulate, even though this meant that hundreds of animals would have to be slaughtered every week to feed the bhikkhus, and even though consumption of the flesh of animals killed especially for their benefit was prohibited to bhikkhus by the Buddha in the very *Vinaya-Pitaka* whose text the Council was then engaged in reciting, checking, and 'purifying'. Buddharakshita's story did not surprise me. For some Burmese monks, I well knew, giving up meat and fish was equivalent to giving up Buddhism.

The morning after my meeting with Buddharakshita, and a few hours after I had sent the last corrected page proofs of the Vaishakha number to the press, Sachin and I left Calcutta. Previously one had always had to cross the Ganges by the ancient, overcrowded paddle steamer. Now launches were plying, and in one of these we took our place. The result was that we reached the opposite shore ahead of most of the other passengers, secured seats in the connecting train without difficulty, slept for most of the night, and arrived in Kalimpong the following afternoon not too much the worse for our journey.

During my absence Anand-ji and Gyan Jyoti's plans for an evening college at the Dharmodaya Vihara had started to bear fruit. Classes were already being held. Before my departure I had agreed to teach the IA and BA classes English and Logic and having had tea and talked with Aniruddha and a few other early visitors I accordingly made my way to the Dharmodaya Vihara and took my first class. After the class I discussed the forthcoming Vaishakha Purnima celebrations with Gyan Jyoti. This year, for the first time since my arrival in Kalimpong (perhaps for the first time ever), the dozen or more Buddhist organizations and institutions of the town were going to celebrate the thrice-sacred day jointly, as well as individually, a committee had been formed for that purpose, and I had been elected general secretary. For the next few weeks much of my time was therefore taken up with committee meetings, consultations with Gyan Jyoti, who had been made treasurer, and discussions with the stewards of the procession that was to be the main feature of the joint celebrations, as well as with the collection of funds for our own Maha Bodhi Society celebrations at Craigside.

Inevitably my routine was affected. Though I taught Aniruddha and Durga most afternoons, and took my IA and BA classes at the Dharmodaya Vihara three times a week, my mornings were broken into and it was more than two weeks before I could resume work on the *Survey*, and then only for a few days. There was no time for the evening sessions of puja, readings from the scriptures, and meditation. Ani-la was in any case in Darjeeling, and after her return to Kalimpong she evinced little or no interest in their being restarted. They had not benefited her as much as I had hoped they would. At the time of my departure for Calcutta she was still liable to black moods, still in the habit of silently handing me letters about her difficulties, and capable of announcing that she had decided to 'go away' and nobody would ever be bothered by her again. Now she was experiencing difficulties in connection with her living arrangements in Tirpai. Two or three months earlier she had moved from her quarters in someone's outhouse into a roomy natural cave in the hillside above the village. With the help of friends she furnished the cave, installed electric light, and made herself otherwise comfortable in her new abode. For a while the French Nun's wonderful 'electrified cave' was the talk of the town, with people walking all the way up to Tirpai from the bazaar just to see it. I had seen it once, when on an outing to Dailo, the wooded hill behind Tirpai, with some of our younger members. Recently, however, there had been friction between Ani-la and her neighbours, and shortly after returning to Kalimpong she tearfully informed me that it was impossible for her to go on living there. Her neighbours did not realize she needed peace and tranquillity for her studies; despite her pleas for silence they continued to shout and quarrel in the vicinity of her dwelling. Worse still, one of them wanted to cut down the row of bamboos that screened the entrance to the cave, thus depriving her of their protection and exposing her to the gaze of passers-by.

The evening sessions of puja, readings from the scriptures, and meditation not having been restarted, Ani-la was seen at Craigside less frequently than before. But Lobsang continued to come, even though there was no rebellious French nun for him to teach, and we continued to work on the article on Tibetan Buddhism he was writing. Not that he had actually written very much of the article. Weeks were to pass before he had produced a sufficient number of pages for me to be able to make a serious start on the work of revision – a work that was to last far longer than I had expected. Meanwhile, we spent our afternoons together discussing Tibetan Buddhism in general and trying to clarify terminology. Though Lobsang was writing the article, in a sense he was not its author, as the material for it was being supplied by Dhardo Rimpoche, for whose knowledge of the Dharma he had the highest regard and with whom he was in regular contact. The Rimpoche was aware, of course, that I was helping Lobsang and aware, therefore, that material supplied to the young Tibetan aristocrat was also material supplied, indirectly, to me, and that I would need to understand it thoroughly if I was to give the article an adequate revision. Sometimes Dhardo Rimpoche seemed to be communicating to me, through Lobsang, material not intended for the article or indeed for publication at all. Thus for four or five afternoons in succession, apparently at the Rimpoche's behest, Lobsang gave me a detailed account of the meditational practices of the *Guhyasamaja Tantra*. So complex were these practices that as soon as he was gone I wrote down what I remembered of them, in this way accumulating quite a sheaf of notes on a highly esoteric subject. It was curious, I reflected. Ever since my first encounter with it, some years earlier, in an article written by a Bengali Indologist, the mere name of the *Guhyasamaja Tantra* had possessed a strange resonance for me. In Nepal a lay Tantric *yogin* had told me that together with the *Prajnaparamita* 'in 8,000 lines' and the *Bodhicharyavatara* it was one of the three foundational texts of Nepalese (Newar) Buddhism. With the *Prajnaparamita* or 'Perfection of Wisdom' literature and the *Bodhicharyavatara* or 'Entry into the Life of Enlightenment' of Shantideva I was already familiar. Indeed, I prized them highly. Was there, then, a hidden spiritual connection between these two texts and the *Guhyasamaja*, and why had Dhardo Rimpoche chosen to reveal to me some of the secrets of Tantric Buddhist meditation?

Whatever the answer to these questions may have been, or even if the latter represented a misunderstanding on my part, one thing at least was clear. Just as our consultations about Ani-la had strengthened the ties between Dhardo Rimpoche and Lobsang, on the one hand, and me on the other, so my work on the article on Tibetan Buddhism was bringing me, through Lobsang, into ever closer contact with the kindly but, seemingly, aloof Gelugpa incarnate lama who was its true author. Thus when a situation arose in which I needed Dhardo Rimpoche's help I had no hesitation in approaching him directly. The situation related to the forthcoming joint Vaishakha Purnima celebrations, now less than a week away. For several days rumours had been circulating in the bazaar to the effect that the (Gelugpa) lamas, of whom there were about a hundred in Kalimpong, were deeply divided, that tensions between the two rival parties were building up, that there was going to be a violent confrontation, and that the clash was due to take place on Vaishakha Purnima day, either in the course of the procession or at the public meeting that was to be held at the Dharmodaya Vihara afterwards. What had led to the division I never discovered, but as the two groups seemed to regard Dhardo Rimpoche and the abbot of the Tharpa Chholing Gompa, respectively, as their leaders, it was these two dignitaries that I initially approached. Dhardo Rimpoche promised to intervene and restrain the lamas who claimed to be his followers, and the venerable old abbot, with whom I had been on friendly terms since my arrival in Kalimpong, gave me a similar undertaking. I also took the precaution of speaking to the representatives of the two *kidus* or lay associations, both of which had become embroiled in the dispute, and warned that any violence on the Vaishakha Purnima, of all days in the year, would bring shame and disgrace on the Buddhists of Kalimpong and particularly on the members of the Tibetan community. These and similar meetings kept me busy for several days, but at length I was satisfied that no untoward incident would be allowed to mar the sanctity of the thrice-sacred day. It was as well I had taken the action I did. Dhardo Rimpoche's followers, who were the more aggressive party and included monks belonging to the Tharpa Chholing Gompa, apparently had been planning to attack the abbot at the meeting at the Dharmodaya Vihara and drive him from the platform.

Feelings within the Kalimpong Buddhist community could indeed run high. Besides the divisions among the lamas, there were serious differences between Tamang and Newar Buddhists, or at least between Dhanman Moktan and the Dharmodaya Vihara, and these, too, I had to settle before I could be certain that everybody would be taking part in the procession and the public meeting. Dhanman Moktan lived in Tirpai and was a dealer in grains. As I had long known, he cherished a violent hatred towards Newars, especially Buddhist Newars, and in particular towards the three (formerly four) Jyoti brothers, who were among the town's leading merchants and the Dharmodaya's principal supporters. For him no epithet was too bad to be applied to the unfortunate Newars. The reason for this inordinate hatred I had yet to discover, though over the years he had told me many a story purporting to reveal the arrogance, perfidy, and meanness of the entire Newar community. One of the more identifiable grounds for his differences with the Dharmodaya Vihara (though not for his unreasoning hatred) related to the ownership of the little one-room vihara situated a few doors from his grain shop. This had long been a bone of contention between him as the (self-appointed) representative of the Tirpai Buddhists and the Dharmodaya Vihara's Kathmandu-based parent body the Dharmodaya Sabha. If the issue was not resolved to his satisfaction, the irascible Tamang declared, he and his supporters would neither take part in any procession that started from the Dharmodaya Vihara nor attend any meeting held on the Vihara's premises. Fortunately I was able, as a friend of both parties, to get them to agree to a compromise. In return for Dhanman Moktan's recognition of the Sabha's ownership of the little vihara, Gyan Jyoti, on behalf of the Sabha, recognized the right of the Tirpai Buddhists to manage it. Thus the co-operation of Dhanman Moktan and his supporters in the joint Vaishakha Purnima celebrations was assured.

Not that Gelug lamas, and Tamangs and Newars, were the only ones whose divisions and differences threatened to mar the unity of the Buddhist community. In Kalimpong there were only four Western

Buddhists (or five if one included Dr Roerich), yet on the eve of the Vaishakha Purnima two of them managed to get into a foolish quarrel that created, for a time, a quite unpleasant atmosphere. The two offenders were Ani-la and Joe. Both were keen to help decorate Craigside for our Maha Bodhi Society celebrations, but knowing that they were not the best of friends, and knowing, moreover, that they possessed very different artistic tastes, I had been careful to demarcate their respective areas of responsibility. Ani-la was to be responsible for decorating the shrine-room, where the morning celebrations would be held, and Joe was to be responsible for setting up the outside shrine, in front of which we would be holding the evening celebrations, when more people were expected to attend. Our younger members were given the responsibility of erecting the Tibetan marquee I had borrowed for the occasion from the Tharpa Chholing Gompa. Having displayed, as I thought, truly Solomonic wisdom, I went to the Dharmodaya Vihara to see Anand-ji, leaving my helpers, young and old, to get on with their respective tasks. But even the wisdom of Solomon was unable to prevent the intransigent French nun and the prickly Canadian upasaka from finding cause for disagreement. Though I had demarcated their respective areas of responsibility, I had omitted to define exactly where one ended and the other began. In particular, I had not made it clear to whose area the casement windows in the back wall of the shrine-room belonged, and during my absence a dispute arose between them over this important point. Ani-la claimed that as the windows were usually kept shut they formed part of the *inside* of the shrine-room and therefore fell within *her* jurisdiction, whereas Joe contended that as they opened outwards they should be considered as being *outside* it and therefore as falling within *his* jurisdiction. The reason for Joe's contention was that he had set up the outside shrine immediately below the windows; if the windows were opened, and the shrine-room's main image turned round, this would create a triptych-like effect, with the image forming the central panel of the triptych and the window-frames on either side of the image the two wing panels. Obviously the idea was a good one, and despite Ani-la's vehement protests Joe not only opened the windows but proceeded to line the inside – now transformed into the outside – of the window-frames with flowers. This high-handed behaviour, as she saw it (and Joe should really have waited for me to return and settle the dispute), infuriated Ani-la, and soon the two Western Buddhists were engaged in an unseemly altercation that dismayed and embarrassed the other helpers. Nor did the matter end there. After Joe had left, Ani-la climbed up on to the outside shrine and threw down the flowers with which he had lined the window-frames. At this point I returned. On learning what had happened I ordered Ani-la to replace the flowers and after the usual hysterics she obeyed.

Joe was very angry the next morning when he discovered what Ani-la had done to his handiwork, and Dr Hudson was even angrier on his behalf. 'Why was *that woman* allowed to interfere?' she kept demanding, of no one in particular, her bony frame trembling with rage. But this was not the time for anger or any other negative emotion. Vaishakha Purnima day had dawned clear and bright; from early morning more than a dozen pairs of hands (including Ani-la's) had been putting the finishing touches to the decorations, and soon it was time for us to welcome Dhardo Rimpoche, to invite him to hoist the five-coloured Buddhist flag, and to conduct him to his throne in the shrine-room. Here he performed puja in Tibetan and gave an address which Lobsang translated into English. I then administered the Refuges and Precepts to the gathering, led the chanting of the Salutation to the Three Jewels, and delivered a short sermon. Later in the morning, after an alfresco early lunch, our members and I went in a body to the Dharmodaya Vihara and took our places in the procession, which had just started moving. Anand-ji and I walked together immediately behind the palanquin containing the image of the Buddha. In front of the palanquin went the red-robed lamas in their yellow ceremonial headgear, some of them carrying flags and banners, others beating drums and clashing cymbals and blowing on various wind instruments, including a pair of twelve-foot copper trumpets. Behind us came a motley crowd of Tibetan, Nepalese, Sikkimese, Bhutanese, Chinese, and Indian lay devotees, many of them in national dress and carrying on their shoulders images and sacred books. The mile-long procession presented a colourful sight as slowly it wound through the High Street and Chowrasta, up past the Scottish Mission compound, and so along the ridge to the Tirpai bazaar and the Tharpa Chholing Gompa, whence it made its way back to the Dharmodaya Vihara by a different route. The public meeting, which took place soon afterwards, though short was no less successful. I addressed the audience in English, after which Anand-ji addressed it in Hindi. On the platform with us, seated in two enormous armchairs, were Dhardo Rimpoche and the abbot of the Tharpa Chholing Gompa. Though some of their respective followers exchanged unfriendly looks, and though the abbot was the object of a few aggressive stares, the two dignitaries greeted each other warmly on their arrival. I was reminded of the Hindu saying that however much

Shiva's ghosts and Vishnu's demons might quarrel the two gods, their masters, remained the best of friends.

The evening celebrations at Craigside were held on the lawn, beneath the Tibetan marquee, and were attended by a couple of hundred people including the new Deputy Commissioner from Darjeeling and the Second Officer of Kalimpong. As in the morning, I administered the Refuges and Precepts, led the chanting of the Salutation to the Three Jewels, and delivered a sermon. This time the sermon was a long one. Taking as my text the words *sukho buddhanamuppado*, or 'Happy is the birth of the Buddhas', from the *Dhammapada* verse 194, I emphasized the fact that the Way to Enlightenment was also the path to supreme happiness. Then came a reading from the Pali Canon descriptive of Siddhartha's attainment of Enlightenment beneath the Bodhi-tree, after which there followed a short period of group meditation. This should have marked the end of the proceedings, but such was the atmosphere that had been created that more than half the people, including the Deputy Commissioner, sat on, as though unable to tear themselves away. If the predominant mood of the morning celebrations had been one of joy, that of the evening celebrations was one of peace and tranquillity. Some sat with eyes still closed. Others contemplated the 'altar' Joe had set up at the far end of the marquee, against the outside wall of the shrine-room, where three tiers of butter-lamps burned and where, above the topmost tier, the sedent Buddha-image that was the focal point of the celebrations looked out from between banks of Madonna lilies.

Chapter Sixteen

GANGTOK, THE VILLAGE CAPITAL

GANGTOK, THE CAPITAL OF SIKKIM, was fifty miles from Kalimpong by road. I had visited the place once before, when at the invitation of Venerable Sangharatana I had joined the official delegation taking the relics of Shariputra and Maudgalyayana, the Buddha's two chief disciples, for exposition in Gangtok and at the Dungkara Gompa in southern Tibet, where the sixteen-year-old Dalai Lama was then staying. On that occasion the government of India, for reasons of its own, had prevented me from setting foot in Tibet, but I had at least seen Gangtok, where twice daily for a week I assisted Sangharatana and Kashyap-ji at the ceremonial expositions of the relics for the benefit of the faithful and where, in the evenings, I gave discourses on the Dharma. Since then, Gangtok and Sikkim had become as remote and mysterious to me as the mythical kingdom of Shambhala, and I had expected to see no more of the Himalayan principality than the snows of Kanchenjunga and its other sacred mountains shining against the blue sky a hundred to a hundred and fifty miles away. Early in December, however, there had come a message from the *Maharaj Kumar* or Crown Prince. He would like to consult me before attending a meeting of the Maha Bodhi Society's Governing Body the following week. Would I mind coming up to Gangtok for a day or two? Not knowing at that time that the Indian authorities, who controlled access to Sikkim, gave invitees of the Palace their frontier passes automatically, I sent back a message to the effect that there might be a delay in my receiving permission to cross the Inner Line. Could His Highness not see me on his way down to Calcutta? He could and he would, and a few days later we accordingly met at Churchill, the Kalimpong home of his sister Princess Pema Tsedeun, where we had a long discussion about the Society's affairs.

The Maharaj Kumar must have found the meeting useful, for towards the end of May there had come a second message inviting me up to the village capital. Not only did the Maharaj Kumar want to consult me again about the affairs of the Maha Bodhi Society; he also wanted me to give a few lectures. The invitation, though welcome, did not come at the most convenient time. It was less than a month after the Vaishakha Purnima celebrations, I had only recently been able to re-establish my daily routine of writing and teaching, and did not want to interrupt it yet again. Moreover, I had been re-reading D.T. Suzuki's translation of the *Lankavatara Sutra*, as well as the three volumes of his *Studies in Zen Buddhism*. I had first encountered the great 'idealist' *sutra* in the early forties, when I was still in my teens and still in England. Though I had encountered it in Dwight Goddard's shortened version *The Self-Realization of Noble Wisdom* (afterwards included in his well-known *Buddhist Bible*), its teaching had impressed me almost as deeply as that of the *Diamond Sutra*, the reading of which, at about the same time, had made me realize that I was, in fact, a Buddhist, and always had been. Reading the work again now, after an interval of thirteen or fourteen years and with, perhaps, a better understanding of Buddhism, I found myself being plunged into a deeply introspective mood that I had no wish to disturb by a sudden change of scene. Nevertheless I thought it would not be right for me to refuse the Maharaj Kumar's invitation a second time, especially as on this occasion a refusal would mean not taking advantage of an opportunity to preach the Dharma. Nor were these the only considerations. Sikkim was a Buddhist state, with a ruler who was a Dharmaraja or Righteous Monarch, and though Buddhists were now outnumbered by (immigrant) Hindus Buddhism was still culturally and socially dominant and it behoved me to see as much of the principality as I could while the present regime was in place. I therefore accepted the Maharaj Kumar's invitation, and taking a volume of Suzuki's *Studies* with me for company left for the village capital at the beginning of June.

During the last few days it had been raining heavily, and though the road between Kalimpong and Gangtok was not blocked by landslides there was plenty of cloud and mist and I caught only an occasional glimpse of the darkly wooded slopes on the other side of the Teesta. At the little market town of Rangpo, where trains of Tibetan mules stood disconsolately around in the rain waiting for their packs to be searched for contraband, I alighted and showed my pass at the West Bengal police checkpoint, after which we were free to cross the frontier by the narrow, swaying suspension bridge. On the Sikkim side a friendly police constable waved us on with a smile that was in marked contrast to the sullen, suspicious looks of the Bengali sub-inspectors on the Indian side of the boarder. As we drove up into the hills clouds parted and mist cleared to reveal clusters of thatched huts and terraces already green with early rice and maize. Gangtok bazaar, where I was set down soon after midday, presented a depressing sight, consisting as it did of little more than a few rows of nondescript shops and miscalled 'hotels', most of them of the open-fronted Indian variety and most of them owned, judging by their names, by Indians. On the hillside behind the bazaar was a scattering of wattle and daub cottages with here and there a modern bungalow. It was not difficult to understand why Gangtok was called the village capital, for apart from the Palace and a few other buildings out of sight higher up the ridge what I saw before me *was* Gangtok, which with its two thousand inhabitants represented the biggest concentration of people in Sikkim.

Fortunately I did not have to contemplate the bazaar for long. A telephone call to the Palace to announce my arrival soon produced the khaki-clad Superintendent of Police to whom had been entrusted the responsibility of welcoming me on behalf of the Maharaj Kumar and conducting me to the State guest-house. Hardly had this functionary gone, after seeing me settled in my quarters, than there appeared another, in the shape of a tall, rather nervous young Sikkimese in a black chuba. This was the ADC, who had come to make sure that I was comfortable and had everything I needed, as well as to inform me where and when I would be giving my lectures. The rest of the afternoon was my own. In the evening I had a visit from Rai Bahadur Densapa, also known as Berniak Kazi, Berniak being the name of his estate and Kazi his title as a Sikkimese nobleman. I had met him on my previous visit to Gangtok, as well as several times in Kalimpong subsequently, and knew him reasonably well. Like the ADC he wore a chuba, in his case brown, but unlike the ADC, who sported a Western-style haircut, he wore his uncut hair in the traditional Tibeto-Sikkimese manner, that is, plaited into two braids that were coiled tightly round the head. Tall and portly, with an exceptionally florid complexion, he was in fact a man of strongly conservative views and one of the pillars of the Sikkimese establishment. At one time or other he had occupied all the major posts in the administration (at the time of my visit he was, I think, in charge of the Department of Ecclesiastical Affairs), and was well known for his capacity for work, his personal integrity, and his loyalty to the Ruling Family – a loyalty that did not prevent him from offering, on occasion, unpalatable advice. He was also well known for his scholarship and for liking nothing more than a good discussion on Buddhist history, or doctrine, or literature. If this was indeed the case, and if it was the hope of having such a discussion that brought him to the guest-house that evening, then probably he was not disappointed, for we talked far into the night and covered a good deal of ground.

The following morning came ebullient, irrepressible Tseten Tashi, the Maharaja's Private Secretary, whom I also knew reasonably well. He was at my reverence's service, he announced in his usual comical fashion, doffing his porkpie hat with a flourish and making an exaggeratedly low bow, and had come to take me to the Palace. To the Palace we therefore went, at dizzying speed, and up a succession of hairpin bends, and in less than ten minutes I was being ushered into the Maharaj Kumar's private sitting-room. Here I found Rai Bahadur Densapa, and talked with him and Tseten Tashi until the arrival of the Maharaj Kumar, upon which they withdrew. Polden Thondup Namgyal, Crown Prince of Sikkim, was in his early thirties and of medium height. Like the members of his entourage, he wore a chuba, off-white in colour and with long sleeves into which he inserted his hands from time to time as if to conceal something. Apart from a pronounced stutter, his most noticeable feature were his eyes, which were black and beady, and could be said to twinkle, especially when he became animated, as he had in Kalimpong when we discussed Maha Bodhi Society affairs. On the occasion of our present meeting, which lasted for the rest of the morning, his eyes twinkled more brightly than ever, especially when we passed from the Society's affairs to the question of the revival of Buddhism in Sikkim, which evidently was very much on his mind.

The Dharma had been introduced into Sikkim in the seventeenth century, its introduction being especially associated with the name of Lhatsun Chempo, a learned Tibetan lama. According to legend, the lama was guided across the mountains by the spirit of Kanchenjunga in the form of a white bird. Subsequently, monasteries sprang up at the spots where he had erected shrines. These monasteries, which eventually numbered more than forty, were divided fairly equally between the Nyingma and Karma-Kagyu Schools. Whatever they may have been like in the past, it was generally admitted that their present condition was on the whole one of serious decline. Hardly any of the lamas were celibate (according to Rai Bahadur Densapa, perhaps *one* of them was) and few lived in the monastery to which they were affiliated. Most lived nearby, with their wives and families, cultivated the land, and gathered at the monastery twice a month to perform rituals. Religious knowledge was minimal or non-existent, and drunkenness and sexual immorality were rife. With the clergy in such a state, it was hardly to be expected that the laity should be remarkable either for understanding or practice of the Dharma, Rai Bahadur Densapa being very much an exceptional figure in this respect. Clearly Buddhism needed to be revived in the State, and clearly it was fitting that the Maharaj Kumar, as the future *Dharmaraja* or Righteous Monarch, should be giving thought to the matter. There could however be no revival of Buddhism without Buddhist education, in the sense of regular, systematic instruction in the fundamentals of the Dharma, and he was therefore trying to ascertain how such instruction might best be given. In the case of the lamas it would probably have to be given with the help of qualified Nyingma and Kagyu teachers from Tibet, and it was to be hoped that from the lamas knowledge would trickle down to their largely illiterate peasant clientèle. But what of the English-educated laity, who together with their Hindu counterparts now formed the most highly influential section of the community? How was the Dharma to be communicated to *them*? Since they were to a great extent alienated from their traditional culture, it would probably have to be communicated in terms that were rational rather than symbolic and not too obviously incompatible with their Westernized outlook. Probably it would even have to be communicated, at least for the time being, by a Western Buddhist, which was where the English monk of Kalimpong came in, the Maharaj Kumar apparently having not forgotten the enthusiasm with which younger Sikkimese Buddhists, in particular, had responded to the lectures I had given four years earlier, in connection with the exposition of the relics of Shariputra and Maudgalyayana.

Thus it was that I was again visiting Gangtok, the village capital, and again giving a series of lectures there. The first lecture took place on the afternoon of the day following my meeting with the Maharaj Kumar, and the second and third on the two succeeding days. I gave all three of them in the secretariat building adjoining the Palace, in a room that with the help of Tibetan painted scrolls, lighted silver lamps, and incense, had been transformed into a veritable temple. Looking round, I could not but contrast the care taken here in Gangtok to create the right kind of atmosphere for my lectures with the very different way things were done in Calcutta. In Calcutta, when I lectured in the Maha Bodhi Society's shabby hall, no care whatever was taken to create the right kind of atmosphere. Jinaratana, who as Joint Secretary was in charge of such things, did not even bother to advertise the lectures properly. Half an hour before I was due to speak a board announcing the title of the lecture and the name of the speaker (invariably described as 'English monk') would be placed outside the entrance in the hope that passers-by would see it and wander in, which fortunately some always did, especially if it was raining. When there was a reception to be given to a visiting politician or other such dignitary, however, no trouble or expense would be spared to decorate the hall and send out invitations, even Devapriya-ji not being free from such opportunism. The fact that no care was taken to create the right kind of atmosphere for my lectures did not mean that I took any the less trouble preparing and delivering them, especially as I had, in addition to those who came in off the street, a small band of regular auditors; but when such care *was* taken, as in Gangtok it patently had been, it was a great encouragement to me and I felt more inspired than ever to give of my best.

Mindful that on the occasion of my previous visit, when I spoke on such basic topics as the Four Noble Truths and the Noble Eightfold Path, some of the younger Sikkimese Buddhists present had declared they had no idea Buddhism taught such wonderful things, I had decided that this time, too, I would stick to fundamentals. I therefore spoke on the Three Jewels, devoting my first lecture to the Buddha, the second to the Dharma, and the third to the Sangha, which enabled me to present the Buddha's teaching not only in its depth but in its breadth. According to a contemporary report, in the course of these lectures, none of which lasted for more than an hour, I gave a survey of practically the whole field of Buddhism. 'The unique status of the Buddha as not only the preacher but the discoverer of the Path to nirvana, the Dharma as the Means to Enlightenment, the treading of the Threefold Way, the practice of meditation, the duties and mutual obligations of monks and laymen, the wrongfulness of supporting Christian missions, the importance of the Guru, and the need for properly trained and educated monks, were topics upon which the Ven. Bhikshu laid particular emphasis.' That I should have laid such emphasis on them was not surprising, for they were among the topics with which I was dealing in the *Survey* and therefore very much in my thoughts.

Though the lectures were held in the secretariat building, which for those without means of transport meant a long uphill climb, all three were well attended, especially the second and third. My auditors included the Maharaj Kumar, Princess Pema Tsedeun, the new Dewan (a plump little Parsee from Bombay whom I had yet to meet), Rai Bahadur Densapa, and Tseten Tashi, as well as members of the Sikkimese nobility and officers of the State, both Sikkimese and Indian. Each lecture was followed by questions and the questions by a discussion which became at times, quite lively. Afterwards I mingled with the audience, greeting old friends and being introduced to people I had not met before. Thus I talked about Tibetan art with Kanwal Krishna, whom I had met in Kalimpong a few years ago and who had given lessons to Burma Raja and to the Maharaja of Sikkim, discussed the teachings of J. Krishnamurti with Moti Chand Pradhan, an elderly Theosophist who once had been Sub-Divisional Officer of Kalimpong, and made the acquaintance of Apa B. Pant, the new Political Officer, who as the representative of the Government of India was the real if unavowed ruler of the little Himalayan principality. Having not forgotten that it was the Government of India that had prevented me, through a previous Political Officer, from accompanying the relics of Shariputra and Maudgalyayana to Tibet, I was inclined to treat the present agent of its authority – and ambitions – in the region with a certain amount of reserve. However, when we had chatted for a while Pant said he would like to have some discussion with me in Kalimpong and naturally I replied I would be happy to see him there.

In between the lectures, and when not busy working on my notes in the guest-house, I was usually out and about seeing places and meeting people. The most interesting place I saw was Enchay Gompa, where I gave a short talk to the fifteen or twenty boy lamas studying at the Tibetan school there. They were a mixed bunch, some of them looking as though they were not at all suited to the religious life, but I gave them what encouragement I could, exhorting them to be faithful to the Dharma and to regard being a lama as a vocation rather than as a profession. The gompa, which was situated on the outskirts of Gangtok, was a large wooden building of the traditional type. As Rai Bahadur Densapa afterwards told me, it was about two hundred years old and a branch of Pemayangtse Gompa in western Sikkim, which was the royal monastery and the biggest and most important Nyingma establishment in the principality. Despite its (indirect) connection with the Ruling Family, however, Enchay Gompa was in a state of considerable disrepair; some of its massive timbers were warped and decayed, and like the old Bhutan Palace in Kalimpong it reminded me of the ruined mansion described in the *White Lotus Sutra*'s Parable of the Burning House. On the day I saw Enchay Gompa I also visited the Sir Tashi Namgyal High School, where Lama Kazi Dawa-Samdup, the translator of *The Tibetan Book of the Dead*, had once wielded the rod as headmaster. Here too I gave a talk, this time to a hundred or more boys who were *not* lamas, and discussed the curriculum with the staff. Discussion turned on religious education in schools and it transpired that only one teacher, a Caste Hindu from Bihar, was against it. On other days I talked with a Superintendent of Police from Shillong, an American journalist, a friend of Phani Sanyal's, a Kazi friend of Ani-la's, and the weaving master from the Cottage Industries Emporium, as well as with various people whom I had known when they lived in Kalimpong. There were also more long discussions with Rai Bahadur Densapa, who seemed anxious to spend as much time with me as possible.

Despite all this external activity I did not altogether lose touch with the introspective mood into which I had been plunged, shortly before the arrival of the Maharaj Kumar's invitation, by the re-reading of the *Lankavatara Sutra* and the three volumes of Suzuki's *Studies in Zen Buddhism*. Whenever I could I had recourse to the volume of *Studies* I had brought with me to Gangtok, and one night, when I had been reading it and reflecting on its contents for two or three hours, I not only found myself in a deeply meditative state but had a new insight into the nature of Zen. This served to confirm my belief that external activity and inner spiritual experience were not necessarily incompatible, and that however valid the distinction between 'introvert' and 'extravert' might be on the psychological level it was one that was transcended by the Bodhisattva's non-dual experience of the Wisdom that is Compassion and the Compassion that is Wisdom.

The confirmation was not untimely. Full as the last few days had been, my final day in Gangtok was to be even fuller. Four or five people came to see me at the guest-house before breakfast, and straight after breakfast the Maharaja's Assistant Private Secretary whisked me off to the Palace for further discussions with the Maharaj Kumar about the revival of Buddhism in Sikkim. These discussions were interrupted by the arrival, at about 10.30, of R.M. Nehru, India's Secretary for External Affairs, and his wife, who were on their way to Bhutan and had decided to halt for half an hour at Gangtok. Mrs Nehru was European. In fact she had been born in Hungary, and was pleasantly surprised to learn that I was of partly Hungarian descent, my mother's paternal grandfather having emigrated from Hungary at an early age. The Nehrus were accompanied to the Palace by the Political Officer and the Dewan, whose name, I now learned, was Nariman K. Rustomji. When they had all gone the Maharaj Kumar and I resumed our discussion, which continued through lunch, which turned from Buddhism in Sikkim to Buddhism in the sense of the general principles of the Dharma, and in which Princess Pema Tsedeun and her husband Pheunkhang-se, and the Maharaj Kumari or Crown Princess, eventually came and joined. What with the friendly, cultivated atmosphere, and the sense that we were united in our common devotion to the Three Jewels, it was one of the most enjoyable discussions I had experienced for a long while, and I was sorry when the time came for me to say goodbye to them all and leave the palace and leave Gangtok. A fortnight after my return to Kalimpong the Maharaj Kumar sent me, through Princess Pema Tsedeun, offerings in the form of sacks of rice, tins of cooking oil, and other no less welcome additions to my scanty stores.

By that time I had again re-established my daily routine of writing and teaching, and was hoping to be able to keep to it, without any further interruption, all through the rainy season and into the autumn. In the event I was more or less successful in doing so. During this period the *Survey* made steady progress, I re-wrote the greater part of Lobsang's lengthy article on Tibetan Buddhism, edited three or four issues of the *Maha Bodhi*, produced the first two issues of *Lumbini* (after which the magazine ceased publication), and at the invitation of the editor of *2500 Years of Buddhism* started writing an essay on 'Cultural and Political Implications of Buddhism for the Modern World'. Though I still gave Aniruddha, Durga, and a few other students individual tuition at Craigside, most of my teaching was done at the Dharmodaya Vihara, where I continued to take the IA and BA classes three times a week as part of the evening college. Besides taking the classes I corrected essays, set question papers, and marked the students' answers, all of which took time. There were also staff meetings to attend. These could be long and acrimonious, the longest and most acrimonious being the one at which my six or seven colleagues and I debated the issue of remuneration. So far we had all given our services voluntarily, it being understood that most of the students were not in a position to pay fees. At the meeting in question, however, Pandit Paramahans Misra, the uncouth, aggressive UP brahmin who took the Sanskrit classes, not only raised the issue of remuneration but was adamant that we should all demand it as our right. The unabashed mercenariness of the Pandit's attitude embarrassed even the least philanthropic among us, though when his proposal was put to the vote only two of our number actually voted against it. The two were Bhaichand Pradhan, the young littérateur who taught Nepali and was the proposal's bitterest critic, and the English Buddhist monk from the Maha Bodhi Society's branch at Craigside who taught English and Logic.

Knowing as I did that any remuneration for the teachers would have to come from Gyan Jyoti, and that the latter's resources were not limitless, I was not very sanguine about the evening college's chances of survival. But it certainly survived long enough for the IA and BA classes I took there to form a substantial part of my routine all through the latter half of the year. For these five or six months my routine was in fact a very demanding one. I had never been as busy, nor worked so hard, in my life, and some of my friends, Ani-la in particular, were of the opinion that I was doing too much and that my health was suffering in consequence. The only variations from my routine were those provided by our full moon day celebrations and other festivals – and by visitors and guests from overseas or from other parts of India.

Chapter Seventeen

BIRDS OF PASSAGE

A FINE AFTERNOON IN THE MIDDLE OF MAY saw me leaving Craigside shortly after lunch and making my way to Sachin's place. For the last few days my young Nepalese friend had been ill in bed, suffering from what his doctor father thought might be appendicitis, and I was going to see him. Accompanying me on my visit was Venerable Saranankara, the slow-spoken, kindly Sinhalese monk with whom I had become acquainted in Calcutta and who for the last two or three weeks had been staying with me. On our arrival at the bungalow where he lived with his family we found Sachin no better than he had been the previous day, and Saranankara proposed that we should perform a *paritta* or 'protection' ceremony for his benefit. Such ceremonies were, I knew, popular in the Theravadin Buddhist world of South-east Asia, just as their more elaborate and colourful Mahayana counterparts were in China, Japan, and Tibet. I did not have much faith in them as remedies for actual disease, though willing to concede they might have a kind of placebo effect, but Saranankara was a firm believer in their efficacy, and as Sachin himself had no objection and as his mother and sisters rather liked the idea of a religious ceremony being performed in their house, I agreed to co-operate. A length of white thread and a brass pot filled with water were accordingly produced, the thread was passed round Sachin's bed and between his hands, and for the next twenty or thirty minutes Saranankara and I chanted the *paritta suttas*, all the while keeping hold of the thread, the ends of which had been allowed to hang down in the water inside the pot. By the time we finished Sachin was fast asleep, and having tied a portion of the thread round his wrist we departed. Saranankara was sure he would wake up feeling much better.

From the hospital compound we made our way not back to Craigside but a little farther up the road, to Tenth Mile. Our destination was the

Homes Studio, where we had arranged to meet Joe, Ani-la, Aryadeva, and Lilian Silburn for a group photograph. Whose idea the group photograph was I no longer recollect. Probably it was mine, in which case I must have thought it would be a good idea to have a record of some of the (mainly Western) Buddhists who were associated with me at that time. Joe, Ani-la, and I were now permanently resident in Kalimpong, though Ani-la and I, at least, were often out of town; but Saranankara, Aryadeva, and Lilian Silburn were birds of passage, spending the hottest weeks of the year in the comparative cool of the hill station. Saranankara and Aryadeva were in fact due to leave the following day, though Miss Silburn would be staying for another fortnight. In the photograph the three monks are seated on chairs. Saranankara, as the seniormost, sits in the middle, looking uncharacteristically glum, with an amused-looking Aryadeva on his right and a faintly smiling Sangharakshita on his left. Between Saranankara and me, a little to the rear, stands Joe, lips pursed as though he had just sucked a lemon and eyes looking piercingly through heavy spectacle-frames. Lilian Silburn, who wears a sari, sits cross-legged on the floor at my feet. Like me, she manages a faint smile. Ani-la, sitting at Aryadeva's feet, has the mournful, resigned expression of one who, in her own opinion at least, is obliged to put up with a good deal of ill usage. She fingers a rosary, but mechanically, her thoughts far away.

It being a studio photograph, none of us looks very natural, with the possible exception of Aryadeva, who appears about to crack a joke, as he often did. Though Ani-la's mournful, resigned expression was quite characteristic of her, she was in fact at that time happier than I had ever known her to be. She had abandoned her electrified cave at Tirpai and moved into a room on the ground floor of the Manjula cottage. As Lobsang and his wife were living in the upstairs flat that had once been Miss Barclay's she had easy access to Tibetan lessons, Lobsang having offered to teach her again. She was also studying daily with Tethong Rimpoche, a Gelug incarnate lama recently arrived from Tibet. But probably what contributed most to her happiness at this time was the fact that with Aryadeva and Miss Silburn in Kalimpong she had two friends with whom she could communicate in her own language. Miss Silburn was indeed staying with her (Aryadeva was staying with me), so that the 'compressed' French nun had someone with whom she could share her thoughts and feelings on a day-to-day basis.

Lilian Silburn was almost the exact opposite of Ani-la, at least in temperament. A quiet, modest, unobtrusive Englishwoman, auburn-haired and of no particular looks, she was (or had been) a student at the Sorbonne and was working on a doctoral thesis on discontinuity in Indian thought, the discontinuity in question being that between the substantialist and non-substantialist philosophies. During the month she was in Kalimpong I saw a good deal of her, sometimes together with Ani-la and Aryadeva but more often on her own. Knowing that my mornings and afternoons were occupied she usually came and had lunch with me and then stayed on for a while afterwards. In fact I soon gave her a standing invitation to lunch, as she was intelligent and well-informed and I greatly enjoyed her company. The *Survey* being very much in my mind, I naturally told her about it and explained the general plan of the work. No less naturally, she told me about her thesis and we discussed some of the points with which she was having to deal. She also spoke of her researches into Kashmir Shaivism, one of the comparatively unexplored areas of Indian philosophy and religion – unexplored, that is, by Western savants and their Indian followers. Jagadish Chandra Chatterjee, the wily old Bengali pandit with whom I had been briefly associated in 1947, was one of the few modern scholars to have investigated this ancient tradition, apparently one of the richest and most complex in the whole field of Indian thought and praxis, and I had read his pioneering book on the subject. Yet scholar though Lilian Silburn undoubtedly was (and her knowledge seemed well on its way to winning Ani-la's accolade of 'formidable'), her approach to Indian philosophy and religion was far from being academic in the pejorative sense of the term. She was as much a devotee as a scholar, though only towards the end of her stay did I learn that her affinities were with Hinduism rather than with Buddhism and that she had taken initiation from a Hindu guru.

Among her more peripheral interests were Indian films, about which we had a long discussion, and graphology and other forms of character analysis. One day I selected from my files specimens of the handwriting of some twelve or fourteen correspondents who were personally known to me and asked her to tell me what she could about their respective characters. Her readings proved to be remarkably accurate. At least they accorded with my own knowledge of the persons concerned. Towards the end of the session, however, it was evident she was tiring and her analyses becoming less confident, as though the task of concentrating on so many different handwritings – and so many different persons – one after another demanded a degree of energy that could not be sustained indefinitely. The other forms of character analysis in which she was interested, and which she showed me, included one I had not encountered before. The subject or analysand was given a sheet of paper and a pencil and asked to draw a landscape containing houses, trees, bushes, ponds, bridges, and other such features. Several of our younger members were desirous of submitting themselves to this novel method of analysis. Saranankara, who like many Sinhalese monks was an amateur palmist, had already told their fortunes for them, and they were eager to learn more about their characters and future prospects. By far the most interesting of the drawings thus produced was the one made by Dawa. The faithful secretary of our little Maha Bodhi Society branch had depicted two solidly built houses, identical in size and every other respect but separated by a thick wall that ran right down the middle of the paper, dividing it into roughly equal halves. There was no door in the wall, and no means of climbing over. Miss Silburn was not surprised when I told her that Dawa's affections were divided between his mother, who had forbidden him to marry a non-Tibetan, and the Nepalese girl with whom he had long been in love and to whom he was secretly engaged. Not that I altogether escaped analysis myself, even if it was only self-analysis. At the intuitive little Englishwoman's suggestion I too drew a landscape containing all the prescribed features, but when I asked her to tell me what it revealed of my character she refused to do so, saying I would have to work it out for myself.

Neither Ani-la nor Aryadeva cared to have recourse to paper and pencil in this way, Ani-la indeed being inclined to pooh-pooh the whole idea of character analysis. Had they cared to have recourse to them the results would probably have been both interesting and informative, especially in the case of Aryadeva, whom I knew much less well than I knew Ani-la. In Ani-la's case I at least knew *what* she was like, even if I found it difficult to understand *why* she was like it, whereas in Aryadeva's case my knowledge of what he was like was limited. Though we had corresponded for several years, ever since his ordination as a samanera by my own teacher Jagdish Kashyap, we had spent very little time together. I had bumped into him once or twice in Darjeeling, and he had stayed with me at The Hermitage for a few days, and that was all. During his stay at The Hermitage he had been an object of great interest to our younger members, some of whom were positively fascinated by him. This was due partly to his height, on account of which his yellow-robed form towered above them all in a way at which they never ceased to marvel, and partly to the fact that he played the flute. His flute was in fact his constant companion, and he played it on the slightest provocation. Sometimes he replied to questions by producing on it a kind of derisory flourish. He did this with Ani-la in particular, especially when he thought she was becoming argumentative or too obsessed with her own problems. This annoyed her intensely. At the same time, he would look at her with an expression of such comical good humour that she could not help laughing in spite of herself. Aryadeva, I reflected, was very good for Ani-la. He handled her much better than I did, or at least handled her in a way that gave him less trouble than my way of handling her gave me. For her part, the French nun was quite fond of her flute-playing compatriot, even though she disapproved of his flippancy and had no great regard either for his mental capacity or his knowledge of Buddhism. Despite his having been ordained by Kashyap-ji, who was a scholar of the first water, Aryadeva's knowledge of Buddhism, as of Indian philosophy and religion generally, indeed was not only rudimentary but extremely patchy, though he made up for this by a perverted intellectual ingenuity which enabled him to detect all sorts of 'correspondences' in the fields of philology and comparative religion. One of the most outrageous examples of his ingenuity in this respect was his 'discovery' that the Abraham and Sarah of the Old Testament were none other than the Brahma and Saraswati of Hindu mythology, and this proved that Hebrew was derived from Sanskrit and that Judaism was a branch of Hinduism. For discoveries of this kind his little band of Hindu admirers in Darjeeling were accustomed to speak of him, much to Ani-la's sardonic amusement, as 'a very great scholar'.

So patchy was Aryadeva's knowledge of Buddhism, and so little interest did he evince in traditional Buddhist practices such as meditation and puja, that even after making all possible allowances for differences of background and temperament I still wondered, sometimes, if he was really a Buddhist. Nor was this my only doubt. So hysterical was his high-pitched, whinnying laughter, so bizarre his thought processes, and so manic the expression in his staring blue eyes, that I also wondered if he was entirely sane. But whether or not he was really a Buddhist, and whether or not he was entirely sane, he certainly regarded himself as a Buddhist (though he may have defined the term in his own way), and claimed to have been one even before leaving France for the East. In Paris he had attended meetings of Les Amis du Bouddhisme, and possessed a fund of anecdotes about the members of the formidable female triumvirate that ruled the tiny French Buddhist organization. One of his most amusing anecdotes related to an encounter between Constant Lounsbery, the expatriate American president of Les Amis du Bouddhisme, and Alexandra David-Neël, the famous explorer and author, who was *not* one of the triumvirate. The encounter took place on Vaishakha Purnima Day, which Les Amis du Bouddhisme was celebrating in a grand, neo-classical building in the heart of Paris. Standing at the top of the steps, Mme Lounsbery was receiving, queenlike, members of the association and specially invited guests. Among the guests was Mme David-Neël, who came wearing her red Tibetan lama costume and brandishing a trumpet made from a human thighbone. Having climbed the steps, she halted directly in front of Mme Lounsbery and blew a blast on the trumpet right in the latter's ear. 'What do you think of *that*, madame?' she demanded triumphantly. 'I think it is not Buddhism, madame,' retorted Mme Lounsbery, quivering with indignation. Whereupon there ensued, according to Aryadeva, a violent argument between the two ladies as to what was, and was not, Buddhism. So violent was the argument that, if he was to be believed, the building rocked.

Though Saranankara, Lilian Silburn, and Aryadeva all spent the hottest weeks of the year in Kalimpong (and Darjeeling, in Aryadeva's case), birds of passage there were who descended on the English monk at other seasons. Some came earlier, some later, than the three with whom Joe, Ani-la, and I had our photograph taken that afternoon in mid-May, when Saranankara and I had visited Sachin and performed a *paritta* ceremony for his benefit. There were those who settled in the town – a few of them at Craigside – for months and weeks together, and those who came and went within a matter of days or even hours. Some were already known to me, either personally or through correspondence, while others were people of whom I had not heard but who had, apparently, heard of me and wanted to meet me. Some, again, were people who, regardless of the length of their stay or the extent of our contact, printed themselves indelibly on my memory – not necessarily to their advantage. Others, on the contrary, left on it only the faintest of traces. Among the latter was a Mr Hobson, of whom I remember only that he was an Australian Theosophist, that he arrived early in the year, and that he stayed with me for several months. He must have given me no trouble (otherwise I would probably remember him better), for when I went down to Calcutta at the end of February I allowed him to stay at Craigside on his own. But if he gave me no trouble he apparently was giving it to someone else. While I was in Calcutta a woman came to see me who had been searching for him for several months and who was, she claimed, his wife. At my suggestion she travelled to Kalimpong to see him. What the result of the interview was I never learned, or have forgotten, but on my return to Kalimpong I found Mr Hobson still quietly living at Craigside.

The bird of passage who printed himself most indelibly on my memory, and by no means to his advantage, was a young Italian named Dosi Angelo. We had met in Calcutta, where I helped him obtain a renewal of his visa, and a week or two later he turned up on my doorstep with a lot of luggage and no money. As he spoke not a word of English, communication was difficult, but with Ani-la's help (either she knew a little Italian, or he a little French) I established that he was from northern Italy, that his family owned a bakery and would be sending him money, and that he had come to India in search of initiation into the mysteries of Tantric Yoga. 'La Yoga Tantrica' was a perfect obsession with him. As I had noticed in Calcutta, he could not meet a new person without asking, in an agitated manner, 'La Yoga Tantrica? La Yoga Tantrica?' as though he fully expected them to have the much coveted object somewhere about them and to be able to hand it to him on the spot, like one of his parents' pastries. Yet though the phrase 'La Yoga Tantrica' was constantly on his lips, and though apart from his creature comforts he seemed to think of nothing else, the twenty-three-year-old Italian gave the impression of being as devoid of religious feeling as he was of consideration for other people. With the possible exception of someone I had known in the Army he indeed was the greediest and most selfish person I had ever met. At mealtimes he grabbed at food without waiting to be served, and on one occasion drank the entire contents of a jug of milk. When it was pointed out to him, with the help of gestures, that his action left the rest of us with no milk for our tea, he protested (in Italian, presumably, though his aggrieved expression made his meaning clear enough), 'But I *wanted* it!'

So disruptive was Dosi's infantile behaviour that when his money came through (and getting it for him involved me in protracted negotiations with the bank and the Sub-Divisional Officer) I insisted he moved to a hotel, which with a very ill grace he eventually did. During his last days with us he spent much of his time in the bazaar, making up for the deficiencies of our admittedly spartan diet. To the astonishment of passers-by, who had not seen a European behave in that way before, he would squat at the roadside cracking eggs on the kerb and dropping the contents into his upturned open mouth. At Craigside he spent his afternoons out on the lawn, reclining in the cane-bottomed armchair I had inherited from Major Cummins and eating the little cakes with the brightly coloured icing that he had bought from the itinerant *roti wallah* or bread man. The armchair was one of the old colonial type, with double-length wooden arms on which one could rest one's legs after the day's work. Having spaced out his cakes along these arms, five or six of them on each side, Dosi would pop them into his mouth one by one, a smile of satisfaction on his pink, rather rat-like features. After his departure for the Himalayan Hotel, where he stayed only long enough to obtain a pass for Gangtok, I did not see him again until, some years later, I ran into him in Calcutta. He still knew no English, though he had picked up a few words of Hindi, was again having trouble with his visa, and was as obsessed as ever with '*La Yoga Tantrica*'.

On the eve of Vaishakha Purnima day, some weeks after Dosi Angelo had left Craigside, I received an unexpected visit from a very different kind of person. She was small, bowed down with age and infirmity, wore the brown robe of an anagarika or 'homeless one', and was shaven-headed. It was Mother Vipassana, the Nepalese nun who had taken a great liking to Buddharakshita and me when, six years ago, we arrived at Kusinara in search of ordination as samaneras or novice monks. Not only had she looked after us, and arranged for us to meet U Chandramani, who we hoped would agree to ordain us. When the old man finally did agree, partly as a result of her intervention on our behalf, she also had constituted herself our *Dharma Mata* or 'Mother in Religion', organizing the preparation of our robes and making the customary food-offerings to U Chandramani and all the other monks (including our newly ordained selves) after the ordination ceremony and doing, in short, everything our biological mothers would have done had they been Buddhists and present on the occasion. Now she had come to say goodbye. She did not have much longer to live, she explained, with a smile of the same peculiar sweetness that had lit up her worn features in Kusinara, and wanted to see me, and pay her last respects, before she died. I was deeply touched, but also a little surprised. Though I knew how devoted she was to Buddharakshita and me I had not imagined that almost the last act of her life, as it turned out to be, would be to travel all the way from Kusinara in order to see me for an hour and bid me farewell. Contrary to Theravadin tradition, I offered her something to eat before she left, and was glad when she did not scruple to accept. It was the least I could do. She had been a real Dharma Mata to me. Without her intervention, U Chandramani might not have agreed to ordain me, and had he not ordained me my life thereafter could well have been very different, and probably much more difficult. That apart, I honoured Mother Vipassana as one truly devoted to the spiritual life and would always cherish her memory.

Another anagarika who came to see me about this time was Magandiya. Like Mother Vipassana she was a disciple of U Chandramani, but unlike her older and more literate sister she lived not at Kusinara but on the hillside above Teesta Bazaar, where she had a cottage and piece of land which she cultivated herself, doing all the digging and planting with her own hands, and where I had once visited her. With her lived her father, the aged Sadhu Lama, who was not a lama in the Tibetan sense but one of the many Tamang Buddhists who were called 'Lama' on account of their forebears having belonged to the Tamang priesthood. In the course of my visit I asked what had led her to become an anagarika. '*Dukkha*, Bhante,' she replied, using the Pali word, 'nothing but *dukkha*.' She did not elaborate, but no elaboration was necessary. The tone of her voice, and the look in her eyes, told me all. Suffering had been her teacher, not books. It was deep personal suffering that had made her turn to the Dharma, giving up all worldly ties and responsibilities save that of supporting and caring for her old father, who was unable to manage without her. Not that as an anagarika she had experienced no suffering. Her life was one of great hardship, even of privation, and I was therefore all the more surprised when she told me, probably during that same visit of mine, that she and Sadhu Lama were planning to make a pilgrimage to Lhasa, as the latter wanted to worship at the holy places there before he died. Lhasa being three hundred miles away, and the passes into Tibet more than fifteen thousand feet up, I privately doubted if this was a very practicable proposition, especially as Sadhu Lama was seventy and Magandiya herself over forty. But months later, around the time of Mother Vipassana's visit, they came to see me at Craigside on their way back to Teesta Bazaar *from Tibet*. They had made their pilgrimage. Sadhu Lama had worshipped in the holy places of Lhasa and could die in peace, his last wish fulfilled. Yet the journey had not been an easy one. To begin with, like true pilgrims they had covered the entire distance on foot, walking there *and* back and taking, altogether, three months to do so. Then they had been snowbound, Sadhu Lama had fallen ill, and when their funds ran out Magandiya had been forced to support the pair of them by begging. But they did not complain, and after I had given them tea they set off down the road with stout hearts, seemingly none the worse for their adventure.

The old Tamang and his daughter were by no means the only people of my acquaintance to go on pilgrimage to Lhasa that year, nor was it only Buddhists, apparently, who went. Opening my door one morning I found crouching on the veranda a half naked sadhu or Hindu holy man. He was extremely dark-skinned, with aquiline features and a shock of black hair, so that I judged him to be from South India. Unlike most sadhus he had an excellent command of English, and was in fact an MA We had not exchanged more than a few words before I realized he was in quite an abnormal mental state, though whether as a result of a nervous breakdown or of an overwhelming religious experience it was difficult to tell. Anyway I took him in, and after staying with us for a few days he set out for Lhasa. From various disjointed utterances I had gathered that he was looking for something (what it was he did not know, or could not say), that it was of supreme importance to him to find it, and that he was convinced he would find it in Tibet. Months later he, too, came to see me on his way back to the plains from Lhasa. This time he wore the maroon robes of a Tibetan lama and was shaven-headed. When I asked him if he had found what he was looking for he answered, simply, 'Yes.'

Like the birds of passage who visited me before Vaishakha Purnima, some of those who winged their way to Kalimpong after the thrice-sacred day came from overseas and some from other parts of India. Gregory (as I shall call him) came from England and was a scion of a family well known in English history. Though he stayed with me for three months, leaving only when I myself left Craigside for yet another rented property, he seems to have made little impression on me, for had it not been for an incident that occurred half-way through his stay I might well have remembered him no better than I remember the shadowy figure of innocuous Mr Hobson.

The incident in question took place late one night. We had been talking for some time, probably about the Buddhist attitude towards psychic powers, when Gregory started to speak about black magic. He was evidently well acquainted with the subject. In graphic detail he described the black mass and other satanic rituals, some of which involved animal – and, he hinted, human – sacrifice. The principal centres of black magic in Europe were London, Paris, and Brighton. In all three cities lived powerful black magicians, some of whom were at enmity with one another and fought, by means of black magic, pitched psychic battles that in some cases resulted in the actual death of one or more of the partici- pants – deaths that doctors and the police were unable to explain. These battles took place, I gathered, mainly between the French and the English black magicians, and so vivid a picture of this supernatural warfare did Gregory paint that, as he spoke, I could see in my mind's eye the psychic missiles winging their deadly way across the Channel from Paris to London and Brighton and from London and Brighton to Paris like so many satanic V-1s and V-2s. There was something else I could see – in the

In the garden of `The Hermitage', Kalimpong with (left to right) Miss Singh, Beena (back), Meera, and Hari-didi, circa 1953

Dr and Mrs B.R. Ambedkar

With (left to right) Ani-la, a French nun; Aryadeva, a French samanera; Saranankara, a Sinhalese bhikkhu; Upasaka Joseph E. Cann; Lilian Silburn, an English scholar

Parinirvana stupa and temple at Kusinara, visited with Dhardo Rimpoche in 1956

With Khemasiri, escorting the Dalai Lama on his arrival at `Everton Villa', March 1957

With Dhardo Rimpoche outside the Maha Bodhi Temple, Bodh-gaya, 1956

With Khemasiri, escorting the Dalai Lama on his arrival at `Everton Villa', March 1957

The 2500th Buddha Jayanti procession arriving at Mela Ground, Kalimpong, May 1957

With Khemasiri, leading the 2500th Buddha
Jayanti procession through the streets of
Kalimpong, May 1957

With Dhardo Rimpoche in front of Ashoka's
column (which marks the birthplace of the
Buddha), Lumbini, 1956

Kachu Rimpoche, circa 1957

Chattrul Sangye Dorje, 1950s

literal sense. In the pupils of the young Englishman's eyes burned two tiny green flames. As he continued to speak, and I to listen, the flames grew steadily bigger and brighter, until eventually the entire room was engulfed in a brilliant green fluorescence. At this point, when I could see nothing but the fluorescence, I realized that something untoward was going on and started mentally reciting the mantra of Avalokiteshvara, the Bodhisattva of Compassion. Immediately the green fluorescence disappeared, and there was my clean-featured companion again, sitting on the other side of the table and still quietly speaking.

Sikkim was not a part of India, and it was certainly not overseas. It was an Indian protectorate and the larger state was represented, as in the days of the Raj, by a resident Political Officer who was the principality's *de facto* ruler. During my visit to Gangtok the new Political Officer, Apa B. Pant, had expressed a wish to have some discussion with me in Kalimpong, and one afternoon in August he accordingly came to tea and we talked at length about conditions in Sikkim and Bhutan and about Buddhism. He was particularly interested, it seemed, to ascertain the extent of Communist influence in the area, especially among members of the younger generation, and though he was responsible to the Ministry of External Affairs in Delhi, which was well known to be riddled with fellow travellers, I formed the distinct impression that personally he was anti-Communist rather than otherwise. He was also concerned to assure me that as Indian High Commissioner in Kenya he had not aided and abetted the Mau Mau terrorists, as alleged in the British press. The reason for his concern was not clear. I was in any case unaware of his having been High Commissioner in Kenya, and probably had not even heard of the Mau Mau before. Perhaps my visitor took me to be more British, or a greater reader of the newspapers, than I actually was.

Chapter Eighteen

BOMBAY REVISITED

TOWARDS THE END OF AUGUST, when I had been living at Craigside for less than a year, the landlord informed me that the property had been bought by a wealthy Tibetan refugee and that the new owner wanted to move in right away. Though I had not been following events in Tibet very closely, I knew the Chinese were tightening their grip on the country and that the Tibetans were becoming increasingly restive. I also knew that members of the aristocratic governing class had started arriving in Kalimpong in greater numbers and that many of them were buying from the Marwaris, at vastly inflated prices, such English-style houses and bungalows as happened to be on the market. It was one of these moneyed new arrivals, I gathered, who had taken a fancy to Craigside and made our landlord an offer the latter felt unable to refuse.

The idea of our leaving Craigside did not disturb me personally, even though I knew that the move to new premises would mean an interruption to my work on the *Survey*. I had put down no roots in the place, and there was nothing about it I would regret as much as I had regretted the loss of the garden when we left The Hermitage. But if the idea of our leaving Craigside did not disturb me personally it certainly disturbed me in my capacity as bhikshu-in-charge of the Kalimpong Branch of the Maha Bodhi Society. Since my arrival in the town more than five years earlier I had conducted Buddhist activities at, and from, as many as five different premises, and well knew the disruptive effect a change of location could have on those activities. But there was no help for it. We had to leave Craigside, a new place had to be found, and I accordingly asked our members and friends to look out for a suitable property that was available at a rent we could afford. In the end it was Chunnilal, our landlord, who found our new home for us and persuaded the owners to let us have it for a hundred and thirty rupees a month, which was still thirty rupees more than we were paying at present. Where the extra money was going to come from I did not know, but trusting it would come from somewhere, as it always did when really needed, I closed the deal and prepared to move.

Everton Villa was situated on the outskirts of the Development Area, not far from Panorama, which meant that it was about two miles from the bazaar. Like Panorama it occupied a broad hillside terrace, and like Panorama it commanded a magnificent view of the Darjeeling foothills, as well as the foothills of western Sikkim. Like Panorama, too, it was not overlooked by any other building and was strangely quiet, not only at night but even during the day. Oblong in shape, and with a roof of so low a pitch that it was almost flat, the isolated, unpretentious bungalow contained three large rooms at the front and three much smaller ones at the back. The middle room at the front, which was very large, opened on to a narrow veranda running the whole length of the building. Behind, there was a kitchen, storeroom, and servants' quarters, and on one side a square of lawn in the centre of which stood a small monkey puzzle tree. Access was by means of a flight of stone steps that from the pukka road connecting the Upper and Lower Cart Roads ran down to the square of lawn. When Chunnilal first took me to see Everton Villa I was not favourably impressed. It had been empty for a couple of years (why, I discovered only later) and presented a shabby, neglected appearance. The roof leaked, some windows were broken, and on the walls of the front rooms patches of mould had developed, so that the air indoors was damp and musty. However, the owners undertook to repair and decorate the place, within little more than a week the work was finished, and on a rainy day in mid-September I moved into our new abode, now smelling of paint and varnish and wearing a brighter, more cheerful look. A few days later came Anagarika Dharmapala's birth anniversary, which we celebrated under Anand-ji's presidentship with the usual speeches in honour of 'the greatest Buddhist missionary of modern times', and the following day I resumed work on the *Survey*.

Not that the work on the *Survey* was merely resumed. I actually put on a spurt, and in the course of the next few weeks not only succeeded in finishing Chapter Three, 'The Mahayana Schools', but also made a good start on Chapter Four, 'The Bodhisattva Ideal', with which the book concluded. What made it possible for me to put on the spurt was the fact that, though I still taught at the Dharmodaya Vihara's evening college, and still gave lessons to Durga and his friends, I was no longer having to devote time to the rewriting of Lobsang Phuntsok's article on Tibetan

Buddhism, the handwritten draft of which had eventually come to comprise more than three hundred foolscap pages. I had finished the work a week before moving into Everton Villa, and had handed the last typed corrected sheets to the grateful young Tibetan aristocrat with a feeling akin to relief. It was well that I had finished it when I did. Dr Kenneth W. Morgan, the American scholar who had commissioned the article, arrived in Kalimpong a few days later, and Lobsang was able to deliver the completed manuscript to him personally in Dhardo Rimpoche's and my presence. The following year, edited and drastically shortened, the article appeared in Dr Morgan's *The Path of the Buddha*, which also contained an article by Kashyap-ji on 'Origin and Expansion of Buddhism'.

As the material for Lobsang's article had been supplied by Dhardo Rimpoche, and as the Rimpoche himself had been educated at Drepung, the manuscript delivered to the American scholar inevitably reflected the more intellectual Buddhism of the great Gelug monastic universities. Towards the end of September, and during the month of October, I became better acquainted with a very different kind of Tibetan Buddhism. This was the ethnic, almost tribal Buddhism of the inhabitants of the Tamang village at Seventh Mile. Despite their living just down the road, so to speak, for one reason or other I had seen much less of these rustic followers of Padmasambhava than I had of their more numerous co-religionists in Darjeeling, but recently they had invited me to give a lecture for their especial benefit in the village school. Down to Seventh Mile one afternoon I therefore went and spoke for an hour and a half on 'The Three Jewels'. So successful was this lecture, which was attended not only by the Tamangs themselves but by their Hindu neighbours, that in the course of the next few months I was invited to give two more lectures and accordingly spoke on 'Meditation and the Mantra *om mani padme hum*' and on 'The Buddhist World'. The first lecture having dealt with the fundamentals of Buddhism, of which I knew the Tamangs to be woefully ignorant, in the second I sought to elucidate a sacred formula with which they were familiar but of which they had little or no understanding, and in the third to give them an idea of the extent and diversity of the religion to which they belonged and of which their own tradition formed a part. At the conclusion of the third lecture I was taken to see the gompa, which stood a little apart from the village. It was very small, and comprised no more than a single whitewashed room at the far end of which, on a low platform, sat three life-size clay images. The images represented Buddha Amitabha, Bodhisattva Avalokiteshvara, and the Precious Guru,

Padmasambhava – the traditional Nyingma triad. All three were of extremely crude workmanship and painted in colours which must have looked gaudy when new. The art of a religion, I reflected, tended to flourish or decline as the religion itself flourished or declined, and if images in a Tamang gompa were crude it was probably because the Nepalese followers of the Precious Guru had long been out of touch with the spirit of the Nyingma tradition.

After seeing the gompa I took tea at the house of a sympathetic Hindu Newar, with whom I discussed the possibility of buying land at Seventh Mile and building a monastery there, for remote as Everton Villa was from the bazaar a wealthy Tibetan refugee was just as likely to take a fancy to it as to Craigside, in which case we should be homeless again. Sooner or later, it seemed, the Kalimpong Branch of the Maha Bodhi Society would have to acquire its own permanent premises. I therefore continued to think of buying land at Seventh Mile, and did so for some time, but nothing ever came of the idea. In any case, shortly after giving my lecture on 'The Buddhist World' I left for Bombay, and when I returned to Kalimpong six months later I had other things to think about.

There were two reasons for my making the trip to Bombay. Towards the end of 1952, after taking part in the re-enshrinement of the relics of the Arahants Shariputra and Maudgalyayana at Sanchi, I had spent three weeks in the city as the guest of Raj Kapoor, the famous film star, who was planning to produce a film with a Buddhist theme and wanted to consult with me about it. During those weeks I struck up a friendship with Arjundev Rashk, the young Punjabi scriptwriter of the film, which was to be called *Ajanta*, after the famous cave temples, and we had kept up a desultory correspondence ever since. Recently he had been urging me to pay another visit to Bombay. Raj Kapoor was again thinking seriously about *Ajanta*, he wrote, and he himself was busy revising the script and badly in need of my assistance. Would I please come as soon as possible? The other reason for my going to Bombay was that the Wadias wanted me to give a couple of lectures there and that I needed, in any case, to discuss with B.P. Wadia the forthcoming publication of the *Survey*, now complete except for the last four sections of Chapter Four. On 1 November, having delivered my usual full moon day sermon the previous night, I therefore travelled down to Siliguri and caught the evening train to Katihar Junction. Fortunately I was not having to make the long journey across the subcontinent on my own, as Sachin had decided to accompany me. He had passed his IA examination, with honours, and after spending two weeks with me in Bombay would be joining college in Calcutta and reading for an Arts degree.

At Katihar Junction, which we reached at two in the morning, we had to wait twelve hours for our connection and it was another twelve hours before we reached Benares. Ten minutes earlier I had been surprised to see the pink sandstone tower of the Mulagandhakuti Vihara appearing above the trees, as I had not realized we would be approaching Benares from the Sarnath side. In the City of Ghats our train arrived after we had been waiting little more than an hour, and soon we were again on our way. Eighteen hours later, when we had enjoyed a good night's rest (Sachin on the luggage rack, I on the bench below), we found ourselves clanking slowly through the insalubrious suburbs of Bombay and steaming, at last, into the soot-blackened neo-Gothic splendours of the Victoria Terminus. My friend Soratha, the Little Monk, was there to meet us. In the absence of a permanent bhikshu-in-charge he was spending his holiday, at Devapriya-ji's request, looking after the Ananda Vihara, one of the Maha Bodhi Society's two centres in Bombay, and it was to the Ananda Vihara that he joyfully took us to stay.

The modest, two-storey building was situated on a busy thoroughfare in the heart of the city, not far from Bombay Central Railway Station, and stood in a corner of the Nair Hospital compound. Vihara and hospital had been built in the twenties by the late Dr Anandrao Nair, a wealthy physician from South India who had become a Buddhist, or at least a very good friend of Buddhism, and who had organized the Buddha Society, Bombay. The hospital was, of course, much bigger than the vihara, and in fact seemed likely to squeeze the latter out of existence. It was also much busier. Not more than half a dozen people came to the vihara from one week's end to the next, Soratha told me, whereas hundreds came to the hospital every day, as I could see for myself by looking out of the window. Moreover, in the centre of the common courtyard between the vihara and the main entrance to the hospital stood a small Hindu shrine, which may or may not have been built by Dr Nair. This was constantly thronged with worshippers, mostly women, either praying for someone's recovery or giving thanks for a cure. None of them even glanced in the direction of the vihara, much less entered its modest portals or sat quietly for a few minutes in front of the big alabaster Buddha, as Dr Nair apparently had hoped they would. The Ananda Vihara was in fact distinctly under-used. Vaishakha Purnima was celebrated every year, and there was the occasional lecture, and that was about all. Soratha, however, was determined that the place should not be under-used while he was in charge, albeit temporarily, and least of all while I was in Bombay and available as a speaker. He had therefore made arrangements for me to give two lectures at the vihara. Quite a few people, it seemed, wanted me to give lectures for them that winter. So much was this the case that not long after my arrival, when I had met Mme Wadia, Rashk, and other friends and had an idea what I would be doing in Bombay, the Little Monk and I drew up a programme of my lectures for the next five or six weeks.

I gave my first two lectures at Aryasangha, the Wadia mansion on Malabar Hill, in what evidently had once been the ballroom. As they were held under the joint auspices of the PEN, the Indian Institute of Culture, Bombay Branch, the Maha Bodhi Society of India, Bombay Branches, and the Indian Council for Cultural Co-operation, both lectures were attended by what the newspapers were accustomed to describe as the cultural élite of Bombay. In the first lecture, 'Buddhism as Doctrine and as Method', I emphasized that the criterion of Truth was pragmatic, and that as Doctrine Buddhism might be defined as a body of teachings the intellectual acceptance of which tended to lead to a course of action eventually resulting in the attainment of Enlightenment. As was famously illustrated by the Buddha's 'Parable of the Raft', Doctrine had only a relative and provisional value, and it was because they were convinced of the relativity of their own doctrines that Buddhists could be undogmatic and, therefore, tolerant. The course of action following from acceptance of the doctrines of Buddhism, and resulting in the attainment of Enlightenment, was threefold, consisting of ethics, meditation, and wisdom. All the methods of Buddhism, comprising its entire practical side, could be included under one or another of these heads. As Method, Buddhism therefore comprised all those practices that were conducive to Enlightenment. After Enlightenment, doctrine or Wisdom meant the actual realization of Truth, and Method the dynamic compassion that caused us spontaneously to help others. Not that we needed to wait for Enlightenment before helping others. Buddhism included both the Path of the Arahant *and* the Path of the Bodhisattva, and helping oneself and helping others were systole and diastole of the spiritual life at *all* its levels.

My second lecture, 'Inspiration – Whence?', given a few days later, was of a more general nature. Though artistic inspiration might appear to come from without, in reality it came from within. The artist was not *wholly* passive; he had an active or creative aspect to his being. Creation meant expression, and expression meant communication, for which a common medium was necessary. Formerly, ideas derived from tradition, especially religious tradition, provided that medium. Not that the purpose of a work of art was to communicate ideas. Its purpose was to communicate feeling (for want of a better term); but feeling could not be communicated without ideas. Though there was no poetry, for example, without intellectual content, poetry was not identical with intellectual content. In modern times, because tradition was breaking down there was no proper medium of communication. We did not know what to believe, and hence there was chaos in the arts. Modern artists were open to low-level inspiration, with results that were often unintelligible, as in the case of Surrealism. The two great difficulties facing the artist today were (*i*) to remain open to high-level inspiration, which could be done with the help of yoga (the poet was, after all, the prophet), and (*ii*) to have a philosophy of life. Ideally, inspiration should come from the highest possible level and be expressed in the most universal terms. Literature should elevate; nowadays it merely depressed.

Both lectures were well received by my cosmopolitan, not uncritical audience, and after each of them I was besieged by people who wanted to ask questions or simply to meet me. The second lecture indeed aroused a quite exceptional degree of interest. This was due partly to the nature of the subject, which was of special concern to the many people present who were involved with the arts, and partly to the fact that having taken the measure of my audience I spoke with considerable feeling and gave what in my opinion was a particularly good lecture. Among the people who besieged me afterwards there was a short, middle-aged woman in a Western-style frock who, being more pertinacious than the rest, was soon claiming my exclusive attention. So excited was she, and so voluble, that it was not easy for me to make out what she wanted to convey. Eventually I gathered that in my lecture I had given utterance to some of her own deepest beliefs, that she painted and meditated, that she considered herself a Buddhist, that she wanted me to meet someone called Dr Mehta, and that she would be coming to the Ananda Vihara in a few days' time and taking me to her place for tea. Thus began a connection that was to last many years and be the occasion, before long, of my making new friends and extending the sphere of my activities.

After the lectures at Aryasangha came the lectures Soratha had arranged for me to give at the Ananda Vihara. I gave them the following weekend, and being held under the auspices of the same group of organizations as before they were attended by much the same kind of people, who, if they came in considerably smaller numbers, at least came out of a more definite interest in Buddhism. Unfortunately the atmosphere of the second meeting, when I spoke on 'Buddhist Meditation', was initially spoiled by some long-winded and unnecessary remarks from the chair. Mme Wadia had introduced my first lecture at Aryasangha by reading aloud one of my poems, Sir H.V. Divatia, the Vice-Chancellor of Ahmedabad University, had introduced the second with a few appropriate words, while the well-known Pali scholar Dr N.K. Bhagwat, who had presided at the Ananda Vihara the previous day, when I spoke on 'Buddhism and the Future of India', had followed up my lecture by heartily concurring with my belief that Buddhism still had much to contribute to the land of its birth. Silver-haired Dr Kaikini, a tall, angular figure in a grey Western-style suit, chose to do things differently. His introduction was a rambling, incoherent discourse in which he perpetrated, in the course of half an hour, more blunders about Buddhism than I had encountered during the previous twelvemonth. Before I could speak on Buddhist meditation I therefore had to explain, *pace* the president of the meeting, what Buddhism did *not* teach. This unpropitious beginning did not prevent my lecture from being a success, and to judge by the length of the ensuing discussion Buddhist meditation was a subject in which many members of the audience were deeply interested. None the less I was dismayed that Dr Kaikini had been able to air his muddled views on such an occasion, especially as he was one of the leading members (an office bearer, I think) of the Ananda Vihara branch of the Maha Bodhi Society, as the Buddha Society had become after Dr Nair's death. If the tiny Buddhist movement of Bombay had many friends like Dr Kaikini, I reflected, it would not need enemies.

Not that the Ananda Vihara was the only Buddhist centre at which I had cause for dismay, or at least for disappointment, that week. Two days after giving my lecture on 'Buddhist Meditation' I spoke at the Bahujana Vihara, Parel, and at the Japanese Buddhist Temple, Worli. The Bahujana Vihara, the Maha Bodhi Society's other branch in Bombay, was situated down a side street in a working-class district dominated by factory chimneys. It consisted of a Sinhalese-style preaching hall, open on three sides and having a stupa at the far end, and a small bungalow for the accommodation of the bhikshu-in-charge. Despite its name, which meant 'Vihara of (or for) the Masses', it did not enjoy much support among the local people, most of whom were in any case Hindus, and according to Soratha it was almost as under-used as its sister vihara in the Nair Hospital compound. Its principal function was to serve as a hostelry for Sinhalese Buddhists, and it was probably no coincidence that my audience that evening included a party of thirty-one monks on pilgrimage from Ceylon. I spoke on 'Dharma-Vijaya', or conquest by righteousness as opposed to conquest by force, and at the conclusion of my lecture I appealed to the monks – their lay guide interpreting – to come forward and assist in the propagation of Buddhism in India, which I said was severely handicapped for want of workers. My appeal fell on deaf ears. For all the response I received, I might as well have appealed to the stupa behind me. The faces of the thirty-one yellow-robed figures betrayed not so much as a flicker of interest. Most of them indeed seemed more dead than alive. At the Japanese Buddhist Temple, where I spoke on 'The Message of Buddhism' to a very attentive audience, the situation was hardly better. The Scheduled Castes Hindus who frequented the place had learned to chant *nam myoho renge kyo*, 'Homage to the Lotus Sutra', to the thunderous accompaniment of the big temple drum, and that was about all. What the *Lotus Sutra* was, and why they were paying homage to it, they did not know, and as the Nichirenite monk or priest who banged the drum for an hour and a half every evening spoke only Japanese he was not in a position to enlighten them.

With the Ananda Vihara being under-used, or even misused, the Bahujana Vihara serving mainly as a hostelry for Sinhalese pilgrims, and the Japanese Buddhist Temple confining itself to drum-beating and chanting in Japanese, it appeared that Buddhism in Bombay was not in a very flourishing condition. I even began to suspect that it had been in better shape during the twenties and early thirties, when Dr Nair organized the Buddha Society and built the Ananda Vihara. This suspicion of mine was soon confirmed. Though Dr Nair had been dead more than twenty years his widow was still living in the city, and shortly after giving my Parel and Worli lectures I found myself partaking of a ceremonial food-offering in the block of flats that had once been the family mansion and listening to her rapturous accounts of what her philanthropic physician-husband had done for the poor of Bombay and for Buddhism. She was in fact very pleased to see me and overjoyed to be able to show me her Buddhist treasures, as she called the various works of Buddhist art Dr Nair had collected over the years. Treasures indeed they were, the collection including as it did magnificent bronze and alabaster Buddhas from Thailand and Burma, Gandharan sculptured panels, Japanese folding screens, Chinese porcelain pagodas, copies of Ajanta frescoes, and large modern oil paintings of scenes from the life of the Buddha, together with a hundred *objets d'art* in ivory, crystal, and sandalwood. Alas! they were all crammed into two or three shuttered rooms and covered in dust. After Dr Nair's death the family's fortunes had declined, Mrs Nair had been obliged to withdraw into a corner of the mansion, letting out the rest, and had neither the space in which to display her treasures nor the means to look after them.

By this time Sachin and I had been in Bombay a fortnight. While I lectured and met Buddhists and sympathizers with Buddhism, he had been looking up old friends who were either studying or working in the city, especially the film actress Malla Sinha and her parents, who were Nepalese and hailed from Kurseong. But now his holiday was over, and it was time for him to leave for Calcutta and for me to get back to the *Survey* and to start helping Rashk revise the script of *Ajanta*. On the evening of the day on which Mrs Nair showed me her Buddhist treasures I accordingly saw my young companion off at VT, as the Victoria Terminus was universally known, and the following day moved to Rashk's ground floor flat at Khar, a newish, middle-class suburb on the western side of the Bombay peninsula. I was sorry to say goodbye to Sachin, especially as for the next two years we would not be seeing much of each other, and sorry to leave the Ananda Vihara, where Soratha and I had enjoyed our usual lively exchanges and where, moreover, I had made friends with a young Burmese monk who happened to be staying there. This young monk was exceptionally good-looking, and I was not surprised to learn that thereby hung a tale. He told me the tale not long after we had got to know each other, and though he told it in a simple, unaffected manner it was the kind of story to which only the colourful, impressionistic pen of a Lafcadio Hearn could really have done justice, in the sense of sketching in its idyllic background, exploiting its romantic interest, and bringing out the characters of the two people involved.

The scene of the story was a small monastery on the outskirts of a village in the heart of rural Burma. There Visuddhisara or 'Essence of Purity', as the good-looking young monk was called, had lived with the learned elder under whose direction he was studying. Each morning, as the custom was, the two monks went into the village with their alms-bowls, moving silently from door to door until they had collected enough rice and curry for their one meal of the day. On festival days and other special occasions, however, the villagers brought food to the monastery and served it to the monks on the broad veranda. Two of the villagers, a mother and her unmarried daughter, were especially assiduous in this respect. By the time Visuddhisara had been at the monastery a few months they were bringing food to him and his teacher every day, so that the two monks no longer had to go into the village with their alms-bowls. One day the daughter came alone. Her mother was ill, she explained. As it happened, Visuddhisara's teacher had gone to visit a colleague in a neighbouring village, so that the young monk and the maiden had the veranda to themselves. When she had served him and he had eaten his fill and chanted a blessing, the maiden prostrated herself three times before him and asked him to excuse her presumption. She had a confession to make, she said – and a proposal. His good looks, and dignified bearing, had impressed her deeply – so deeply that she had fallen in love with him. As her mother's only child, she would inherit the house where they lived, along with some land. If his reverence wished, he could give up the yellow robe and marry her. He would not have to work, and they could live happily together for the rest of their lives. She would be a good and faithful wife to him, and he would have no cause to regret his decision. The proposal took Visuddhisara completely by surprise. He had never contemplated marriage, nor had he ever felt any romantic interest in the maiden. Since he kept his eyes lowered in the presence of women, as a monk should, he had not even realized before how beautiful she was. None the less he promised to consider her proposal. Whereupon she prostrated herself three times and left.

During the next few days Visuddhisara looked deep into his own heart. What he saw shining there, like a vein of gold in the depths of a mine, was a desire to be a monk for the rest of his life, and though tempted by the proposal he had received, and conscious that in Burma it was possible to leave the yellow robe without dishonour, he knew he had no alternative but to be true to that desire. When he and the maiden next had the veranda to themselves he therefore told her that much as he appreciated her offer he wanted to remain a monk and strive for nirvana. Deeply disappointed, she prostrated herself in silent acceptance of his decision. Nor was her proposal mentioned between them again. But she and her mother still came to the monastery every day, bringing food for him and his teacher, and continued to do so right up to the time of his departure for Bombay.

Simply and unaffectedly as Visuddhisara told his story, I found it difficult to know which to admire more, the firmness with which the young monk had rejected the maiden's proposal, or the good grace with which she had accepted that refusal. A Western woman, I reflected, might not have given up so easily. The manner in which the two actors in the little drama had acquitted themselves in fact reflected credit on them both, as well as on the traditional culture of Buddhist Burma, within which they had grown up and whose values had no doubt influenced their behaviour.

Chapter Nineteen

THE PRESENCE IN THE CORNER

THE SUBURB TO WHICH I HAD MOVED was on the local railway line. From the station a road ran north, and from this road, at regular intervals, the still unmade-up roads extended east towards the middle of the peninsula and west towards the coast. Rashk's flat was located in a square white building, very similar to all its square white neighbours, which was situated near the end of 18th Road, one of the last side roads to the west. It was a small flat, consisting, besides the usual offices, of a lounge, a bedroom, and a kitchen. The lounge was furnished, Western-style, with a sofa, two armchairs, a coffee table, and a bookcase containing, as I soon discovered, a stack of *Time* magazines, numerous American and Russian novels (*not* the classics), and the ten-volume official biography of Mahatma Gandhi. Here I was installed, Rashk having come and fetched me and my small luggage from the Ananda Vihara, and here for the next two months and more I stayed. The lounge was very quiet, as was the rest of the flat and, indeed, the whole building. This was due principally to the road not being a through road but coming to an abrupt end at the edge of a piece of waste ground, beyond which were only the huts of the dark-skinned fisherfolk who, until a few centuries ago, had been the sole occupants of the seven islands that were now the city of Bombay.

In circumstances thus propitious it did not take me long to settle down, and two or three days after moving to Khar I resumed work on the *Survey*. As my custom was, I worked on it in the morning, usually managing to complete three or four foolscap pages before lunch. After lunch I rested and read, dipping into Rashk's bookcase, and in the afternoon or evening – sometimes until late at night – my scriptwriter friend and I would discuss the story line, or the dialogue, of *Ajanta*, as well as the Hindi novelette he was writing. At least such was our routine initially. Before a week had passed Rashk was having to spend much of the day out on business of his own, sometimes leaving the flat early in the morning and not returning until 11 or 12 at night, to the ill-concealed annoyance of his young wife, who disliked spending the whole day with only the two teenage maidservants for company. For my part, I did not mind having extra time in which to work on the *Survey*, especially as B.P. Wadia was getting the manuscript typed and had started sending me bulky instalments of typescript for correction. Nor did I mind having extra time for the exploration of Rashk's bookcase, and besides reading several of the modern American and Russian novels, of which only Hemingway's *The Old Man and the Sea* really impressed me (I had not read any Hemingway before), managed to get through Kenneth Walker's *Venture with Ideas* and Axel Münthe's *The Story of San Michele* and to make a start on the multi-volume *Mahatma*.

My exploration of his bookcase led to some lively discussions with Rashk, when he was at home, and I formed the impression that he was happier to talk about literature than to finish revising the script of *Ajanta*, to serious work on which we got down only several weeks later. His tastes were very different from my own, modern American authors being the principal occupants of his literary Valhalla, and William Faulkner the god of his particular idolatry. At that time my knowledge of American literature was confined to Emerson, Poe, Walt Whitman, and Harriet Beecher Stowe; of the moderns I knew nothing, and if, years later, I got round to reading Faulkner (and certain of his contemporaries) this was to some extent due to my discussions with Arjundev Rashk at Khar in the winter of 1955–56. Not that our discussions at his flat, and in taxis and Irani tea-shops on our occasional joint forays into town, were by any means restricted to literature. They ranged over a variety of topics, from politics to sex, and from Buddhism to the Japanese film. We also talked about ourselves. At least Rashk talked about himself. As I already knew, his mother tongue was Punjabi, and his preferred literary medium Urdu, in which he had written poetry ('Rashk' was not his surname, i.e. caste name, but his poetic *nom de plume*, and as such rightly to be enclosed within single inverted commas). What I did not know was that he had not been born in India. He had been born and brought up in Burma, in Rangoon. At the time of the Japanese invasion, when he was still in his teens, he and his family had fled as refugees to India, making the last part of their journey on foot through the jungles of Burma and Assam. In this connection he had a curious story to tell. Like the tale told me by Visuddhisara, it was one to which only the pen of a Lafcadio Hearn (in this case the Hearn of the late Japanese ghost stories), or perhaps, in a different style, the pen of a Somerset Maugham, could have done justice.

A year or so before the invasion he had consulted an astrologer about his future. Not that he had much faith in astrology then, he explained, but most Hindus believed in it, even English-educated ones, and being on the threshold of manhood, and uncertain which direction in life to take (his real ambition was to be a poet), he thought he might as well find out what the stars had to say on the subject, if indeed they had, or could have, anything to say on it. To his surprise the astrologer, after making his calculations, professed himself extremely puzzled. He could tell his client what he saw, he declared, but not its meaning. What he saw was a broad track through dense jungle. On either side of the track, for its entire length, human skeletons were lying, and along this track, between the skeletons, his teenage client was walking, tired and hungry, with the sun blazing overhead and the vultures circling. A year or so later the prediction – for such it turned out to have been – was strangely and tragically fulfilled. With what remained of his family, Rashk told me, a more sombre expression than usual clouding his pleasant, irregularly-shaped countenance, he had found himself in just such a jungle as the astrologer had described, stumbling along just such a track, fleeing as fast as his failing strength permitted from the advancing Japanese troops. He must have passed thousands of skeletons, their bones picked clean by vultures – the remains of those Indian and European refugees, indistinguishable now in death, who had fallen exhausted by the wayside and perished before they could reach safety. As a result of this experience, he said in conclusion, he had developed a certain amount of faith in astrology. At least he no longer dismissed it out of hand. There were good astrologers in Bombay, one of whom came to the flat every month and gave him the benefit of his – or the stars' – advice and guidance. That this was the case I already knew, having seen a thin, elderly brahmin arriving one morning and being shown into the bedroom, where he remained closeted with Rashk an hour for what, the latter afterwards told me, was a professional consultation. What I did not know was that before I left Bombay I would be having, in connection with that same elderly brahmin, a curious story of my own to tell.

As a Buddhist, I had no faith in astrology, in the sense that I did not believe that the relative positions of the stars and planets determined events on Earth, including events in individual lives. Had not the Buddha (as Bodhisattva, in the Jataka Book) scornfully demanded, in words my rationalist friend Anand-ji was fond of quoting, *'Kim karissanti taraka?*

What can the stars do?' Yet the resemblance between Rashk's experience, as he journeyed on foot through the jungles of Burma and Assam, and what the Rangoon astrologer had predicted, was too close to be explicable in terms of pure coincidence. A clue was perhaps to be found in the fact that the astrologer had, as it appeared, spoken of *seeing* the track through the jungle, the human skeletons, and his client walking between them. Perhaps it was a case, not of his having predicted Rashk's future in accordance with calculations made on the basis of a reading of the stars, but rather of his having 'seen' that future clairvoyantly by means of a precognitive faculty that had been brought into play as a result of the intense concentration the making of those calculations required. Be that as it may, one story about the occult led to another, as usually happened when that fascinating subject was broached, and I think it was on this occasion that I told Rashk about my own precognitive experiences as a teenager, when I 'saw' what was going to happen to me (though not was going to happen to others) half an hour or so beforehand, as well as about my 'seeing' Buddharakshita clairvoyantly one night when he was several hundred miles away. I did not, however, tell him about a strange experience that had befallen me much more recently, under his own hospitable roof, and in the very room in which we were sitting. I did not tell him about it, partly because it was not occult in the sense that clairvoyance and precognition were occult, being an experience of an entirely different order, and partly because I had no words with which to describe it.

It was an experience of Presence or, perhaps I should say, of *a* Presence. Though what was present was definitely not a thing but a person (not that Presence and person were really distinguishable), equally the presentness was not that of any particular person. Moreover, the Presence was spatially located. 'It' occupied a certain corner of the room, the one nearest the door, which, as I sat cross-legged on the sofa writing, was to my left. Objectively speaking, it was a strange experience, but though I recognized it, intellectually, as being strange, I never *felt* it to be so. There was nothing 'spooky' about the Presence, and when it was 'there', in its usual corner (not that it had any dimensions), I felt quite comfortable with it and at home. It always 'appeared' (not that I ever actually saw anything) when I was alone, perhaps when I had been alone for some time, and while I was writing. By now the end of the *Survey* was in sight, and I was working on the penultimate and antepenultimate sections of the last chapter, which dealt, respectively, with 'The Thought of Enlightenment' and 'The Ten Perfections'. As this whole chapter, and these two sections in particular, were devoted to the Bodhisattva Ideal, 'the perfectly ripened fruit of the whole vast tree of Buddhism', as I then believed it to be, I could not forbear wondering, later on, if there had been a connection between my 'strange' experience and the lofty ideal about which I was writing. Might not the Presence have been that of a Bodhisattva, or even of the Buddha? But this was only speculation *after* the event. What I experienced at the time was Presence, or *a* Presence. Not any particular person, good or bad, human or divine. Just personalimpersonal *Presence*.

The Presence appeared when I was *alone*, or rather, it did not appear when I was not alone. But I was not often alone, especially after Rashk, his outside business apparently concluded, started bethinking himself of the unfinished script of *Ajanta* and of the work we were supposed to be doing on it together. The time I was least alone, both before and after our getting down to serious work on the long-neglected script, was the evening, this being the time, usually, when Rashk's friends called on him and when we, though more rarely, went to see them. His friends were all men (at least I remember no women, though he appeared to be acquainted with some of the wives), and most of them belonged to, or were connected with, the film industry, whether as producers, directors, actors, scriptwriters, musicians, or artists. The friend of whom we saw most, and whom I got to know best, was tall, portly Jairaj, a South Indian in his early or middle forties who, Rashk told me, had played the hero in more than thirty Tamil 'mythological' films. What was of greater interest to me, he also happened to be a nephew (by marriage, I think) of Sarojini Naidu, the Nightingale of India, on whose poetry, shortly after my arrival in India, I had written an article. Like other members of Rashk's circle, he had a genuine interest in religion and philosophy, as his library attested, and we had more than one discussion on these subjects. Producers excepted, most of those who worked in the film industry were, I found, much less interested in their actual jobs than they were in doing other things. Rashk himself, I remembered, had told me, on my earlier visit to Bombay, that he wrote film scripts only because he could not afford to write poetry. Similarly, Achrekar, who was Raj Kapoor's art director (and designer of the *Maha Bodhi Journal's* new cover) would rather have been painting pictures, and Abbas, a more successful scriptwriter than Rashk, would have preferred to be adding another popular novel to his *œuvre*.

Besides the people I met of an evening, there were those I saw in the course of my forays into town, both with and without Rashk. As my work on the *Survey* drew to a close (I must have finished it early in the New Year) these forays became not only more frequent but longer and more of the nature of excursions. On four or five of these I gave lectures, and on one of them presided over the World Religions Day meeting organized by the Baha'i community. This last-named event, which went off even better than the organizers had dared hope, was attended by representatives of an astonishing variety of religions, sects, and cults. Bombay was not just a cosmopolitan city, not just a whole world in itself; it was a world within which there was a multitude of sub-worlds, religious, cultural, linguistic, and so on, most of which overlapped only to a limited extent. During the months of December and January I became acquainted, or better acquainted, with at least three of these sub-worlds, one cultural (if the film industry sub-world could indeed be so categorized), one religious, and one socio-religious, as well as with the three outstanding personalities by which they were severally dominated. As there was no overlap between the three sub-worlds, and as in each of them I appeared in a different capacity and functioned in a different manner (though still as a Buddhist monk), during this period I was leading, in a sense, three different lives, or part-lives, and expending my energies in three different directions. Often all three lives, or part-lives, were lived on different days of the same week, even at different hours of the same day, so that in the interests of consecutive narration each 'life' is best dealt with separately from the other two. As Ruskin observes in *Praeterita*, his autobiography:

> Whether in the biography of a nation, or of a single person, it is alike impossible to trace it steadily through successive years. Some forces are failing while others strengthen, and most act irregularly, or else at uncorresponding periods of renewed enthusiasm after intervals of lassitude. For all clearness of exposition, it is necessary to follow first one, then another, without confusing notices of what is happening in other directions.

What is true of successive years may be equally true, sometimes, of the days and weeks of two successive months, even if in their case it might be a question, not so much of forces failing and strengthening as of different forces being deployed at different times, according to circumstances.

The part I played within each of my Bombay sub-worlds was to a great extent determined, at least initially, by my relationship with its leading personality. In the film industry – certainly in the important part of it that was R.K. Films – the leading personality was Raj Kapoor. On my 1952 visit to the city, when he had shared with me his ideas for a film with a Buddhist theme to be called *Ajanta*, we must have met a dozen or more times. Miss Nargis, his principal leading lady, was usually by his side. This time we met only twice or thrice, and he was alone, in the sense that Nargis was not there. As before, we met at The Cottage, Raj Kapoor's private quarters at R.K. Studios, Chembur. At our first meeting, after I had gone on to the set and seen some shooting, discussion naturally soon turned to *Ajanta*. Though we discussed it at some length, indeed, until quite late in the night, I formed the impression that his mind was really on other things. This impression was not unconnected with the fact that in the course of the evening he had brought out from an inner drawer, with the air of a card-player revealing a winning hand, a sheaf of black-and-white photographs of his latest 'discovery' – an attractive Anglo-Indian girl whom he had met, quite by accident, in Delhi. She had the makings of a fine actress, he assured me, his eyes gleaming, and he had promised her a leading role in one of his films. On our way back to Khar Rashk enlightened me as to the background of the story. Relations between Raj Kapoor and Nargis were strained, and he was looking for a new principal leading lady. Whether she was to be given the leading female role in *Ajanta* he did not know. Personally, he did not think Nargis could be so easily replaced. But, with or without Nargis, Raj Kapoor would, he was confident, make the film. Achrekar had already designed costumes for it and created, in his room at R.K. Studios, a plaster and clay model of the main set. Rashk was also confident that the film would be a financial success and that Raj Kapoor would be happy to give me, out of the proceeds, the 20,000 rupees that would be required for the monastery I wanted to build in Kalimpong. Perhaps I would call the monastery the Ajanta Vihara!

The next time Raj Kapoor and I met at The Cottage he was in a very different mood, in fact in a very different mental state altogether. Nor was he alone. Not that it was Nargis who was with him. On this occasion he had for companion the bottle of Black Label on which it was his habit, apparently, to rely for moral support at times of crisis or when he was feeling particularly sorry for himself. The plain truth was that he was drunk, though not so drunk that we were not able to have a long, if rather inconsequential, discussion which he insisted on tape-recording for the benefit of posterity. The discussion was punctuated by maudlin outbursts in which he lamented the loss of his 'discovery' and upbraided her for her treachery, deceitfulness, and ingratitude. She had ruined his life, he declared, to heart-rending sobs. She had destroyed him. Once again it was Rashk who enlightened me as to the background of the story. The Anglo-Indian girl had come to Bombay (R.K. Studios had flown her there). Her screen tests had proved highly satisfactory, and Raj Kapoor had become more convinced of her talent, and more infatuated with her, every day. But last week there had come a message. Would he meet her in town at a certain fashionable restaurant? On entering the place he found, to his astonishment, that his 'discovery' was not alone. She was with a good-looking young man. He was still more astonished when she introduced the young man as her fiancé. They were going to be married quite soon, she said. 'But what about your film career?' a shocked Raj Kapoor had demanded, clutching at a straw. 'Oh my fiancé is a multi-millionaire,' she replied. 'He's ready to make as many films for me as I want.'

The leading personality in the Society of Servants of God was Dr Dinshah Mehta. This was the same mysterious Dr Mehta whom the short, middle-aged woman who had claimed my exclusive attention after the second Aryasangha lecture had been so anxious I should meet. True to her word, she had come to the Ananda Vihara a few days later and taken me to her Marine Drive flat for tea. There I learned that Dinoo Dubash, as she was called, was a Parsee by birth but a Buddhist at heart, that she was a Montessori teacher, having trained with Mme Montessori herself in Italy in the thirties, that she was an insomniac, that the rest of the flat was occupied by her Montessori school, and that she wanted to give a thousand rupees for the Buddha Jayanti. In between she scolded the cook, gave me (or tried to give me) a sumptuous tea, and showed me her Buddhist books, many of them heavily underlined, as well as her water-colour paintings, among which there was a series of striking 'portraits' of the blue-eyed, golden-haired figure who had appeared to her in meditation and whom she believed to be the Buddha Maitreya. I also learned that Dr Mehta was by profession a naturopath, in fact a well-known one, that my hostess had once been a patient of his, and that he had founded the Society of Servants of God three years earlier. Originally it had been called the Society of Servants, Miss Dubash confided, not without a smile of good-natured amusement, but people thought it was a domestic servants' agency and kept telephoning about cooks and bearers, and Dr Mehta had been forced to change it. She herself was not a member of the Society (at least, not a member of the inner circle!), nor did she believe in all its teachings, or accept everything Dr Mehta said, even though it was supposed to come from God, but she liked the

Society's emphasis on meditation and for that reason sometimes attended its meetings.

Despite her excitedness and volubility – her skittishness, even – Dinoo Dubash was, I could see, an essentially serious-minded person, with a genuine devotion to the spiritual life. She was like a little babbling brook, whose excess of foam, as it skips and dances down from the hills, conceals the depth and translucency of its water. I was therefore all the more disposed to treat seriously her reiterated wish that I should meet Dr Mehta and see what I thought of the Society of Servants of God, without allowing myself to be inhibited by the fact that its members were dedicated to the service of a being in whose existence good Buddhists did not believe. As it happened, I had already been approached by a stout, shifty-eyed young representative of the Society and invited to address the Servants of God on 'Love and Devotion in Buddhism', and one morning three weeks after taking tea with Dinoo Dubash accordingly found myself being escorted, by the same shifty-eyed young man, from Khar to the flat on Malabar Hill that was the Society's headquarters.

The flat was located on the ground floor of Mayfair, a block of luxury apartments not far from the Hanging Gardens. From the gloomy hallway there was a dark, narrow passage between what seemed to be wooden cubicles, and at the end of this passage a sunny room furnished, Indian style, with white-covered mattresses and bolsters. Opposite the door, his back against the far wall, sat a grizzled-haired, grossly corpulent figure in close-fitting muslin tunic and white cotton jodhpurs. On the floor beside him rested a telephone set, while in front of him a portable electric fan, swivelling energetically from side to side, sent a swathe of cold air in his direction. He welcomed me cordially, if with a certain solemnity, a smile of satisfaction on his grey, flabby features, after which the two of us got down to a serious discussion, mainly about meditation, that lasted for the remainder of the morning and well into the afternoon. Several members of the Society were present, as was Miss Dubash, but apart from the last-named, whose tongue could not be easily restrained, they were content to lean back against their bolsters and listen. After lunch, eaten from *thalis* in the same room and solemnly blessed before being served, Dr Mehta (for indeed it was he) read to me from what he called The Scripts. The Scripts, I gathered, were the written records of the 'guidance' he had received, over the last few years, when in a state of deep meditation. They were of various lengths, though none of them comprised more than a couple of thousand words. Some were in verse, some in prose. The verse Scripts, which were the shortest, reminded me, in their general tone and tenor, of the earlier, shorter *suras* of the Koran. But long or short, in verse or in prose, and regardless of their actual subject-matter, whether hortatory or consolatory, practical or deeply metaphysical, all the Scripts from which Dr Mehta read that afternoon were couched in the first person singular. Who, then, was the speaker? According to the Society, and indeed The Scripts themselves, it was none other than God. It was God who, through the Servant of Servants, Dr Mehta, directed the affairs of the Society and the lives of its members. The Scripts were thus a species of divine revelation, similar in content, if not in form, to the revelations vouchsafed by the prophets and founders of religions in the past, from Zoroaster to Muhammed.

That the members of the Society (at least the members of what Dinoo Dubash had called the inner circle) believed its affairs, as well as their own lives, to be personally guided by the Almighty meant that their involvement with it had a special significance for them. It also meant that the involvement had a certain depth of seriousness. Something of that seriousness was apparent in the faces of the thirty or more people who, later on in the afternoon, squeezed into the room to hear me speak on 'Love and Devotion in Buddhism'. I was glad to have the opportunity of speaking on this subject. Indeed, it may have been of my own selection. Even in a city like Bombay, supposedly the cultural as well as the commercial capital of India, the few who knew anything at all about Buddhism usually thought of it as a sturdy rationalism, or sterile agnosticism, in which there was no place for devotion, and I wanted to disabuse the Servants of God, at least, of any such idea, and in this way remove whatever prejudice they might have had against Buddhism. Love was of three kinds, depending on whether it was directed towards a person or an object superior, or equal, or inferior to ourselves. The first kind of love was called *shraddha*, the second *maitri*, the third *karuna*, and on each in turn I spoke at some length, giving examples from the Pali scriptures and explaining how it was to be developed. In Buddhism the principal object of *shraddha* or devotion was the Buddha, the Enlightened human teacher, the embodiment of Reality, just as in the theistic religions it was the Creator. I also emphasized that *shraddha* was to be balanced by *prajna* or wisdom, even though the predominantly emotional factors of bliss, joy, and equanimity played an important part in spiritual life right up to the attainment of nirvana. Nirvana itself was both absolute wisdom and infinite compassion. Since the Buddha had no superior, and no equal, in relation to ordinary humanity it was compassion that was the most prominent aspect of Enlightenment. Compassion was characteristic of

Buddhism – perhaps its most important teaching. It was because of the compassion he felt that the Buddha spent his life showing the Path to others. His actions had all been the spontaneous overflow of his love for sentient beings.

My talk was well received and followed by a discussion, initiated by Dr Mehta, on meditation as a source of nutrition. This enabled me to describe the four kinds of nutriment recognized in Buddhism, as well as to relate how the Buddha, in the course of his early struggles for Enlightenment, had refused to allow the *devas* to provide him with celestial nourishment. These particulars Dr Mehta seemed to find especially interesting. The Servant of Servants indeed had followed my talk with close attention, and a week or two later, when I attended a lecture on 'The Economic Structure of Islam' (in Urdu, which I could not follow very well), he asked me to give another talk and engaged me in further discussion about meditation. This second talk, which I gave a few days later, was on 'The Buddha and the Spiritual Life in Buddhism'. I spoke for nearly two hours, and whether on account of the concentrated, meditative atmosphere of the meeting, or because I was upheld by the sustaining power of the Buddhas and Bodhisattvas, I gave what I afterwards thought was one of the best talks I had ever given, and probably the profoundest. At any rate, the audience was sufficiently impressed, and it was evident that some of its members, at least, were beginning to realize that there was more to Buddhism than they had imagined. In the weeks that followed I paid several more visits to Mayfair and had further discussions with Dr Mehta about meditation, as well as about Buddhism. He also read to me from The Scripts, of which there were about two thousand. At least this was the figure given by the youngish woman in a white sari who appeared to be Dr Mehta's chief disciple and who, I subsequently learned, ran the quality control business that was the Society's principal source of income. Sundri Vaswani, as her name was, also told me that a large proportion of The Scripts had been received in the first year or so of the Society's existence, when Dr Mehta had 'sat for guidance' several times a day. Nowadays he sat for it only occasionally, she said – a little regretfully, I thought. None the less, before leaving Bombay perhaps I would have an opportunity of being present when he sat and seeing him receive guidance in meditation.

It so happened that I did have an opportunity. There was no meeting at Mayfair that evening, and only the members of the inner circle were present in the room. Besides Dr Mehta himself, this consisted of Sundri Vaswani and her brother Hira (the shifty-eyed young man); Durgadas

Birla, a minor member of the famous business family, and his bespectacled wife; and Father Mascarhenas, an elderly, disaffected Goanese Catholic priest who was fond of denouncing, at least within the walls of Mayfair, the iniquities of what he termed 'the Roman racket'. Proceedings began with a kind of group meditation. Dr Mehta then went into what appeared to be a trance state, turning up his eyes until only the whites were visible. After a while he closed them, his right hand was seized with a violent trembling, and snatching up a pen he began scribbling furiously on the top sheet of the stack of paper that had been kept in readiness before him. I was sitting beside him, on the same mattress, and observed that his eyes remained closed during the whole time he was writing and that he could not see what he was doing. Sheet after sheet he covered, Sundri snatching away each one as it was finished and making sure the sheet underneath was so positioned that his pen did not run off the paper. When seven or eight sheets had been covered he suddenly stopped, and his head slumped forward on to his chest. God had again spoken and given his guidance. Another Script had come into existence. When the light was switched on, I saw that the Servant of Servants' face was greyer than ever, and that he was bathed in perspiration.

The socio-religious sub-world of the Scheduled Castes Federation was much bigger than the religious sub-world of the Society of Servants of God. I had met Dr B.R. Ambedkar, the leading personality of the Federation, in 1952, after having been in correspondence with him two years earlier. On that occasion we had met at Rajgir, his residence in Dadar, in the heart of industrial Bombay, and I had asked him, probably with his recent article 'The Buddha and the Future of His Religion' in mind, whether he thought Buddhism had a future in India. His reply was an indirect one. *He* had no future in India, he declared bitterly (he was at that time in the political wilderness), as if his own future in India and that of Buddhism were inextricably interconnected. But his attitude, or at least his mood, had since changed. Having realized, after a lifetime of unsuccessful campaigning, that the Caste Hindus were not going to give up their traditional inhuman treatment of the Untouchables, as the Scheduled Castes and Depressed Class people were popularly known, he had come to the conclusion that he and his followers would have to change their religion. They would have to become Buddhists, Buddhism being a religion that was of Indian origin, that was rational, and that treated men (and women) according to their worth, not their birth, i.e. not according to their (hereditary) caste. Within the last few months he had twice visited Buddhist Burma, and only days before our second meeting, which took place on 25 December, he had installed an image of the Buddha in the temple that had been built by members of the Scheduled Castes community at Dehu Road, near Poona.

We met not in Dadar but in the Fort area of Bombay, in Dr Ambedkar's office on the top floor of Buddha Bhavan, one of the buildings of the Siddharth College of Arts and Science. In appearance he was greatly altered. At the time of our first meeting his demeanour had been belligerent, and his expression grim and lowering, and though inclining to corpulence he had seemed in good health. Now, three years later, he was quieter and more subdued, and so crippled by arthritis that, as he explained when apologizing for receiving me sitting down, he could stand only with difficulty. But though quieter and more subdued he had, as it seemed, made up his mind that he and his followers should become Buddhists, and was even now drawing up plans for the revival of Buddhism in India. These plans he explained to me at some length, adding, with evident emotion, that he intended to devote the rest of his life to Buddhism. Mrs Ambedkar, who stood beside him as he sat behind his desk, appeared to support his plans, and from time to time intervened to reinforce a point he had made, especially when his energy flagged. For my part I explained, in response to Dr Ambedkar's enquiries, that formal conversion to Buddhism consisted in 'going for Refuge' to the Three Jewels, i.e. the Buddha, the Dharma, and the Sangha, and in undertaking to observe the five basic principles of ethical behaviour. One could 'take' the Refuges and Precepts from any monk or other senior Buddhist. All the same, he and his followers would be well advised to take them from someone like U Chandramani of Kusinara, probably the seniormost monk in India, rather than from a junior monk like myself (Ambedkar had asked me if I would be willing to perform the conversion ceremony for them), as the Buddhist world would probably then take their conversion to Buddhism more seriously. Before we parted the Scheduled Castes leader asked me to write to him recapitulating what I had said about conversion. He also asked me to explain to his followers what conversion to Buddhism really meant. On my acceding to both these requests, he promised to see that a talk was organized for me by his lieutenants in the city.

Dr Ambedkar was as good as his word, with the result that on New Year's Day I addressed a gathering of some 3,000 people on 'What it Means to Become a Buddhist'. It was not the first time I had spoken to members of the Scheduled Castes community on this burning topic, as it was fast becoming for all of them. Only days before my meeting with Dr

Ambedkar I had addressed the residents of the so-called Harijan Colony at Khar, and had afterwards explained to its elders the implications of conversion to Buddhism. Compared with the meeting now organized for me by Dr Ambedkar's local henchmen this had been a very small affair, and it was clear that there would be no conversion to Buddhism, at least not on a mass scale, unless the Scheduled Castes leader himself took the first step. The meeting took place at Worli, on a piece of waste ground overlooked by a row of chawls or tenement blocks, and since many of Ambedkar's followers were factory workers who did not get home much before eight o'clock it did not begin until quite late. By that time there was a cold wind blowing, so that when I at last rose to speak I was shivering in my thin cotton robes. With the President of the Bombay Branch of the Scheduled Castes Federation of Bombay giving a running translation into Marathi, I addressed the gathering for more than an hour, speaking as simply as I could and confining myself to fundamentals. Becoming a Buddhist meant going for Refuge to the Buddha, the Dharma, and the Sangha, I explained, just as I had to Dr Ambedkar, as well as undertaking to observe the Five Precepts, but one could not truly go for Refuge unless one understood what it was to which one went for Refuge. The greater part of my talk was therefore devoted to explaining that the Buddha was a human being who had gained Enlightenment by his personal efforts, not an *avatar* of the god Vishnu; that the Dharma or Teaching of the Buddha was the principial Way to Enlightenment, especially as represented by the three 'trainings' of Morality, Meditation, and Wisdom, and by the Noble Eightfold Path; and that the Sangha was the spiritual community of the Buddha's disciples – past and present, monk and lay.

In speaking about the Dharma Refuge I was at pains to emphasize that in Buddhism the word 'dharma' possessed a meaning quite different from that which it bore in Hinduism. In the latter it meant one's duty as determined by the (hereditary) caste to which one belonged. If one had been born as a brahmin, one's duty was to study the Vedas and receive offerings; if as a *shudra*, to serve the members of the three higher castes. If one had been born as an untouchable then, of course, one's duty was to remove night soil and animal carcasses and to avoid polluting Caste Hindus by coming into contact with them. According to Hinduism one could no more change one's dharma than one could change one's caste. It would be a sin even to try to change it. In Buddhism, however, the Dharma, in the sense of the Way to Enlightenment, was the same for all human beings, regardless of caste, which in any case was not recognized by Buddhism. Becoming a Buddhist and practising the Dharma meant, among other things, breaking free from the caste system, and from untouchability, and following a path of ethical and spiritual development that was for the benefit of oneself and others.

Sitting there on the bare ground, my poorly clad and mostly illiterate audience followed my talk with the closest attention and in a silence that was broken only by the applause that greeted any remark of which they particularly approved. Not surprisingly, the greatest applause was reserved for my comments on caste and untouchability. From the warmth with which the organizers congratulated me on my talk after the meeting, I left Worli that night with the impression that provided Dr Ambedkar lived long enough Buddhism did have a future in India.

Chapter Twenty

NATURE CURE CLINIC

DR MEHTA'S NATURE CURE CLINIC AND SANATORIUM occupied a spacious compound in a tree-shaded avenue immediately behind the Poona Railway Station. It consisted of two buildings, one much larger than the other. The larger of the buildings was a tiled, barn-like structure consisting of a central hall surrounded by eight or ten suites of small rooms, hall and rooms alike being paved with black flagstones. The smaller building, which must once have been servants' quarters, was situated in a corner of the compound, on the same side as the front entrance of the larger building. It occupied an important place in the history of India, or at least in the history of the Independence movement, Mahatma Gandhi having stayed there a number of times in the forties, with his entourage, and taken treatment from Dr Mehta, who was his personal naturopathic physician and the manager of two of his three 21-day fasts. The smaller building was therefore called Bapu Cottage in his memory, Bapu or 'Father' being the name by which the Mahatma was known to his more intimate associates. The room where he had lived and worked was kept much as it had been in his day, and his bed, writing table, and spinning wheel could still be seen. Flush with the top of the rear wall of the compound was the stone platform from which he was wont to address the people who had gathered in the adjacent Railway compound for his evening prayer meeting.

On my arrival at the Clinic, one day towards the end of January, I could not help noticing that the larger of the two buildings had a shabby, neglected look, and that the paths surrounding the garden between it and the rear wall were overgrown with weeds. Though the occasional patient still convalesced there, the Clinic had been inoperative for two or three years, Dr Mehta himself having not so much as visited the place during that period, despite the fact that his wife and his two small children were living at Bapu Cottage. But recently things had changed. God had spoken. Guidance had come to the effect that a branch of the Society of Servants of God should be established in Poona, at the Nature Cure Clinic, that the Union Government Minister of Planning, Sri Gulzarilal Nanda (a former patient of Dr Mehta's), should be invited to address the inaugural meeting, which was to be on a grand scale, and that Bhikshu Sangharakshita should be invited to preside. Even though I did not, indeed as a Buddhist could not, believe that the guidance received by Dr Mehta in meditation came from God (though I was willing to concede it might come from a source higher than his own conscious mind), the knowledge that I was the object of what the Servants of God regarded as nothing less than the personal attention of the Almighty gave me a peculiar sensation, the more especially as I also knew that the question of whether or not I would accept an invitation that had actually come for me 'in guidance' was one of intense interest and concern to Sundri and the other members of the inner circle. In the end, having consulted with Dinoo Dubash (who was of the opinion that the Society could do with a good dose of Buddhism), I decided to accept. My decision was in no way determined by the fact that the invitation *might* have come from a higher source. The reason for my acceptance was that I was glad of an opportunity to visit Poona and, possibly, make contact with the Buddhists there, of whom I had heard there was a considerable number. Thus a day towards the end of January saw me arriving in Poona by Deccan Queen, being met at the station by Miss Dubash, and by her being conducted to the Nature Cure Clinic in Tadiwalla Road. Dr Mehta was already there, having arrived a few days earlier, together with members of the inner circle, and I was soon accommodated in a suite of rooms across the hall from his own.

The inaugural meeting of the Society's Poona branch was indeed on a grand scale, at least so far as the preparations were concerned. An enormous square stage, replete with white mattresses and bolsters, had been erected in the space – once a garden – between the main building and the rear compound wall. This was surmounted by a canopy, at the four corners of which hung curtains, so that from a distance the structure had the appearance of a four-poster bed of Brobdingnagian proportions. On the ground in front of the stage were row upon row of white mattresses. Strings of fairy lights hung between the buildings, and from branch to branch of the giant flame-of-the-forest trees. Yet despite the elaborate preparations the meeting was poorly attended. It must have been a long time since Gulzarilal Nanda, a wiry, Gandhi-capped figure with a black walrus moustache and a surprisingly bass voice, had addressed so small an audience. Even I usually had a bigger one. But though there could not have been more than seventy people down there in front of us on the white mattresses, the Union Minister for Planning made a cheerful speech, in which he eulogized Dr Mehta and the Society in very general terms, while I, for my part, spoke of the need for a sense of direction in life. People might talk about ideals, I declared, but a man could know what his ideal was only when he knew himself. Human beings lived on two levels, the animal and the rational, between which they oscillated. But beyond the rational mind there was the level of the superconscious, and beyond that the transcendental or divine. The aim and object of human life was to live at those higher levels, which were attainable through the practice of concentration and meditation. Those attending the present inaugural meeting would, I hoped, feel that they had been shown the way to a higher life.

In the evening there was a concert, the principal performer being a professional singer of devotional songs who, accompanied by her mother, had travelled from Ahmedabad for the occasion. Madhuribehn, as she was called, had a dark, pock-marked face and a pair of brilliant black eyes, and must have been in her middle or late thirties. In her green silk sari, and with flowers in her sleek black hair, she presented a distinctly queenly appearance as she sat facing the audience that had gathered in the flagstoned hall beneath the gently whirring ceiling fans. Her face, especially when she was singing, wore a kind of triumphant smile, such as one saw on the faces of certain gods and goddesses in ancient Hindu temples. She sang accompanying herself with a sort of sistrum, as well as on a stringed instrument of a type with which I was unfamiliar but which was not a sitar, and from the first notes that the strong, rich voice plucked so confidently out of the air it was evident that Madhuribehn was a perfect mistress of her art. Song after devotional song she sang, with a vitality, and an intensity of expression, that raised the emotional temperature of the crowded hall by several degrees and no doubt brought some of her auditors nearer to a higher level of consciousness than I had been able to bring them with my presidential address. Though I had been privileged to hear some fine renderings of devotional songs, by singers both professional and non-professional, the present performance was of an entirely different order, and I could well understand why the saints and sages of the Hindu *bhakti* tradition should have come to regard sacred music as constituting an independent path to the realization of the divine.

The Poona branch of the Society of Servants of God having been duly inaugurated, and the stage dismantled and taken away, the Nature Cure Clinic was a very quiet place. Besides Dr Mehta, Sundri, and Hira, the only persons left in the main building were me and Parvati, a middle-aged woman with permed white hair, dark glasses, and an exaggeratedly English accent who was, it seemed, still under Dr Mehta's care and semi-convalescent. Dr Mehta was staying on in Poona because he had received guidance to this effect in meditation, and I was staying on because Dr Mehta had invited me to do so, though whether the invitation came from him or from God *through* him was unclear. Whichever may have been the case, I was glad to be there. Poona was very pleasant in winter. It was cooler than Bombay, and much less humid, and despite the blue skies and brilliant sunshine the heat was not oppressive. In subsequent years Poona was to become one of my favourite places in India, and one of the principal centres of my activities. On this first visit, however, I saw nothing of the city *proper* (as my Indian friends would have expressed it), being content to enjoy the peace and quiet of the Nature Cure Clinic, a peace and quiet broken only by the sound of the occasional train and the high-pitched, incessant note of the brain-fever bird, as well as to join the rest of our little community in the daily routine that had soon been established. There was a group meditation in Dr Mehta's room early in the morning, while it was still dark, followed by a second one after breakfast and a third in the evening. In between I read, talked with Dr Mehta, and took a constitutional stroll along the weed-grown paths that bordered what had once been the garden. Meals were taken out of doors, in the courtyard of Bapu Cottage, at a table set beneath one of the giant flame-of-the-forest trees. Thus the days and weeks passed. It was an idyllic existence, such as would not have been possible in strife-torn Bombay, which had been the scene, shortly before my departure, of serious disturbances in connection with the demand, by the Marathi-speaking section of the population, for a separate Maharashtra State with Bombay as its capital. Rashk and I had happened to be in town at the time of the worst of these disturbances, when the police opened fire on a crowd of demonstrators at Flora Fountain, in the heart of the Fort area, killing six people and injuring many others.

In a letter to Dinoo, written in the fourth or fifth week of my stay at the Nature Cure Clinic, I gave my new friend a glimpse of what life was like there at the time. Though she was, I knew, eager to know how I was getting on at the place, it was not possible for me to satisfy her curiosity in a letter, or even in many letters. Having apologized for not writing earlier, and expressed the hope that we might meet in Bombay before she left for her pilgrimage to Ceylon and Japan, I therefore proceeded to give her more news of common friends than of myself.

> Dr is keeping quite well [I wrote]. He has been reading several extracts from Buddhist books, and repeatedly refers to the Buddha's life and teachings. He is even thinking of making a small Buddhist shrine here. Gulbehn is quite cheerful, and of course as active as usual. She and I have become well acquainted, and she too likes to hear about Buddhism. We chant the Buddhist prayers or verses from the *Dhammapada* together every day before meditation. You would like it! Mrs Rasma Mistri is coming every day. She too is very Buddhist-minded. Sundri and Hira are as busy as ever, and bear the main brunt of the work. Probably you have heard that the Society will be publishing a journal called 'Living Silence', and that Hira will be publisher, Sundri editor, and myself associate editor. Parvati has not been keeping well and has been confined to her bed for several days. On the whole the atmosphere here is very good, with everybody friendly and cheerful.

One of the reasons Dr Mehta was keeping quite well was, probably, that he had taken to joining me on my constitutional stroll round the garden, instead of remaining indoors on his *gaddi* all day as was his custom in Bombay. At the time of my arrival at the Clinic Gulbehn, his wife, had not been at all cheerful. The fact that her long-absent husband had chosen to stay in the main building with his disciples, rather than at Bapu Cottage with her and the children, had hurt her deeply, and initially she had refused to have anything to do with the inauguration of the Society's Poona branch. Friends had interposed, however, and eventually she was persuaded to attend the evening concert. By the time I wrote to Dinoo she had more or less adjusted to the situation and, as mentioned in my letter, she and I had become well acquainted. At first, thinking I was a disciple, she had been a little wary of me, but on learning that this was not the case, and that I no more believed that The Scripts came from God than she did herself, her attitude had changed. Like Dr Mehta she was a Parsee, and like him she wore *khadi*, the coarse cotton handloom cloth that was the mark of the Gandhian true believer and which took, in her case, the form of a baggy, Gujerati-style sari that was really much too thick and heavy for such warm weather. Unlike her husband, however, Gulbehn was a follower of the way of Martha, rather than of the way of

Mary, being no less convinced of the importance of good works than he was of the value of meditation. She indeed was a kind, open-hearted woman, with a quite exceptional willingness to be of service to others.

Though Gulbehn attended the group meditations she always left straight afterwards, so that my principal contact with her was at meal times. These were pleasant, sociable occasions, over which Dr Mehta presided in patriarchal fashion, with his wife at his elbow and his servants in attendance. In the days when the Nature Cure Clinic and Sanatorium was a thriving institution, and he one of Poona's (and Bombay's) best-known physicians, he and Gulbehn had, it seemed, kept open house, and even now old friends and ex-patients would drop in at meal times and be invited to join us at the big round table. Sometimes Dr Mehta afterwards told me their histories. Many of them, like the Buddhist-minded Mrs Rasma Mistri mentioned in my letter to Dinoo, were Parsees, and many, I noticed, were more than a little perplexed by their host's transition from naturopath to divinely-guided guru and unsure how to relate to him in his new capacity. One who was not at all perplexed was Mr Bo, as everybody called him, a lean, hatchet-faced, jovial Italian who had been interned at Dehra Dun with Lama Govinda and who, after the War, had settled in Poona and made a living for himself as general handyman and amateur inventor. Mr Bo was not perplexed because he did not believe in God and could, therefore, cheerfully dismiss Dr Mehta's claims to divine guidance and continue to treat him as he always had done. He was in fact a militant atheist, an ardent socialist, and a sworn enemy of the Roman Catholic Church, with an inexhaustible fund of stories and jokes that were very much at the expense of popes, cardinals, bishops, priests, and the whole clerical fraternity. Some of his stories and jokes were extremely funny, and Mr Bo's comically fractured English and expressive gestures ensured that they lost nothing in the telling. Dr Mehta did not much relish these *jeux d'esprit*, though Gulbehn and I enjoyed them immensely, nor did he really like being treated as though he was still just the eminent naturopath and not, as he believed himself now to be, the recipient of God's guidance to the Society, India, and the world. Sometimes he tried to bring God into the conversation and assert his own new character, but with Gulbehn there to remind him of the past this was not always easy, especially when she produced, as she did on one occasion, photographs of the famous 'Greek Statue' posing performances he had given thirty years previously, when he was not only mad about body-building but a thoroughgoing agnostic. These trials the Servant of Servants bore with reasonable good humour, secure in the conviction that (as he used to tell me afterwards) a prophet had no honour in his own country, or at least in his own house, and that this was proof positive of his being a prophet. Once he confided to me that he was sure the Buddha must have had difficulties with Yashodhara, even though there was no mention of this in the Buddhist scriptures.

Our more serious discussions usually took place after the second meditation or when we were strolling round the garden later in the day. As Gulbehn was in the kitchen of Bapu Cottage, Sundri often away in Bombay on quality control business, and Hira out running errands in the bazaar, we were usually undisturbed. Though Dr Mehta did, no doubt, repeatedly refer to the Buddha and his teachings, more often than not in an attempt to discover parallels with his own experiences, our discussions covered a good deal of ground, from Nature Cure to the ethics of hunting (he confessed to having been a great *shikari* in his time), and from Indian politics to the Moral Rearmament movement (he had known Dr Frank Buchman). As a result of these discussions we became better acquainted, and I could not but acknowledge that while Dr Mehta's manner could be a trifle portentous there was a simple, human side to his character, and that whatever reservations I might have about the nature of the guidance he received he was, in fact, undoubtedly a man of broad sympathies, deep understanding, and great personal integrity. One day he told me the story of his conversion from agnosticism to a life of Godguidedness. Towards the end of what was to have been a fast to death he had heard a Voice. The Voice told him to terminate the fast, which he had undertaken because he was at the end of his tether intellectually, and terminate it on its fiftieth day. Many more such spiritual experiences followed, but on account of his agnostic convictions he was unable to accept them. The inner struggle had lasted seventeen years. In the end he had asked for a sign, a sign had been given him, and thereafter he had 'accepted' to follow the guidance vouchsafed him – by God, as he believed – when he was in a state of deep meditation. That was just over two years ago. Since then his whole life had gradually changed. He had founded the Society of Servants of God, and now all his activities were based on the guidance he received in meditation, as the activities of the Society also were.

Meditation, and the acceptance of the guidance received in meditation, indeed formed the principal themes of Dr Mehta's teaching. With much of what he said about meditation I was in complete agreement, especially as it was evident that he spoke more from personal experience than from books. Guidance was another matter. Though the actual content of the guidance received might be acceptable, it was acceptable, so far as I was concerned, only because it was in agreement with my own reason and experience and with the Buddha's teaching, *not* because it was said to come from God. And of course sometimes that content was unacceptable. Dr Mehta himself was inclined to see any refusal to accept guidance (that is, the guidance that came for one through him) as being simply a matter of the ego's resistance to divine grace. But as I pointed out, the fact that one did not follow the guidance that came through him did not necessarily mean that one's life was unguided. Take my own case. I was a Buddhist; I followed the guidance given by the Buddha in the Buddhist scriptures, and felt no need to look for guidance elsewhere. Rather grudgingly, Dr Mehta admitted that it was possible to be guided in this 'general' way, though he added that such guidance was much less reliable than that which came for one through a God-guided personality with which one was in actual contact. The *most* reliable kind of guidance was, of course, that which came to one directly from God, when one was in a state of deep meditation, which was the way his guidance came to him. But the vast majority of people were incapable of reaching such a state and their guidance had, therefore, to come to them indirectly. Those who were not God-guided had to submit themselves, unconditionally, to the guidance of those who were. This was one of the great laws of spiritual life.

The upshot of this exchange (and others like it) was that during the second half, especially, of my stay at the Nature Cure Clinic I made a special effort to deepen my meditation. Though I had been meditating for a number of years, my achievements in this field were far from commensurate with my aspirations. There were experiences of the bliss and peace of the lower *dhyanas*; there were visions, usually of the Buddha or Avalokiteshvara; there were flashes of insight, not always in connection with the meditation itself: and that was about all. What I now had to do, I felt, was to achieve a level of meditative experience which would enable me to receive whatever might be the Buddhist equivalent of Dr Mehta's 'guidance', for much as I rejected the possibility of guidance by God (a being in whose existence I did not believe) I was well aware that for real spiritual progress to take place the ego, or 'defiled mind-consciousness' (as the Yogachara termed it) needed to open itself to the influence of what I was later to call 'the transcendental outpourings of the Absolute'. Just how that deeper – or higher – level was to be achieved was not clear, but I trusted that if I was able to stay long enough in the lower *dhyanas* the inherent momentum of those states, together with my intense desire to be truly guided, would be sufficient to carry me further. Conditions were favourable. The Nature Cure Clinic was quiet and peaceful, I was meditating three times a day with a small group of spiritually-minded people, at least one of whom appeared to have an extensive acquaintance with 'meditative states', and I had no worries about my livelihood. In order to be able to review my daily and weekly progress (or otherwise) I started keeping a meditation diary. I had kept one once before, during my wandering days, but after two years it was so bulky that I discontinued it and eventually burned it. The present diary, which I kept from the morning of 1 February to the evening of 7 March, was a much less weighty affair. The entries were no more than rough notes, meant for my own eyes, but even so, like dried flowers long pressed within the pages of a book, they had the power to evoke in after years a sense of the experiences of which they were mementoes.

Though progress during those five weeks was by no means uniform (there were occasions when my concentration was poor), overall I succeeded in achieving higher states of consciousness than usual and staying in them longer. Often I experienced what I described in my diary as 'positive peace', by which I meant a peace that was not merely the absence of conflict but which had a definite nature of its own, cool, refreshing, and vibrant. Sometimes this peace came percolating into my consciousness from a level even higher than the one I had attained, like water trickling down through the soil. At other times it was felt in the body. On the evening of 7 February, for example, as my diary records:

Concentrated quite easily. Neither quite in nor quite out of ordinary mind. Experience of positive peace in crown of head. This descended and spread throughout whole body. Experience of ascending and descending at same time. All kinds of movements and explosions of energy in the body, though not exactly in the physical body. As though some healing, at the same time destructive, force, was pulling and stretching and kneading the mind.

Dr Mehta explained, when I told him about these experiences, that there was a conflict between grace descending through the topmost chakra and effort ascending through the lower chakras, the point of meeting being at the third or navel chakra. It may have seemed so, but nevertheless I did not find the explanation entirely satisfactory, especially as I tended, in any case, to be wary of employing the language of 'chakras' and 'kundalini'. To me such language, together with its underlying philosophy, smacked not so much of Buddhism as of Hinduism. Be that as it may, besides *positive peace* I also experienced feelings of intense love and devotion towards the Buddha (especially in the form of Amitabha) and Avalokiteshvara, which was not often the case with me. Sometimes these feelings were accompanied by the corresponding visionary experiences, but more often there would be an awareness of the transcendental 'person' in question without my being conscious of any particular form. On several occasions this awareness was so strong that I was able to put questions and receive answers. Not that I heard any words, whether my own or the Buddha's. I pronounced the words of my questions sub-vocally, and those of the Buddha's answers were imprinted directly on my consciousness without being pronounced at all. The first such experience occurred on the morning of 11 February, the diary entry for which reads:

> Concentrated. Feeling of total dissociation between past and present life. Doubt. Awareness of answer: 'Whatever leads to etc … is My Dharma'. Decided to ask more questions, as follows:
> Q. What should be my attitude towards surroundings after returning to K.?
> A. Absolute detachment. This detachment is positive. Must be detached even from the Buddha. Detachment as taught by the Buddha transcends both attachment and detachment in the ordinary sense.
> Q. How behave towards people?
> A. Buddha first and everyone else second. – Awareness of shortcomings in this respect.
> Q. What about acquiring land etc.?
> A. This will be settled after your return. You must be ready to be anywhere and nowhere.
> Awareness of the Buddha's presence, though rather faintly (*sic*). Reflected whether these awarenesses were genuine guidance. Concluded that since they were in agreement with the Scriptures and were not unreasonable they could be accepted.

The diary entry for the evening of the following day, 12 February, records a similar experience:

> Good concentration. Sensation of positive peace descending. Asked, 'What should I do?' Awareness of answer came at once – 'Nothing'. Experience of emptiness and stillness. Self reduced to

an absolute pinpoint. This state lasted for some time. Awareness: 'Whatever works you may have to do later on, in the midst of them you will have to maintain this state of mind.'

Experiences on subsequent days included visions of 'flowers' made as though of flame, and of jewels of intense light, sensations as of a light trying to break through, as well as of vastness and emptiness, and an awareness of the importance and meaning of the *White Lotus Sutra*. My predominant experience, however, especially during the second half of the month, was one of increasingly intense feelings of love and devotion towards the Buddha and Avalokiteshvara. On one occasion I felt in the region of the heart a love and peace so strong that I was unable to bear it and had to stop meditating for a while. There was also a sensation as of someone touching me on the heart, and an experience of my 'heart chakra' being suddenly opened. During this period the Bodhisattva of Compassion, Avalokiteshvara, featured no less prominently in my experience than did the Buddha, and it was not without significance that his name should be mentioned in my last diary entry, for the evening of 7 March, which ran:

> Fairly good concentration. Feeling of devotion. Awareness of universe as it appears in the eyes of A[valokiteshvara]. Again feeling of devotion. Consciousness of peace descending from a great height.

More often than not I discussed my experiences with Dr Mehta, and sometimes he told me about his own. One morning he had a vision of three monks meditating under the influence of the Buddha – which was probably indicative of his growing interest in Buddhism. But though we spent much of our time discussing meditation, and though meditation and the acceptance of the guidance received in meditation formed the principal themes of his teaching, the Servant of Servants' life had not changed so much since his conversion that he had forgotten the secular and humanist ideals of his unguided days. Whether owing to his Parsee family background or his Gandhian associations he still had an active social conscience. He continued, for instance, to be strongly opposed to the caste system, especially to its most abhorrent manifestation, the practice of untouchability. His opposition was not only theoretical but practical. As I had soon discovered, the servants at the Nature Cure Clinic, who had been with him and Gulbehn for decades, were Marathi-speaking members of the Scheduled Castes and, therefore, potential converts to Buddhism. Perhaps they would know whereabouts in Poona the Buddhists with whom I wanted to make contact lived. In the event they did not know, any more than did Mrs Mistri, or Mr Bo, or any of the other visitors I questioned on the subject, and I began to think that the 'considerable number' of Poona Buddhists of whom I had heard in Bombay had a purely mythical existence.

Dr Mehta was of the same opinion. At least, during all his years in Poona he had not come across a single Buddhist. He did, however, believe that conversion to Buddhism would be very much to the advantage of the Scheduled Castes people, and when I told him about my meeting with Dr Ambedkar he at once suggested I should write to the Scheduled Castes leader inviting him and Mrs Ambedkar to spend a few days at the Nature Cure Clinic and continue our discussions there. The place being a nursing home, whatever medical facilities he might require would be available. Whether because he could not spare the time, or because the institution's Gandhian associations did not appeal to him (he and Gandhi had been political opponents), Dr Ambedkar did not take up the invitation, and when we did meet, ten or more months later, it was in a different place, and under very different circumstances.

Chapter Twenty-One

2,500 Years of Buddhism

THE BUDDHIST ERA HAS ALWAYS BEEN REGARDED as beginning with the *parinirvana* or final passing away of the Buddha. According to the traditional Sinhalese reckoning, which is accepted by all Theravadin Buddhists but which modern scholarship has shown to be incorrect, the *parinirvana* took place in the year 544BCE. Thus the 1956 Vaishakha full moon day, which fell on 24 May, marked the completion of 2,500 years of Buddhism – the Vaishakha full moon day being the anniversary, according to late Sinhalese traditions, not only of the Buddha's attainment of Enlightenment but also of his birth and his *parinirvana*. The year from the Vaishakha full moon day of 1956 to that of 1957 was accordingly celebrated as the year of the Buddha Jayanti by Buddhists all over the world, not excluding those whose own traditional chronologies differed from that of Ceylon but who, in the words of a Japanese scholar at the time, 'were glad to collaborate with Theravadin Buddhists in their 2,500th year ceremonies honouring the Buddha.'

India was not a Buddhist country, and its Buddhist population was tiny, consisting of perhaps a quarter of a million people scattered mainly along its northern borders. Moreover, India was a secular state. None the less, Prime Minister Nehru and his colleagues had decided that India should join the Buddhist countries of South-east Asia in celebrating the Jayanti and that the cultural, as distinct from the religious, celebrations should be sponsored by the Union government. Preparations had been set in train and a programme drawn up. On the eve of the Vaishakha full moon day Pandit Nehru would lay the foundation stone of a monument to the Buddha in New Delhi, thus inaugurating the nation's Buddha Jayanti celebrations, and the following day, 24 May, the President of the Republic, Dr Rajendra Prasad, would address a mass meeting. The occasion would be marked by special programmes on All-India Radio, by the publication of a volume entitled *2500 Years of Buddhism*, and by the issue of commemorative postage stamps. Foreign Buddhists visiting the Buddhist holy places would be able to travel on the railways for half the usual fare, and facilities at the holy places themselves would be improved. The main celebrations, however, would take place in the month of November, in the cooler weather, when an exhibition of Buddhist art would be held in New Delhi, as well as a meeting of UNESCO and an international symposium on 'Buddhism's Contribution to Arts, Letters, and Philosophy'. A documentary film on the life of the Buddha would also be released.

To a minority of orthodox Caste Hindus the idea of the Government of India sponsoring the Buddha Jayanti celebrations even to a limited extent was anathema. One of their number, a certain Acharya Neminath of South India, went so far as to publish a pamphlet in which he accused the Government of violating the Constitution by spending public money on the celebration of Buddha Jayanti, called on them to 'keep themselves absolutely away from all religious functions', and incidentally admitted that it caused him 'heart burnings' to hear national leaders praising Buddhism as the best of religions. As usual, such people wanted to have it both ways. They wanted to be able to claim Buddhism as a branch of Hinduism; at the same time, they did not want Buddhism to be praised or patronized. Replying to the Government's orthodox Hindu critics, Dr S. Radhakrishnan, the Vice-President of India and Chairman of the Buddha Jayanti Celebrations Working Committee, pointed out that: 'When we call ourselves a secular State we do not mean that we are worshippers of comfort, security, and worldly goods. We mean by it respect and appreciation of all faiths that have found a home in this country.' Judging by the way in which preparations for the Jayanti were going on all over India the majority of Indians agreed with Dr Radhakrishnan. The State Governments had drawn up programmes of their own, as had a number of public bodies. The Government of Bihar proposed to shower the Maha Bodhi Temple at Bodh-gaya with rose petals from a helicopter. More prosaically, the Government of Bombay planned to drop leaflets.

The Maha Bodhi Society's Buddha Jayanti celebrations were to take place mainly at its Calcutta headquarters and at its centres in Sarnath and Bodh-gaya, and unlike the government-sponsored celebrations they were to be of a predominantly religious character. The dozen or so other centres were expected to organize celebrations of their own, and Devapriya Valisinha, the Society's General Secretary, had toured the country visiting them and exhorting the bhikkhus-in-charge to rise to the occasion and enlist the support of the local people. He had not visited Kalimpong, which was off the beaten track, but on my returning there, towards the end of April, I found that a public meeting had been held in the Town Hall and a Buddha Jayanti Celebrations Committee set up with, as was usual on such occasions, Rani Chunni Dorji as Chairman, Gyan Jyoti as Treasurer, and Bhikshu Sangharakshita as General Secretary. I had been away six months. From Poona, after saying goodbye to Dr Mehta and the Nature Cure Clinic, I had gone to Bombay, and from Bombay I had made my way to Calcutta, though I did not leave the former city without spending a few days at Khar with Rashk. No doubt we discussed the script of *Ajanta*, and no doubt my friend gave me the latest news of Raj Kapoor, but my principal memory of those days relates to something of a very different order.

Before my departure for Poona I had given Rashk, at his request, the date, time, and place of my birth, and these details he had communicated to his personal astrologer, the thin, elderly brahmin whom I had seen arriving at the flat one morning. The latter had drawn my horoscope and made certain calculations, and one afternoon, at Rashk's suggestion, he came to tell me what the stars had revealed. The first thing they had revealed was that I had broken my vow of *brahmacharya* or chastity. I had broken it on a certain date in February. When I told him categorically that I had done no such thing the old man became quite furious, declaring that the stars could not lie and that if he was proved wrong he would throw his books in the Ganges. I could only conclude that, supposing the stars *could* reveal the state of one's brahmacharya and that the brahmin's calculations *were* correct, I must have got my birth hour wrong, which was in fact more than likely. The stars had revealed not only my immediate past but also my remote future. I would have many disciples, the brahmin assured me, but when I was fifty (or it may have been sixty) I would give up being a monk and after that I would have more disciples than ever.

These revelations gave me food for thought as the train sped towards Calcutta. In the first place my friend's astrologer was a brahmin, and orthodox brahmin householders were notoriously hostile to non-brahmin ascetics, especially if the latter happened to belong, as I did, to one of the great non-Vedic traditions. What better way could there be of undermining people's faith in such ascetics than by casting doubts on the purity of their morals? Rashk knew me well enough to believe me when I gave the stars the lie, despite his (qualified) faith in astrology, but others who came to know what the brahmin had said might well think that I must have broken my vow of brahmacharya in Poona and was no longer a true monk. As for the revelation about my future, this could be understood as an attempt to induce me to give up the monastic life by appealing to my religious ambitions. But I had no wish to give up the monastic life, and no ambitions of the kind the stars' – or the brahmin's – prediction seemed to envisage. Even if I had entertained such ambitions I would in any case have stood a better chance of realizing them by remaining a monk in my old age than by giving up being one. Elderly ex-monks, in my experience, were much more likely to lose such disciples as they had than to attract new ones in even greater numbers. However that might be, there was little doubt that astrology was a powerful weapon, quite irrespective of its truth or falsity, and that people could be manipulated by its means. Politicians of every party had their personal astrologers, just as Rashk had, and these were said to exercise, through the advice they gave their powerful clients, an enormous influence behind the scenes. Businessmen too had their astrologers, as did film actors and others connected with the cinema industry. Astrology in fact dominated large and important areas of Indian life, and to the extent that it tended to play on people's hopes and fears, on their greed, hatred, and delusion, those areas could be said to be dominated by the forces of Mara the Evil One. It was therefore no wonder that the Buddha should have included astrology among the 'low and lying arts' in which his monk disciples were not to engage. – With reflections such as these did I beguile the tedium of my two-day journey.

In Calcutta I stayed, as usual, at the Maha Bodhi Society's headquarters building, behind the Sri Dharmarajika Vihara in College Square, and as usual the greater part of my time there was spent attending to the work of the *Maha Bodhi Journal*, the last five or six issues of which I had been obliged to bring out on the wing. The Vaishakha full moon day was fast approaching, and therewith the time for the appearance of the Journal's special Vaishakha number. It would be the third such special number I had brought out, and since it would also be the 2,500th Buddha Jayanti number I was anxious that it should be bigger and better than any of its predecessors. Despite the intense heat I set to work with a will, editing the articles I had collected, choosing the illustrations, which this year included two in full colour, commissioning a cover design, changing printers (for two issues only), reading proofs, and writing the editorial and much of the Notes and News section.

For the last four months my editorials had dealt, in one way or another, with the forthcoming Buddha Jayanti. The January editorial, which was entitled 'The Coming Year', drew attention to the fact that, as many indications showed, Buddhism was capable of meeting a very definite need, satisfying a spiritual hunger, not only in the East but in the West. The Vaishakha Purnima of 1956 would therefore present the whole Buddhist world with a unique opportunity – and a challenge. It would present a challenge, because opportunities, besides revealing our strength, also exhibited our weakness.

> The great weakness of the Buddhist world today [I continued] is lack of unity. By unity we do not, of course, mean mere external uniformity, much less still simply a keeping up of friendly social relations. We mean by unity an effective recognition of the fact that despite differences of presentation and interpretation, both *yanas* and all schools of Buddhism accept, teach and follow that Threefold Path of Morality, Meditation and Wisdom, leading to Enlightenment, wherein consists the very essence of the Dharma of the Lord Buddha. The nearer we approach to actual practice of the essentials of the Teaching the nearer we shall approach to each other. That 'unity is strength' is none the less true for being a truism. The nearer we approach to each other the more effectively shall we be able to take advantage of the opportunity, to meet the challenge, which the coming Anniversary represents. Only a united Buddhism will be able to fulfil the old prophecy that from this year the Dharma will begin to overspread the whole earth.

The editorial for February struck a different note. Entitled 'The Inner Preparation', it reminded readers of the *Maha Bodhi* that Buddhism had its origin in the fact that, five-and-twenty centuries ago, a man sat under a tree in the forests of north-eastern India and *meditated*. Buddhism had been able to spread so wide outwardly because the sources of its inspiration lay so deep within. In this fact there was an important lesson for us today. Preparations for the 2,500th anniversary of the *parinirvana* had been going on for some time, and the celebrations promised to be the grandest with which the name of Buddhism had ever been associated, but there was one question which those who were in any way connected with these events had to ask themselves:

> What is the inner basis of all these manifestations of zeal for the Buddhist cause? Is it a love of pomp and circumstance, of the parade and pageantry of religion? Is it merely faith? Or is it,

again, merely an opportunistic taking advantage of a particular conjunction of circumstances of the historical order?

The tree of Buddhist revival can shoot high only if its roots are planted deep in the soil of our hearts. The modern Buddhist movement must be based not on faith, not on unreflecting enthusiasm, – much less still on meaner motives, – but on actual realization of the import of the Dharma.

To such a realization there is only one way: Meditation. The Buddhist texts are unanimous that the Truth can be discerned only by the mind which has been thoroughly purified by the systematic practice of meditation. Not to the intellect, not to the emotions, but only to the mind which is at equilibrium in *samadhi* do there arise those flashes of insight which destroy all wrong views, such as belief in a creator God and the reality of the ego-soul or *atman*, and which eventually culminate in the attainment of that *Aryan* knowledge which constitutes the Path to Supreme Enlightenment.

Hence we urge upon all our readers the necessity of making, during the coming months, a special effort not only to study and propagate the Doctrine but to realize it through meditation.... On an occasion so auspicious as the one we shall be celebrating shortly, we should make every effort to raise our consciousness to the highest possible level. For only if it proceeds from within without will the modern movement of Buddhist revival be truly successful. Without underrating the part played by external organization, it may be said without fear of contradiction that it is the inner preparation which is the more important. To that inner preparation, therefore, let us devote ourselves during the coming months, so that the coming Vaishakha Purnima will be an anniversary not merely in the history of Buddhism but in our own spiritual life.

The March and April editorials suggested other ways of making a special effort in honour of the Buddha Jayanti. In the former, entitled 'Buddhism and the Indian Languages', I appealed to 'our friends in every corner of the Buddhist world' to inaugurate, as part of their Jayanti programme, a movement to have as much Buddhist literature as possible translated into as many Indian languages as possible, and in the latter, entitled 'Buddha Jayanti Among the Birds', I pleaded for a measure of vegetarianism. A measure of vegetarianism, I pointed out, besides demonstrating our much-advertised *maitri* for the animal creation, would go a long way towards enabling birds and beasts to participate in the Buddha Jayanti celebrations.

> Buddhist pilgrims to India in particular would be well advised to abstain from fish and meat during the period of their pilgrimage. Whether rightly or wrongly, the average Indian is deeply shocked at the spectacle of Buddhists, especially monks, who even while on pilgrimage are unable to control their palate to the extent of forgoing, even temporarily, this particular article of diet.

Now, in my fifth editorial of the year, for the 2,500th Buddha Jayanti number, I was concerned to point out that the present anniversary did not mean that the Buddhist world, with twenty-five centuries of history behind it, was now justified in resting still more comfortably and complacently upon its laurels. Rather did it mean that, enriched by twenty-five centuries of experience, it could now prepare itself for a concerted effort to make the limits of the Dharma conterminous only with the limits of the globe itself. The May editorial was therefore entitled 'Ring in the New' and concluded, after referring to the duty of the Buddha's followers to spread the Dharma:

> Let us, therefore, on this unprecedentedly solemn and auspicious occasion, vow to make so great an effort for the world-wide dissemination of the Dharma that when, after two and a half millenniums, we celebrate the five thousandth Anniversary of the *Maha Parinirvana*, we shall do so in a world united by a common allegiance to the Buddha, the Dharma, and the Sangha.

The aspiration was a grandiose one, but what with the preparations for the Buddha Jayanti, and the rumours of the impending conversion of Dr Ambedkar and his followers to Buddhism, at the Maha Bodhi Society's headquarters at that time there was, perhaps, a whiff of triumphalism in the air.

Triumphalism or no triumphalism, the work of editing the 2,500th Buddha Jayanti Vaishakha number, together with that of seeing two or three booklets through the press, left me with scant leisure for other things. I was able, none the less, to see a little of Soratha, now back in Calcutta after his spell as locum at the Ananda Vihara, and to spend a few evenings with Sachin. My Nepalese friend was now a student at St Paul's College, the prestigious Anglican missionary institution where Phani Sanyal was Professor of Economics and, I believe, at that time warden of the hostel where Sachin was staying. Talking with Sachin naturally brought the image of Kalimpong very vividly before my mind's eye, especially as we exchanged news of common friends and reminisced about the early days of the YMBA, and I longed more than ever to escape from the stifling heat of the plains to the comparative cool of the hills, and from the noise and bustle of the headquarters building to the tranquillity of Everton Villa. Fortunately it was not many days after writing my editorial on 'Ring in the New' that I was able to give the print order for the last forme of the Vaishakha number, pack my bags, and summon a taxi to take me to Sealdah Station.

Once back in Kalimpong it did not take me long to slip into the duties my fellow citizens had assigned me and start organizing the procession and public meeting that was to be the town's principal contribution to the Buddha Jayanti celebrations. As I had organized functions of this sort before, and was well acquainted with the various people whose co-operation would be required, this did not prove difficult. Moreover, I had a regular assistant in the form of a young Thai bhikkhu from Shanti-niketan. Khemasiri was in India to study English, but finding he did not make much progress at the Visvabharati University, where he and the other young Thai bhikkhus spent much of their time talking together in their own language, he had decided that the best thing he could do would be to go and stay with the English monk in Kalimpong for a few months. Quiet, modest, and diligent, he not only helped me organize the town's contribution to the Buddha Jayanti celebrations but thereafter spent several months with me as my assistant, friend, and companion. Not that Khemasiri's was the only help I received during the run-up to the Buddha Jayanti. Besides Dawa, Durga, and others of our members and friends there were occasional helpers from outside Kalimpong. One of these was Dr Kalidas Nag, the Chairman of the editorial board of the *Maha Bodhi*. Following Devapriya-ji's example, he was touring the Maha Bodhi Society's centres with a view to stimulating interest in the Buddha Jayanti. Unlike Devapriya-ji, he had included Kalimpong in his itinerary, and in the course of the two days he spent in the town his affable looks and charming manners captivated everybody he met. Another such helper was Narada Thera, the doyen of the English-speaking bhikkhus of Ceylon, whose public appearance, at least, was less than a complete success.

I had met Narada Thera in Kathmandu in 1951, and in 1952 I had shared a tent with him at Sanchi, where we had disagreed as to whether or not vitamin tablets counted as food and whether or not, therefore, a monk could take them after twelve o'clock without breaking the Vinaya. (According to Narada Thera they were not, and he could; according to me they were, and he could not.) My last meeting with him had taken place in Calcutta, at the Maha Bodhi Society's headquarters building, where one evening he took me aside and pumped me for information about the strictness with which the Society's bhikkhus observed certain minor monastic rules. He also spoke about the higher stages of the Path, but in such a way that I formed the distinct impression that he wanted me to think he was an Arahant. Be that as it may, he concluded by saying, in a confidential would-you-believe-it tone of voice, 'Do you know, Avuso, some people actually think I am a *hypocrite*.' (Avuso or 'Friend' was the correct mode of address from a senior to a junior monk.) 'Yes, Bhante,' I responded brightly, 'I have heard as much.' 'Oh dear, Avuso, have you really!' he exclaimed, shocked and momentarily flustered by this unwelcome confirmation of his worst suspicions. The truth was that although Narada Thera was a great favourite with the Theravadin laity, mainly on account of his pedantically strict observance of the Vinaya, he was not very popular with his fellow Sinhalese bhikkhus, the majority of whom tended to regard him as something between a joke and a fraud. Many were the stories that were in circulation about him. Soratha had told me a number of them, some of them very funny and to be appreciated only by those acquainted with the finer points of the Vinaya and the jealous, proprietary attitude of the Sinhalese laity towards its monks. Indeed, it seemed that all the stories ever told in the monasteries of Ceylon about hypocritical monks had come to be related, over the years, of the unfortunate Narada Thera, just as in India all the jokes ever told about dim-witted Sikhs had come to be related of Sardar Baldev Singh, Pandit Nehru's bearded and turbaned Minister of Defence.

But hypocrite or not, the elderly Sinhalese monk was a prominent figure in the Buddhist world, and on learning of his arrival at the Dharmodaya Vihara I at once went and invited him to give a public lecture. He accepted the invitation with alacrity, whereupon I not only publicized the meeting extensively but personally urged everybody I met to attend, saying that Venerable Narada was the most famous Buddhist monk in Ceylon, that he was well known as an author and speaker, and that he had lectured on Buddhism in many Western countries, all of which was perfectly true. When the time came the Town Hall was therefore crowded. Unfortunately what should have been one of the highlights of the run-up to our Buddha Jayanti celebrations turned out to be a near disaster. Narada Thera's lecture was dull and platitudinous in the extreme and delivered, from what were evidently old notes, in a high-pitched voice and with an air of benign condescension. People were bitterly disappointed, some of them afterwards going so far as to compare the Sinhalese monk's abilities as a lecturer with my own in a way that was by no means to his advantage. Friends wanted to know why I had praised Narada Thera so highly. But an incident which occurred before he began to speak created, perhaps, an even less favourable impression than the lecture itself.

As my custom was, I had arranged for the speaker and chairman (on this occasion me) to occupy the Town Hall's tiny stage and for the more distinguished members of the audience, including bhikkhus and lamas, to occupy the first two rows of chairs in the auditorium. No sooner had Narada and I taken our seats on the stage, however, than my elder brother in the Order insisted that the bhikkhus (but not the lamas) should join us there, nor was he satisfied until, with much hauling and scraping of chairs, and a good deal of confusion, the eight or ten bhikkhus in the audience were all squeezed together with us on the stage. But that was by no means the end of the matter. Narada Thera had not been speaking for more than a few minutes when a yellow-robed figure slipped into the hall and unobtrusively took a seat in the back row of the auditorium. It was Anand-ji's disciple Sumedha. He had been to see me in Bombay, and at my request Dr Bhagwat had agreed to teach him Pali; but having no real interest in study he was now back in Kalimpong and again staying at the Dharmodaya Vihara. Not realizing that the meeting would be starting on time, he had turned up late. Narada Thera's eagle eye at once spotted the new arrival and, interrupting his lecture, he called upon him to come forward and take his rightful place on the stage. 'That's all right, Bhante,' protested Sumedha, in his uncultivated Hindi (which the Sinhalese monk did not understand), 'I'm fine where I am, thanks.' But Narada Thera, who was accustomed to having his own way, continued to call upon the recalcitrant samanera to come forward until the latter, deeply embarrassed to be the centre of everyone's attention, eventually made his way to the stage, where an extra chair was somehow squeezed in among the rest. Having seen him merged with the other yellow robes, Narada Thera turned to the audience and observed, in his blandest manner, 'I am glad to see that the good people of Kalimpong know how to show proper respect to the members of the Holy Order.'

This was not to be my last experience of Theravadin orthodoxy, as represented by the doyen of the English-speaking Sinhalese monks. Wishing to be hospitable, I had not only invited Narada Thera for lunch but made sure that Padam, my cheerful Nepalese cook-bearer, prepared a more elaborate meal than usual. Moreover, knowing what a stickler my guest was for the observance of the twelve o'clock rule (the rule that prohibited monks from taking solid food after midday), I had made sure that the meal was ready by eleven o'clock, for which time the Thera was invited. But eleven o'clock came and went, then 11.30, and still there was no sign of him. What could have happened? By 11.45 I was feeling distinctly worried on his account, as it was an unheard-of thing for an orthodox Theravadin monk to be late for a meal. Eventually, at 11.55, a panting, perspiring figure in yellow could be seen hastily descending the flight of rough stone steps that led from the road to Everton Villa. It was Narada Thera! Realizing that if he missed his lunch he would probably have to fast until the following day (except for vitamin tablets), and not wanting Padam's meal to be wasted, I told Naginda, who had invited himself to lunch that day (as he often did), to put the clock back half an hour and position it prominently on the dining-room table. No sooner had he done this than in rushed a distraught Narada Thera. 'Avuso, Avuso,' he gasped, 'Am I late, am I late? I lost my way! Those Dharmo-daya people misdirected me!' 'Don't worry, Bhante,' I replied, 'you're not *very* late.' Whereupon Narada Thera saw the clock. 'Oh!' he exclaimed, with evident relief, 'I thought it was later than that' – and lost no time in sitting down to the meal. He was careful, I noticed, not to look at his own watch. Even if Narada Thera was not exactly a hypocrite, there were clearly times when he regarded the apparent observance of the Vinaya as being of greater importance than its real observance.

But with the Vaishakha Purnima almost upon us I had little time to think about such things. According to an ancient prophecy, the 2,500th Buddha Jayanti would mark the beginning of a period of revival for Buddhism, and if this was the case it was to be hoped that the pseudo-orthodoxy of the Narada Theras of the Buddhist world would soon dissolve like mist in the light of a truer understanding of the Buddha's teaching. Indeed, when at last the snows of Kanchenjunga flushed with the dawning of the great day, and as Khemasiri and I made our way up to the Tharpa Chholing Gompa, it really did seem that the Buddhists of Kalimpong, like those of the rest of the Buddhist world, were ringing in a new cycle in the history of their religion. Five-coloured Buddhist flags fluttered everywhere, incense smoked from braziers in front of shops and houses, and on all sides the sound of chanting could be heard. On arriving at the gompa we found that two thousand people had gathered to take part in the procession, and it took me some time to organize them into their different sections. According to a report I subsequently wrote for the *Maha Bodhi*, the procession was led by more than a hundred Tibetan lamas, 'all magnificent in their ceremonial robes of silk brocade, who blew trumpets and clarinets, beat upon drums, and swung censers in which incense burned. A beautiful image of the Lord Buddha, pictures of His Holiness the Dalai Lama, and banners of victory, Buddhist flags and emblems were borne in the procession. Nearly a thousand devotees carried on their backs huge volumes of the Buddhist Scriptures in Tibetan.' What I did not write was that although the procession was led by the hundred Tibetan lamas in their ceremonial robes of silk brocade, the lamas themselves were led, by popular demand, by Khemasiri and me in our yellow cotton robes. Down from Tirpai to Eleventh Mile we led them, along the main road, through the narrow, shop-lined streets of the upper bazaar, and so to the Mela Ground. The Mela Ground was a level open space that had been cut out of the hillside between the High Street and the lower bazaar. As its name implied, it was really a fairground, though in my time only football matches were ever held there. It was surrounded on three sides by tiers of seats, also cut out of the hillside, and at intervals there were broad flights of steps. Down one of these flights of steps Khemasiri and I led the lamas, the rest of the procession behind them, and began following the lines of the maze which, with the help of Pheunkhang-se and two other Tibetan officers, I had marked out on the floor of the Mela Ground the previous day. Back and forth we went, from one side of the Mela Ground to the other, until by the time we had reached the end of the maze, and the tail of the procession was descending the steps, the entire space was a sea of red robes and colourful national costumes from which rose, like the masts and sails of ships, the still more colourful Buddhist flags and banners of victory.

In the afternoon the Mela Ground was the venue of a public meeting. Sri S.N. Roy, the current Sub-Divisional Officer, presided, and the guest of honour was Sri S.R. Das, the Chief Justice of India, who was a regular visitor to Kalimpong and with whom I was well acquainted. Speeches in various languages were delivered, including one in Tibetan by Jigme Dorji, the *de facto* Prime Minister of Bhutan, and one in English by me. Immediately after the meeting prayers – as one could not help calling them in English – were chanted by a large congregation of Tibetan lamas in front of the gilded and jewelled Buddha image that had been lent for the occasion by Rani Dorji, who was also responsible for the tasteful appearance of the shrine. Later, the Kalimpong branch of the Maha Bodhi

Society and the other Buddhist institutions of the town held special functions in honour of the day at their own premises.

On the following day a meeting was held at the Town Hall especially for students, when the results of the Students' Essay Competition were announced and prizes distributed. A variety entertainment, including dramatic sketches dealing with the life of the Buddha, was also given. Though I had organized the meeting I was unable to be present, as I was in Gangtok, taking part in the second and third days of the Buddha Jayanti celebrations being held there. Tibetan Buddhist chronology, which was followed in Sikkim, differed from that of Theravadin South-east Asia by several centuries, but in 1956, the year of the 2,500th Buddha Jayanti, the Tibetan *Shaga Dawa* or anniversary of the Buddha's Enlightenment, and the South-east Asian (and Indian) Vaishakha full moon day, happened to fall, miraculously, on the same date, so that Himalayan Buddhists could join in the Buddha Jayanti celebrations without feeling that they were being unfaithful to their own traditions. Besides services in all the monasteries of Sikkim, the previous day had seen a public meeting in Gangtok, and the next day, shortly before my arrival in the village capital, the Buddha's image had been taken in procession from the Palace Temple. I gave my first lecture that evening, and the second the following evening, both of them being given at the White Memorial Hall under the presidentship of the Maharaj Kumar. In the first I spoke on 'Tradition and Progress' and in the second on 'Buddhist Meditation'. Both lectures were well attended, members of the Sikkimese nobility and officers of the State being particularly prominent in the audience.

On my previous visit to the Village Capital I had been a guest of the Palace and had stayed at the Palace guest-house. This time I was the guest of Apa B. Pant, the Political Officer, and stayed with him and his family at the Residency, where he lived in much the same style as his British predecessors, employing the same aged Lepcha butler and dining off the same silver plate on formal occasions. The Residency had been built some fifty or sixty years earlier, in a superior version of Himalayan Mock Tudor, and commanded a view of the snows that was unequalled even in Gangtok. It was surrounded by extensive lawns, the lawns were bordered by flower beds, and the flower beds were backed by shrubs and blossoming trees, behind which rose the dense enclosing mass of the Sikkim jungle. The space occupied by the whole *mise en scène* – house and outbuildings, lawns and flower beds – seemed to have been carved out of the jungle, so that as I looked across the front lawn at the tree ferns and giant rhododendrons I was reminded of the way in which, in the Garden of Eden as seen by the fallen Archangel in Book IV of Milton's great poem, 'the verdurous wall of Paradise up sprung'. Wandering in the grounds of the Residency, with their combination of the cultivated and the wild, it was easy to imagine oneself in the Garden of Eden, and I could not help wondering if any of Apa Sahib's English predecessors, walking there in the cool of the evening, had not been reminded of the lines in *Paradise Lost* describing that ideal scene.

I did not have much time to wonder. My stay was a short one, and I was soon back at Everton Villa, catching up with correspondence and attending to the work of the *Maha Bodhi*, for which I now had to write notices of some of the many special numbers that newspapers and periodicals of all kinds had brought out in honour of the 2,500th Buddha Jayanti. I did not have any classes to teach at the Dharmodaya Vihara. As I had feared, the strain of remunerating the teachers had eventually proved too much for Gyan Jyoti's limited resources, and during my absence in Bombay the evening college had collapsed, not without a certain amount of recrimination. For me personally the fact that I no longer had regular classes to teach was not without its advantages. It meant that I was now less tied to Kalimpong (not that I had been much tied even before), and in the course of the late summer and early autumn I was away twice, visiting three places and giving three series of lectures, while during the month of November I was away on pilgrimage to the Buddhist holy places with Dhardo Rimpoche and others as a guest of the Government of India.

In Calcutta, where I spent much of August attending to Journal work, my lectures were given as three of the 'Thursday lectures on Buddhism' which now formed part of the regular activities at the Maha Bodhi Society's headquarters. On successive weeks I spoke on 'Buddhism and Modern Thought', on 'Buddhism and the Arts', and on 'Buddhism and the Social Order'. What prompted me to speak on the last subject, other than the simple desire to explore the relation between Buddhism and various departments of human life, I do not know, though the fact that Dr Ambedkar and his Scheduled Castes followers were, as it now seemed, about to embrace Buddhism, may have had something to do with it. However that may have been, the president at this lecture was my old teacher Kashyap-ji, in accordance with whose injunction I had stayed in Kalimpong to work for the good of Buddhism. Having established the Pali Postgraduate Institute in Nalanda, the site of the ancient 'monastic university, he was now editing the entire Pali Tipitaka – the Canon of Theravadin Buddhism – in *Devanagari* characters for publication by the Government of Bihar. As we discussed this enormous project, which was to occupy him for many years, I recalled an incident which had occurred six or seven years earlier, when I was staying with him at the Benares Hindu University. Indicating the palm of his hand, he had one day exclaimed, with reference to the same forty-five-volume Tipi-taka, 'Sangharakshita, I have it all *here*!' I certainly could not claim to have the Tipitaka, or even a small portion of it, in the palm of my hand, but texts like the *Sutta-nipata*, the *Udana*, and the *Itivuttaka*, if not my constant companions, were often in my thoughts and had long been a major source of inspiration.

The three lectures I gave at Shantiniketan, in the first week of September, were given under the auspices of two different departments of the Visvabharati University and one of its campus organizations. At Cheena Bhavan, under the auspices of the International Club, I spoke on 'Buddhism as a Religion for Life', under the auspices of the English Department on 'Eastern Thought and English Literature', and under the auspices of the Philosophy Department on 'The Philosophical Interpretation of the Buddha's Personality'. The 'philosophical' interpretation in question was that of the subtle and mysterious doctrine of the *trikaya* or 'three bodies', according to which the Buddha possessed, in addition to the earthly body perceived by gods and men, a sublimely beautiful ethereal body that was perceived only by highly advanced Bodhisattvas and other Buddhas, and an unmanifested body which, besides including the two previous bodies, was the Supreme Reality of all individual persons and things and the goal to be realized through transcendental wisdom. Lobsang Phuntsok had dealt with the trikaya doctrine in his article on Tibetan Buddhism, and my own exposition drew on his account, which was in turn based upon oral explanations given him by Dhardo Rimpoche. The trikaya doctrine was important, in my view, not least because it served to illustrate the fact that, enlightened *human being* though the Buddha was, his enlightened humanity possessed – as did the unenlightened humanity of all men potentially – dimensions undreamt of in the modern, secular conception of what constituted humanity. That the Buddha possessed three 'bodies' was, of course, a distinctively Mahayana teaching, originally promulgated by the Yogachara School on the basis of earlier, uncoordinated traditions, and it was mainly to the Mahayana that I devoted the two lectures I gave in Gangtok the following month. The first of these was on 'Hinayana and Mahayana', the second on 'The Six Paramitas'. Both lectures were given in the White Memorial Hall, the Maharaj Kumar again presiding. To the Buddhists in my audience, including the Maharaj

Kumar, the question of the relation between the Hinayana and the Mahayana was of more than academic interest. In recent years they had become increasingly aware that the Hinayana, as represented by the Theravadin bhikkhus with whom they came in contact in India, differed widely from the Mahayana, as represented by the Nyingma and Karma-Kagyu lamas of Sikkim. Was the Hinayana the original Buddhism, of which the Mahayana was only a corrupt and degenerate form, as the bhikkhus (and some Western orientalists) tended to believe? Or was the Mahayana a higher, more developed form of Buddhism, to which the Hinayana was only introductory, as the more learned lamas asserted? Or, again, were the two yanas complementary? These were questions which Western Buddhists, too, were having to face, and I had attempted to deal with them in Chapter Two of *A Survey of Buddhism*, on which the Gangtok lecture on 'Hinayana and Mahayana' was partly based.

In between my visit to Calcutta and Shantiniketan and my visit to Gangtok, and my visit to Gangtok and my tour of the Buddhist holy places, I spent my time in Kalimpong organizing full moon day meetings at Everton Villa, editing (and writing for) the *Maha Bodhi*, helping Khema-siri with his English, and doing my best to follow Dr Johnson's justly famous injunction that a man 'should keep his friendship *in constant repair*'. I did more than follow it. Besides keeping old friendships in repair, whether through personal contact or by means of correspondence, in the course of the brilliant autumn days I made two new friends, who came to be as much associated, in recollection, with Everton Villa, as Sachin and Durga were with The Hermitage and Mitra and Lalit with Craigside. Autumn seemed to be the season of friendship, as spring was the season of love. In an essay written in the year of my arrival in Kalimpong, when I was still intoxicated with the mingled grandeur and loveliness of my surroundings, I had not only linked autumn with friendship but cele-brated both in the highly lyrical terms that then came naturally and spontaneously to my exultant twenty-five-year-old heart.

> Beautiful indeed is the Indian Autumn [I wrote], but most
> beautiful of all here in the foothills of the Himalaya. The rains are
> over and gone, and one has no longer to huddle day after day
> within doors listening to the thunder of them on the roof, or
> watching the jagged lightning as it glares from end to end of the
> sky swollen with black clouds. Doors and windows are all open
> now, open to the warm golden sunlight glistening on the grass,
> on the long green hair of the earth, as she emerges from the rains

as a naiad with dripping locks from the river. The human heart
also expands and opens, unfolding petals of brotherhood and
love. People meeting in the cool of the evening eagerly renew the
acquaintanceship of last year, and friends who have not met for a
season, turning aside from the highways and the heat at noon,
lose themselves in the cool of the forest and once more wander
hand in hand through the deep silence of innumerable trees.

The friends who wandered hand in hand were friends in the strict,
non-sexual sense of the term, not lovers, for in India it was possible for
two men to hold hands in public without this giving rise to unwarranted
suspicions. Whether Narayanmani and Taranath ever wandered hand in
hand, in the forest or anywhere else, I do not know, but I became
acquainted with them at about the same time. They were good friends,
and they often came to see me together. Both were of Nepalese stock,
Narayanmani being a Hindu Newar and Taranath a Chhettri. One was
fair-complexioned, religious-minded, and cheerful; the other sallow-
featured, philosophically inclined, and somewhat cynical. Though different in temperament, the two young men were not without common
interests, the chief of these being Buddhism and English literature, which
were the usual topics of discussion among the three of us and between
me and one or the other of them when they came to see me independently.
Both had been away at university for a couple of years, returning to
Kalimpong only in the vacations, which was the principal reason we had
not met earlier, though each had heard of me through friends or relations.
Taranath, who was the elder of the two, had spent some time in Calcutta
after graduation. There he had become engaged to an Anglo-Indian girl
from Darjeeling. His engagement did not, however, prevent him from
being something of a Don Juan, which, as he was extremely good-
looking, he did not find it very difficult to be. Partly on account of their
having seen a little of the outside world, both Narayanmani and Taranath
possessed a greater degree of emotional and intellectual maturity than
did their more stay-at-home contemporaries, so that in the course of our
discussions I was often able to share my deeper thoughts and feelings in
a way that it was not possible for me to do with anybody else in
Kalimpong at the time.

Besides being religious-minded, in a devotional kind of way, Narayanmani was sensitive almost to the point of being psychic. Once, when
staying at Everton Villa overnight, he woke me in the early hours of the
morning by calling out to me, from the bed he occupied near my own,

'Bhante, who is that lady standing in the doorway?' I could see no lady, and thinking that he might be dreaming with his eyes open (though he sounded wide awake) I asked him to describe what he saw. 'She is not very young and not very old,' he replied, 'and she is wearing a white sari with a red border.' Enquiries subsequently revealed that Everton Villa had been occupied, some years previously, by a Bengali family; the lady of the house had died, and her ghost was believed to haunt the place, which was why it had remained unoccupied for so long. The white sari with a red border was typical of the Bengali married woman whose husband was living, the red border being torn off if she was so unfortunate as to become a widow. Narayanmani's experience may or may not have been connected with some odd experiences of my own. The room in which we had been sleeping, and in the doorway of which the ghost – if ghost it was – had appeared to him, was both my bedroom and study, and the table at which I worked stood directly beneath the window. When I worked there in the evening, as I usually did, I would hear a sound as of handfuls of gravel being tossed against the glass. When I went outside on to the veranda to look there was nobody there, neither was there so much as a speck of gravel to be seen on the ground beneath the window. After the first three or four nights I took no further notice of the phenomenon, and eventually came to accept it as a normal part of life at Everton Villa.

Not all the friends I made around this time were Nepalese, nor were they all from Kalimpong. Simmons and Marcia Roof were Americans, Vaidyasekera was Sinhalese, and Michael Junius was German, and so far as their immediate antecedents were concerned all four hailed from Shantiniketan. The precise nature of the Roofs' connection with that seat of the muses was unclear, but Vaidyasekera was a student there (he had organized my recent lectures), as was Michael Junius, who was studying Indian classical music at Sangeet Bhavan and learning to play the sitar. Simmons and Marcia, who as Americans were no doubt accustomed to comfort, stayed in a rented bungalow on the Homes Estate above Tirpai, while Vaidyasekera and Michael stayed with me at Everton Villa. The five of us (plus Khemasiri) met frequently, as there were few days when the American couple did not take a taxi to my place and spend a good part of the afternoon and evening there. Simmons was in his early or middle thirties. Tall and inclining to corpulence, he had a smooth manner and exuded complacency to a degree that bordered on the ludicrous. Only when we had been acquainted several weeks did I learn that he was a Unitarian minister and in India on a sort of study sabbatical. Marcia, who was of about the same age as her husband, was slim, nervous, and intense. As soon became evident, she was in love with Michael (a situation Simmons appeared to accept), who was at least ten years her junior and the veritable embodiment of blond Teutonic young manhood. For his part, Michael was not interested in Marcia, except as a friend, and was in fact soon in blatant pursuit of Taranath, who was then staying with me and who, on more than one occasion, had to take refuge in my room from the young German's importunity. Michael was, however, a pleasant enough companion, and already both an expert musician and a serious musicologist. Early each morning he played his sitar for an hour or more, starting while it was still dark, and I would wake up to the sound of the plangent notes of the appropriate raga coming from the shrine-room, where I had allowed him to practise and where, after he had finished, I would go and meditate.

Though the Roofs came to see me so often, the only visit of theirs of which I have a distinct recollection is associated, in my mind, not so much with the American couple themselves as with the figure of someone they very much wanted to meet and who, at their request, I had invited to have lunch with the three of us at Everton Villa.

Like others in India on a study sabbatical, Simmons Roof was gathering material for a book. It was to be a book about the spiritual life, as illustrated by his personal religious quest, and in this connection he was anxious to meet as many spiritual personalities, both Hindu and Buddhist, as possible. Being now in Kalimpong he wanted to meet a real lama. I do not know if he had met Dhardo Rimpoche, if indeed the latter was in Kalimpong at the time, but it so happened that I had recently become acquainted with a Nyingma lama who had impressed me greatly. I had become acquainted with him through Ani-la. On my return from Bombay I had found the volatile Frenchwoman in a state of great excitement. She had found a new guru! He was a most remarkable man, and she had met him in the strangest fashion!

Little by little the story of the meeting came out, Ani-la's words tumbling over one another in her eagerness to tell me everything at once. She had been wandering in the mountains of western Sikkim on her own, in a state of deep depression, thinking that life was not worth living and that the only course left her was to commit suicide. Thus wandering, not caring in which direction she went, she came upon a small clearing in the forest. A tent had been pitched in the clearing, and in front of the tent sat a shaven-headed, red-robed figure whom she at once recognized as a lama. Her curiosity aroused, she approached and saluted him in her best

Tibetan, and the two got into conversation. The lama, it transpired, was from Tibet. He was on his way to Pemayangtse Gompa, the premier Nyingma monastery of Sikkim, where he was to be installed as abbot. According to tradition, he had to enter the monastery on a certain auspicious day. That day had not yet come, and in the meantime he was staying on his own in the forest and meditating. Having satisfied the French nun's curiosity, he naturally expected her to satisfy his, a white woman in monastic garb no doubt being the last person he had expected to meet in the forest-clad mountains of western Sikkim. She was a *getsulma* or novice nun, Ani-la explained. Who had ordained her? Dhardo Rimpoche, a Gelug incarnate lama who lived in Kalimpong. Which *sadhana* or spiritual practice was she doing? She was doing the sadhana of Manjughosha, 'He of the Gentle Voice', the Bodhisattva of Wisdom. So far the interrogation had proceeded along familiar lines, but at this point the strange lama's expression changed. 'No,' he said, in a stern but kindly manner, 'you are *not* doing the Manjughosha sadhana. You have not done it for six months.' Ani-la was overwhelmed. It was true. Being angry with Dhardo Rimpoche she had stopped doing the sadhana he had given her at the time of her ordination and had not done it for exactly six months. The lama must have read her thoughts. He was a real lama. She would become his disciple.

The upshot was that Ani-la had spent some time at Pemayangtse Gompa, after the lama's installation, and there received teachings from him. Nor was this all. Within weeks of my returning from Bombay and hearing Ani-la's account of how she had found her new guru, the lama himself had spent a few days in Kalimpong, and I had met him. On my not only telling Simmons Roof the French nun's story, just as she had told it to me, but adding the information that the lama was even now paying a second visit to Kalimpong, both he and Marcia begged me to arrange a meeting. Thus it was that I had invited the lama to have lunch with the three of us at Everton Villa.

Kachu Rimpoche was a cheerful, straightforward, down-to-earth person who certainly did not give the impression of being possessed of supernormal powers of any kind. He was undoubtedly very knowledgeable, however, and over lunch, and for some time afterwards, Simmons plied him with questions on a wide variety of topics, with me acting as interpreter and translating the Unitarian minister's questions from English into Nepali and the Nyingma incarnate lama's answers from Nepali into English. As the discussion progressed, the questions Simmons asked related to topics of a more and more abstruse nature. All the Rimpoche's answers, as well as his additional explanations, were clear and to the point, especially when the question related to meditation, of which he evidently had extensive personal experience. Sometimes the alternation of question and answer was so rapid that I had difficulty keeping up with my translations. Eventually, when Simmons had put a highly philosophical question regarding the nature of nirvana, I noticed the Rimpoche had started replying to it without waiting for me to translate it for him. He was replying not to the words of the question, which were in a language he did not understand, but to the thought (and possibly also to the feeling) behind the question, which it seemed he was able to comprehend directly, without having to rely on its verbal expression. For some reason Simmons failed to notice this, but after the Rimpoche's departure he and Marcia expressed themselves entirely satisfied with the meeting, which had exceeded their expectations.

According to Buddhist tradition, *parachittajnana*, knowledge of the minds of others, was one of the mundane *abhijna* or superknowledges. Though a sign of attainment in meditation, its development was not essential to the realization of Enlightenment. That Kachu Rimpoche was able to know Simmons's mind, if such indeed had been the case, did not in itself mean that he was far advanced spiritually. None the less, the meeting at Everton Villa left me more impressed by him than ever and anxious to continue the acquaintance, despite the fact that he was living in western Sikkim and I in Kalimpong. As it happened, he was of much the same mind, with the result that in subsequent years we met a number of times and he came to occupy an important place in my life as friend and teacher.

Chapter Twenty-Two

HOLY PLACES AND EMINENT BUDDHISTS

BY THE END OF THE THIRTEENTH CENTURY Buddhism had almost disappeared from India as an organized religion. Assimilation by Hinduism, withdrawal of royal patronage, centralization of learning in grand monastic universities, and the destruction of those universities by Muslim invaders from the north-west, had all played a part in the process, though the relative importance to be attributed to each of these factors remains a matter of dispute among scholars. During the next six hundred years the situation did not greatly change, so that when India achieved independence in 1947 Buddhist communities were to be found only in the border areas, principally those in the north (Ladakh and Himachal Pradesh) and in the north-east (Sikkim, Assam, and the North-East Frontier Agency). As part of the Buddha Jayanti celebrations, some fifty representatives of these communities had been invited to tour the Buddhist holy places as guests of the Government of India and to spend four days in Delhi in the same capacity. Among the Eminent Buddhists from the Border Areas, as the invitees were officially designated, were two from Kalimpong, in the persons of Dhardo Rimpoche and me, for both of us had by that time resided in the town long enough, and played a sufficiently prominent part in its Buddhist activities, to be regarded as the *de facto* representatives of the place's rather heterogeneous Buddhist population.

The tour started from Calcutta, and it was outside the national tourist office in that city that we all assembled on the morning of 29 October. Many of those who gradually filled the little compound were monks. There were shaven-headed, yellow-robed bhikkhus from West Bengal and Assam (none of them, unfortunately, known to me) and shaven-headed, red-robed lamas from Ladakh and NEFA, besides long-haired, red-robed figures from some indeterminate border region who may or may not have been monks and who presented, in some cases, a rather fantastic appearance. There were also laymen in a variety of national and regional costumes, from Nepalese coat and jodhpurs to Tibetan-style kaftan. Some of my fellow Eminent Buddhists were bewildered, even disoriented, by the experience of being suddenly plucked from a remote village or monastery and set down in the heart of the biggest city of India, especially as they knew neither Hindi nor English and could communicate, in a few cases, only in their own local dialect. This meant that the stylish young Bengali woman who was in charge of the tourist office and responsible, apparently, for getting us to Howrah Station, did not have an easy time ascertaining their identities and inducing them to board one of the waiting buses. At times, indeed, she was reduced to darting hither and thither, sari-end floating out behind her, pushing and shoving the more uncomprehending of them in the direction she wanted them to go – an unceremonious proceeding to which the more elderly and conservative among them clearly took exception. Eventually, however, she succeeded in getting everyone on board, and half an hour later we were being off-loaded at the station and escorted to the special train that was to take us to the holy places and which was to be our home for the duration of the pilgrimage.

In the course of the next week we visited Bodh-gaya, Rajgir, Nalanda, Sarnath, Kusinara, Lumbini, Sanchi, and Agra, as well as seeing two or three of the enormous dams the government was constructing as part of one of its ambitious hydroelectric power schemes. What with the time it took the train to get from one pilgrimage centre to another, and the time it took the coach to convey us from the railway station to the temple or archaeological site that was our objective, we rarely were able to spend more than an hour or two at any of the holy places we visited, with the result that in most cases my impressions of them are not very distinct. Of some of the most important holy places, including Bodh-gaya, I have indeed no recollection at all, at least so far as the present pilgrimage is concerned. My only really vivid recollections are of Sarnath and Kusinara, and these are recollections not so much of the places themselves as of certain incidents that took place in them, one of which was ultimately to affect the whole course of my life and thought as a Buddhist and as a monk. As for the dams we were taken to see, my only recollection of these is of standing in front of one of them with Dhardo Rimpoche and his shaking his head and remarking, with a smile, 'Such things don't *really* solve the problem of human suffering.' If the organizers of the tour had hoped that the Eminent Buddhists from the Border Areas would be no less impressed by the temples of modern India, as Pandit Nehru was fond of calling dams and power stations, than they were by the ruined shrines of the ancient Buddhist holy places, then they were doomed to disappointment.

Sarnath was one of the four principal places of Buddhist pilgrimage, together with Lumbini, Bodh-gaya, and Kusinara, the Buddha having preached there, to his five former companions, what had come to be known, in English, as his 'First Sermon', but which was much more likely to have been more of the nature of an informal talk. In the course of the last seven years I had visited Sarnath at least four or five times, more than once staying there for a few days, and was familiar with its excavated area, dominated by the massive bulk of the Dhamekh Stupa, its two or three modern temples or monasteries, its archaeological museum, and its Birla *dharamsala* or pilgrims' rest-house, as well as with the half-dozen Sinhalese bhikkhus who ran the Maha Bodhi Society's activities there and cared for the Mulagandhakuti Vihara, the pink sandstone temple built by Anagarika Dharmapala in the late twenties and early thirties. Since my last visit much had been done in the way of improvement. Lawns and flowerbeds had been laid out, giving the whole place a serene, park-like appearance, and beyond the excavated area, not far from the Mula-gandhakuti Vihara, a deer park had been created, Sarnath having been in the Buddha's day a place of refuge for deer and other wild creatures. As soon as we had paid our respects to the Dhamekh Stupa, which according to an ancient inscription marked the exact spot where the Buddha had delivered the First Sermon or, in traditional parlance, 'turned the Wheel of the Dharma', Dhardo Rimpoche and I and the rest of the Eminent Buddhists were led to the Mulagandhakuti Vihara. Here a reception by Venerable Sangharatana and his yellow-robed colleagues awaited us. Before it could begin there was a point of protocol to be settled. The Vihara consisted of a spacious rectangular hall, the walls of which were covered with frescoes, with a kind of chapel at the far end. The floor of the chapel, which contained a life-size gilded image of the Buddha, was a foot or so higher than the floor of the hall. On entering the Vihara the bhikkhus in our party automatically went and sat inside the chapel, where the Maha Bodhi Society bhikkhus were already seated, leaving the lamas to occupy the floor of the hall along with the laity. Some of the lamas, as Sonam Topgay Kazi, the Sikkim representative, was not slow to point out to Venerable Sangharatana, were however celibates, like their Theravadin counterparts. Would it not therefore be better, he politely enquired, if these lamas sat inside the chapel with the bhikkhus, rather than in the hall with him and the other lay members of the party? As I knew from my own acquaintance with him, Sangharatana was more open-minded than most Theravadin monks, and I was not surprised when, after he had briefly consulted with his colleagues, the celibate lamas were invited, to their evident satisfaction, to sit with the bhikkhus on the higher, more honourable level.

On the opposite side of the excavated area from the Mulagandhakuti Vihara stood the modest structure that was the Burmese temple. It was in this temple, almost exactly six years earlier, that I had received my bhikkhu ordination, and I naturally did not want to leave Sarnath without visiting the place, paying my respects to the resident monk, U Kittima, and renewing my commitment to the monastic life. On entering the compound I saw a number of Burmese pilgrims, all in national costume and smoking cheroots, and either strolling about or squatting on their heels beneath the big, shady trees. But there was no sign of U Kittima, and no one seemed able or willing to tell me where he was or even if he was on the premises at all. At length there emerged from the servants' quarters the brahmin woman who, as I knew, was U Kittima's cook, and the young man, her son, who acted as the temple manager. As soon as she recognized me the woman uttered a great cry and threw herself at my feet. Babaji wanted to throw her and her son out, she exclaimed, bursting into a flood of tears. She had served him faithfully for twenty years and more. She had been a good wife to him and now he wanted her and her boy to leave the place. Where would they go? What would they do? Would I please write to Big Babaji in Kusinara and ask him to tell Babaji not to turn her out? Would I speak to Babaji himself, who for the last two or three weeks had been staying in Benares and who had vowed not to return until she was gone? 'You all know Babaji and I were living together,' she pleaded. 'You all know my son is his son too. Please help us.'

I had not known that U Kittima's cook was also his concubine, though his brother bhikkhus in Sarnath (and Kusinara) had evidently been privy to what was going on. Nor had I known that the young man in the lungi who acted as the temple manager was the Burmese monk's son, though when I looked at him, as he stood there beside his mother, arms stoically folded, the resemblance was obvious. The distraught woman's revelations therefore came as a complete surprise to me and for some minutes I did not know what to say, especially as several Eminent Buddhists who wanted to see more of Sarnath had accompanied me to the Burmese temple from the Mulagandhakuti Vihara and were clearly wondering what was amiss. There was no question of my writing to 'Big Babaji', whom I was in any case hoping to meet the following day when the party visited Kusinara and who of course was none other than U Chandramani, from whom I had received my samanera or novice ordination in 1949. Neither was there any question of my speaking to U Kittima, whom I had always regarded as being very much my elder brother in the Monastic Order. When I had recovered from my astonishment I therefore simply assured the discarded cook-concubine of my sympathy, and expressed the hope that Babaji would change his mind and allow her to stay, after which I left the Burmese temple without having renewed my commitment to the monastic life and in a state of considerable perplexity.

That taciturn, scholarly U Kittima was, as it appeared, 'a layman in the guise of a monk' was not a matter that concerned him alone, or even one that concerned only him and the unfortunate woman he now wanted to dismiss from his service. It was a matter that concerned the whole Theravadin monastic order, or at least that branch of it to which he and I both belonged. It was certainly a matter that concerned me personally. U Kittima had been present at my bhikkhu ordination. He had taken part in it, sitting inside the *sima* or consecrated area with the other members of the ordaining chapter. It was he who, as presiding monk of the Burmese temple, had signed my ordination certificate, testifying that I was 'properly ordained as a Bhikkhu according to the Vinaya of Theravadi Bhikkhus.' If at the time of my ordination he was 'a layman in the guise of a monk' and if, as I had been told, the presence of such a person inside the *sima* as a member of the ordaining chapter invalidated the proceedings, then my ordination was technically null and void and I was not in fact a bhikkhu. What, then, was I? While I was certainly not 'a layman in the guise of a monk' in the way that U Kittima was, I was technically a layman none the less, in that according to the Vinaya I was neither bhikkhu nor samanera and there was no fourth category of male ecclesiastical persons to which I could belong. Yet I did not feel myself to be a layman. I was as much committed to the spiritual life, and to being a monk, as I had been before that fateful visit to the Burmese temple, and did not have the slightest wish to return to the life of the world. Indeed, I knew myself to be more committed to the spiritual life, and to being a monk in the true sense, than were many bhikkhus of my acquaintance, technically valid though their ordinations may have been. But if according to the Vinaya I was neither bhikkhu nor samanera, and if I did not feel myself to be a layman, then what was the basis of my commitment to the spiritual life? What was it that enabled me to live as a monk and work for the good of Buddhism? Such were the questions that passed through my mind as I rejoined my fellow Eminent Buddhists and boarded the coach that was taking us back to Benares, and it was to be many years before I found a satisfactory answer to them. Meanwhile I had no alternative but to live as though I had, in fact, been validly ordained and was a bhikkhu in the technical Vinaya sense.

Kusinara was about 150 miles from Benares, and if we did not see the site of the Buddha's *parinirvana* or 'final passing away' the following day we certainly saw it the day after that. Like Sarnath, it had been much improved since my last visit, and as that visit had occurred in 1949 there were even more changes for me to take note of here than in Sarnath. In my eyes not all the changes counted as improvements. The brand-new temple with the big 'Ajanta-style' horseshoe windows that now housed the ancient thirty-foot-long recumbent image of the Buddha was no doubt a fine building, but it entirely lacked the atmosphere of the primitive structure, hardly bigger than the image itself, in the gloom of which, seven years ago, Buddharakshita and I had meditated each morning with only two or three flickering candles between us and the enormous face of the dying Master. Other changes were even less welcome. The half-crazy Chinese monk who lived in a peepul tree, and who burned candles on different parts of his body, had come down from his tree. But he had not only come down. He had built himself a cottage, and was even now building a kitchen on to the cottage with bricks taken from inside the exposed rim of the newly excavated Angyar Chaitya, the mound marking the spot where the earthly remains of the Buddha had been cremated. A party of coolies was busy dislodging hundreds of bricks with crowbars and removing them in baskets. When some of us went and complained to the Archaeological Department overseer he flatly denied that anything of the sort was happening, whereupon we insisted on his accompanying us to the spot and seeing with his own eyes what the coolies were doing. Either there had been gross negligence on somebody's part or somebody had been bribed. Whichever it was, serious damage had been done to an ancient and important Buddhist monument.

Though Kusinara had been much improved since my last visit, few changes had taken place in the dimly-lit, sparsely-furnished ground floor room where Buddharakshita and I had been favoured with our first interview with U Chandramani and where my former preceptor now received as many of the Eminent Buddhists as could be squeezed into the limited space. Very little was said, conversation being hardly practicable in the circumstances and the visitors being for the most part content, in any case, simply to sit there and have the old man's *darshan*. At one point, however, as slowly he surveyed the different faces in the room, U Chandramani's gaze fell upon me. 'Is it Sangharakshita?' he asked wonderingly, as if unable to believe his eyes. I confirmed that it indeed was, but though he seemed pleased to see me there was no further exchange between us. We had not met for seven years. For my part, though *I* was pleased to see *him*, and though the occasion brought back poignant memories of my samanera ordination at his hands, the brahmin woman's plea for help still rang in my ears and I was uncomfortably aware that U Chandramani, too, had known of U Kittima's liaison with her and had therefore been, in a sense, a party to it. Despite his eighty years he still presented a fairly robust appearance as he sat there, cross-legged, on the same old cane-bottomed armchair, but his face was more deeply furrowed and the flesh hung a little more loosely on his bones. He also looked a little tired. This was not surprising. He had not long returned from an exhausting trip to Madhya Pradesh, where on 14 October, in Nagpur, he had formally initiated Dr Ambedkar and his wife into Buddhism, after which the Scheduled Castes leader had himself administered the Three Refuges and Five Precepts, together with twenty-two vows of his own devising, to more than a quarter of a million of his followers, thus inaugurating the movement of mass conversion of Untouchables to Buddhism. Before taking leave of U Chandramani the Eminent Buddhists, at Sonam Topgay's whispered suggestion, dug into pockets and shoulder bags with the result that we were able to place at his feet a small pile of currency notes.

Lumbini was not in India but in Nepal, so that in order to reach it one had to cross the border, but apart from having my photograph taken with Dhardo Rimpoche in front of the pillar that marks the spot where the Blessed One was born I remember nothing of our visit to the place. I do have a vivid recollection, however, of the evening the Rimpoche and I spent in Gorakhpur, where our special train was kept at the station for two nights in a siding and whence we were conveyed by coach first to Kusinara and then to Lumbini. Gorakhpur was an old-fashioned town with, it appeared, a predominantly Hindu population. At least that was the impression we formed as we made our way to the bazaar area, for there was a Hindu festival in progress and everybody was taking part. Night had already fallen and the houses and open-fronted shops, and the innumerable little wayside stalls, were all lit not by electricity but by the soft golden glow shed by myriads of tiny oil lamps. Despite the fact that a festival was being celebrated there was little noise, and an atmosphere of deep peacefulness prevailed. As though in a dream – a dream filled with the smell of incense and crushed flowers – we drifted down bylane after bylane and from stall to stall. Many of the stalls were selling beautifully painted and decorated wooden or clay figures a few inches high. Who or what the figures represented, or whether they had a connection with the festival, we did not know, any more than we knew what the festival itself was all about. Nor did we want to know. I myself was perfectly content simply to observe the scenes through which we passed, taking in colour, shape, and movement as it were for their own sake, without thinking about what I saw. 'In the seen only the seen, in the heard only the heard....' Though we obviously were strangers to the town, nobody accosted us, or tried to sell us anything, or bothered us in any way. It was almost as though we were invisible, so that we returned to the train well pleased with our nocturnal outing and favourably impressed by Gorakhpur.

By this time the tour was more than half over, and something like a friendship had begun to develop between Dhardo Rimpoche and me, as well as between the pair of us and the two other occupants of our compartment. These were Sonam Topgay Kazi and S. Yhonzone. Sonam Topgay was a friend of the French nun, in fact the same Kazi friend who had come to see me in Gangtok on the first of my recent visits to the village capital. Small, light-complexioned, and invariably attired in the traditional chuba, he worked as a translator in Apa Pant's office, where he had acquired a reputation, I afterwards learned, for elusiveness. Though broad in his Buddhist sympathies, he was a convinced follower of the Nyingma tradition and the personal disciple of some of its most distinguished living masters. It was from him, in the course of one of our many conversations during the tour, that I first heard of Dzogchen, the highest Nyingma teaching. He possessed, in fact, a good general knowledge of Tibetan Buddhism and was acquainted with learned lamas of every school. In Benares he had taken me to see a Gelug lama whom he particularly esteemed, both for his learning and his asceticism. We found the lama, whose name was (I think) Sherab Gyaltsen, occupying a tiny whitewashed room whose sole contents were a mat, two or three Tibetan books, and a small tin suitcase that served him as a desk. He was overjoyed to see us and with Sonam Topgay as interpreter he and I were able to have a short conversation. All he wanted to do was study, he told me enthusiastically, his eyes shining. It was in order to study that he had come to Benares, as despite his advanced age (I judged him to be about fifty) he wanted to learn Sanskrit. On our taking leave of him he looked round the room for something to give me. But there was nothing there. Whereupon he looked inside the tin suitcase, but except for a few dried apricots it was empty. But he was not to be defeated. As though seized by a sudden inspiration, he broke the string of his rosary and gave me a bead, saying, 'Many millions of mantras have been said on this bead. Please accept it with my blessing.'

The fourth member of our quartet, S. Yhonzone, was a Tamang schoolmaster from Kurseong with whom I was already acquainted as a result of the visits I had paid to that place. Like Sonam Topgay, he was about my age, but unlike that staunch traditionalist he preferred Western dress, as did most English-educated young Nepalis in the Darjeeling area. For the purpose of the tour, however, he had decked himself out in a light blue coat and jodhpurs, complete with a black conical cap. Though a Tamang, and therefore technically a Nyingmapa, he knew little or nothing about the Nyingma tradition or, for that matter, about any form of Buddhism. Consequently he did not find it easy to join in the doctrinal discussions with which Dhardo Rimpoche, Sonam Topgay, and I passed the time between holy places, and when he did join in it was usually only to reveal an ignorance and a confusion that would have been laughable had they not been so lamentable. But though not very bright he was sincere and well-meaning, and in the course of the tour the three of us did our best to inculcate a few basic Buddhist ideas and to clear up at least some of his confusion. Occasionally our quartet received a visit from Dhondup Lhendup, the leader of the NEFA contingent, who had studied with me for a few months in Kalimpong, in the days when I was living as the guest of Burma Raja, and whose good looks had been much admired by Marco Pallis. Since then he had graduated, joined the Indian Administrative Service, and been posted to a sub-division in the depths of NEFA. There, I had heard, he exercised despotic sway, enjoying unlimited access to the local liquor and the local women. Absolute power had corrupted absolutely. The first time he appeared in the doorway of the compartment I hardly recognized him. Gone were his looks, he had put on weight, his eyes were bloodshot, his gaze dull and vacant. In the crumpled navy blue suit he was wearing he looked like a middle-aged man, though he could not have been more than thirty. When I told Marco Pallis, a few years later, about the change that had taken place in my old pupil, he was quite distressed, and exclaimed, 'Oh, he was *so* good-looking!'

Whenever the Eminent Buddhists were ferried from a railway station to a holy place Dhardo Rimpoche and I would sit together in the middle section of the coach. Initially this occasioned astonishment, even indignation, on the part of the yellow-robed members of the party. Like most Theravadin bhikkhus they were great observers of protocol, and the first time we had to board a coach, which must have been when we visited Bodh-gaya, they made sure that they got on first and occupied the front seats. Their red-robed counterparts, on the contrary, motioned others to precede them with a polite 'After *you*.' When we were all on board, the leader of the Assam bhikkhus turned round in his seat, saw me sitting with Dhardo Rimpoche a dozen rows back, and called out, 'Come and sit in the front with us! You're a bhikkhu too!' But I stayed where I was, and as I sat with the Rimpoche for the rest of the tour he and the other bhikkhus eventually concluded that I was a renegade from their ranks and could not be relied on to help them maintain the prestige of the Theravadin monastic order. From our position half-way down the coach my companion and I could not only see what was going on in front of us but hear what was going on behind. Often we heard squeals and scuffles. These sounds came from the back seat, which extended for the entire width of the coach. In the middle of this seat, facing the aisle, sat a stout, youngish woman who, we had been told, was a Bhutanese nun. She wore a short, apron-like skirt that barely reached to her knees, leggings, a little jacket, and a conical hat with a feather in it, and her round, rosy face was always wreathed in smiles. On each side of her sat two or three shaven-headed, red-robed lamas. Every now and then one of the lamas would pinch her plump thigh (hence the squeals), whereupon she would turn in his direction and try to give him a slap (hence the scuffles). While she was thus engaged, a lama on the other side would pinch the *other* thigh, whereupon she would turn round and try to hit *him*. Everyone seemed to enjoy this little game, including the dignified Bhutanese abbess, said to be a relation of the king, who from a seat nearby regarded the proceedings with an indulgent smile. At any rate, both the lamas and the nun enjoyed it sufficiently to play it every time we were in the coach for more than a few minutes.

Friendship implies a degree of mutual knowledge, and the fact that something like a friendship had begun to develop between Dhardo Rimpoche and me meant that we had got to know each other better. In Kalimpong this had hardly been possible, as we met only at intervals and usually on some formal occasion. Moreover, we were both rather reserved, whether by nature or as a result of having had, in his case a Gelug monastic training, in mine an English upbringing. None the less, each had definite feelings of goodwill towards the other, while from my side there was an appreciation of the Rimpoche's unusual qualities. That appreciation naturally increased during the tour, as well as in Delhi afterwards, when the fact that we were constantly together meant that I got to know him much better than before, even as he, no doubt, got to know me better. Though he had many positive qualities, the two that impressed me most were his uniform kindness and generosity and his unfailing mindfulness. The latter consisted, not only in an entire absence of anything resembling forgetfulness or inattentiveness, but also in a degree of foresight and preparedness that was almost supernatural. In later years I was to say that Dhardo Rimpoche was never caught napping. On the tour itself there occurred an incident which strikingly exemplified this quality of his. The officials who were responsible for looking after the party and organizing its transport used to tell us each morning which places we would be visiting that day. One morning they told us we would be visiting a certain dam in the morning and in the afternoon, after returning to the train for lunch, a certain holy place. Unfortunately there was somehow a mix-up. An hour after leaving the train we found ourselves not at the dam, as we had expected, but at the holy place. This in itself did not really matter, but thinking that we would not be needing them until the afternoon none of us had brought any candles or incense sticks. None of us, that is, except Dhardo Rimpoche. As we were lamenting the fact that we would be unable to offer worship in the proper manner, he produced packets of candles and bundles of incense sticks from beneath his voluminous robes and smilingly distributed them among us. Strange to say, there proved to be enough candles and enough sticks of incense for everyone.

If Sarnath meant the Dhamekh Stupa, and Kusinara the colossal image of the recumbent Buddha, then Agra – our last stop before Delhi – meant the Taj Mahal. It was the first time either Dhardo Rimpoche or I had seen that 'one solitary tear hanging on the cheek of time', as Rabindranath Tagore characterized Shah Jahan's masterpiece. Having seen so many photographs and paintings of the famous monument, not to mention the plastic models that were on sale at every railway station, I was more than half afraid that the beauty of the original had been spoiled for me and that I would be disappointed. Nor was it really to be expected that any building on earth could live up to the superlatives that had been heaped upon the Taj Mahal. In the event I was *not* disappointed. The Taj Mahal far exceeded my expectations. It was incomparably more beautiful than I had imagined it to be. It was also very much bigger. The perfect proportions of the building and its flanking minarets, as shown in a hundred pictures, had led me to think of it as small and dainty, but as the Rimpoche and I walked from the high red sandstone gateway, along one of the paths bordering the long watercourse in whose depths it was reflected, it grew steadily bigger until eventually the dazzlingly white marble mass loomed over us almost blotting out the blue sky. Inside it was cool and comparatively dark, especially in the crypt containing the actual tombs of the woman in whose memory the Taj Mahal had been built and the grieving emperor who had built it. A few months later, recalling the visit, I composed a quatrain in which the love and death – eros and thanatos – that were everything inside the crypt were contrasted with the life and hate that seemed to be everything outside it. The fact was that I had visited the Taj Mahal at the time of the Suez Canal crisis, when 'voices prophesying war', ancestral and other, could be heard on all sides. But it was not only the prospect of war which dismayed me. I was also dismayed by India's adoption of the double standard. I had not expected this. Had there not been an ethical dimension to the freedom struggle, and had not independent India so far shown a marked tendency to occupy the moral high ground in international affairs? Yet here was Pandit Nehru, the Prime Minister, vigorously condemning the Anglo-French action in Egypt while at the same time responding to Soviet Russia's invasion of Hungary, and its crushing of that country's nascent reform movement, simply with a mild expression of concern. India's foreign policy, it seemed, was in reality no more guided by moral considerations than was that of less Pecksniffian nations.

On our way back to the station from seeing the Taj Mahal and the Agra Fort a strange thing happened. Dhardo Rimpoche and I both saw the words 'Buddha Vihara' on the end of a small roadside building. This was not strange in itself, even though none of the other Eminent Buddhists on the coach saw them. What was strange, as we discovered afterwards when we compared notes, was that whereas the Rimpoche had seen the words in Roman script I had seen them in Devanagari. Obviously we ought to investigate, for where there was a Buddha Vihara there were bound to be Buddhists and we had not expected to find any Buddhists in Agra. As none of our Eminent Buddhist colleagues was willing to accompany us, some of them indeed being of the opinion that both the Rimpoche and I had only *thought* we saw the magic words, the two of us got into a rickshaw and set off on our own. Finding the route taken by the coach did not prove easy, and it took us a long time to locate the area in which the building we sought was situated; but eventually we did so, and there it was, and there were the words 'Buddha Vihara' – in *both* scripts. It was a rather nondescript building, and consisted of little more than a single chamber and a veranda. Peering through the grille in the wooden doors, we saw inside a Buddha image of the traditional Burmese type. A Hindu temple had evidently been turned into a Buddhist place of worship. As there was no one to be seen, it being by that time about ten o'clock and very dark, I seized the rope of the large bell that hung, Hindu-style, inside the veranda, and gave it several sharp tugs, producing a corresponding number of loud clangs. Soon several dozen poorly dressed men, women, and children from the nearby hutments had gathered on the veranda. Despite the presence of the Buddha image on the shrine, which an elderly man now opened, they seemed uncertain whether they were Buddhists or not, nor did they know much about Buddhism, though I gathered that a few of the men had attended Dr Ambedkar's mass conversion ceremony in Nagpur the previous month. Though surprised by our sudden appearance in their midst, especially at such an hour, they were pleased to see us, and pleased when I gave them a twenty-minute impromptu talk on Buddhism. Dhardo Rimpoche and I therefore returned to the station well satisfied with the success of our expedition and glad we had followed our instinct in the matter.

In Delhi the Eminent Buddhists were guests of the Government of India for four days, after which we were expected to shift for ourselves. Some of us found shelter at the local branch of the Maha Bodhi Society and at the Ashok Vihara, Mehrauli, which had been founded by Venerable Veera Dhammavera, the Cambodian monk I had met in Calcutta the previous year, but which an Englishwoman married to a well-known Indian communist was trying to wrest from his control. During the days that we were still government guests we continued to live in our special train, whence we were conveyed each day not to a Buddhist holy place or a dam but to a meeting or reception. Our first meeting was with the President of India, Dr Rajendra Prasad, and it took place at his official residence, Rashtrapati Bhavan, the palace-like building that had once been the Viceroy's House. As it was his government that had invited us to tour the holy places as its guests, we naturally wanted to express our gratitude for the invitation to Dr Prasad, and I had been elected to perform this office on everybody's behalf. Besides thanking him, I made a number of requests. These requests had been agreed among the Eminent Buddhists beforehand, and related to such matters as facilities for worship at the Vajrasana in Bodh-gaya, the acquisition of land in Bodh-gaya by Border Area Buddhist organizations, the protection of the Angyar Chaitya in Kusinara, and the provision of scholarships for

Tibetan-speaking border area Buddhists who wished to study Sanskrit, Hindi, and Pali. To all our requests Dr Prasad gave a sympathetic response, promising to refer them to the appropriate authorities. Only one request did he reject, and that was made not by me but by the leader of the Assam bhikkhus. Seeing the president was in what he must have thought was an indulgent mood, he asked if he and his fellow bhikkhus could stay on in the capital as the government's guests, and at its expense, for an extra two weeks. Dr Prasad could not help smiling at this absurd request, and stroking his walrus moustache replied, as gently as he could, that he did not think that would be possible, whereupon the bhikkhu sat down looking crestfallen and discomfited.

When I made the requests on which we had all agreed I noticed that as soon as I mentioned Bodh-gaya the president stiffened in his seat and his expression, hitherto kindly, became grave. He evidently thought I was about to raise the vexed question of the Bodh-gaya temple, control of which the Buddhists had been demanding since the time of Anagarika Dharmapala. But I knew it was unwise to ask for something the other party would never give, especially when the asking was likely to cause offence. Devapriya Valisinha had told me that Rajendra Prasad, though not a brahmin, was a staunch Hindu, and that in pre-Independence days, when he was president of the Indian National Congress, he had once approached him regarding the Bodh-gaya temple. In the course of the interview Prasad warned him that if the Maha Bodhi Society persisted in campaigning for Buddhist control of the temple he would personally lead a counter-campaign and see to it that the Buddhists had no say at all in its affairs. People seemed to feel strongly about the Bodh-gaya temple, but while it was natural that Buddhists should want to be in control of their own holiest shrine it was difficult to understand why Hindus should want to hold on to a place that had come into their possession as a result of a series of historical accidents. When it became clear that I was *not* going to raise the Bodh-gaya temple question the president relaxed and his face resumed its previous kindly, almost fatherly, expression.

At our meeting with the Vice-President, Dr S. Radhakrishnan, we had no requests to make, and he did practically all the talking. Indeed, he treated us to a glib homily on the subject of the inseparability, even the unity, of *prajna* and *karuna*, Wisdom and Compassion, which Sonam Topgay translated into Tibetan for the benefit of the Tibetan-speaking delegates and over which they afterwards shook their heads. That a non-Buddhist layman should take it upon himself to address Buddhists, including lamas, on one of the profoundest Mahayana teachings struck them as extremely odd. When we met Pandit Nehru there were neither requests from us nor any lecture from him. Dr Rajendra Prasad had received us in a sort of throne room, sitting on a dais and flanked by uniformed ADCs and attendants in scarlet tunics. At the meeting with Dr Radhakrishnan there had been much less formality, the Vice-President receiving us in his drawing-room and addressing us from an easy chair. At Pandit Nehru's house, where we were given lunch and met Indira Gandhi and her two young sons, Sanjay and Rajiv, there was no formality at all. After the lunch, for which we sat, Indian-style, at individual small tables decorated with flowers, Pandit Nehru took me into the garden to show me the pair of giant pandas he had recently been given by the government of the People's Republic of China. Despite their keeper's enticements, they refused to come down from their eucalyptus tree and all I was able to see of them was two black-and-white patches high up amid the grey-green foliage. Much as one might disagree with Pandit Nehru's foreign policy statements there was no disputing the fact that he was a friendly and charming person and the perfect host.

Dr Radhakrishnan's homily may have occasioned some head-shaking on the part of Tibetan-speaking Eminent Buddhists from the Border Areas, but he at least had attempted to meet us on our own ground. No such attempt was made at the reception we were given by the Hindu organizations of Delhi. The reception took place under a *shamiana* in the grounds of the Buddha Vihara, the little temple that was part of the Maha Bodhi Society's Delhi centre and a sort of Buddhist annexe to the huge Lakshmi Narayan Temple next door, both of them having been built – the latter 'in grand and cakey style' – by a philanthropic Hindu multi-millionaire. Evidently our hosts had decided to take the Buddhist threat seriously. The capital's seven or eight leading Hindu scholars and intellectuals had been invited to address us, with the result that we had to sit through more than two hours of speeches. There were speeches in Hindi and speeches in English, long speeches and short speeches. But regardless of whether they spoke in Hindi or in English, or for a longer or a shorter time, all the speakers harped on a theme that was only too familiar to me. They all told us, with varying degrees of emphasis, that Buddhism was only a branch of Hinduism and that there was no difference between the two religions. The Buddha himself had lived and died a Hindu, and his teaching was no more than a restatement of the teachings of the Upanishadic sages. Buddhists were really Hindus, and it was very wrong of them not to want to be included in the Hindu fold but to want, instead, to set Buddhism up as a separate, independent religion.

They should give up their narrow-mindedness and intolerance, recognize that Buddhism was part and parcel of Hinduism, and allow themselves to be absorbed by the one true universal Hindu Sanatana Dharma.

The message had not been repeated more than four or five times before the Eminent Buddhists, together with the other Buddhists in the audience, started becoming restive under the onslaught. There were signs of unease, even of indignation. Eventually two or three of my colleagues whispered to me that the Hindus ought not to be allowed to have things all their own way. I therefore sent a note up to the chairman asking if I might reply to the speeches (they were ostensibly speeches of welcome) and thank the organizers of the reception. Not suspecting anything, he agreed. I began innocently enough. We were grateful to the Government of India for inviting us to Delhi; we were grateful for having been given the opportunity of worshipping in the Buddhist holy places (I did not mention that as non-Hindus we had not been allowed to enter the Vishwanath Temple in Benares), and we were grateful to the Hindu organizations of Delhi for having arranged the present reception. All this I said at some length, and in the kind of language that was customary on such occasions. But having said it, I changed my tune. 'When you invite someone to your house for a meal,' I told the speakers, 'you offer them the food that they like. You do not offer them food that for one reason or another is unacceptable to them. For example, you would not offer a vegetarian non-vegetarian dishes. Now you know very well that Buddhists do *not* agree that Buddhism is "only" a branch of Hinduism, or that the Buddha lived and died a Hindu. You know that such ideas are quite unacceptable, even repugnant, to them. Yet having invited us to your house for a meal, so to speak, *this* is the fare you insist on setting before us. It is not a reception. It is an insult.' These words of mine created consternation on the platform. Several speakers started up to protest that they had not intended to hurt the feelings of the Buddhists, while the chairman, who had himself shown signs of unease during some of the speeches, did his best to conclude the proceedings on a conciliatory note. Next morning a report of the reception appeared on the front page of the *Statesman*, and though I was not quoted verbatim the report made it clear that Buddhists did not agree that Buddhism was a branch of Hinduism.

Once the meetings and receptions were over (and there were several others, of all of which I have only a faint recollection), the Eminent Buddhists from the Border Areas were free to go their separate ways. Dhardo Rimpoche and I, and the other two members of our quartet, continued to keep in touch and to go out and about in one another's company. A visit that Dhardo Rimpoche, Sonam Topgay, Yhonzone, and I made together ended in a way that was not only unexpected but also amusing and even instructive, as did a visit that Sonam Topgay and I made on our own. The first visit took the four of us back to Rashtrapati Bhavan, while the second took the two of us to the Ashoka Hotel, where the foreign delegates to the Buddha Jayanti celebrations had been accommodated. One of the President's ADCs was Yhonzone's cousin. This cousin had invited Yhonzone for lunch at his quarters, which were in Rashtrapati Bhavan. When the day came our Kurseong friend insisted that the rest of us should accompany him and that we should *all* have lunch with his cousin. As we had not been invited, Dhardo Rimpoche, Sonam Topgay, and I naturally demurred, but Yhonzone was so positive that there would be plenty for everybody, and that his cousin, with whom he was on the best of terms, would be very pleased to meet us, that in the end, rather against our better judgement, we allowed ourselves to be persuaded.

Plump, sleek, smiling Captain Tamang was indeed pleased to meet us, and an hour passed in light general conversation. But of lunch there was no sign. Half an hour more passed. Still there was no sign of lunch. Eventually, when the atmosphere had become rather strained, Yhonzone asked his cousin *sotto voce*, in Nepali, when he thought lunch would be ready. Captain Tamang replied, smoothly, that he had not expected so many people and that the chicken curry his cook had prepared would only be enough for two. 'Couldn't we divide it up and make it do?' asked Yhonzone in desperation. But Captain Tamang was afraid they couldn't. At this point, when Yhonzone was sweating with embarrassment, Sonam Topgay intervened, also speaking in Nepali. Obviously there had been a misunderstanding, he said, in his usual quiet, courteous tones. But there was no cause for concern. He would be happy to take the two venerable ones into the city and give them lunch at a restaurant. Leaving an apologetic Yhonzone and a sleek, still smiling Captain Tamang to enjoy their chicken curry (of which I, at least, would in any case have been unable to partake), we caught an auto-rickshaw to Connaught Circus and had a belated lunch at Gaylord's. Over the meal we chuckled, good-naturedly, at our well-meaning but naïve friend's *faux pas*, and I was reminded of the famous apologue of the Town Mouse and the Country Mouse. As Captain Tamang was doubtless explaining to Yhonzone at that very moment, the city was not the village, and the free and easy behaviour appropriate to backward, out-of-the-way Kurseong was out of place in sophisticated, cosmopolitan Delhi.

Not long afterwards it was Topgay and I who found ourselves in the position of Country Mouse, at least so far as political naïvety was concerned. We had gone to the Ashoka Hotel to meet Narada Thera, whom we found well pleased with himself for having taught the youthful Muslim bearer not to offer him a banana without first removing the skin (bhikkhus were not allowed to peel their own bananas), and not to offer it without repeating the traditional Pali formula. He had great hopes for the Dhamma in India, he told us. People were very receptive. After we had left Narada Thera it occurred to me that we ought not to leave the hotel without trying to meet at least some of the delegates from the Communist bloc countries. There was a Buriyat head lama from Soviet Russia, for instance. Having obtained his and his secretary's room numbers at the reception desk we made our way upstairs. The two rooms were adjacent to each other. Rather gingerly, we knocked on the right-hand door, which was the head lama's. After a second and a third knock it opened to reveal a burly layman who looked out at us with an unfriendly, even hostile, expression without saying anything. We had knocked on the wrong door. Or rather, we had knocked on the right door, but the right door was the wrong door, the secretary having installed himself in the room supposedly occupied by the head lama and vice versa. It was an old trick, and we had been taken in by it. None the less, Sonam Topgay asked the burly layman, first in Tibetan and then in English, if it would be possible for us to meet the lama, but he appeared to understand neither language, and after a few minutes shook his head and closed the door.

I had also hoped to meet the members of the Buddhist Association of China, but thinking I would probably have no more success with them than Sonam Topgay and I had had with the Buriyat head lama I abandoned the idea. In any case, the Association was little more than the willing or unwilling tool of Chairman Mao's regime, and its members' principal function, when travelling abroad, was to make, in the name of the Buddhists of China, statements supporting the regime's current position in international affairs. But if I did not meet any Chinese Buddhists I at least saw a good deal of ancient Chinese Buddhist art. The Government of India had sponsored an exhibition of Buddhist art as part of the Jayanti celebrations. Each of the participating countries had its own individual section, the contents of which had been selected and arranged by native experts. One thus was able to see that the Buddhist art of each country possessed a certain distinctive quality, which pervaded all its expressions and was found at all periods. Sikkimese and Bhutanese Buddhist art were usually subsumed under Tibetan Buddhist art, but seeing them in bulk, as it were (both sections took the form of a shrine), I was struck by the extent to which both differed not only from the art of Tibet but even from each other, Sikkimese art being more 'feminine', Bhutanese art more 'masculine'. But rich and varied though the exhibition was, many of the exhibits not having been seen outside their own country before, probably the biggest and most striking section was the one devoted to Chinese Buddhist art, and the most striking feature of that section, in my eyes, were the murals from Central Asia (or rather, from that part of Central Asia that was now part of the People's Republic of China). I had never seen anything like them, though they were not the originals but only full-scale copies and though they reproduced, apparently, the changes that had taken place over the centuries in the colour of the pigments that had been used. Unfortunately, picture postcards were not available, but images of the famous meeting between Manjughosha the Bodhisattva of Wisdom and the elder Vimalakirti, as described in the *Vimalakirti-nirdesha*, as well as of flying *apsarases* (or 'fairies') and angular Buddhas with extraordinary, multi-coloured haloes, lingered in my mind for many years afterwards.

It was a far cry from communist China, where Buddhism was in decline, to democratic India, where it was being revived and where, a month earlier, more than a quarter of a million people had been converted to Buddhism at a stroke. I had not been able to be present at the ceremony, as my invitation arrived late, when I had already made arrangements to visit Gangtok. Realizing the importance of the step Dr Ambedkar and his followers were about to take I had, however, sent a message to be read out on the occasion:

In these days when there is so much lip-sympathy for Buddhism and so little real devotion, it is a refreshing and stimulating contrast to find a great national leader boldly breaking away from outworn creeds and obsolete dogmas and openly taking refuge in the Buddha, the Dharma and the Sangha. Even if Dr Ambedkar stood alone to-day his conversion to Buddhism would be an event of epochal significance. But he does not stand alone. With him on this historic occasion are tens of thousands of his devoted followers, bent upon emulating his noble example. With him are Truth, Justice and Compassion. With him, as he stands with his face towards the glorious Sun of Buddhism as once more it rises upon this land, are all those mighty spiritual forces which elevate the human mind and conduce to true progress. With him is the future of India.

I had also written an editorial about the forthcoming conversions for the October number of the *Maha Bodhi Journal*. The editorial was entitled 'The Tide Turns', and in it I sought, *inter alia*, to remind readers of the background against which the conversions would be taking place.

Let none think that Dr B.R. Ambedkar has taken this momentous step hastily or without due consideration [I wrote], or that he had embarked upon this truly revolutionary course without full consciousness of its socio-religious implications and its far-reaching historical significance. It is perhaps five-and-twenty years since Dr Ambedkar first declared that though he had been born a Hindu he did not intend to die a Hindu. Twenty-five years is a big enough slice of anybody's life, and a period of time sufficiently long for the pondering even so momentous a step as the changing of one's religion. Brahminical clamours to the contrary notwithstanding, Dr Ambedkar knows what he is doing, and his followers know what they are doing, too.

Not theoretical considerations merely but their own bitter experience of all the unspeakable cruelty, the soul-searing injustice and systematic relentless inhumanity through the ages has eventually convinced them that Hinduism is incapable of reformation and that the only course now open to them is to break away from it and embrace Buddhism.

Within the Buddhist fold they will find not only social emancipation but, what is even more important, a way of life conducive to the attainment both of happiness here and hereafter and that unshakeable deliverance of mind which is the gist of the Buddha's teaching. They will also find the hand of brotherhood stretched out to them from every side, not only welcoming but assisting and supporting them as they make their first step along the Noble Eightfold Path.

My own hand was certainly stretched out to them, literally as well as metaphorically. Coming to know that Ambedkar was in Delhi, whither he had returned from Nagpur a few days after the conversion ceremony, I decided to go to see him and personally congratulate him on his great and historic achievement. Most of the Eminent Buddhists from the Border Areas were still in the city, waiting to receive the Dalai Lama and the Panchen Lama when they arrived at the end of the month, and I was able to persuade them to accompany me, even though many of them had not heard of Ambedkar before and did not know that he had been responsible for the conversion of hundreds of thousands of people to Buddhism.

Thus it was with representatives of several different Buddhist traditions that I descended, one fine morning in the second week of November, on Dr Ambedkar's modest residence in Alipore Road. As there was no room big enough for him to receive us all in, chairs were set out in the compound, and there, in a semi-circle, we sat facing our host in the hot sunshine. The Scheduled Castes leader – now a Buddhist leader – sat behind a small table, his wife at his side. I saw at once that he was far from well, and that the brown, pear-shaped face beneath the pith helmet looked tired and haggard. So tired and haggard did it look, and so full of suffering the dark eyes, that I apologized for disturbing him, saying that we had come simply to pay our respects and to congratulate him on his conversion to Buddhism. It had been my intention that we should stay no more than fifteen minutes, but in the event we stayed two hours. Ambedkar was unwilling to let us go. Or rather, he was unwilling to let me go, for it was solely to me that he addressed himself throughout the meeting, to the exclusion of Dhardo Rimpoche, Sonam Topgay, and the rest of the Eminent Buddhists. He was a deeply worried man. The movement of mass conversion had been successfully inaugurated, but what of the future? There was still so much to be done.... From the way he spoke, sitting there with arms resting on the table and lowered head, it was clear that the weight of his responsibilities had become almost too much for him to bear and that he wanted to transfer some of that weight to younger shoulders. Indeed, I had the distinct impression that the shoulders to which he wanted to transfer some of it were my own. Be that as it may, the meeting was undoubtedly tiring him. The broken sentences came from his lips with increasing difficulty, and at ever longer intervals. Eventually, when his head was already resting on his outstretched arms, his eyes closed in utter weariness. Whereupon, to his doctor wife's evident relief, we all quietly left.

If Dr Ambedkar was an old man who had started a new Buddhist movement, the Dalai Lama was a young man who represented an ancient Buddhist tradition. Whereas one was beholding the sun of Buddhism once more rise upon India, albeit amid clouds, the other would see that sun set upon Tibet for no one knew how long. Though it had been known for several months that the Government of India had invited the Dalai Lama to attend the official Buddha Jayanti celebrations in Delhi, only in October was it known that he would definitely be coming. Certain obstacles stood in the way, the Chinese authorities had declared, and it would not be possible for His Holiness to leave Tibet. But Pandit Nehru had intervened, the obstacles had been swept aside, and now it was certain that the Dalai Lama would be coming. He would be coming at the end of November, and the Panchen Lama would be coming too. The news was received with great satisfaction by the Indian public, and official and unofficial agencies alike prepared to give the two Grand Lamas a rousing welcome. They arrived in Gangtok on 24 November, and the following day the three planes carrying, respectively, the Dalai Lama, the Panchen Lama, and the Maharaja of Sikkim, touched down one after another at Palam airport, where tens of thousands of people had gathered to receive them. Each in turn was welcomed with the traditional white scarves, inspected a guard of honour, and was introduced to ministers of the Central Government and members of the Diplomatic Corps, some of whom also offered scarves. The Dalai Lama himself was welcomed by Dr Radhakrishnan and Pandit Nehru, and when the formalities were over, and the last diplomat had been introduced, he advanced towards the waiting bhikkhus. According to the newspapers, Delhi had never seen so many yellow-robed Buddhist monks as were then gathered on the tarmac (there were no red-robed lamas, apparently because the authorities feared they might take advantage of the opportunity to demonstrate against the Chinese occupation of Tibet). The monks came from all the South-east Asian Buddhist countries, as well as from India itself and from Nepal. There was even a yellow-robed figure from the United Kingdom. The only bhikkhu in Delhi who was *not* there was Narada Thera. The Dalai Lama was junior to him in monastic ordination, he had declared, and it would be highly improper for him to go to the airport to receive him. The Dalai Lama ought to come to *him*. None of the other bhikkhus seemed to be in the least bothered about who was junior in ordination and who senior, and as the Dalai Lama drew near everybody thronged joyfully round the youthful hierarch, catching him by the hands and reciting Pali verses invoking on him the blessings of the Buddha, the Dharma, and the Sangha. For several minutes he remained standing there in our midst, blinking in the strong sunlight and smiling, a maroon island in a sea of brilliant saffron.

A day or two later, thanks to Sonam Topgay, I was able to meet the Dalai Lama privately and to exchange a few words with him. We met at Hyderabad House, where he had been taken from the airport after giving *darshan* there and making a short speech. It was also at Hyderabad House, I think, that I met him in company with two or three other British Buddhists, one of whom was Christmas Humphreys, Founder-President of the Buddhist Society, London, who had recently returned from Kathmandu after attending the fourth conference of the World Fellowship of Buddhists. I had already been to see him in his room at the Ashoka Hotel, and had been struck by his extreme coldness. Ten or twelve years ago in London I had not noticed it, but here in India, where Buddhists and Hindus alike tended to be warm and friendly rather than otherwise, it was very noticeable indeed. Besides being a cold person, the Founder-President of the Buddhist Society was a Theosophist (not that the two things were necessarily connected), or was at least as much a Theosophist as he was a Buddhist. When it was his turn to be presented to the Dalai Lama he not only sank to his knees in stately fashion, rather as a camel does, but produced a copy of Mme Blavatsky's *The Voice of the Silence* and asked the Dalai Lama to sign it for him. What was the book, His Holiness naturally wanted to know. 'It is a Buddhist scripture', Humphreys replied. Whereupon the Dalai Lama signed. Years later, when I was again in London, I heard him tell members of the Buddhist Society that *The Voice of the Silence* was a genuine Buddhist sutra and that the Dalai Lama had personally authenticated it as such.

Chapter Twenty-Three

DEATH OF A HERO

AT THE TIME OF MY DEPARTURE FROM POONA the previous March Dr Mehta had urged me to see him again as soon as I could, and spend more time in his company, and this I had promised to do. Having attended the UNESCO Seminar on Buddhism in Delhi (which I did after paying a flying visit to Agra and Sarnath) I therefore decided not to return to Calcutta by the direct route but instead to make a detour and see the Servant of Servants in Bombay, where he was now staying. On 29 November I accordingly left the capital, and some forty hours later arrived at *VT*. Before going to Mayfair I spent a few hours with Dinoo Dubash, who recently had written to me expressing her disillusionment with Dr Mehta. In my reply I reminded her that she was a Buddhist, and that she had been attending meetings of the Society of Servants of God simply because she found it helpful to the leading of her own Buddhist life, particularly as regards meditation. The minute she found the association no longer helpful she was justified in breaking it off. Personally speaking, I added, I accepted Dr Mehta's 'guidance' only to the extent that it accorded with the Buddha's teaching, which meant that in *his* sense I did not accept it at all. Whatever was discordant I rejected, and before leaving Kalimpong I had written him a letter in which I made my position clear. In the course of my meeting with Dinoo, which took place in her flat, I was able to reinforce these points, as well as to emphasize that if her disillusionment with Dr Mehta was accompanied by any emotional disturbance it meant that there was a personal attachment from which she should try to free herself. My words were not without effect, and I left my voluble Parsee friend less upset by her disillusionment with the Servant of Servants and more confident that in ceasing to attend the Society's meetings she had done the right thing.

At Mayfair I was welcomed very warmly by Dr Mehta and Sundri, as well as by Durgadas Birla and some of the other friends I had made there and at the Nature Cure Clinic earlier in the year. Dr Mehta's welcome, I could not help noticing, despite its warmth was not unmixed with something of the satisfaction a good shepherd feels on seeing a wandering sheep return at last to the safety of the fold. But there was no question of my having returned to the fold, for even if I could be regarded as belonging to the ovine species (which I rather doubted) I belonged to a different flock, had my fold elsewhere, and hearkened to the voice – however distant – of quite another Master. Though the pasturage at Mayfair was indeed green, and though I could happily have grazed on it for a while (Dr Mehta wanted me to go on a meditation retreat there), I knew that it was essential for me to be on my way and that I could not spend more than a few days with my Bombay friends. *How* I knew this I was unable to say, any more than I was able to say *why* it was essential for me to be on my way. I did not hear an inner voice, neither did I have a sudden intuition. It was simply that I knew, clearly and certainly, that *I had to be on my way*, and accordingly fixed my departure for 5 December. Dr Mehta was not at all happy that I would be going so soon, and did his best to persuade me to postpone my departure until later in the month. Indeed it would be good if I postponed it indefinitely. Making plans was nothing but a form of ego-assertion, he solemnly assured me, and the more one allowed the ego to assert itself the more difficult it became for one to surrender to the Divine and accept its guidance. As if to reinforce his words, a few days later there came a Script. It came in the usual manner, when we were all seated in meditation and Dr Mehta had gone into a kind of trance state, and among its various directives there was one for me. The Buddhist monk Sangharakshita, the mysterious entity behind The Scripts declared, should postpone his journey to Calcutta and remain at Mayfair, in the company of 'My Servant Dinshah (i.e. Dr Mehta)', for at least a few weeks.

Believing as Dr Mehta and the members of the Society did that the entity behind The Scripts was God, they naturally also believed that the 'guidance' given in these communications, whether for themselves or anyone else, was to be followed unquestioningly. Dr Mehta therefore renewed his efforts to persuade me to postpone my departure, and to his urgings Sundri added hers. Now that God himself had spoken it was in their eyes no longer simply a matter of my refusing to accede to the wishes of my friends but rather, what was an infinitely more serious matter, of my resisting – even rejecting – the 'guidance' that had come for me from the Divine through the Divine's chosen instrument, the Servant of Servants. Emanating as it did from such an exalted source, the guidance was obviously in my best interest, and any reluctance on my part to accept it must be due, they broadly hinted, to that root of all evil, ego-assertion, which despite my having committed myself to the Buddhist way of life evidently was still able to prevent me from surrendering wholeheartedly to the Divine. I did not blame Dr Mehta and Sundri for putting this construction on my failure to accept the guidance that had come for me. Believing as they did, it was hardly possible for them to put any other construction on it. Far from blaming them, indeed, I recognized that their efforts to persuade me, not so much to postpone my departure, as to *accept God's guidance*, were motivated by a genuine concern for my spiritual welfare and were the expression, therefore, of true, if misguided, friendship. Had I not known, with such clarity and certainty, that it was essential for me to be on my way, I would probably have stayed a little longer in Bombay, simply in order to please them. As it was, the fact that they were now pressing me to postpone my departure because I had been 'divinely guided' to do that meant that I had to confront the issue squarely and explain, as I had already explained in the letter I had written Dr Mehta from Kalimpong, that I did not accept the latter's 'guidance' unconditionally. In fact, I added, I was of the opinion that it was positively wrong to do so. Having made my position clear I felt much better, though I was not sure how Dr Mehta would take my plain speaking. In the event he took it quite well, probably because he was not unaccustomed to people 'resisting the guidance' (was not his own wife still resisting it?), and was prepared to be patient and wait for them to come round to his way of thinking. At any rate, he and Sundri stopped trying to persuade me to postpone my departure, and for the remainder of my stay at Mayfair I joined them in their thrice-daily meditation sessions, and talked with Dr Mehta, without reference being made to my unwillingness to accept divine guidance. I also arranged for one of the Society's evening meetings to be addressed by another Buddhist speaker.

The speaker in question was Christmas Humphreys. Having attended the Fourth Conference of the World Fellowship of Buddhists in Kathmandu, the Founder-President of the London Buddhist Society was now on his way back to the United Kingdom and making a brief stopover in Bombay. Besides being curious to know what the Society's members would think of Zen Buddhism (Humphreys's chosen topic, on which he had written several books), I had a Boswellian desire to see what two such dissimilar characters as the English criminal lawyer-cum-Buddhist and the Parsee naturopath-cum-guru would make of each other and how they would get on together. The audience at Humphreys's talk consisted of much the same kind of people as those who had attended my own talks a year earlier. Few of them had even heard of Zen before and though the tradition was, supposedly, of Indian origin, its 'style' was so foreign to them as to be virtually incomprehensible. As his custom apparently was, Humphreys emphasized the irrational, anti-intellectual, iconoclastic side of Zen (probably a useful emphasis in concept-ridden, tradition-bound India), illustrating his points with some of the more outrageous Zen anecdotes. He was a fluent and forcible speaker, at times even a fiery one, but the fire was the cold fire of the intellect, not the warm fire of the heart, and I could see that although the audience was impressed by his dramatic, not to say histrionic, manner of delivery, they were not moved. As for Dr Mehta, he sat through the talk motionless, eyes upturned so that only the whites were visible, and from the rambling, inconsequential nature of his summing up afterwards, in the course of which he spoke about '(sexual) union at the highest level', it was clear that there had been no meeting of minds between him and Humphreys and that he had perhaps not even been listening to what the latter said. The truth was that the two men could hardly have been more different. Despite his (reluctant) assumption of the prophet's mantle, Dr Mehta was very human, whereas there was something inhuman about Humphreys. If the former was easy to like (as Dinoo was later to observe, he had 'a way of melting one'), then to like the latter would, I imagined, be a rather difficult task. However that may have been, on my departure from Mayfair Dr Mehta's softer side was very much in evidence, and he bade me an almost tearful farewell; at the same time, he was full of dark forebodings about my failure to 'follow guidance' and predicted that all my plans would come to nothing.

Though sorry to part from my God-guided friend, I did not allow his forebodings to disturb me, and my predominant feeling as I caught the overnight train to Nagpur was one of satisfaction, even relief, that at last I was acting on the knowledge that it was essential for me to be on my way. Why it was essential for me to be on my way I did not know. Dr Mehta had predicted that all my plans would come to nothing; but it was not because I had plans that needed to be carried out immediately that it was essential for me to be on my way. I was on my way simply because it was essential I should be on my way. True, I was on my way to Calcutta, where I would be editing the next issue of the *Maha Bodhi Journal*, and I would be breaking my journey in Nagpur in order to make the acquaintance of the newly converted Buddhists, who had invited me to spend a few days with them and deliver some lectures. But it was not because I had to do these things immediately that it was essential for me to be on my way. I could just as easily have edited the next issue of the *Maha Bodhi Journal* in Bombay, and just as easily have given my Nagpur lectures two or three weeks later. I was on my way because it was, I knew, essential for me to be on my way, though why it was essential I did not yet know. Before leaving Bombay I wired the date and time of my arrival in Nagpur to A.R. Kulkarni, the elderly brahmin advocate, and secretary of the Buddha Society, with whom I had stayed on my previous visit and who had arranged for me to speak at the University and elsewhere.

On the occasion of that visit, more than two years earlier, my arrival in Nagpur had attracted little attention. Only Kulkarni was waiting on the platform to receive me, and he had taken me to his – or rather his brother's – house in Dharampeth by taxi with a minimum of fuss. This time it was very different. As the train came to a halt I saw that the platform was a solid mass of excited, white-clad figures. There must have been 2,000 of them and I realized, with a shock of astonishment, that they were all new Buddhists and that they had come to receive me. Kulkarni was also there, and on my emerging from the carriage he and the office-bearers of the Indian Buddhist Society (which Ambedkar had founded a year or two earlier, and which had been responsible for the organizing of the mass conversion ceremony) pushed their way through the crowd towards me. I was profusely garlanded, and then to repeated shouts of 'Victory to Baba Saheb Ambedkar!' and 'Victory to Bhikshu Sangharakshita!' was led to the waiting car and escorted to Dharampeth and the Kulkarni residence. Since my previous visit Krishna, Kulkarni's elder nephew, had married, and as he and his wife now occupied the room where I had stayed I was accommodated in the wooden outhouse that Kulkarni had built for himself at the end of the back yard. Here I was left to undo my bedding roll and spend the rest of the afternoon recovering from my journey.

But this was not to be. I had arrived in Nagpur at one o'clock. Less than an hour later, when I was still settling into my new quarters, there was a sudden commotion in the yard outside and a few seconds later three or four members of the Indian Buddhist Society burst into the little outhouse. 'Baba Saheb' was dead. He had died in Delhi the previous night. The bearers of these dire tidings were not only in a state of deep shock but utterly demoralized. They were barely able to tell me that the Society's downtown office was being besieged by thousands of grief-stricken people who, knowing of my presence in Nagpur, were demanding that I should come and speak to them. Obviously it would be impossible for me to address so many people without a microphone and loudspeakers. I therefore told my visitors to organize a proper condolence meeting. They should organize it for seven o'clock that evening. I would address the meeting and console people for the loss of their great leader as best I could. There being no time to lose, my visitors departed without further ado, taking with them others who had arrived after them, and I was left to consider my own reactions to the news of Ambedkar's death. Though shocked, I was not surprised. At the time of our last meeting he was evidently a very sick man, and I had been astonished to learn, before my departure from Delhi, that he had flown to Kathmandu in order to attend the Fourth Conference of the World Fellowship of Buddhists. There, as I afterwards heard, he was given a standing ovation by the assembled delegates and addressed them, by popular demand, on 'Buddha and Karl Marx'. Returning to Delhi on 1 December, he visited the exhibition of Buddhist art, attended a meeting in honour of the Dalai Lama, and passed some time in the Rajya Sabha or Council of States, of which he was a member. The evening of 5 December was spent receiving a deputation of Jain leaders, listening to a record of his favourite Buddhist devotional song and, apparently, working on the preface to his book *The Buddha and His Dhamma*. At 6.30 the following morning, when I was on my way to Nagpur, his wife had entered his bedroom to find him dead.

The condolence meeting was held in the Kasturchand Park, which was little more than a large open space part of which was occupied by a small pavilion. Roads apparently debouched into it from a number of directions, for on my arrival there at seven o'clock, by which time night had fallen, it was the dark centre of a gigantic wheel the golden spokes of which were formed by the lighted candles carried by the long columns of mourners who were converging on the place from all over the city. As the columns entered the park I saw that the men, women, and children carrying the candles were all clad in white – the same white that only seven weeks ago they had worn for the conversion ceremony. Whether on account of their demoralized state, or because there was not enough time, the organizers of the meeting had done little more than rig up a microphone and loudspeakers. There was no stage and, apart from a petromax or two, no illumination other than that provided by the thousands of candles. By the time I rose to speak – standing on the seat of a rickshaw and with someone holding the microphone up in front of me – about 100,000 people had assembled. Under normal circumstances I would have been the last speaker, but on this occasion I was the first. In fact as things turned out I was the only speaker. Though some five or six of Ambedkar's most prominent local supporters one by one attempted to pay tribute to their departed leader, they were so overcome by emotion that, after uttering only a few words, they burst into tears and had to sit down. Their example was contagious. When I started to speak the whole vast gathering was weeping, and sobs and groans filled the air. In the cold blue light of the petromax I could see grey-haired men rolling in agonies of grief at my feet.

Though deeply moved by the sight of so much anguish and despair, I realized that for me, at least, this was no time to indulge in emotion. Ambedkar's followers had received a terrible shock. They had been Buddhists for only seven weeks, and now their leader, in whom their trust was total, and on whose guidance in the difficult days ahead they had been relying, had been snatched away. Poor and illiterate as the vast majority of them were, and faced by the unrelenting hostility of the Caste Hindus, they did not know which way to turn and there was a possibility that the whole movement of conversion to Buddhism would come to a halt or even collapse. I therefore delivered a vigorous and stirring speech in which, after extolling the greatness of Ambedkar's achievement, I exhorted my audience to continue the work he had so gloriously begun and bring it to a successful conclusion. 'Baba Saheb' was not dead but alive. To the extent that they were faithful to the ideals for which he stood and for which he had, quite literally, sacrificed himself, he lived on in them. This speech, which lasted for an hour or more, was not without effect. Ambedkar's stricken followers began to realize that it was not the end of the world, that there was a future for them even after their beloved Baba Saheb's death, and that the future was not altogether devoid of hope.

While I was speaking I had an extraordinary experience. Above the crowd there hung an enormous Presence. Whether the Presence was Ambedkar's departed consciousness hovering over the heads of his followers, or whether it was the collective product of their thoughts at that time of trial and crisis, I do not know, but it was as real to me as the people I was addressing.

In the course of the next four days I visited practically all the ex-Untouchable 'localities' of Nagpur, of which there must have been several dozen, and addressed nearly thirty mass meetings, besides initiating about 30,000 people into Buddhism and delivering lectures at Nagpur University and the Ramakrishna Mission. My locality speeches were rendered simultaneously into Marathi by Kulkarni, who despite being nearly twice my age not only kept pace with me but did full justice to the energy and passion with which I spoke. As he had done on the occasion of my previous visit, he maintained a detailed record of my engagements which he afterwards wrote up in article form. When the time came for me to be again on my way I had addressed altogether 200,000 people and forged, incidentally, a very special link with the Buddhists of Nagpur, indeed with all Ambedkar's followers. As I wrote to Dinoo from Calcutta a few weeks later:

> ... I think I can say without vanity that I created a tremendous impression. Dr Ambedkar's followers told me that they felt my being there at that critical juncture was a miracle and that I had saved Nagpur for Buddhism. Had I not been there, there is no knowing what would have happened. At first people felt that the end of the world had come. But after listening to my speeches – which were very strong indeed – they felt full of hope and courage and determined to work for the spread of Buddhism. On the last day of my visit I gave no less than eleven lectures. The last meeting was held at 1.30 in the morning, when fifteen thousand people were converted to Buddhism.

Nor was that all. The events of the last four or five days had had their effect on me as well as on my auditors. My letter to Dinoo continued:

> My own spiritual experience during this period was most peculiar. I felt that I was not a person but an impersonal force. At one stage I was working quite literally without any thought, just as one is in *samadhi*. Also, I felt hardly any tiredness – certainly not at all what one would have expected from such a tremendous strain. When I left Nagpur I felt quite fresh and rested. Now let us see about the rest of the programme.

By the rest of the programme I presumably meant the work that had been awaiting me at the Maha Bodhi Society's headquarters, where I spent six or seven weeks seeing the December 1956 and January 1957 issues of the *Maha Bodhi Journal* through the press, as well as bringing out my dialogue 'Is Buddhism for Monks Only?' and essay 'Buddhism and Art' in booklet form with funds provided by Dinoo. A considerable portion of the Notes and News section of both the December and January issues of the Journal was taken up by reports of the arrival in India of the Dalai and Panchen Lamas, their participation in the Buddha Jayanti celebrations in Delhi, and their subsequent pilgrimage to the principal Buddhist holy places. Newspaper coverage of the activities of the two hierarchs was extensive. People were fascinated by the exotic visitors from beyond the Himalayas. The fascination was due partly to the Lamas' extreme youth (both were in their early twenties), partly to their being celibate monks, and partly – perhaps above all – to the fact that after being surrounded for centuries with an aura of remoteness, inaccessibility, and mystery, the Dalai and Panchen Lamas of Tibet were now treading the soil of India and could be seen and heard and even photographed. Despite the Chinese Government's efforts to ensure equal treatment for the two visitors (efforts which so far as official protocol was concerned were entirely successful), the Dalai Lama inevitably attracted more attention than the Panchen. The press regularly – and incorrectly – referred to him as the God King of Tibet ('God King Worships Relics' was a typical headline). Commentators also observed that the Dalai and Panchen Lamas were markedly different in temperament, the former being jovial and outward-going, the latter thoughtful and reserved. During their stay in Delhi Pandit Nehru had given them a choice of films. The Dalai Lama, characteristically, had asked to see a Marx Brothers film, while the Panchen Lama, no less characteristically, wanted to see *War and Peace*.

By the time the Lamas came to Calcutta, which was when they had been in India for about two months, a note of criticism had started to creep into the newspaper coverage, which hitherto had been uniformly favourable, even adulatory. Many people were shocked to learn that two such great religious personalities as the Dalai and Panchen Lamas were not vegetarians, as were the vast majority of Hindus, all Jains, and some Sikhs. But as I well knew, vegetarianism formed no part of Tibetan Buddhism, though the Tibetans did not maintain, as some Burmese did, that one could not be a (Theravadin) Buddhist *and* a vegetarian. There also were complaints that the two Lamas lived in a lavish style more appropriate to secular princes than to religious leaders and exemplars – a contradiction perhaps inherent in the very nature of their position in theocratic Tibet. An instance of this lavishness which excited particular comment occurred while they were in Calcutta. They were staying at the Grand Hotel, the best hotel in the city. One day they both decided they needed haircuts. A barber was accordingly sent for, and with the aid of a pair of clippers soon reduced their redundant locks to the regulation monastic length. For this service they each tipped him two thousand rupees. The size of the tip excited comment because if the Lamas gave two thousand rupees each for a haircut (in Kalimpong I gave one rupee, which was the top rate), then the rest of their expenditure was, presumably, on a correspondingly grand scale, which meant that each of them would be spending lakhs of rupees every month. What the two Lamas and their advisers seemed not to realize was that in India, unlike in Tibet, spirituality tended to be associated, in most people's minds, with poverty rather than riches, simplicity rather than ostentation.

It was in his suite at the Grand Hotel, after he had received his haircut, that I had my second private meeting with the Dalai Lama. Having learned that he (though not the Panchen Lama) would be spending a week or so in Kalimpong before returning to Tibet I wanted to invite him to Everton Villa for a reception in his honour by our branch of the Maha Bodhi Society. Probably as much on account of the name of the Maha Bodhi Society, with which he was by this time well acquainted, as for any other reason, he accepted without demur. The reception was to be held on 27 January, four or five days after his arrival in Kalimpong. As this was not far off, I left Calcutta as soon as I conveniently could, which happened to be the very day the Dalai Lama himself left. Before my departure I had written the editorial for the January issue of the *Maha Bodhi*. It was headed simply 'Dr Ambedkar'. After giving a résumé of his eventful career, I wrote:

> A lifelong student of religions, Dr Ambedkar had step by step come to the conclusion that [Hindu] orthodoxy was incapable of reformation, and that the victims of age-old socio-religious oppression and exploitation in India could be freed from their disabilities only by embracing Buddhism. Towards this consummation he gradually bent more and more of his energies. Some, even among his own people, opposed him, feeling perhaps that no mere 'religion' could solve a problem of such tremendous complexity. But Dr Ambedkar's faith in Buddhism stood firm as a rock. With characteristic boldness, he declared that he was going to become a Buddhist even if nobody else became one. But when the time for taking the momentous step came far from taking it alone he carried hundreds of thousands with him. All over India, wherever the name of Dr Ambedkar was honoured, people gathered in their thousands and in their tens of thousands to take refuge in the Buddha, the Dharma, and the Sangha.
>
> Before the movement of mass conversion could reach its height Dr Ambedkar, worn out by the labours of a lifetime, died. Some

there were who thought that with his death the movement would come to an end, or at least receive a serious setback. Never were prophets more false. The ashes of his funeral pyre were hardly cold before the movement gathered a momentum beyond the expectations of the most wildly optimistic. Nay, even as all that was mortal of him was consigned to the flames the sacred chant 'Buddham Saranam Gacchami' rose spontaneously from the lips of tens of thousands of mourners there. Since then reports have come in of mass conversion ceremonies at Nagpur, Poona, Ahmedabad, Agra, and a score of other important centres. Great as Dr Ambedkar's influence was during his life, evidently it is greater still in death.

Chapter Twenty-Four

'WHERE THE THREE YANAS FLOURISH'

ONE OF THE FIRST THINGS I DID after my return to Kalimpong was to buy a special cup and saucer for the Dalai Lama. It was the Tibetan custom to offer a guest three cups of tea, and when the guest was an important incarnate lama the Chinese-style cup would be of porcelain or jade and its stand and lid of gold and silver studded with semi-precious stones. The Kalimpong branch of the Maha Bodhi Society possessed no such cup, neither did it have the means of purchasing one, but at least we should serve the Dalai Lama tea in a brand-new cup and saucer, I thought, and that cup and saucer should be the finest the Himalayan Stores was able to supply. We also erected a throne of the traditional type, consisting of five (or was it seven?) square Tibetan-style mattresses piled one on top of the other, covered with a rug, and backed by a brocade cushion the upper edge of which was draped with a white ceremonial scarf. This throne was set up in the shrine-room of Everton Villa, the walls of which were hung with silk for the occasion. There was also an archway of greenery and bunting at the entrance to the building.

The Dalai Lama arrived on the morning of the appointed day, which happened to be a Sunday, accompanied by the current Sub-Divisional Officer and by members of his entourage. On his arrival I, Khemasiri, Dr Singh, and Dawa offered him ceremonial scarves on behalf of the Reception Committee and conducted him down the flight of steps leading from the road to our centre. At the bottom of the steps I had stationed monk-musicians from the Tharpa Chholing Gompa, and it was to the sonorous rumblings of their giant trumpets that the Dalai Lama passed between the rows of assembled members and friends who, with lighted incense-sticks in their hands, lined the path between the steps and the entrance to Everton Villa. On entering the shrine-room he prostrated himself three times before the image of the Buddha (the standing one Lama Govinda had given me), performing each prostration in the elaborate Tibetan manner. Having rearranged his voluminous upper robe, he then remained standing for about ten minutes as he chanted Tibetan verses in praise of the Enlightened One. He chanted in a deep, resonant voice, smilingly scattering grains of rice as he did so. When he had finished he took his seat on the improvised throne and Dawa poured him his first cup of tea. As I afterwards discovered, in Tibet it was considered a great honour to be allowed to pour tea for the Dalai or Panchen Lama, and those who had enjoyed that privilege were permitted to wear their cap turned up at the side in a particular manner. How aware of all this our young secretary was I do not know, but he certainly filled the Dalai Lama's cup slowly and mindfully, with the lowered eyes and deferential inclination of the body that were second nature to a Tibetan in such circumstances.

Our guest having taken a few sips of tea, as etiquette prescribed, I read out the address of welcome I had prepared. To this the Dalai Lama replied in Tibetan, an English version of his speech being supplied by Sonam Topgay, whose services the Government of India had, it seemed, placed at the Tibetan hierarch's disposal. In the course of his reply the Dalai Lama expressed his satisfaction at finding a 'young branch' of the Maha Bodhi Society at Kalimpong and exhorted its members to follow the teachings of the Lord Buddha. I then presented him, on behalf of the branch, with an ancient palm-leaf manuscript of a Pali Abhidhamma work and a complete set of our publications in English and Nepali, including a two-volume bound set of the twenty issues of *Stepping-Stones*. The Dalai Lama spent the remainder of his visit, which lasted for about an hour, bestowing individual blessings on all those present, who filed past him for that purpose, offering white scarves and flowers as they did so. I noticed that he blessed everybody with the 'double-handed blessing', that is, by placing both hands firmly on each individual head, at the same time smiling broadly. In Tibet itself, apparently, he would simply have touched them lightly with a bunch of coloured ribbons fastened to the end of a stick. Among the recipients of the double-handed blessing were a number of local Tibetans who, having got wind of the fact that the Dalai Lama was visiting our centre, had taken advantage of the opportunity to have the *darshan* of their revered leader. After his departure they drank up what remained of his third cup of tea (actually, the third topping up), sharing the precious drops among themselves with the kind of devotion with which, I imagined, pious Catholics took holy communion. Before leaving they thanked me warmly for making it possible for them to have such close contact with His Holiness. They could not have had it otherwise, they averred, as the members of Kalimpong's Tibetan community were finding it difficult to get so much as a glimpse of him.

On my arrival the following morning at Bhutan House, where the Dalai Lama was staying, I saw that this was indeed the case. There was a police guard on the gates, and Tibetans who had come for the Dalai Lama's *darshan* were being refused admission. This was because the Chinese Government wanted that there should be as little contact as possible between the Dalai Lama and the Tibetan population of Kalimpong, who were known to be strongly in favour of independence for Tibet and opposed to the continued occupation of their country by the Red Army. I and the rest of the little party from the Maha Bodhi Society's branch had no difficulty gaining admission, as the Dalai Lama had asked us to call that morning. We found him seated in the Dorji family's richly appointed chapel, where he was apparently putting up, and where, four years earlier, Anand-ji and I had recited *suttas* over the dead body of Raja S.T. Dorji and I had delivered the funeral sermon. The Dalai Lama received us with his usual cordiality, and after a few minutes' conversation presented me with a Buddha-image, block prints of two Tibetan scriptures (the *Prajnaparamita* or *Perfection of Wisdom 'in 8,000 lines'* and the smaller *Lamrim* or *Stages of the Path* by Tsongkhapa), and a signed and sealed photograph of himself, plus a cash donation. We were then smilingly dismissed.

While there were people in Kalimpong who wanted to see the Dalai Lama but could not, there were others who, although they had no wish to see him, were nevertheless obliged to do so. The Government of India was eager that the Dalai Lama should visit a modern educational institution, just as it had been anxious that the Eminent Buddhists from the Border Areas should see dams as well as holy places. In Kalimpong what better institution was there for him to visit than the famous Dr Graham's Home, where five hundred orphans of mixed descent were housed, clothed, fed, and educated, and which was in many respects a model of its kind? The Homes authorities were therefore informed, through the Sub-Divisional Officer, that the Dalai Lama would be visiting the place and that he was to be shown round. To the Scottish Presbyterians who ran the Homes this was far from being welcome news; many of the teachers and house-parents were convinced that Tibetan Buddhists were devil-worshippers and practised black magic. Now they were being required to welcome the chief devil-worshipper himself on to their premises. But there was no help for it. Christian missionaries were being attacked in the press, restrictions had already been placed on some of their activities, and the Homes authorities dared not risk incurring the Central Government's displeasure by refusing to receive the Dalai Lama who was, after all, a State guest. If only something would happen to prevent his coming to the Homes! Perhaps God would prevent it if they prayed hard enough. The more bigoted teachers and-house parents therefore held an all-night prayer meeting before the Dalai Lama was due to arrive, but their united prayers no more availed to keep him away from the Homes than the Tantric 'rites of destruction' ordered by the Lhasa Government in 1950 had availed to halt the steady advance of the Red Army into Tibetan territory. The chief devil-worshipper came the next day as planned, breakfasted with Mr Duncan, the whey-faced Superintendent of the Homes and his family, saw the school, met the children, and by all accounts thoroughly enjoyed his visit.

The Dalai Lama was not the only important Tibetan religious leader I saw in the New Year, nor the one with whom I had the most contact. Happening to meet Sonam Topgay in the bazaar one day, a few weeks after the Dalai Lama's return to Tibet, I learned that there was a celebrated Nyingma lama staying at Tirpai and that my Sikkimese friend had come from Gangtok in order to see him and pay his respects. The lama's name was Sangye Dorje (Buddhavajra in Sanskrit), but he was commonly known as Chattrul Sangye Dorje. 'Chattrul' meant something like 'without affairs' or 'without concerns' and the sobriquet had been bestowed on him on account of his complete indifference to such things as organized monasticism and ecclesiastical position. It was not even clear whether he was a monk or a layman. He roamed freely from place to place, no one knowing where he was going to turn up next or how long he would stay. He was an accomplished yogi, having spent many years in the solitudes of eastern Tibet, meditating; and if popular report was to be believed, he possessed many psychic powers and was a great magician. Despite his indifference to organized monasticism and ecclesiastical position, Sonam Topgay added, and his frequently bizarre and eccentric behaviour, Chattrul Sangye Dorje was highly esteemed by several prominent members of the Gelug hierarchy. Once, when in Lhasa, he had bestowed a number of esoteric Tantric initiations on the Regent of Tibet (whether this was Reting Rimpoche or his successor my friend did not say). At the conclusion of the ceremonies, which lasted several days, the Regent made the customary offerings which, his position being what it was, were extremely valuable. Chattrul Sangye Dorje swept them all on to a cloth, tied the cloth up into a bundle, and handed the bundle to the

Regent, saying, 'Look after it for me'. Whereupon he resumed his wan-
derings.

Sonam Topgay's account intrigued me. In fact I was fascinated by his
picture of the unconventional lama whom, it was evident, he very much
admired. (Later I discovered that Chattrul Sangye Dorje, though not an
incarnate lama, was widely revered as one of the three great Nyingma
gurus of the century.) Seeing my interest, Sonam Topgay observed that it
would not be difficult for me to meet the lama, who notoriously did not
stand on ceremony and who was very accessible – once you had succeeded in tracking him down. He moreover hinted that although Chattrul Sangye Dorje was highly unpredictable, and one could never be sure
how he would respond to a particular request, he *might* be willing to give
me Tantric initiation. In any case, I ought not to miss the opportunity of
meeting so great a lama and obtaining his blessing.

The result was that a day or two later, on Friday 8 March, I left Everton
Villa soon after breakfast and made my way through the bazaar and up
to Tirpai. With me was the French nun, who had stopped by early that
morning and who, on learning I was going to see Chattrul Sangye Dorje,
had asked if she might accompany me. Though I would really have
preferred to go without her, I raised no objection, as she was again
experiencing 'difficulties' in connection with her Tibetan studies and I
thought the lama might be able to help her, especially as she was by this
time beginning to be no less disappointed with Kachu Rimpoche than
she had been with Dhardo Rimpoche. What I had expected the famous
Nyingma lama to look like I cannot say, but on meeting him I received a
shock. He was of indeterminate age, perhaps somewhere between thirty
and forty, his coarse black hair was cut short, like a monk's, and he was
clad in a nondescript maroon garment lined with what appeared to be
grubby sheepskin. What I was most struck by however was his face,
which was coarse and unrefined almost to the point of brutality, and
could easily have passed for that of a horny-handed peasant with no
thought beyond his pigs and poultry. At the same time, his whole being
communicated such an impression of strength and reliability that one
could not but feel reassured, and it was not long before the two of us were
deep in conversation. As was proper, Chattrul Rimpoche (as my Sikkimese friend respectfully called him) took the lead, and asked me a number
of questions, first about the Vinaya or Monastic Code and then about the
Abhidharma. This seemed to be the standard procedure in Tibetan
religious circles. At my first meeting with the abbot of the Tharpa
Chholing Gompa, I recalled, the old man had questioned me closely

about the Vinaya before moving on to more abstruse topics. Apparently the idea was that one should make sure one was operating within the same universe of discourse as the other person, and that the two of you had a common medium of communication (a medium that was not merely linguistic) and only *then* proceed to engage in serious discussion. On the present occasion I must have answered Chattrul Rimpoche's questions to his satisfaction, for from the Abhidharma we progressed – through what intermediate steps I no longer recollect – to meditation and meditational experiences, and eventually I found myself telling him about Dr Mehta's 'guidance' and asking him to what extent he thought this could be accepted. Perhaps not surprisingly, as we were both Buddhists, his reply was in agreement with my own conclusions. Teachings and directives received in a state of trance, whether by oneself or by another person, were not to be accepted uncritically but were to be subjected to the test of reason and experience and compared with the Buddhavachana, or Word of the Buddha, as explained by the enlightened masters of India and Tibet.

By this time I had developed considerable confidence in the Rimpoche, and I therefore asked him to tell me who my *yidam* or tutelary deity was. Though unable to accept Dr Mehta's 'guidance' on his (or its) own terms, I had taken very much to heart his insistence that in the spiritual life the best and most reliable guidance was that which came from beyond one's ego. For me it could not come from God, but perhaps it could come from one or other of those transcendental beings who according to the Buddhism of Tibet (as of that of China and Japan) were the different, infinitely various, aspects of the Buddha's *sambhogakaya* or 'body of glory' – the supra-historical 'body' in which he communed with advanced bodhisattvas and they with him. Chattrul Rimpoche showed no surprise at my request. In fact he seemed rather pleased, and after a moment of inner recollection told me that my yidam was Dolma Jungo or Green Tara, the 'female' bodhisattva of fearlessness and spontaneous helpfulness, adding that Tara had been the tutelary deity of many of the great pandits of India and Tibet. In other words, I had an *affinity* with Green Tara, in the sense that she was the transcendental counterpart of my own mundane nature and that I could, therefore, more readily come to a deeper understanding of myself through devotion to her. Having told me my yidam, the Rimpoche proceeded to bestow the appropriate initiation. First he gave me the ten-syllabled mantra, which he pronounced very forcibly in the Tibetan manner, after which he explained the sadhana or spiritual practice that would enable me to visualize Green Tara and call down her blessings on myself and all sentient beings. The latter he did at some length, so that it was mid-afternoon when I finally bade him a grateful farewell, having spent more than four hours in his company. My mood was one of considerable elation. Before leaving Tirpai I called on the aged Tibetan artist who lived there and commissioned from him a thangka or scroll painting, which I would be needing as an aid to visualization. The French nun, for her part, was more cheerful than she had been for a long time, Chattrul Rimpoche having spoken to her about her Tibetan studies and persuaded her to give up the fast on which she had embarked in order to force someone to do something about the difficulties she was experiencing in connection with them.

A few days later the Rimpoche came to see me at Everton Villa. Though he probably arrived unannounced, he must have been accompanied by Sonam Topgay, for he explained the Green Tara sadhana to me again and gave me further instructions about its practice. I had already committed his previous explanations to writing and therefore was able to check what I had written with him and make sure I had got the details of the sadhana absolutely right. As soon as the thangka I had commissioned was ready I would start practising. A new phase in my spiritual life was about to begin. Hitherto I had been a Theravadin monk practising meditation with the help of the Theravadin tradition of *anapana-sati* or respiration-mindfulness. From now on, while remaining a Theravadin monk, I would be practising meditation with the help of the Mahayana-cum-Vajrayana tradition of mantra-recitation and deity-visualization. This did not mean that previously I had not valued the Mahayana and Vajrayana, any more than it meant that in future I could afford to dispense with the practice of respiration-mindfulness. I had always valued the Mahayana and Vajrayana very highly. Mahayana scriptures like the *Diamond Sutra* and the *Lankavatara Sutra* and Vajrayana works such as *The Life of Milarepa* and *The Golden Rosary of the Precepts of the Gurus* had been important sources of inspiration from very early on in my Buddhist career. It was after reading the *Diamond Sutra* at the age of sixteen that I realized I was a Buddhist and in fact always had been one. But though the Mahayana and the Vajrayana meant so much to me, and though I had derived abundant inspiration from their respective canonical literatures, I had not practised any of the distinctively Mahayana or Vajrayana methods of meditation. Now I was taking up the Green Tara sadhana, and the fact that I was so doing marked an important transition in my spiritual life.

Changes of a more external nature were also imminent. In the course of his visit Chattrul Rimpoche elicited from me the information that

Everton Villa was only a rented property, that our lease would expire in September, that it would be difficult for us to find an equally suitable property that was to let, and that although my real aim was to establish a permanent monastic centre in Kalimpong there seemed at present little likelihood of my being able to do so. The centre, I explained, would be dedicated to the study, practice, and dissemination of the total Buddhist tradition, for I had long been convinced that, in the noble words of Dr Edward Conze, 'the doctrine of the Buddha, conceived in its full breadth, width, majesty and grandeur, comprises all those teachings which are linked to the original teaching by historical continuity, and which work out methods leading to the extinction of [ego-]individuality by eliminating the belief in it.' The Rimpoche's response to this information was as categorical as it was unexpected. There was no doubt that I would establish a permanent monastic centre in Kalimpong, he assured me. In fact I would establish it quite soon, and I should call it 'The Vihara Where the Three Yanas Flourish (or Blossom)'. Having given the as yet non-existent monastery its name in what I afterwards described as a mood of high spiritual inspiration, Chattrul Rimpoche addressed to me the Tibetan original of the following stanzas:

> In the sky devoid of limits, the teaching of the Muni is
> The sun, spreading the thousand rays of the three *sikshas*
>   [i.e. morality, meditation, and wisdom];
> Continually shining in the radiance of the impartial disciples,
> May this Jambudvipa region of the Triyana be fair!

> In accordance with his request, [made] in the Fire-Monkey Year
> On the ninth day of the first month by the Maha Sthavira
>   Sangharakshita,
> This was written by the Shakya-upasaka, the Vidyadhara
> Bodhivajra: [may there be] happiness and blessings!

Notwithstanding what was said in the first line of the second stanza, the stanzas were not in response to any request of mine. The Rimpoche produced them quite spontaneously. That he should cast them in the form of a response to a request was probably no more than literary convention, even as his styling me Maha Sthavira or 'Great Elder' when I was only a simple bhikshu was just the normal Tibetan politeness.

The fact that Chattrul Rimpoche had named my future monastery *of his own accord* greatly impressed my Tibetan friends, especially those of the Nyingma persuasion. According to Kachu Rimpoche, who came to see me shortly afterwards, it was exceptionally auspicious, as whatever

Rimpoche Chattrul Sangye Dorje named was sure to prosper. I was pleased to hear this, but before the Triyana Vardhana Vihara – as I had decided the place should be called in Sanskrit – could prosper it had to come into existence, and as yet there was no sign of this happening. It was not that I doubted the reliability of the Rimpoche's prediction, but 'quite soon' was a relative term and could as well mean next year as this year, or even the year after next.

In the event, my dream of a permanent monastic centre was transformed into a reality much sooner than I had dared hope. The turning point in its fortunes came less than six weeks after Chattrul Rimpoche's visit, when I was in Calcutta, having flown to the City of Dreadful Heat (as it now was) from Cooch Behar after a short lecture tour in the Doors, an important tea-growing area near the Bhutan-Assam border where there were many thousands of Nepalese Buddhists. In Calcutta I saw the Vaishakha number of the *Maha Bodhi Journal* through the press, gave weekly lectures in the hall of the Sri Dharmarajika Vihara, and spent time with friends like Soratha and Sachin. One day I received a batch of redirected mail from Kalimpong. Among the letters there was a rather disturbing communication from the landlord of Everton Villa. Though our lease did not expire till September, he wrote requiring us to move out by 15 May, as the property had been bought by a Tibetan who insisted on immediate occupation as one of the conditions of the sale. It looked as if the Maha Bodhi Society's Kalimpong branch would soon be homeless. The next letter I opened was from Marco Pallis, and in it my old friend promised very substantial assistance towards the realization of my plans. Having been buffeted one minute by the 'worldly wind' of loss, I was being assailed the next by that of gain, and it was not easy for me to contain my feelings of joy, thankfulness, and relief. We would not be homeless, after all, and I would be able to establish my permanent monastic centre! The plans to which Marco Pallis referred were, of course, the ones I had already outlined to Chattrul Rimpoche and which had prompted him not only to give the monastery its name but to predict its establishment 'quite soon'. Earlier in the year I had written to four or five people asking for their help in acquiring a place of our own in Kalimpong, as owing to the influx of Tibetans, who were buying up properties right and left, it would be impossible for me to find another suitable place when the lease on Everton Villa expired. So far the only response to my appeal had come from Dinoo, who had promised a thousand rupees. On the strength of Marco Pallis's promise of very substantial assistance (he did not mention the actual figure) I was in a position to start looking for a property and entering, perhaps, into preliminary negotiations.

There were three properties which I knew to be for sale and which were, severally, suitable for conversion into a small monastic centre, besides being of a price that might be within my reach. Two of the properties were situated down at Seventh Mile, not far from the Tamang village, the other at Chebo Busti, on the Lower Bridle Road, a mile or so beyond Chitrabhanu and Manjula. On my return to Kalimpong on 21 April, after spending exactly a month in Calcutta, I viewed each one of these in turn. It did not take me long to make up my mind. The Chebo Busti property was far and away the most suitable, and the most attractive, comprising as it did a stone cottage, sheltered on the north and south by magnificent Kashmir cypresses, and four acres of terraced hillside land. The cottage, which was perched on a rocky spur high above Fifth Mile, faced due west and commanded a panoramic view of the foothills of both the Darjeeling and Sikkim sides of the River Rangit. The only drawback was that the property's asking price was somewhat higher than I had expected.

Fortunately, in the course of our occupancy of Everton Villa I had got to know the landlord's plump Bihari manager. Taking him into my confidence, I told him I was willing to move out of Everton Villa by 15 May provided I could move into the Chebo Busti property at the same time, but that I would be able to move into the latter only if I bought it and that I would be able to buy it only if the price was right. As his employer stood to make a very handsome profit if the sale of Everton Villa went through, and was therefore desperate to have me out by the stipulated date, Ramsingh promised to do what he could to help. The result was that there followed ten or twelve days of intensive negotiations, with Ramsingh acting as intermediary between me and the Marwari owners of the Chebo Busti property, and, I suspected, between the latter and the landlord of Everton Villa as well. At the end of that period I found myself accompanying Ramsingh to Lakhmichand Kaluram's High Street office and there making my final offer in person. 'Nineteen thousand rupees,' I said, as previously instructed by the plump Bihari; 'nineteen thousand and not a rupee more.' 'No, I can't let it go at that price,' protested the yellow-turbaned figure behind the desk. Whereupon, as also instructed by Ramsingh, the organizer of this little comedy, I rose to my feet, expressed regret at our inability to reach an agreement, and strode briskly to the door. Before I was half-way there I was called back. My offer was accepted, and I was free to move into the property even before all the formalities had been completed.

A few days later, on 13 May, the Maha Bodhi Society's Kalimpong branch held its last full moon day meeting at Everton Villa. It was the full moon day of the month Vaishakha, the anniversary of the Buddha's attainment of perfect Enlightenment, and therefore marked the end of the Buddha Jayanti year – the year celebrating twenty-five centuries of Buddhism. For the tiny movement of Buddhist revival in India – a movement now augmented by hundreds of thousands of converts from among the followers of Dr Ambedkar – it had been a memorable year, even though it remained to be seen how deep or how lasting an impression the government-sponsored celebrations had made on the national psyche. It had been a memorable year for me too. In fact it had been a veritable *annus mirabilis*, a year of wonders. I had visited the principal Buddhist holy places in the company of Dhardo Rimpoche, I had met the Dalai Lama, I had forged a special link with the newly-converted followers of Dr Ambedkar, I had received Tantric initiation from Chattrul Rimpoche, and I had been enabled to establish in Kalimpong a vihara that would serve both as my personal headquarters and as a centre of living Buddhism. Nor was that all. *A Survey of Buddhism,* brought out a few months earlier by the Indian Institute of Culture, was already attracting highly favourable notices – notices that were to culminate in its publication being hailed by one Buddhist reviewer of Ceylon, a leading scholar, as the principal event of the Buddha Jayanti year.

The week following the full moon day was spent making the newly-acquired property habitable, as it had been left unoccupied for more than a year and was badly in need of repair and decoration. In the course of these proceedings I discovered that it was to Chebo Busti that the Burmese Princess had gone to stay after the death of my old friend Burma Raja, and that the hut in which she was then supposedly living, subsisting on greens from the garden, was none other than the substantial, oak-panelled cottage that I was about to transform into the Triyana Vardhana Vihara. But there was no time for reminiscence. On Thursday 23 May, assisted by the friends who were staying with me, I dismantled the shrine with its much-travelled standing Buddha image and set it up in its permanent quarters, in this way formally marking the move from the old to the new premises. Next day I was off to Gangtok, where I was to give a series of lectures, leaving the others to finish the business of moving. Having completed its first two and a half millennia, Buddhism had entered upon its second, which according to tradition was to culminate in the appearance of Maitreya, the Buddha of Love; and I, a tiny cell in the multi-dimensional body of the Sangha or Spiritual Community, was about to enter upon a new period in my Buddhist life.

Index

The Windhorse symbolizes the energy of the enlightened mind carrying the Three Jewels – the Buddha, the Dharma, and the Sangha – to all sentient beings.
Buddhism is one of the fastest growing spiritual traditions in the Western world. Throughout its 2,500-year history, it has always succeeded in adapting its mode of expression to suit whatever culture it has encountered.
Windhorse Publications aims to continue this tradition as Buddhism comes to the West. Today's Westerners are heirs to the entire Buddhist tradition, free to draw instruction and inspiration from all the many schools and branches. Windhorse publishes works by authors who not only understand the Buddhist tradition but are also familiar with Western culture and the Western mind.

For orders and catalogues contact

WINDHORSE PUBLICATIONS	ARYALOKA
UNIT 1-316 THE CUSTARD FACTORY	HEARTWOOD CIRCLE
GIBB STREET	NEWMARKET
BIRMINGHAM	NEW HAMPSHIRE
B9 4AA	NH 03857
UK	USA

Windhorse Publications is an arm of the Friends of the Western Buddhist Order, which has more than forty centres on four continents. Through these centres, members of the Western Buddhist Order offer regular programmes of events for the general public and for more experienced students. These include meditation classes, public talks, study on Buddhist themes and texts, and 'bodywork' classes such as t'ai chi, yoga, and massage. The FWBO also runs several retreat centres and the Karuna Trust, a fund-raising charity that supports social welfare projects in the slums and villages of India.
Many FWBO centres have residential spiritual communities and ethical businesses associated with them. Arts activities are encouraged too, as is the development of strong bonds of friendship between people who share the same ideals. In this way the FWBO is developing a unique approach to Buddhism, not simply as a set of techniques, less still as an exotic cultural interest, but as a creatively directed way of life for people living in the modern world.

If you would like more information about the FWBO please write to the

LONDON BUDDHIST CENTRE	ARYALOKA
51 ROMAN ROAD	HEARTWOOD CIRCLE
LONDON	NEWMARKET
E2 0HU	NEW HAMPSHIRA
UK	NH 03857
	USA

ALSO FROM WINDHORSE

SUBHUTI
BRINGING BUDDHISM TO THE WEST:
A LIFE OF SANGHARAKSHITA

Born in London, Dennis Lingwood realized that he was a Buddhist at the age of sixteen. Conscripted during the Second World War, army life took him to India where he stayed on to become the Buddhist monk, Sangharakshita. By the mid-fifties he was an increasingly active and forthright exponent of Buddhism, and had established a uniquely non-sectarian centre in Kalimpong.

As hippies flocked eastward in the sixties, Sangharakshita returned to England to establish the Friends of the Western Buddhist Order. This movement has been pioneering a vital form of Buddhism for the modern world. It is also at the heart of a Buddhist revival in India – the land where Buddhism was born 2,500 years ago.

Sangharakshita's story is proof that it is possible to live a truly spiritual life in the modern world.

208 pages plus 12 pages of photographs, index
ISBN 0 904766 69 1
£9.99/$18.95

SANGHARAKSHITA
FACING MOUNT KANCHENJUNGA

In 1950 Kalimpong was a lively trading town in the corner of the world where India runs into Nepal, Bhutan, Sikkim, and Tibet. Like a magnet, it attracted a bewildering array of guests and settlers: ex-colonials, Christian missionaries, princes in exile, pioneer Buddhologists, incarnate lamas from the Land of Snows – and Sangharakshita, the young English monk who was trying to establish a Buddhist movement for local youngsters.

In a delightful volume of memoirs, glowing with affection and humour, the author shares the incidents, encounters, and insights of his early years in Kalimpong. These include a brush with the Bombay film industry, a tour with the relics of the Buddha's chief disciples, a meeting with Dr B.R. Ambedkar, a friendship with Lama Anagarika Govinda, and much more.

Behind the events we witness the transformation of a rather eccentric young man into a unique and confident individual, completely at home in his adopted world, and increasingly effective as an interpreter of Buddhism for a new age.

512 pages
ISBN 0 904766 52 7
£11.95/$24.00

SUBHUTI
SANGHARAKSHITA: A NEW VOICE IN THE BUDDHIST TRADITION

Today Buddhism is a growing force in Western life, sowing the seeds of a spiritual, cultural, philosophical, artistic, and even economic revolution. Among the personalities at the heart of this development is a remarkable Englishman: Sangharakshita. Sangharakshita was one of the first Westerners to make the journey to the East and to don the monk's yellow robe. In India he gained unique experience in the main traditions of Buddhist teaching and practice. His involvement with the 'mass conversion' of ex-Untouchable Hindus to Buddhism exposed him to a revolutionary new experiment in social transformation. More recently he founded one of the most successful Buddhist movements in the modern world – pioneering a 'living Buddhism' that seems ideally suited to our times.

Highly respected as an outspoken writer and commentator, he has never been afraid to communicate his insights and views, even if they challenge venerated elements of Buddhist tradition.

But what are those insights and views? How have they arisen and developed? Here one of Sangharakshita's leading disciples offers an account of his evolution as a thinker and teacher.

328 pages, Index
ISBN 0 904766 68 3
£9.99, $19.95

SANGHARAKSHITA
LEARNING TO WALK

At the age of sixteen Dennis Lingwood discovered that he was a Buddhist – and that he had always been one. This realization was to become the motive force behind a life in which Lingwood – now better known as Sangharakshita – has played a major part in the introduction of Buddhism to the West.

But how and why should a teenager, living in England in 1941, come to such a realization? If there are any clues then they will surely be found in this volume of early memoirs, for here, in an evocative portrait of a child's life in London between the wars, the author has traced the events and influences that led to his surprising conversion.

192 pages
ISBN 0 904766 45 4
£5.95

SANGHARAKSHITA

A Survey of Buddhism

Now in its seventh edition, *A Survey of Buddhism* continues to provide an indispensable
study of the entire field of Buddhist thought and practice. Covering all the major
doctrines and traditions, both in relation to Buddhism as a whole and to the spiritual life
of the individual Buddhist, Sangharakshita places their development in historical
context. This is an objective but sympathetic appraisal of Buddhism's many forms that
clearly demonstrates the underlying unity of all its schools.
'It would be difficult to find a single book in which the history and development of
Buddhist thought has been described as vividly and clearly as in this survey.... For all
those who wish to "know the heart, the essence of Buddhism as an integrated whole",
there can be no better guide than this book.' *Lama Anagarika Govinda*
'I recommend Sangharakshita's book as the best survey of Buddhism.' *Dr Edward Conze*
544 pages, Bibliography, Index
ISBN 0 904766 65 9
£12.99, $24.95